FATHER HENRY YOUNG
(Painting in the Convent, Portland Row).

An Apostle of Catholic Dublin

Father Henry Young

BY

MYLES V. RONAN, P.P., D.Litt.

BROWNE & NOLAN LIMITED
THE RICHVIEW PRESS CLONSKEAGH
1944

DECLARATION

In conformity with the decree of Pope Urban VIII, dated March 17, 1625, I declare that if in the course of this work I should give the name of Saint to those not officially recognised as such; and if I make mention of such facts and revelations as might bear the character of the miraculous or prophetic: I do not in any way presume to take upon myself to express, on either persons or facts, a judgment which is reserved to the Church, nor in any way whatsoever to forecast decisions which belong to her alone.

Nihil Obstat :

IOANNES KELLY,
Censor Theol. Deput.

Imprimi potest :

✠ IOANNES CAROLUS,
Archiep. Dublinen.,
Hiberniae Primas.

Dublini, die 5° Martii, anno 1944.

FOREWORD

Lady Georgiana Fullerton's *Life of Father Henry Young* (1874) was a beautiful and timely reminder to the people of the day of the virtues and zeal of the great priest who laboured in city and country, almost throughout the entire diocese of Dublin and in many places outside the diocese, for over half-a-century. It kept alive the memory of the " Curé d'Ars of Dublin." It interested me as a boy when I received the book as a Catechism premium. It interested me more when, a few years ago, I found his name in the parochial records of the parish of SS. Michael and John and of St. Michan's. These records throw new light on his activities. These activities could not be adequately appreciated unless the Catholic and social background of Dublin of the period was depicted. Moreover, the position of his father as a prominent woollen merchant, one of the zealous supporters of the Church in Dublin in its emergence from the Penal Laws, necessitated an inquiry into the position of Catholics in Dublin in the middle eighteenth century. Thus, the pursuit of Father Young has become a survey of Catholic and social Dublin. He was an assistant or curate in most of the city parishes, and so the conditions of these parishes must be described. This work has become a sketch of Catholic life in Dublin between 1749 and 1869, namely, between the last of the Penal Laws and the Disestablishment of the Protestant Church.

Many friends have helped me with important material—the Sisters of St. Joseph's Asylum, Portland Row ; the Presentation Sisters, George's Hill ; the Ursuline Sisters, Cork ; the Poor Clare Sisters, Harold's Cross ; the Evening Office Confraternity of SS. Michael and John's ; the late Most Rev. Dr. Mulhern, Bishop of Dromore ; the Rev. M. Campbell, Newry ; the Rev. Denis McGrath, C.C., SS. Michael and John's ; the Rev. R. Burke Savage, S.J. ; Miss Helen Landreth, and the officials of the Public Record Office and Record Tower, Dublin Castle. To them I return sincere thanks for, without their aid, I should have been unable to add much to Lady Fullerton's *Life*. Above all I am indebted to Mr. Patrick McGrath, East Essex Street, for allowing me to use his priceless collection of old Dublin publications. Lastly, I wish to thank Rev. Michael Clarke, C.C. ; Mr. V. Grogan, M.A., B.L. ; Miss Eleanor Moylan and Miss Noreen O'Hagan for valuable assistance in putting my MS. into proper form.

MYLES V. RONAN.

ST. MICHAN'S,
8th September, 1943.

" Social History sometimes suffers from the reproach that it is vague and general, unable to compete with the attractions of political history either for the student or for the general reader, because of its lack of outstanding personalities. In point of fact there is often as much material for reconstructing the life of some quite ordinary person as there is for writing a history of Robert of Normandy or of Philip of Hainault ; and the lives of ordinary people so reconstructed are, if less spectacular, certainly not less interesting. So I believe that social history lends itself particularly to what may be called a personal treatment, and that the past may be made to live again for the general reader more effectively by personifying it than by presenting it in the form of learned treatises. . . . The present age differs from the centuries before it in its vivid realisation of that much-neglected person, the man in the street. . . . To-day the historian is interested in the social life of the past and not only in the wars and intrigues of princes. . . . As Acton put it, ' The great historian now takes his meal in the kitchen ' . . . . In the long run history is made by the lives of ordinary men and women."— (Eileen Power, *Medieval People*—Pelican Books.)

CONTENTS

		PAGE
FOREWORD		iii
PROLOGUE		ix

I. THE CATHOLIC REVIVAL IN DUBLIN :

1. Dublin in the Eighteenth Century 1
2. Dublin Catholics in Industry and Commerce . . 10
3. Catholic Priests in the City of Dublin . . . 14
4. The New Catholic Chapels 18
5. Catholic Schools in the City of Dublin . . . 31
6. Convents of Nuns in the City of Dublin . . . 41
7. The Beginnings of Catholic Literature in Dublin . 47
8. Catholic Charity in Eighteenth-Century Dublin . . 52

II. THE CAMPAIGN FOR CATHOLIC RELIEF :

1. The Catholic Committee 57
2. The Dublin Corporation opposes Catholic Relief . 61
3. Henry Grattan supports the Catholics . . . 64
4. Archbishop Troy's Pastorals 66
5. Archbishop Troy and Emmet's Rising . . . 71

III. THE YOUNG FAMILY :

1. A Dublin Merchant 77
2. Henry Young's Boyhood 80
3. Vocation to the Priesthood 84
4. Henry Young in Rome 87
5. Father Young in St. Michan's 91
6. Father Young at Harold's Cross 94
7. Father Young and Prince Hohenlohe . . . 102
8. Death of Father Young's Parents 110
9. Father Young's Brothers and Sisters 116

IV. FATHER YOUNG AND PAROCHIAL ORGANISATIONS :

1. St. Michan's Parish :
   a. Christian Doctrine Confraternity . . . 123
   b. Devotion to the Sacred Heart 126
   c. Classical and Mercantile Academy . . . 128
   d. New Church 130
2. Dr. Blake at SS. Michael and John's . . . 131
3. Father Young and the Purgatorian Society . . 138
4. Father Young and the " Catholic Directory " and
   " Evening Office " 147
5. The Evening Office Confraternities 157

CONTENTS—*Continued.*

PAGE

6. The Christian Doctrine Confraternity :
   a. Protestant Opposition 163
   b. Sweep Department 170
   c. Classes 174
   d. Branches 181

7. The Temperance Movement 189
8. Dr. Yore at St. Paul's 195

V. FATHER YOUNG'S MISSIONARY WORK :

1. The Jubilee of 1826 206
2. Father Young's Missions :
   a. In Co. Wicklow 210
   b. In Garristown and Baldoyle . . . 217
3. The Cholera Plague of 1832 219
4. Father Young again on the Mission 231
5. Father Young and Devotion to the Immaculate Heart
   of Mary 236
6. Father William Young's Mission in Cornwall :
   a. Missions 243
   b. Publications 250
7. Fathers James and Henry at Finglas . . . 255
8. Father Young in St. Catherine's 257
9. Father Young and Daniel O'Connell . . . 266
10. Archbishops Murray and Cullen 270

VI. FATHER YOUNG'S LAST YEARS :

1. Father Young at St. Joseph's, Portland Row . . 279
2. Father Young at St. Joseph's, Clondalkin . . . 282
3. Father Young returns to Portland Row . . . 285
4. Father Young's Last Years 292
5. Last Illness and Death 296

EPILOGUE—DISESTABLISHMENT OF THE PROTESTANT CHURCH IN
   IRELAND 303

INDEX 307

PROLOGUE

As Father Henry Young was born some six years before the repeal of the chief Acts of the Penal Code (1792), and as his father had to struggle against many disabilities under that Code, a short review of it will be useful.

The Code falls chronologically into two parts—from the "Reformation" to the Revolution of 1688, and from 1688 to 1749.

In the first period the aim of the penal legislation was the complete suppression of Catholic worship, and the forcible stamping out of "Recusancy" or refusal to conform. The Dublin Parliament of 1560 enacted that "all persons refusing to take the Oath of Supremacy were shut out from ecclesiastical, civil, or military office," and Catholics were fined 12d. for every absence from Protestant service on Sundays and Holidays.

With the Revolution of 1688 under William of Orange a new epoch begins. Compulsion of Catholics to recognise the English Monarch as Head of the Church in Ireland was given up, and so also was the attempt to force Catholics to attend Protestant Service. William abandoned the idea of James I to make one nation out of the English and Irish, and, recognising that the Irishman could not be turned into an Englishman, aimed at his impoverishment. The Catholic might keep his religion, but, if he did, he was to be reduced to the hewer of wood and drawer of water. Land, political power and riches were to be the monopoly of the Protestant. Thus, an ingenious series of laws, popularly known as the Penal Laws, were devised to impoverish and weaken in every way all dissenters from the Established Church, but especially Catholics.

The new penal code begins with an Act of the English Parliament of 1691. Then came Acts of the Irish Parliament. Firstly, foreign education was forbidden; and no papist was to teach school publicly or in private houses, except to the children of the family. Subsequent Acts reaffirmed and strengthened this, widening its scope, and increasing the penalties on Popish schoolmasters. An Act of 1709 " forbade any Papist in trade to have more than two apprentices, except in the hempen or flax manufacture."

As to Catholic worship—no longer illegal—the new Code attempted to suppress it by the gradual extinction of the existing Catholic priesthood. All Regular priests and all clerics exercising ecclesiastical jurisdiction, were banished (1697). Thus, no bishop was to exist in Ireland, and, consequently, no ordination of priests was to take place. As a matter of fact (in 1708), out of the twenty-six Irish dioceses there were only two bishops in Ireland, one of whom was in a Dublin prison, and the other was bed-ridden. Yet, the Code allowed priests from the Continent to enter Ireland.

The Irish Colleges on the Continent provided priests in abundance for the Irish dioceses. To counteract this move the Code added another Act that any Popish priest coming into the kingdom should be deemed a Popish Regular and thus liable to imprisonment and transportation on the first conviction, and to death for High Treason on the second.

Yet, the stream of secular priests into Ireland continued, and the Government recognised its inability to stem it. It devised, however, a means of curbing their activities, which was then considered sufficient but which turned out to be in favour of the priests. It passed an Act for the " Registering of the Popish Clergy " to stop the " Further Growth of Popery " (1703).

I

THE CATHOLIC REVIVAL IN DUBLIN

1. Dublin in the Eighteenth Century

No city in Europe increased more in size and magnificence during the seventeenth and eighteenth centuries than the city of Dublin. In 1610, its walls, including those of the castle, did not take up an Irish mile, its streets and lanes numbered about thirty, and there were 15,000 people within the walls and 11,000 without. In 1765, the length of the city from east to west was little short of three miles, and its breadth about two miles; there were no fewer than five hundred streets and lanes, and the population was over 150,000. In 1821 there were 750 streets, squares, lanes, etc. and 20,000 houses, with a population of about 225,000.

In 1610, Thomas-street and James's-street (outside the city walls) were completely built on as far as James's-gate, but the district between these streets and the river Liffey was waste with the exception of a row of houses in West New Row and the adjoining area occupied by St. John's Hospital without the New Gate. By the year 1765 the district had been considerably built on and was occupied, around New Row and Bridge-street, by the warehouses, shops and dwellings of merchants and traders.

South of the great highway of Thomas-street and James-street were the Liberties, namely, districts not under the city jurisdiction. The chief of these was St. Thomas-court (Earl of Meath's) Liberty. This was the great industrial centre. It was supplied with a splendid stream formed from a small stream that rose at Tymon near Tallaght and which was augmented by water from the Dodder. The united stream was brought by the Civic Fathers, between 1245 and 1254, as a water supply for the city, to James's Basin. Only a third of the stream went to the Basin, whilst two-thirds went through the Liberty of St. Thomas-court to turn the mills of St. Thomas's Abbey. This deflection of the stream took place at the Tongue, Mount Argus. When the industries were established in the Liberties, in the seventeenth century, many branches were provided for their use from the St. Thomas-court stream, then called the Earl of Meath's Watercourse. The woollen manufacturers inhabited the Coombe, at Pimlico, and a district afterwards named Weavers' Square, with its high gabled roofs and attics. The silk-weavers lived mainly in the Spitalfields, so called after a similar district in London.

The chief industrial wealth of Dublin came from the woollen manufacture which was established by English and Huguenot weavers who settled there (*c.* 1618) with their families on account both of the cheapness of labour and of the excellent quality of the wool. By the year 1698 twelve thousand Protestant families were employed in the industry. As its prosperity was a source of jealousy to England, duties amounting to a prohibition were laid on the export of woollen cloth in 1699, and soon afterwards export to England and Wales was wholly forbidden. Many prosperous weavers were reduced to poverty. After the introduction of Spanish wool into Ireland a revival took place which was supported by the Dublin Society, in 1733, by the establishment of a woollen warehouse in Castle-street and by the encouragement of the home consumption of cloth.

Arthur Young remarks in his *Tour* (1779) that since 1748 " Ireland had perhaps made greater advances than any other country in Europe." This prosperity was unfortunately nipped in the bud by the American war of 1775. The repeal, in 1779, of the prohibition Act of 1699 against the woollen industry gave an important impetus to its revival, but yet, according to the Parliamentary Committee, in 1784 not one-third of the looms that had been employed in the industry ten years previously were in use. In 1792 there were 60 master-clothiers and 400 broad looms in the Liberties employ-ing 5,000 persons.

Silk-weaving in Dublin was also originated by Huguenots. In 1730, 800 looms were working, employing 3,000 persons. By 1763, owing to foreign competition, the number of looms was so much reduced that the Irish Parliament granted £8,000 to the Dublin Society to encourage the industry. A Silk Warehouse was opened in Parliament-street in 1765 and was patronised by the nobility and gentry. The industry almost immediately revived, and 3,000 looms were soon at work, employing 11,000 persons.

In the Spring of 1779, however, 19,000 persons connected with the weaving trade in Dublin alone were out of work, and the economic situation as a whole was so bad that public feeling was thoroughly aroused. In imitation of the Americans resolutions were passed against the importation or consumption of any English manufactures. Hostile demonstrations were made, and Dublin was flooded with ballads and satirical verses. The Volunteers declared for free trade and a free Parliament. Yet, in 1784, 5,366 of the 11,270 persons normally employed in the silk industry were idle.

An Act of 26 George III (1785) prohibited the Dublin Society from financing the silk industry, foreign competition again made itself felt, and the Silk Warehouse was closed in 1786. By 1791 another revival had set in, and 1,200 looms were again in use. The Rebellion of 1798, which naturally led to a generally disturbed state in the country, and the Napoleonic wars gave the silk manufacture in Dublin another set-back, and immediately before the Union the industry was in a state of decline.

Under the old commercial restrictions Ireland could not import raw cotton from the colonies, or, owing to high duties, compete with English cloth. When the restrictions were removed in 1779 a decided stimulus was given to the Irish cotton manufacture. The Dublin Parliament laid duties on all imported cottons, and gave large grants to private individuals to establish factories. Yet, it encouraged English weavers to settle in the Liberties. The Dublin Society made grants for the purchase of new machinery and gave bounties on the sale of manufactured goods. Several factories were established in the neighbourhood of the capital, and one was established in Cork-street. About 1786, at least 1,600 cotton-weavers were employed in Dublin. Again, the French wars brought havoc to the Dublin industry.

Whilst Ireland's exports to Great Britain more than doubled between 1748 and 1779, her linen exports trebled. Her linen trade received a severe blow from America's non-importation

resolutions aimed against England. It soon regained its
former position and dominated the market. Linen was the
most important of the Irish manufactures in the eighteenth
century. It was free from the restrictions placed by the
English Government on other Irish industries, and it received
extensive grants from the Irish Parliament—by way of com-
pensation, no doubt, for the suppression of the woollen trade.
Ireland was specially suited both by climate and soil for the
industry, and the manufacturers did a good business with
America. The progress of the trade was particularly rapid
during the period of Grattan's Parliament, when it is said to
have actually trebled. In 1779, 18,836,042 yards of linen
cloth were exported, but by the time of the Union the export
had risen to 35,903,292 yards.

Before the localisation of the industry in the North—
towards the end of the century—Dublin was the great distributing centre for the linen trade. The Linen-Hall in the
street of that name, off North King-street, was erected by
1728 to deal with the enormous increase of business. Ultimately it took the shape of six large courts surrounded by
stores, and contained 557 rooms, including an elegant coffee-
room. A Yarn-Hall was built nearby. The sale commenced
every day at 9 a.m. and continued until 4 p.m. As the business
of the Hall lay principally amongst certain important towns
of Ulster, the streets in the vicinity of the Hall received the
names of Coleraine, Lisburn, Lurgan and Derry. Here
wholesale merchants and drapers gathered to arrange sales ;
here yarn and cloth were stored ; and here the Trustees of
the Linen Board met weekly to supervise the trade. Up to
1816 the volume of trade passing through the Hall amounted
to three-eighths of the total export from Ireland. In 1820 the
value of the linens entered at the Hall amounted to £560,780.

Belfast was rapidly developing as a port, and had begun to
do a direct trade with England. The trade of Dublin gradually
fell off, and the Linen Hall, though retained for some years
as a warehouse, ceased definitely to be used as a market
in 1828.[1]

Besides those industries Dublin had brewing and distilling.

[1] Maxwell, *Dublin Under the Georges*, 213-19, 235.

Beer was not a favourite beverage among the Dublin people, and the high duty placed on its import into England, in the early eighteenth century, hampered the development of the industry. In order to discourage "the drinking of spirits [which] had become a great national evil," the Irish Parliament, in 1791, passed a measure, initiated by Grattan, to encourage brewing by the reduction of excise duties. Its result was that, by 1818, there were thirty-five breweries in Ireland of which Guinness's Brewery, founded early in the eighteenth century, was the chief.

Commerce kept pace with the industries. In 1784, 2,083 ships were invoiced at the port of Dublin, with a tonnage of 228,956. The old Custom-House, erected in 1707, near Essex (Grattan) Bridge, became inadequate for the increase of commerce, and the first stone of the present building was laid, 8th August, 1781. It was completed in ten years, the first edifice of its kind in Europe.[1]

A distressing feature of eighteenth-century Dublin was the excessive drinking of spirits among the poor. In 1792 the Government tried to discourage distilling, that had greatly increased between 1780 and 1792, by raising the excise on spirits. No measures, however, to restrict the consumption of spirits in Dublin under the Georges were very successful, partly owing to the half-hearted measures taken by a Government anxious to maintain its revenues and partly to the widespread existence of illicit stills. By 1818 there were nine distilleries in Dublin, and an export trade was not long in developing.

Lecky says that Dublin "in the middle of the eighteenth century was in dimensions and population the second city in the Empire, containing, according to the most trustworthy accounts, between 100,000 and 120,000 inhabitants. Like most things in Ireland it presented vivid contrasts, and strangers were equally struck with the crowds of beggars, the inferiority of the inns, the squalid wretchedness of the streets of the old town, and with the noble proportions of the new quarter, and the brilliant and hospitable society that inhabited it."[2]

[1] McGregor, *Picturesque Dublin*, 182–96.
[2] *Ireland in the Eighteenth Century*, I. 319.

The English visitors to Dublin were impressed by the air of gaiety in the houses of the well-to-do which went with a peculiarly splendid way of living—a multiplicity of servants, great profusion of dishes on the table, abundant wine.

Dancing commenced at 11 o'clock, and, with an interval for supper at 1 o'clock, continued until 6 a.m. Every night in the winter there was a ball or party. The chief public place of entertainment was the Rotunda Gardens and Assembly Rooms where concerts, masquerades, card-parties, and balls were held, "the most elegant amusements of Dublin" according to Malton. By day the road to claret-drinking Blackrock, with its military band in the Park and its dance halls on the green sward overlooking the baths, and its *bon-ton* rivalling anything in England, was "as much crowded with carriages as the most populous streets in the city."[1]

"Among the higher classes," says Lecky, "there are some traces of an immorality of a graver kind than the ordinary dissipation of Irish life." Again, he says : "The ostentatious profusion of dishes and multiplication of servants at Irish entertainments which appeared so strange to English travellers, and which had undoubted bad moral effects were merely the natural results of the economical condition of the country which made both food and labour extremely cheap."[2] Arthur Young found servants' wages on an average 30 per cent. cheaper than in England.[3]

The servant problem was an important one from the Catholic point of view. "Though servants had low wages they had many perquisites. Mrs. Delany of Delville, Glasnevin, says that they were generally permitted to eat up the remains of the huge dinners of the period, and they were not kept under very severe discipline. Like their masters they drank a good deal ('impersonations of whiskey,' said Lady Morgan). They were 'the proudest, laziest, the most profligate, insolent and extravagant set of mortals anywhere to be found on the face of the globe,' said a writer in the *Hibernian Magazine* of 1778. The truth was that there were

---

[1] Maxwell, op. cit., 84–85.   [2] Op. cit., I. 323, 326.

[3] *Tour in Ireland*, II. 232.

too many domestics."[1] These dinners, says Mrs. Delany, were given once or twice a week.

It may be presumed that the majority of the servants in these houses were Catholics. Protestant girls would naturally be more attracted to the industries in Protestant hands. Moreover, one of the enticements to Catholic girls attending Mixed Schools was that at the end of their schooling they would be fitted out and apprenticed to Protestant mistresses.

Although, due to lack of statistics, it is difficult to estimate the exact proportion of the Catholic to the Protestant population, it is calculated that, in 1812, Catholics were six to one in Dublin. It may be taken that, in 1798, when the population was about 175,000, the proportion was about the same. Catholics naturally formed the great majority of the poor of the city. The deplorable state of the poorer classes in Ireland in the eighteenth century was largely due to the rapid and immense increase in the population. In 1695 the population was about 1,034,000, but in 1821 it was 6,801,827.

The various restrictions on Irish industries in the eighteenth century had spread poverty not only among those engaged in them, but on thousands of others in the Liberties who depended on their prosperity.

Besides all this there was an immense loss to the nation through absentee landlords—the Irish country gentry—living in England, which affected city as well as country. In 1769 the yearly value of the income spent by them in England was given as £1,208,982. "The removal of such a large sum which ought to have been spent in the country was undoubtedly one of the chief causes of Irish poverty."[2]

The Irish Parliament (1771–72) passed an Act that in every city and county there should be one Corporate Body for the relief of the poor of which the Protestant Archbishop or bishop was to be President, and the chief magistrate, parliamentary representatives, and sheriffs were to be members. This Corporation was to erect as soon as possible in its district a House of Industry to provide for four classes—disabled men, disabled women, male vagrants and beggars, and

---

[1] Maxwell op. cit., 86.   [2] Ibid., 18–19.

strolling women. Parliament made no provision for the support of those houses, but recommended the project to the charitably disposed. Dublin Corporation, having granted £100, considered that it had no further responsibility. The Corporate Body of Dublin got the ministers of the city parishes to issue licences on parchment to such poor as were eligible to beg and a metal badge with the name of the parish inscribed. The badge cost the beggars 18d. each, and confined them to begging in their own parish. In 1773, charity sermons were preached in the Protestant churches of the city for the new House of Industry ; Catholic chapels were not allowed to have charity sermons. Up to June, 1773, a total of £2,800 had been received from these sermons and from other subscriptions.

In July, 1773, an old malt-house, designated as " two large commodious houses " in Channel-row (North Brunswick-street) was taken by the Corporate Body and fitted up for the reception of the poor of Dublin, including the " badged " as well as the strolling beggars who had been regarded by the " citizens " as " a nuisance and disgrace." The House was opened—8th November—but " the black cart" had to be sent round the streets, and beadles with muskets had to be provided to force the poor to enter the House. The food was of the poorest kind for some years, and there was no means of treating the sick and infirm who were taken into the House. Better accommodation for all classes of inmates was provided in 1787, and two dining-halls served as chapels— for Protestants and Catholics, who had their separate chaplains. Archbishop Troy nominated the Catholic chaplain, who was appointed by the Governors. In 1791, a new House of Industry was built on an adjoining plot. A proper infirmary was built in 1803, called the Hardwicke Hospital, and 1808, the Dominican Convent, then vacated by the nuns who went to Clontarf, became the Richmond Surgical Hospital (the convent chapel became known as the chapel ward). In 1814 the Whitworth Medical Hospital was built to the south of the new House of Industry.[1]

As to the conditions of the poor in 1798 a contemporary

[1] King Moylan, *Dub. Hist. Rec.* I., No. 2, pp. 41–49 ; No. 3, pp. 67–68.

gives detailed description. Though the environs of Dublin were delightful, according to visitors of the eighteenth century, the city was bad—narrow streets and dirty-looking houses, filth and squalor, poverty, disease, wretchedness, and indescribable misery. The city streets were occupied principally by "working manufacturers, by petty shopkeepers, the labouring poor, and beggars, crowded together to a degree distressing to humanity. A single apartment in one of these truly wretched habitations, rates from one to two shillings per week, and to lighten this rent, two, three, or even four families became joint tenants. As I was usually out at early hours on the [statistical] survey, I have frequently surprised from ten to sixteen persons, of all ages and sexes, in a room not 15 feet square, stretched on a wad of filthy straw, swarming with vermin, and without any covering, save the wretched rags that constituted their wearing apparel."[1] One house in Braithwaite-street, in the Coombe area, sheltered 108 people. The average for the populous streets of this area would be at least 28 to each house. The sanitary conditions of the poor were appalling and the wonder is that the plague of typhus had not made its mark more frequently.

In these circumstances it is not to be wondered at that whiskey drinking became the order of the day and of the night. An enormous number of dram-shops were licensed to sell raw spirits. The Catholic distillers were kept busy, and the Catholic poor were their best supporters. Employers complained that they could not get their work done and that travellers spent their time in the inns rather than in the market. The Grand Jury of 1788 complained that this whiskey drinking, not only led to loss of health, but " prevented the industry, and debauched the morals of the people, and hurried them into the most shocking excesses of riot and vice."[2]

A report (in 1800) from Mr. Grimshaw, an inspector employed by Dublin Castle, states that he has paid several visits to the Liberties and finds that they are " a scene of the most abject poverty, depraved morals, deplorable sickness,

[1] Rev. Mr. Whitelaw, Vicar of St. Catherine's (Warburton, Whitelaw and Walsh, *Hist. of Dub.*, I. vii.)
[2] Maxwell, op. cit., 114–19.

and a magazine of fury." He tells of the "putrid effluvia of every kind," and that "the provisions suspended in the shambles must be contaminated." [1]

Slaughter-houses, distilleries, glass-houses, lime-kilns, and many other industries, made the atmosphere of the Liberties putrid. Life there must have been a difficult one, morally and physically. The poverty and discontent had something to say to the Rising of 1798. But the distress was not confined to that area ; naturally, it had its repercussions on adjacent areas. Its influence on the parishes of St. Michael and St. John is shown in the following document.

A memorial of the ministers and churchwardens of the parishes of St. Michael and St. John was sent to Charles Marquis Cornwallis, Lord Lieutenant of Ireland, in 1798, on the poverty of the parishes. It stated that " these two small parishes contain upwards of 1,600 poor persons who try rather to conceal their distress " ; that " rice was one of the best substitutes for their ordinary food " and that " the Lord Lieutenant had furnished the city with rice at a low price. Many sick and crippled have been unable to make their way to the places of distribution. The benefit of the provision should be more largely extended to the poor. Rich people in these parishes are very few, and their subscriptions are inadequate." The memorialists request " that their parochial committees of distribution should receive such portion of the rice imported by your Excellency for the poor of this city, at such periods of time, and at such reduced terms as your Excellency shall think fit." [2]

2. Dublin Catholics in Industry and Commerce

The Dublin Craft and Merchant Guilds had become definitely Protestant about the year 1650, and, with the support of the Dublin Corporation, composed of the members of the Guilds, were determined on making it impossible for Catholic craftsmen and traders to carry on their business. That was more than fifty years before the penal law (1709)

---

[1] C.S.O.P. II, Record Tower, Dublin Castle, 515/83/10.
[2] Ibid., 544/331/2.

forbidding " any Papist in trade to have more than two apprentices, except in the hempen or flax manufacture." At a meeting of the Common Council of Dublin held after Christmas of the year 1652 the Council ordered " that none shall be admitted into the assemblies of any of the corporacions of this Cittie unlesse hee bee a Protestant, and that noe freeman take any to bee an apprentise but such as are or wilbee and continue in the Protestant religion."[1]

Yet, a few years afterwards, the French Protestants or Hugenots received the favour of freedom of religion and of industry. Lord Lieutenant Ormonde wrote, 30th November, 1665, to Michael Boyle, Protestant Archbishop of Dublin : " having taken into our consideration that there are many Protestant strangers of France and other foreign nations now residing in this Citie of Dublin and Kingdome of Ireland, and for that it is hoped the number of them will receive great increase from the incouragement that is given to strangers by a late Act of Parliament tending to the propagation of the Protestant religion and the settlement of Manufacturers in this Kingdom (14–15 Car. II c. 13), etc."[2] The Huguenots were granted, by the Archbishop, St. Mary's Chapel of St. Patrick's Cathedral for their services, which they continued to use up to 1816. They confined themselves almost entirely to the district of the Liberties.

Before the end of the seventeenth century Archbishop Boyle's wishes were fulfilled as many " Protestant strangers of France " found their way to Dublin after the revocation of the Edict of Nantes by Louis XIV (1685). Several petitions were presented by these strangers to the Guild Merchants to have free liberty of trading in Dublin which were granted.

Moreover, at this time, the Protestant Archbishop of Dublin and the Earl of Meath had granted jurisdiction to the Craft Guilds of the City within their Liberties. The Earl of Meath's Liberty was, roughly speaking, bounded by Thomas-street, Dolphin's Barn, Harold's Cross, and Clanbrassil-street, and New-row in the Coombe. It included Meath-street and most of the industrial area. The Archbishop's Liberty,

[1] *Calendar of Ancient Records of Dublin*, iv. 38.
[2] Lawlor, *Fasti o St. Patrick's* (App. by Le Fanu, pp. 277–78).

adjoining the city, included St. Patrick's-street, St. Kevin-street, and the New-street.

The Protestant Guild system included practically the whole ambit of industry in the city and the Liberties ; the tanners, feltmakers, cutlers, painter-stainers, stationers, plasterers, bricklayers, paviours, coopers, curriers, brewers and malsters, and combers.

How were Catholic craftsmen and traders to find a means of subsistence in face of all these restrictions and privileges ? The ban of the Dublin Corporation of 1652 led to illicit trading by Catholics who were supported by their co-religionists. Within fifty years the Dublin Catholic traders within the city jurisdiction (outside the Archbishop's and Earl's Liberties) had so increased their trade that the authority and power of the Protestant Guilds had visibly declined. From 1700 onwards the decline was rapid. The Protestant Guilds no longer exercised a monopoly over industry and commerce, and a monopoly was essential to the very existence of the Guilds. They were blind to the writing on the walls of old Dublin, and they were blind to the forces that were making themselves felt within their own ranks. The two pillars of the old Catholic Guild System, fraternity and equality, were discarded, and the spirit of capitalism made its appearance. Protestant workers combined against their Protestant masters and were met by repression but, ultimately, many of them joined the popular political cause. The Protestant Craft Guilds degenerated into political clubs against Catholic relief measures.

Occasionally a little relaxation in the Guild by-laws took place, as, for example, when the Feltmakers' Guild passed a resolution in 1764 that Roman Catholic Feltmakers might be members of the Guild provided they had served seven years' apprenticeship. But the by-laws of the Guilds, and the oaths taken by freemen on admission to exclude Catholic boys from being initiated into the mysteries of any art or craft in the city of Dublin, made it practically impossible for Catholic boys to become apprentices to Guild craftsmen.[1]

The Catholic traders, with their two apprentices severally

[1] Webb, *Dublin Guilds*, pp. 8–49, 241–47.

allowed by the Penal Code (1709), by their tenacity and the fraternal spirit of the old Catholic Guild System, not only became prosperous, but broke down the Protestant Guild system. Catholic comradeship between the people and the traders and craftsmen developed ; it was a struggle for existence for all, and Catholic solidarity won through. The second half of the eighteenth century saw the Catholic traders and craftsmen occupying most important positions in the industrial and commercial life of the city.

Arthur Young, an English Protestant, gives in 1779[1] an interesting picture of the Catholic religion and industry of the day, though, in regard to the industry, he spoke of it in general, and does not appear to have gone round the back streets of the city where the Catholic traders and craftsmen were carrying on their illicit business. However, his picture is important as showing that the penal laws against Catholic industry as a means to the breaking down of the Catholic religion were futile. He says : " It is no superficial view I have taken of this matter [Catholic religion] in Ireland, and being at Dublin at the time a very trifling part of these [Penal] laws was agitated in Parliament. I attended the debates, with my mind open to conviction, an auditor [listener] for the mere purpose of information. I have conversed on the subject with some of the most distinguished characters in the kingdom, and I cannot after all but declare that the scope, purport, and aim of the laws of discovery as executed are not against the Catholic Religion which increases under them, but against the industry and property of whoever professes that religion. In vain has it been said, that consequence and power follow property, and that the attack is made in order to wound the doctrine through its property. If such was the intention, I reply, that seventy years experience prove the folly and futility of it. Those laws have crushed all the industry, and wrested most of the property from the Catholics, but the religion triumphs ; it is thought to increase."

He also pointed out that " an aristocracy of five hundred thousand Protestants " crushing " the industry of two millions of poor Catholics " could " never advance the public interest."

[1] *Tour Through Ireland* (1776–79) pt. 2, p. 34.

The Catholic religion in Dublin triumphed and increased because of the triumph and increase of the illicit Catholic traders and craftsmen. It was they who made possible the existence of the 1704 priests among them, built or reconstructed the penal-time chapels into the respectable places of worship they were in 1749, supported the schools that were kept by secular and regular priests, and by lay teachers, in back rooms in tenement houses, and who supported the Catholic Orphan Societies that were then essential in every parish to prevent the Catholic orphan and foundling from falling into Protestant hands.

3. CATHOLIC PRIESTS IN THE CITY OF DUBLIN.

According to the Act of 1703 [1] "No Popish Parish Priest shall keep or have any Popish Curate, Assistant, or Coadjutor .... such Popish Priest and Priests that shall neglect to register him or themselves and remain in this kingdom after the said twentieth day of July, shall be esteemed a Popish Regular Clergyman, and prosecuted as such."

The framers of the Act understood the " parish " to mean the Protestant or civil one. The Catholic parishes in 1704 did not coincide with that arrangement. For instance, the Catholic parish of St. Catherine's included the three Protestant parishes of St. James, St. Catherine and Kilmainham. Though it had only one canonical parish priest it was allowed three priests by the Act.

In the case of St. Michael's parish, which included five Protestant parishes, namely, St. Michael's, St. John's, St. Werburgh's, St. Bride's and St. Nicholas's Within the Walls, there was only one canonical parish priest, but four other priests were allowed by the Act. Similarly, in the case of St. Michan's parish, which included the three Protestant parishes, St. Michan's, St. Paul's, and St. Mary's, there was only one canonical parish priest ; but two others were allowed by the Act. St. Audoen's, which did not include any other civil parish, had one popish priest. Though there were eleven

---

[1] " Act for Registering the Popish Clergy." *Irish Ecclesiastical Record,* June, 1876, pp. 880–85.

Protestant parishes in the city there were only five Catholic parishes, but according to the terms of the Act eleven priests were allowed, six of whom were in reality curates of the canonical parish priests.

Thirty-four " Popish Parish Priests in the City and Co. of the City of Dublin . . . were Register'd at a General Sessions of the Peace held for the Co. of the said City, at the Tholsel[1] thereof, the 13th of July, 1704, and were since Return'd to the *Council Office in Dublin*."

Of these 34, 24 lived in the vicinity of Cook-street, Thomas-street, and Francis-street, and 10 lived in St. Michan's parish. Yet, only 11 were registered for the city proper, and the remaining 23 for the districts of the Co. of the city, including such distant districts as Lusk, Killossery, Ballyfermot, Tany (Dundrum) and Tully. No doubt, these parish priests of the Co. of the city had their illegal curates officiating in the various parishes, whilst they resided in the back streets of the city. The interesting point that emerges from all this is that the Catholic citizens must have had abundant Masses from these 34 priests in the 5 parish churches. Masses were suited to the occupations of the people, and were as early as 5 o'clock and as late as 11 o'clock on week-days.

Besides these 34 priests, there were " Register'd at a General Sessions of the Peace held for the County of Dublin, at Kilmainham, the 13th day of July, 1704, and were since Return'd up to the *Council Office in Dublin*," 36 Popish Parish Priests. Practically all resided in their parishes.

In the city and county of Dublin there were 70 registered parish priests, not counting the illicit curates of the Co. of the City of Dublin and of the County of Dublin. Of the 34 priests, for the city and Co. of the City of Dublin, only 4 were ordained in the diocese—by Archbishop Russell (1683–92)— 12 were ordained in other dioceses, 3 of whom were ordained

---

[1] The Tholsel (tolcetum, le Tolsey, Tollbooth or commercial exchange) stood at the corner of St. Nicholas-street and Skinners-row (Christchurch-place) as far back as 1311. It was used for many purposes—a commercial exchange, the City Hall, Courts, Parliament, Quarter Sessions, banquets, etc. In the late seventeenth century it was rebuilt in elegant style—the Hotel de Ville of Dublin—" worthy of its dignitie."

by Archbishop (Blessed) Oliver Plunkett at Ardpatrick, and 18 were ordained on the continent, chiefly in Spain. Only about one-fifth of them were over 50 years of age in 1704, the rest were almost equally divided between the thirties and the forties. Thus, when the penal time chapels were being reconstructed (about 1723) at least half of those priests were still alive and engaged in the work of reconstruction.

In 1709 a further penal enactment was passed whereby all registered priests were to take the Oath of Abjuration disclaiming any right to the Crown on the part of the Stuart Pretender. Father Cornelius Nary, P.P., St. Michan's, wrote in 1724 : " It is certain that of eleven hundred Roman Catholic priests who were registered pursuant to the Act of Parliament for that purpose, not above thirty-three priests ever took the Oath of Abjuration, and of these thirty-three one-half are now dead."[1]   It would seem these thirty-three priests were the pastors of the City and County of the City of Dublin ; otherwise they could not have carried on their ministrations in these areas. On 19th December, 1713, Parliament " ordered that all Justices of the Peace and Clerks of the Crown and Peace throughout this kingdom do immediately after next quarter sessions certify to this House what popish registered priests have taken the Oath of Abjuration and what priests, having neglected to take the said Oath, do still exercise their functions of priests."

Who was the one priest of the thirty-four Dublin pastors who did not take the Oath of Abjuration ? Was he Father Nary himself ? He says in his pamphlet : " There are some clauses in it [the Oath] to the truth of which no Roman Catholic—at least I am convinced I cannot—in conscience swear."[2]

Father Burke remarks : " The vast mass of those [priests] known and registered were living as outlaws in defiance of government. This fact is borne out by authorities on both sides." Father Nary was not living as an outlaw, but quite peacefully as parish priest of St. Michan's. In spite of his

---

[1] *The Case of the Catholics of Ireland Humbly Represented to both Houses of Parliament* (Burke, *Irish Priests in the Penal Times*, p. 197).
[2] Apud Burke, p. 185.

inability in "conscience" to swear "to the truth" of the clauses, he says : "I shall only remark that to my certain knowledge many a man as well Protestant as Catholic has taken the oath with aching hearts and no other way willingly than as a sailor in a storm throws his goods overboard to save his life."[1] It is to be presumed that Father Nary imitated the sailor and thereby remained one of the thirty-four Dublin pastors.

The friars began to return to Dublin early in the eighteenth century. The Franciscans came to Cook-street in the early years of George I, their first guardian being Father Sylvester Lloyd in 1717. The Dominicans came to Bridge-street about the same time. They retired from there to Little Denmark-street in 1764 and their chapel became the parish chapel of St. Audoen's. The Augustinians returned to Dublin early in the eighteenth century, their prior, Father Byrne (disguised under the name of Colonel Byrne), taking an old stable off Thomas-street near the old tower of St. John's Hospital, outside Newgate. The Discalced Carmelites returned to Wormwood Gate about 1710 ; they had previously been there in 1625. They moved to Lower Stephen's-street in 1760. The Calced Carmelites returned in 1728, and remained in Ash-street until 1780, when they removed to the select quarter of French-street (Upper Mercer-street).

Two Jesuits came to St. Michan's in 1712, namely, Father Milo Byrne and Father Michael Murphy, to assist the secular clergy in Mary's Lane Chapel. They also opened a Classical school, in which they taught Philosophy. Father Murphy was arrested in 1718 for saying Mass and keeping school, but was some time afterwards released, and continued his priestly and professional work until his death in 1736. The Jesuit Fathers continued their work right through the eighteenth century. Father Mulcaile (Mulhall), S.J., came to St. Michan's in 1763. When the Society of Jesus was suppressed in 1773 he continued his services as a secular priest in the parish, as other Jesuits did in other parishes. He enlarged the old school, No. 3 George's Hill, where he lived, and educated 600 to

---

[1] Apud Burke, p. 186.

800 boys, clothed 200, and fed and clothed 30 or 40. The house still stands as portion of the premises of the Presentation Sisters.

4. THE NEW CATHOLIC CHAPELS.

(a). South City

The recognition of Popish Parish Priests by the Act of 1703 was an important stage in the progress of the Church in Ireland. The office of Parish Priest presumed a place of worship for his parishioners which was then implicitly recognised in the Act. No longer would the 1704 Parish Priests of Dublin City be content to offer Mass in the houses of widows, in outhouses and stables in back streets and lanes. As the returns asked for by the Government in 1731 contain detailed references to the chapels erected before 1714 (I George I), we know that some of the Mass-houses were erected before that year, and presumably shortly after the Act of 1703. Thus, even in Queen Anne's reign (1702–14) the parish priests had availed themselves of the freedom for places of worship. But it was after her death, when George I came to the throne, that Dublin Catholics felt a sense of security and began to remodel the dwelling-houses and turn them into respectable places of worship. This renaissance of the Church in Dublin was due almost entirely to the munificence of the Catholic merchants, traders and craftsmen, who had grown prosperous and influential.

The first movement in the direction of remodelling the old chapels, of which we have documentary evidence, was that of Canon Rivers, parish priest of St. Catherine's, who, about 1723, enlarged his chapel in Dirty-lane (present Bridgefoot-street, north of Thomas-street), and added galleries on three sides from the floor.[1] In this arrangement he was only following one that was begun a hundred years previously in the case of the Jesuit chapel in Back-lane. Sir William Brereton,[2] in describing this chapel as it was in 1630, states :

---

[1] Donnelly, *Dub. Par.*, II. 222.
[2] *Travels in Holland, the United Provinces, Scotland, and Ireland*, 1634–35. Donnelly, *Dioc. of Dub.*, 18th cent., *I.E.R.*, Aug. 1889, p. 721.

" The pulpit in this church was richly adorned with pictures, and so was the high altar, which was advanced with steps, and railed out like cathedrals ; upon either side thereof was there erected places for confession ; no fastened seats were in the middle or body thereof, nor was there any chancel ; but that it might be more capacious there was a gallery erected on both sides, and at the lower end of this church. . . ." This plan of oblong room, with three galleries, and free space on the floor, was carried out in the reconstructed Mass-houses.

So widespread throughout the city had been the urge to remodel the old Mass-houses that the Government became alarmed, and an Act was passed to *Prevent the Further Growth of Popery in this Kingdom* (1731). The Lord Mayor, the Seneschals of the Liberties (Archbishop's, and Earl of Meath's) and the Ministers and Churchwardens of the several parishes, were ordered to return an account of all Mass-houses, Nunneries, Fryeries, and Popish Schools that might be found to exist in their several districts. This return[1] conveniently provided a Catholic Directory for the year.

The following is a summary of the returns :

Parishes	Mass-houses	Priests		Schools
St. James's . . .	1	(secular)	3	2
St. Catherine's . . .	1	(secular)	5	2
,, ,, . . .	2	(friars)	15	—
St. Audoen's . . .	1	(secular)	40 or	3
,, ,, . . .	1	(and friars)	50	—
St. Nicholas's Without .	1	(secular)	8	16
,, ,, ,, .		(friars)	7	—
St. Michael's . . .	1	(secular)	5	3
,, ,, . . .		(friars)	5	—
St. Michan's . . .	2	(secular)	—	12
St. Mary's . . .	1	(secular)	1	—
St. Andrew's . . .	1	(secular)	7	2
	12		106	40

The parish chapels were St. James's, Watling-street ; St. Catherine's, Dirty-lane ; St. Michael's, Rosemary-lane ;

[1] *Archivium Hibernicum* (1915), IV. 131 seq.

St. Nicholas's, Francis-street ; St. Michan's, Bull-lane; St. Paul's, Arran-quay, and St. Mary's, Liffey-street. Besides these were the chapels of the Religious Orders : the Augustinians, John's-lane ; the Discalced Carmelites, Wormwood-gate ; the Dominicans, Bridge-street ; the Franciscans, off Cook-street ; the Capuchins, off Church-street, and the Calced Carmelites, Ash-street.

In 1731, the Minister and Churchwardens of the parish of St. James reported that " there is one Mass House on ye South side of St. James's Street in ye said Parish in which service is performed by three Preists or reputed Preists ; built or repaired in ye beginning of Kg. George ye 1st's Reign . . . as alsoe a private Masshouse or Chappell in Dolphin's Barn . . . built in ye Reign of King George the first."   St. James's Mass-house was built in 1724, when St. James's parish was separated from St. Catherine's, in a long yard near a brewery that is now merged into Guinness's premises. As the site was found inconvenient, the chapel, according to the 1749 report,[1] " was since removed to Watling Street, near St. James's Gate, the Sacristy being near the well. The altar is adorned with several pictures, among which are those of St. James the Elder and Ignatius Loyola—on the altar is a gilded tabernacle, six candlesticks—there is a gallery, pulpit, pews, etc."

For the parish of St. Catherine the Protestant minister reported in 1732, that there were 3 Masshouses, one rebuilt since 1st George I (1714), 20 priests, 2 schools, and a weekly conference held from November, 1730, to March, 1731, by one Lahy. The Lord Mayor's return differed from the Minister's report in some important details. It gave 4 Mass-houses, 24 priests, and 6 schools. The Vicar of St. Catherine's entered into further particulars. He certified " that in the parish of St. Catherine within the liberty of the city of Dublin there are three Mass houses or popish Chappels, one in Dirty-lane, it is attended by ye popish registered parish priest and four assistant priests his Curates.

" One other Mass house is in St. Johns lane, belongs to the fryars Augustines and is supplied by about eight priests, four of five of which are resident in sd. parish.

[1] Donnelly, *Roman Catholics*, 1749 (C.T.S., 1904).

" One other Mass house is at the bottom of New-row near where Wormwood Gate stood and belongs to the fryars Carmelite and is supplied by about seven priests, six of whom are resident in sd. parish, sd. Mass house has been lately rebuilt and enlarged.

" And we do further certify that sd. Mass houses were erected before the reign of King George the first [1714].

" And that in ye part of the ye parish which lyes in the liberty of St. Thomas Court there are reputed popish schoolmasters but no nunnery or Private chappel that we know of."

It is interesting to note that the Act of 1704 forbidding any assistants or curates of the parish priests had become a dead letter. The parish priests had many curates, and the friars had their chapels and community. Nothing was done at this time (1731) to curtail the activities of curates or regulars, even in face of the returns required by the Act to " Prevent the Further Growth of Popery." The parish priests and regulars continued to embellish their chapels, and to make them small continental churches. Fortunately, through the industry of Bishop Donnelly, we have a perfect picture of these reconstructed Mass-houses of Dublin.

As to St. Catherine's parish, the Report of 1749 states that the Dirty-lane chapel was " a convenient building with a handsome altar well decorated. The altar piece is Our Saviour bearing His Cross." Of the John's-lane chapel it says that " it fell down a few years ago, but has been rebuilt by subscription, and is one of the most regular built chapels in Dublin, the altar is wainscotted and embellished with pillars, cornices, and other decorations. The altar-piece is a painting of the Crucifixion, and on the altar stands a gilt tabernacle, twelve gilded candlesticks with large wax tapers and with artificial nosegays. The Sacristy is large and commodiously fitted up. Here are two paintings, one of St. Augustine, the other of his mother, Monica. The pulpit is very neat and the confessionals in good taste, and placed under the gallery which serves for a choir. Over the Sacristy are the lodging chambers of the Friars."

Of the Discalced Carmelite chapel at Wormwood-gate the 1749 Report states : " The altar piece is a painting of the

V.M. giving the Scapular to St. Simon, on whose side stand
St. Martin Consinus and St. Angel, Martyr, saints of that
Order. On the other side are the Kings, Popes and Cardinals
who were friends of this Order. Underneath this picture,
paintings of the Crucifixion : on the Epistle side the Ascension,
and St. Theresa : on the Gospel side the Assumption and
St. John of the Cross. Near the pulpit stands a small altar.
There are neither confessionals, pews or vestry, but there are
two galleries. The house adjacent lodges five friars, who have
no provincial in Ireland, but only a vice-Provincial, who
may be suspended at the pleasure of the General of the
Order."

The 1731 report for the adjoining parish of St. Audoen's
gives " two Mass-houses, one in Cook-street, and the other
in Bridge-street . . . neither of which has been built since the
first year of the reign of King George the first . . . there are
between forty and fifty regular and secular priests who reside
in Cook-street, Bridge-street, and Back-lane in said parish,
five or six of whom lodge in the houses adjoining the Mass-
house in Bridge-street, and as many more in the houses
adjoining the Mass-house in Cook-street . . . the number of
them that officiate [at the said Mass-houses] we find it impracticable to discover (those of their Profession being entirely
upon their Guard)." The Mass-house in Cook-street was
St. Audoen's ; that in Bridge-street the Dominican friary.

The Cook-street chapel, opposite Keisar's lane (from
Cornmarket to Cook-street ; extinct), had been the Dominican
chapel in James II's reign, but, on their banishment after the
Battle of the Boyne, became the parochial chapel of St.
Audoen's. According to the report of 1749, " the chapel is
not long since rebuilt with a house contiguous for the reception
of their priests. Between the Pulpit and Sacristy stands the
image of the B.V.M. with a diadem on her head, the Infant
Jesus on one arm and a sceptre in the opposite hand. There
are two galleries with confessionals."

The Dominican chapel, in the courtyard off Lower Bridge-
street, was the most ornate of the old chapels. According to
the 1749 report, " the altar makes a grand appearance, partly
gilded and partly painted, the pillars are lofty, the altarpiece

a large painting of Crucifixion. Besides other pieces there
was the taking down of Our Saviour from the Cross, the
Nativity of Christ, the Assumption, St. Michael fighting the
dragon, and St. Dominic receiving the Rosary from the
V.M. Before the altar, which is always well adorned with
tapers, hangs a silver lamp, and a plate of silver hangs upon
the tabernacle door. Near the pulpit the Lord Kingsland has
a large pew, on which is his coat of arms. There is a convenient Sacristy, several pews and two galleries, in the lower
of which are the confessionals, in the upper the choir. The
devotion of the Rosary is much used here, an essay on which
has been published by Father Richardson as a conventual
of this house, where six friars are commodiously lodged, who
have a superior, also kitchen and servant's room."

Within a few hundred yards of Cook-street parish chapel
was another parish chapel, that of St. Michael's. The Report
of 1731, made by the Churchwardens, stated : " there are
Two Popish Mass houses in our Parish, in which . . . about
Ten Priests officiate, about five in each Mass house, which
Mass houses . . . have been subsisting in said Parish, about
Twenty years, excepting that about five years ago, one of
them, who was kept over a stable, in Skipper's Lane that was
Ruinous, and since fallen down, was removed to Rosemary
Lane, about twenty yards from said former Mass house, to
another Stable in Our Parish, which was repaired and fitted
for their Purpose." The Report of 1749 says that it was
Father Clinch, C.C. (the P.P. was then Dean Russell), who
removed the chapel from Skipper's Lane to Rosemary Lane,
about 1726 or 1727, and " who procured collections for it.
The altar-piece is a large painting of the Crucifixion, placed
between two pillars, and the chapel is built in this form
[L shaped] in which are three galleries. That on the Gospel
side serves as a Communion altar and for Confessionals ;
that in the middle opposite the altar is for the better part of
the congregation, and in the front of the gallery on the epistle
side (which serves for the Choir) is the pulpit. It is the only
chapel in Dublin that has not a tabernacle on the altar."
The Blessed Sacrament was reserved on a side altar according
to continental custom.

At the back of St. Michael's chapel was the other Mass-house of 1731, the Franciscan friary, separated from it by a wall. This was " Adam and Eve chapel, so called from a sign of that name near it in Cook-street." The sign-board was that of an inn which stood at the corner of a passage from Cook-street to the stable taken by the Franciscans. The stable was remodelled into a chapel, and became, before 1749, a respectable place of worship. " The altar-piece," says the Report of 1749, " is a large painting of the Crucifixion and of the Assumption and Annunciation : behind the pulpit which stands on the Epistle side, is a room for the preacher to rest in ; there is a small altar under the new gallery facing the great altar, which was raised at the expense of the Freize-mongers in High Street. There are two galleries, that on the Epistle side serves for a choir, and the other side is full of pews, and was built at the sole expense of one Major Stafford. Adjacent to the chapel is a house that lodges eight Friars with a closet to each chamber." Each friar had a separate room ; the house was, therefore, of large dimensions.

In the parish of St. Nicholas Without the Walls of Dublin, the 1731 Report states, " that there now is, and has been for many years a Mass House, commonly known by the name of St. Francis's Chappel in St. Francis-street ; in which there are eight priests constantly officiating and if we are rightly informed, several more. We also find, that there is another large Mass-House or Friary erected in Ash-street in the said Parish, since his present Majesties accession to the Throne, to which seven priests or friars belong, and that several others, as we are informed, officiate in it."

The Francis-street chapel was built on the site of the pre-Reformation Franciscan friary " in the latter end of the reign of King Charles II " (c. 1685), says the 1749 Report, " by the care of one Barnewall, a Franciscan friar, for the use of his order, who held it until the friars were by law banished (c. 1690) and then it became a Mass-house for secular priests."

Archdeacon Austin (1709–40) embellished the chapel and made it a plain oblong building, 80 x 40 ft., which corresponds with the nave of the present church. He also restored the Franciscan cloister, on the north side of the chapel, and made it a residence for himself and his curates. The Christian Brothers' school now stands on the site.

"The altar-piece," the Report continues, "four pillars and the steps, are all of Kilkenny marble. It is adorned with the pictures of the Assumption, St. Peter, St. Thomas, St. Paul, and St. Nicholas. . . . It is flagged, but has no apartment for a vestry. Near the pulpit stands another [altar] dedicated to St. Anthony of Padua, which is now in disuse. The choir is abovestairs, and the dormitory of the friars serves now for the priests' lodgings."

Ash-street chapel belonged to the Calced Carmelites and was built shortly after 1728. "The altar-piece is a painting of the Crucifixion, on each side of which are those of the prophets Elias and Eliseus in Carmelite Habits, the former of whom that Order boasts as their founder. A handsome branch hangs before the altar ; near which is a pulpit and four galleries. Adjacent to the chapel is a convenient house, sufficient for the reception of six Carmelites."

In 1782 Dirty-lane chapel was moved to Meath-street by Archdeacon Birmingham, P.P. It was an octagon chapel, and was the first departure from the penal time type of building, apparently modelled, exteriorly at all events, on some continental church. The old system of galleries was, however, continued for greater accommodation. Archdeacon Birmingham was fortunate in acquiring such a site off the important thoroughfare of Meath-street, and he must have received it from the Earl of Meath, as it was within the boundaries of the Earl's Liberties.[1] As no chapel should front a main thoroughfare, according to the law of the time, the Archdeacon built an imposing brick presbytery between it and the street—another departure from the penal time lodgings of the clergy over their chapel. St. Catherine's parish, therefore, was the first to emerge from the penal-time chapel, apparently through an understanding and a friendship between the Archdeacon and the Earl.

The present Catholic parish of St. Andrew was created in 1709 and its first chapel, a converted stable at the rere of Lord Ely's house in Hawkins's-street, was in use as early as

[1] See Ronan, *Poddle River*, R.S.A.I., LVII (1927), 42. (Map).

1717. The Churchwardens of St. Mark's Protestant church reported in 1731 that they had " discovered " this old stable where " seven priests celebrated Mass, and two Popish schools." The 1749 Report states that the chapel is old and not uniform ; " they talk of rebuilding it." A storm blew it down in 1750 ; that sealed its fate. Shortly afterwards the Royal Dublin Society purchased Lord Ely's house and gave the parish priest of St. Andrew's a site for his chapel in the old Fleet Market between Poolbeg-street and Lazers-hill, with an entrance from both thoroughfares. It became later (after 1780) known as Townsend-street chapel and did duty from 1750 until 1834, when the present church in Westland-row was built. Several of its relics were removed to the modern church, notably the valuable altar painting of the Descent from the Cross, which still is an ornament behind the high altar.

(b) North City

On the north side of the Liffey was the important parish of St. Michan, the oldest city parish, dating back to Danish days, to the year 1096. Its patron saint was of the sixth century, apparently one of the Welsh missionaries who came to aid the Patrician missionaries in spreading the Gospel. Mochoroc of Delgany, Canoc of Kilmacanogue, and Sanctan of Bohernabreena, were also Welsh missionaries. Michan, at the Ford of the Hurdles across the Liffey, is commemorated in the *Martyrology of Donegal*, at 25th August, as " Michen ó Chill Michen i n-Ath-Cliath." His cill was apparently a hostel at the ford for the wayfarers on the Slighe Cualann from Tara to South Leinster. His mission was to preach to them ; the Celtic colony on the banks of the Poddle, with its cills of St. Michil-le-Pole, St. Brigid, St. Kevin, and St. Patrick on the Island, was already well provided for.

For the growing Norse colony in Ostmantown (corruptly, Oxmantown) Bishop Samuel Ó hAingli built the splendid church of St. Michan's in 1096 on a site granted by Murtogh Ó Briain, King of Dublin (in the present Church-street). St. Mary's Abbey had been already in existence for some years. Between St. Michan's and the Abbey the Dominicans erected (about 1224) St. Saviour's on land (site of present Four Courts) granted them by Henri de Loundres, Archbishop of Dublin.

In penal times the first Mass priest whose name has survived in connection with the district was Father Nicholas Netterville, S.J., between 1604 and 1607,[1] and the first parish priest recorded was Father William Browne (1615–50). In 1618 the Catholics had Mass said for them in " a back-room of Shelton's house beyond the bridge, at the corner of the so-called Hangman Lane " (Hammond-lane, off Church-street). According to the *Visitation of Archbishop Bulkeley*[2] (Protestant Archbishop of Dublin) of the year 1630, " the most part of the parishioners are recusants [Catholics] who go to one Browne to hear Mass." The houses of Patrick White and the Widow Geydon are mentioned later as Mass-houses.

The first parish priest to set up a definite Mass-house in St. Michan's parish was Dr. Nary (1702–38). In 1704, he was registered as 46 years of age, living in Church-street, and parish priest of St. Michan's, Oxmand-town, ordained in Kilkenny, 1682, by James, Bishop of Ossory. Between 1702 and 1704 he transformed an old building at the corner of Bull-lane and Mary's lane into a chapel, and lived in Bull-lane after 1704.

The chapel is thus described in the 1749 Report : " In St. Mary's lane is a parochial Chapel whose jurisdiction extends from one side of Boot lane [Arran St.] to one side of Church-street inclusive. It was built by subscriptions obtained by the solicitation of Dr. Cornelius Nary ; 'tis a large but irregular piece of building. The altar-piece is a painting of the Annunciation of B.V.M. and on the Epistle side stands a large image of B.V. with Jesus in her arms, carved in wood, which statue before the dissolution belonged to St. Mary's Abbey. On the Gospel side stands the pulpit, and opposite it a choir enclosed, near to which is a large Sacristy. There is another altar near the pulpit, over which is a large painting of the crucifix, and under it the picture of Francis Xavirius ; there are three galleries here, several pews and confessionals.

[1] Battersby, *Jesuits in Dublin*, p. 60.
[2] Ronan, *Archivium Hibernicum*, VIII., 58.

The decorations of the altar are much the same as those mentioned in the chapel of Liffey-street. It has been lately repaired by the care of Mr. Dennis Byrne, Titular Dean of St. Patrick's, and parish priest of said chapel."

The statue of the Blessed Virgin is now happily honoured in the Carmelite church, Aungier-street, through the anti-quarian interest of Rev. Dr. Spratt, O.C.C. The picture of St. Francis Xavier was intended to do honour to the Jesuit Fathers for their services in the parish, but it has long since disappeared.

Up to 1707, St. Michan's was the only parish on the north side of the Liffey. In that year two new parishes were carved from it—St. Paul's and St. Mary's—to provide for the people of the new districts of King's-street and Queen's-street (called after Charles II and his consort) on the west (begun about 1664), and Capel-street, Jervis-street, Stafford-street, etc. on the east (begun about 1676). The latter district had formed portion of the lands of St. Mary's Abbey ; hence the name of the new parish. For a few years before 1707, Father John Linegar (afterwards Archbishop of Dublin, 1734–57) hired a room in Mary-street to serve as a Mass-house. The new chapel in Liffey-street was erected in 1730.

This chapel continued to serve for nearly one hundred years. It was situated at the rere of the present houses on the west side of Liffey-street from No. 21 to No. 26. The chapel and its furnishings are minutely described in the Report of 1749 : "This chapel, though small, is neat, altar railed in, steps ascending to it of oak ; fore part of the altar covered with gilt leather, and name of Jesus in glory in the midst. On the altar is a gilt tabernacle, with six large gilt candlesticks, and as many nosegays of artificial flowers. The altar piece carved and embellished with four pillars, cornices and other decorations gilt and painted. The picture of the Conception of the B.V.M., to whom the chapel is dedicated, fills the altar-piece ; and on each side are paintings of the Apostles Peter and Paul. Opposite the altar hangs a handsome brass branch for tapers, near it is a neat oak pulpit, on the sounding board of which is a figure of a gilt dove, representing the descent of the Holy Ghost. In said chapel is a small sacristy, four decent confessionals, two galleries, several pews for better sort, and two sprinkling pots of black marble in chapel yard."

Part of the furniture so described was transferred to the Pro-Cathedral, Marlboro'-street, which was opened in 1826. The " pillars and cornices " are those which now form the handsome superstructure of the side altars, while the " picture of the Conception of the B.V.M." is in the hall of No. 83. With the opening of the Pro-Cathedral the old chapel in Liffey-street was finally closed and soon after devoted to secular use.

St. Paul's parish was erected in the western portion of St. Michan's in 1707 on account of the laying out of Oxman-town with new streets and buildings by the Corporation in 1664 and the rapid increase in population.   The parochial chapel was at the back of Nos. 11 and 12 Arran's Quay,[1] but, in 1708 (7th December), at the Sunday Evening Devotions, a beam fell, killed three people, and injured several others. It was this accident, broadcast in the Press of the day, and other similar accidents in the miserable chapels, which appealed to the good sense of decent Dublin Protestants.   As parish priests were tolerated in 1704, why should they not be allowed suitable chapels ?   With the death of Queen Anne in 1714 the parish priests and friars took courage and began to rebuild their old chapels.   The Augustinian chapel of Hammond-lane, of James II's reign, had been demolished after the Battle of the Boyne and all its materials were sold.   The parochial chapel was an adjoining warehouse until 1730, when Rev. Dr. Fitzsimons, P.P., built a chapel on the Augustinian site with an entrance from Hammond-lane and Arran's Quay.   The 1749 Report states that " it has a good gallery, convenient sacristy, near to which an additional building is made, where the priests lodge."   The buildings stood in a kind of courtyard, similar to the Lower Bridge-street arrangement, with dwelling houses on two sides.   The chapel, mainly in this condition, did duty for over a hundred years, as there was no suitable site available for a new church.

Besides the parochial chapel on Arran's Quay, and the chapel-of-ease in the Dominican Convent in Channel-row, a

---

[1] In No. 12 was born the renowned Edmund Burke, 1728.

third chapel was mentioned in the Government Report of
1731—that of the Capuchin Fathers, which was erected in
1720. It stood off a narrow passage between Church-street
and Bow-lane. Their first return to Dublin after the so-called
Reformation was to Thomas-street and Audoen's Arch, but,
after the famous attack in 1630, they, like the other Religious
Orders, had to leave the city, but they assisted the parochial
clergy in country districts. One honoured name that survives
in the documents of the period was that of Father Barnaby
Barnewall of Shankill, who laboured around Killiney under
the name of Teige O Murroghowe, and said Mass for the
people in his brother's Castle of Shankill.[1]

In James II's reign, the Capuchins returned to the city
and took up their old residence at Audoen's-arch, but, after
the Battle of the Boyne, they retired again to the country as
assistant-priests. One of them, John Weldon, was reported
by the Government as lodging in Luke Dowdall's in Smith-
field, in 1697. To him, apparently, is due the subsequent
coming of the members of the Order to the Church-street
district. The chapel in the laneway is thus described in the
1749 Report : "Church Street chapel was fitted up in the
year 1720, for the use of the Capuchin Friars (who in the reign
of King James II lived at St. Audoen's Arch), by Father Joseph
Evers, Superior of the Order : and in 1730 was entirely
repaired by contributions collected by Father Alexis Dowdall,
Superior also of the said Order. The chapel is small and neat
and the altar decent. The Altar-piece is a Crucifixion, though
formerly it was a painting of Our Saviour taken down from
the Cross, which piece is much admired by Connoiseurs. There
are two images, one of the B.V.M. with Jesus in her arms.
The other of St. Francis with the Capuchin Habit.[2] Here
is a gallery which serves for choir with a vestry, but no
confessionals."

This chapel was rebuilt about 1796, and the reconstructed
building was known afterwards as " The Old Chapel." The

[1] *Archiv Hib.*, *VIII*, 82. Father Angelus, *Irish Capuchins*, p. 53 ff.

[2] Father Angelus (op. cit., p. 61, n.) states that in the present Convent in Church-
street there is " a painting of the Crucifixion and another of the Taking Down from
the Cross." Apparently these are the paintings referred to. It is consoling to know
they are preserved. Very few of those old paintings are extant.

Capuchins resided in various streets in the district, and eventually settled in North King-street. In 1819 there was a thorough repair of the Old Chapel, " the expense of which was defrayed by the collections made at a series of sermons, preached in the evenings of the last Lent but two [i.e. 1819], by the Rev. Mr. Keogh, a Religious of this Order, and Parish Priest of Baldoyle and Howth. The Religious of this establishment, consisting of the Provincial, Guardian, and six other clergymen, have a house in the chapel-yard, to which there is a passage from Bow-street."[1]

5. CATHOLIC SCHOOLS IN THE CITY OF DUBLIN.

By the Act of 1691, as we have seen, no papist was to teach school publicly, and, though popish parish priests were allowed to function by the Act of 1703, yet the popish school-master was still debarred from keeping a public school. Catholics were to be brought up in ignorance so that they might be impoverished and reduced to the position of mere serfs. Yet many a popish schoolmaster broke the law. In 1705, a case is recorded in the Dublin Corporation Assembly Roll[2] of a conviction against Charles Grey, popish school-master, " for keeping a Popish school, contrary to the Act of Parliament in that case made," and he was fined £20, with three months' imprisonment. Having spent the three months in prison, he petitioned to have the fine reduced, and the Assembly ordered " that the said fine of twenty pounds be reduced to sixpence by reason of his great poverty, and giving security of the good behaviour not to be guilty of the like offence for the future."

The penalties against Catholic schoolmasters were increased in 1709 (8 Anne, c. 3), and a person of the Catholic religion instructing youth in learning publicly or in a private house should be taken to be a " popish regular clergyman," and incur all the penalties and forfeitures. This Act meant that he was liable to imprisonment and transportation on the first

---

[1] McGregor, 155. The foundation stone of the present church on the site was laid, 12th June, 1868, by Cardinal Cullen, and the sermon was preached by Father Tom Burke, O.P.

[2] Cal. Anc. Recs. Dub., VI. 342.

conviction, and to death for high treason on the second conviction. It was the same penalty that a Jesuit or a friar incurred.

Under this penal enactment against Catholic teachers, Protestant " Charity Schools " flourished so " that the whole nation may in time be made both Protestant and English." Dean Swift showed himself not the great liberal that some modern writers would have us believe, but a proselytiser of the first order. As Dean of St. Patrick's Cathedral, he established (1712), within his exclusive jurisdiction of the area in the vicinity of the Cathedral, two " Charity Schools " for 20 boys and 10 girls,[1] namely, the children of papists of the district, and furnished them with clothes, books and schooling. After their schooling, he apprenticed them to Protestant masters and mistresses, with an allowance of £3 5s. in money, besides a new suit of clothes, a Bible, a Book of Common Prayer, and a book called *The Whole Duty of Man*. The school children were admonished to attend carefully daily service in the Cathedral, and they were assiduously instructed in the Church Catechism. " Trained up in the manner mentioned," said Swift in his *Wretched Condition of Ireland*, " and then bound apprentices in the families of Gentlemen and citizens they will prove a strong check upon the rest." The example of these perverted Catholic children of the Liberties, schooled, clothed, provided with money and Protestant tracts, apprenticed to Protestant craftsmen, and to the mistresses of Protestant houses, was to be a reminder to the less materially inclined Catholics of the Liberties of the beneficence of the great Dean of St. Patrick's. What with penal laws against school teachers, and the " Charity Schools " of St. Patrick's, the parish priests of St. Catherine's and the adjoining parishes had a difficult task to provide any kind of education, and to counteract the influence of the " Charity Schools."

Notwithstanding the severe penalties, the number of Catholic schoolmasters in Dublin actually increased. According to the report of 1731 on the " State of Popery in Ireland " there were in the city of Dublin 45 schools and 29 outside the city. In St. Catherine's parish, " in the Liberty of St.

---

[1] Corcoran, *State Policy in Irish Education*, 100.

Thomas Court there are two reputed popish schoolmasters. In Earl Street [a school] kept by Taddeus Norton.[1]   In Pimlico kept by Egan Smith.   In Pool Street kept by Charles Condran.   In Braithwaite Street kept by Mary Carolan." Another portion of the Report gives the names of some female teachers who kept schools in this area :   " In Mill Street kept by Catherine Anderson.   In New Row on the Poddle kept by Catherine Hanley.   In the Coombe kept by Mary Murphy. In Fordoms Alley kept by Terence O'Brien and Mary O'Brien. In Truck Street kept by Margaret Teelan.   In New Row on the Poddle kept by Cornelius Hanley."[2]

In the parish of St. Nicholas Without " there are," according to the same Report, " sixteen Popish schoolmasters, some of whom are Priests or Friars."[3]   The Calced Carmelites conducted a school here.   In the parish of St. Michael there were three schools, " two of which teach Book keeping & Mathematicks onely, and the other, Writeing & Arithmetick onely." In the parish of St. Audoen's there were " Three Popish Schools, one in Bridge-Street, one in Cook-Street, and the other in St. Audoen's Arch."   It is likely that the Dominicans, the Franciscans, and the secular clergy conducted respectively those schools in connection with their chapels, and that the higher mathematics and book-keeping were taught for the advantage of the sons of Catholic merchants and traders. In St. James's parish, either in the chapel in James's-street, or in a "house adjoining . . . a Popish school is kept by one Carey a reputed Priest, and at the west end of ye said street another Popish school kept by one Patrick Keef."[4]

The solitary example of a prosecution by the Dublin Corporation of a Catholic schoolmaster would seem to show that Civic and Government authorities saw that the task was too great to suppress every illicit school held in back rooms in back lanes, or even to know where these schools were.   It would have required an enormous staff of detectives to keep

[1] Tadhg O Neachtain, a Gaelic poet. He composed a versified list in Irish of Irish literary men residing in Dublin, mainly during the years 1726-29, with whom Tadhg was acquainted. Three priests, friends of the O Neachtain family, are honoured with first places. (T. F. O'Rahilly, Gadelica, p. 156.)
[2] Archiv. Hib., IV. 148.
[3] Ibid., 146.
[4] Ibid., 140, 138, 139.

track of them, and the Corporation was not inclined to pay the expense. Thus, between 1709, the year of the first Act against Popish schoolmasters, and 1731, the year of the Report, the growth of Catholic schools was enormous. In 1731, there were 26 on the south side of the city, and at least 12 on the north side. After the Report of 1731 of this extraordinary growth of Catholic schools there is no evidence of any interference with them. In fact, with the embellishment of the Catholic chapels, continuing between 1723 and 1749, the urge of Catholic activities seems to have been quickened. A useful stimulus in this direction was the viceroyalty of Philip Stanhope, Earl of Chesterfield,[1] 1745–47, who favoured the policy of toleration to Catholics. He was the father of that famous remark with regard to Dublin Castle bureaucracy, that Ireland was ground down by " deputies of deputies of deputies."

The first Catholic school built, as a school, was in Meath-street, at the back of the octagon chapel, about 1782, ten years before the penal law against Popish schoolmasters was repealed. We do not know how many boys and girls it accommodated, but it may be presumed that a few hundred would have been the limit. It is very likely that the parish priest, Archdeacon Birmingham, would have enlisted the services of the various teachers, men and women, who had been carrying on their illicit teaching in the back rooms of the parish. Yet, the accommodation was by no means adequate for the populous parish.

At the west-end of the parish was the Protestant parochial school, in the Earl of Meath's Liberties. In 1786, " the first Sunday-school established in this city, and in Ireland, was opened " by the Protestant curate of St. Catherine's. " The female children assembled in the parochial school-house, which the Governors lent for that purpose ; and the boys were accommodated by the Earl of Meath, an anxious friend to

---

[1] It was he who planted the elms in Phoenix Park, threw the park open to the people, and erected the Phoenix monument. Did he erect the Phoenix as a symbol of Catholic Emancipation, or was he ignorant of the meaning of the name " Phoenix Park " ? The stream, *Fionn-uisge* (clear stream) rises at the back of the Viceregal-lodge and flows through the park northwards of the Magazine Hill into the Liffey. It was from that stream the park derived its name.

the institution, with the use of the Court-house of the Liberties of Thomas Court and Donore. From 300 to 500 children of all denominations generally attended, and exclusive of the usual course of reading, writing and arithmetic, the sacred scriptures were admitted and read, but without any selection, explanation, or comment whatever."

Apparently, the Earl of Meath was the patron, if not the originator, of this idea of a school for all denominations. The accommodation being "insufficient for the continually increasing numbers in that poor but populous part of the city, an idea was conceived of erecting a school for the purpose, on a large scale, and with every necessary convenience." The school was finished in 1798, mainly due to the " unremitting exertions of Mr. Ephraim Bewley," a member of the Quakers, who were numerous in the parish and who " induced so many respectable and opulent citizens to contribute liberally." The Quakers took an anxious and decided part in the promotion of the Institution. The Sunday-school continued until 1811 when it was opened as a day-school. This Sunday-school system, and its successor, were considered by the promoters " to be the best adapted to the peculiar circumstances of the children of the poor, in a district where Roman Catholics are to all other sects conjunctively as 9 to 1 ; and it has been attended with success."[1]

The inference from all this is that the Catholic day-school in Meath-street was entirely inadequate and only touched the fringe of the Catholic population. Moreover, Catholic young boys and girls were engaged in the industries of the district, bringing in a few shillings a week to help the home, and had no means of education except through the Sunday-school of School-street, where they were taught things useful to them in their industrial work, writing and arithmetic. This Sunday-school system was taken up in other districts, much to the embarrassment of the Catholic clergy.

About this time, the population of the civil parish of St. Catherine's was 20,176, Catholics about 18,000 and Protestants 2,000.[2] The children of school-age would be about

[1] Warburton, Whitelaw and Walsh, *Hist. of Dub.*, 852–54.
[2] Ibid., 847.

2,000—1,800 Catholics and 200 Protestants. Not one-half of those children went to school, to the day-school of Meath-street or to the mixed Sunday-school. The difficulty was to get the children engaged in industries to go to any school on Sunday or to Catechism classes in the Catholic chapel. They were tired after their labours of the week, and sought their freedom.

The Sunday school was not the only opposition to the Meath-street school. The rich and influential Protestants had a powerful body at their back to support them in the scheme for a large day school, namely, the Erasmus Smith Board. A Committee of the Governors reported in 1803 that " in the four parishes within the liberties of the City of Dublin there is no school for the instruction of Protestant children, except the Parochial Schools which only receive a limited number of children, and one small school kept in Truck Street by a man of the name of Fox. . . . Not less than 300 Protestant Children are without any means of instruction and of course exposed to all the evil consequences of ignorance, idleness, and superstition. This calls all the more strongly for our attention, as numbers of Protestant parents have been impelled by a desire of giving their children some education to send them to Roman Catholic schools where they are liable to imbibe the principles of that religion with their daily instruction. We recommend that a school for boys and another for girls be immediately established in that quarter [the Coombe] in which they shall be instructed in the principles of the Christian Religion. One good meal is to be given in the middle of the day to secure good attendance."

As a matter of fact, the Coombe was on the borders of two Liberties, the City's and the Earl of Meath's, and was not the place for making up for the deficiencies of education for Protestant children " within the Liberties of the City of Dublin." However, the Committee reported that they desired the ground and lease of a house for this school in the Coombe and Pimlico, in the Earl of Meath's Liberty. The site chosen was in Pimlico, upper part of the Coombe, on the Earl's property, and the Committee recommended, in 1804, the costs of building, £902 2s. 6d., which were returned for payment in 1806, as £1,411 2s. 9d. In 1807, the Committee returned the attendance as 105 girls and 150 boys, and they recommended that a Catechist be appointed "to have general superintendence of the school, and particular charge of religious instruction of children, and shall distribute such premiums as the Board shall think fit to order and to disburse any money entrusted to him by the Board . . . £10 yearly for purchasing shoes for the most deserving on the 1st November." For our present purpose, the interesting points in this report are that the schools were erected not in the City Liberty, that the Protestant parson was the superintendent, and that only 255 children were in attendance in 1807.[1] Yet, it is admitted that no distinction in the matter of religion of the children was made for 15 years.[2] That most of the children who were enticed to attend were Catholics is abundantly clear.

The Erasmus Smith School in Pimlico was in St. Catherine's parish. According to Mr. Whitelaw, an indefatigable worker on parochial returns, the number of Protestants of all denominations in his own parish of St. Catherine, in 1818, was 2,000, whereas Roman Catholics were 18,000.[3]

As the population did not vary very much between 1803 and 1818, the school-going children in 1807, namely 255, attending the Erasmus Smith School, could not have been mainly Protestant.

When the Governors of the Sunday School closed it down in 1811, apparently sure of their ground in that department, they made it a parochial school, evidently for girls, as the boys were well catered for in the Erasmus Smith School. Yet, in 1818, the attendance at this Protestant parochial school consisted only of 50 girls. In that year the Erasmus School was confined to Protestants, 160 boys and 155 girls. The children did not come from St. Catherine's parish, but from the neighbouring Protestant parish of St. Luke, in the Eastern Liberties, the majority of whose 1,000 'souls' were Protestants.[4] The Protestant parochial school of that parish

[1] Archives, Erasmus Smith Endowment.
[2] Warburton, Whitelaw and Walsh, *Hist. of Dub.*, 860.
[3] Ibid. 847. Though the Protestant Authorities ordered returns of the religious population of the various parishes of the diocese no satisfactory return had been made between 1766 and 1818.
[4] Ibid., 847, 860.

in 1818, could only muster 30 poor children who were clothed and breakfasted. Thus, the Erasmus Smith School, founded to provide for poor Protestants in the city, was, between 1807 and 1818, chiefly for the poor Catholics of St. Catherine's parish, and became in 1818, a high-class school for the better class of St. Luke's parish. The withdrawal of the Catholic children from the school in 1818 was apparently due to the Catholic opposition in that year to mixed schools of another kind (of which later).

Meanwhile, a pioneer of Catholic education in Dublin had arisen in St. Michael's parish ; this was Father John Austin, S.J. He was born, 12th April, 1717, in Austin's Grounds (New-street, Coombe), was recommended for the Jesuits by Dean Swift (whose Grammar School of St. Patrick's he attended) for his poetry, entered the Society of Jesus in Champagne, 27th November, 1735, and, after his ordination, returned to Dublin in 1750. He became assistant-priest of St. Michael's, Rosemary-lane, and lived in Archbold's Court, off Cook-street.

Immediately he " established a school in Cook-street in which John O'Keeffe the dramatist, and the majority of the Roman Catholic youth of the metropolis received their education."[1] It was known as the Seminary. In 1760 he opened the famous seminary in Saul's Court, off Fishamble-street. One of his most famous pupils was Thomas Betagh who joined the Society of Jesus, and returned to Dublin in 1773. The Society was suppressed in that year, and Father Betagh, with Fathers Mulcaile and Fullam, also members of the Society, assisted Father Murphy, C.C., and Father Austin as teachers in Saul's Court. This seminary or classical school was the first of its kind in Dublin to give a higher education to the sons of the wealthy Catholic merchants, traders, etc. It prepared them for commercial and industrial pursuits, and for the priesthood.

Father Austin died, 29th September, 1784, in his 66th year, and was buried in St. Kevin's churchyard, Camden-lane, near Dermot O'Hurley, the martyred Archbishop of Cashel (1584). A monument, with suitable inscription, was erected in 1786.

[1] *Irish Builder*, 1891, p. 223.

He was succeeded at Saul's Court by Father Betagh (born at Kells, 1738). The school became almost a diocesan seminary for Dublin and Meath. Many eminent priests were educated here—Daniel Murray (afterwards Archbishop of Dublin), Patrick Coleman (P.P. of St. Michan's and Vicar-General), M. B. Keogh, Capuchin (P.P. of Howth), Michael Doyle (C.C. of SS. Michael and John's), William Yore (P.P. of St. Paul's and Vicar-General), etc. No fewer than ten of its pupils joined the Society of Jesus.[1]

Father Betagh is mentioned in 1784 as a curate of St. Michael's. In that year Father John Murphy, his fellow curate and teacher in Saul's Court, was appointed parish priest in succession to Father John Field (1767–84), a relative of the great musical composer of Nocturne fame. Immediately, Father Betagh instituted his poor schools, known to the present day as " Dr. Betagh's Schools." The first was an evening school in Schoolhouse-lane (Ram-lane). For some reason Father Betagh removed the school to an outhouse at the back of Skinners-row (Christ Church-place).[2] As Bishop Blake, in one of his sermons (1821), said, Father Betagh established the free schools that no poor boy might be excluded from the benefit of education—poor apprentices, poor servant boys, poor illiterate young men, who were supplied gratis with every requisite in religious instruction, reading, writing, cyphering, book-keeping and mathematics. He encouraged the poorest of them by giving them yearly a suit of clothes ; this was taking a leaf out of the Protestant book. The number of those who attended the school is given as 300 daily, of whom he clothed 40 every year at his own expense. In all, he is said to have put 3,000 children and adults through his hands, and Dr. Blake says of him that up to his 73rd year (1811) he would sit down in a cold damp cellar every night to hear the lessons of children and adults. It was all a great effort to equip Catholics to take their place in the industrial and commercial life of the city.

Another school founded by Father Betagh was in Derby-square (off Werburgh-street), which became the great centre

---

[1] Battersby, *Dublin Jesuits*, 108.
[2] Archbishop Troy, in one of his letters to Dublin Castle, insisted on the protection of this school from the military in 1798. (See p. 164).

of the Christian Doctrine and Evening Office Societies of
St. Michael's. It was at this school that James Clarence
Mangan, the gifted poet, received all his education (c. 1811).

It should be mentioned here that Dr. Betagh was appointed
parish priest of St. Michael's in 1799, and soon afterwards
became Vicar-General.

We have no information about schools in St. Michan's
parish for about fifty years after the so-called Reformation.
In pre-Reformation days the monks of St. Mary's Abbey
educated the sons of the Anglo-Norman gentry, and of the
poor labourers. One of the claims they made against their
suppression was that their monastery was also an educational
centre. This carried no weight with Henry VIII and his
advisers, who provided no substitute for the education of the
gentry or the poor, notwithstanding all their promises to erect
English Schools. The only makeshift of a school was that
in Schoolhouse Lane, near St. Audeon's, which the Civic
Fathers had to finance. Henry VIII, having received all the
precious stones, gold and silver, of the monasteries, churches
and shrines, had no money to devote to the education of the
people of which he made such a boast.

In St. Michan's parish the Jesuits were the successors of the
Cistercians in education. About 1597, Father Henry
Fitzsimon, S.J., returned to Dublin, and set up a chapel in
a room in Lucy-lane, afterwards called Mass-lane (present
Chancery-place), and conducted a school. He was joined,
in 1603, by two other Jesuits, Fathers Kearney and Lennon,
but their efforts came to an end in 1617, when the Jesuits
were suppressed. The Jesuits returned in 1685, under James II,
with the Religious Orders, but, with them, they had to close
their chapel and school, in 1690.

This expulsion of the Jesuits and of the members of the
Religious Orders did not mean that education was dead in
the city, or in St. Michan's parish. Wherever there was a
chapel there was a school of some sort, in the chapel itself,
or in an adjoining room, in a tenement house, or in an outhouse. The secular priests in charge provided for the needs
of the people, and were their principal teachers, but they had
lay men and women who were sufficiently educated to assist

them in teaching the rudiments—reading, writing, and casting accounts. Notwithstanding the penal laws against education, these illicit schools thrived in the back-rooms. The Registration of the Popish Parish Priests, 1703, put great heart into the pastors in regard to the education of their flock, and they conducted their schools, secretly, but with greater courage, and with extraordinary success.

The 1731 Report states that there were twelve schools in St. Michan's parish—the largest number mentioned for any parish :

A Latin school kept by Phil. Reilly on ye Inns.
     do.   by Murphy in Bow Lane.
An English school by McGuirk in Church-street.
     Do.   by Lyons in Church Street.
     Do.   by Hearnon in   do.
     Do.   by Cullen in Pill Lane.
     Do.   by Neal in Hamon Lane.
     Do.   by McGloughlin in Hamon Lane.
     Do.   by Carty in Phrapper Lane.
     Do.   by Ward in Mary's Lane.
     Do.   by Burke in   do.
     Do.   by Gorman in Bow Lane.[1]

6. Convents of Nuns in the City of Dublin.

The first nuns to come to Dublin in the Post-Reformation period were the English Benedictines of Dunkirk, among whom were several of the daughters of Irish lords and gentry. They came to Merchant's Quay in 1614 but had to quit their residence in 1630.

The second coming of the Benedictines was from the Irish Convent of Ypres at the request of King James II (1687) who granted them a patent foundation (5th June, *a.r.* VI)

---

[1] This was probably the Maurice O'Gorman, clerk of Mary's Lane Chapel, in the middle eighteenth century, who taught Irish to Major-General Charles Vallancey who became a noted Irish antiquarian. (Hammond, " Major Sirr," *Dub. Hist. Record,* IV., No. 2 p. 65.)

for one convent, one abbess and nuns in Ireland, to be called " our first and chief Royal Monastery of Gratia Dei." [1]

The site selected was Channel-row (present North Brunswick-street) in the new fashionable quarter. The convent was to receive £100 per annum from the Exchequer. The King presided at the dedication ceremony performed by Archbishop Russell in 1689. "Thirty young ladies of the best families in Ireland " were entrusted to the Abbess, Dame Butler, for their education. Eighteen of them asked permission to join the order but were refused by the Abbess as the War of the Revolution had been far advanced. " The only one who was professed was a lay sister who accompanied the Abbess from Ypres. The King honoured the ceremony with his presence, and from his royal hand she received the veil." [2]

After the Battle of the Boyne, King William's soldiers ransacked the convent and seized the church plate. Dame Butler, notwithstanding the promise of protection of the Duke of Ormonde, her relative, returned to Ypres with her community.

The next Order of Nuns which came to Dublin was that of the Poor Clares from Galway. They founded a convent in Ship-street in 1625, but, like the Benedictines of that time, they had to quit, retired to Athlone, then to Nuns' Island, Galway, and eventually to Spain, in 1652, the Cromwellian period. They returned to Galway, apparently in James II's reign, where they remained until 1712, when their convent was suppressed. Of all places in Ireland, they sought refuge in Dublin, and, with the sanction of Archbishop Byrne, and " encouraged and invited by the Duchess of Tyrconnell," they settled in the former Benedictine Convent in Channel-row. This re-erection of the convent, in Queen's Anne's time, was proclaimed a few days afterwards, 20th September, 1712, and Archbishop Byrne, Rev. Dr. Nary, P.P. of St. Michan's, and Father John Burke, provincial of the Franciscans, were ordered to be taken prisoners for exercising ecclesiastical jurisdiction contrary to the laws of the kingdom,

[1] Harris, *King William III*, app. no. 38.
[2] *Dominican Annals,* p. 189.

and all the laws in force against papists were ordered to be strictly carried out.[1]

It does not appear that either the Archbishop, the parish priest, or the provincial was apprehended, but three of the nuns were arrested, brought before the courts, and acquitted through the influence of some relatives. The convent was searched, and all books and papers were seized.

Dr. Nary, who had received them into the Royal Benedictine House, and who had presumed too far on his own standing with the authorities, advised the Poor Clares to take a less pretentious house, one not designated "a convent." The Duchess of Tyrconnell provided them (1715) with such a house in North King-street (opposite the present St. Paul's Protestant Church). Here, in 1728 (in the more tolerant reign of George I), they built a chapel, referred to in the Government Report of 1731 as a private Mass-house, which served as a chapel-of-ease to the new parish of St. Paul's, and which had a handsome altar and an organ in the gallery which was presented by the Countess of Fingall. The Poor Clares became two separate communities in 1751, one portion, under the jurisdiction of the Archbishop, occupying premises firstly in Russell's Court, and, in 1752, in Drumcondra-lane (present Upper Dorset-street), and the other remaining in North Brunswick-street).

The Royal Benedictine Monastery in Channel-row had a third occupant Order, the Dominican nuns, who, like the Poor Clares, came from Galway (March, 1717). Though the Poor Clares were content to live in retirement, the Dominicans set out to succeed the Benedictines in the matter of education. Young ladies of the old Catholic families offered themselves as postulants, and others as pupils of the boarding-school that was opened in 1719. The nuns, in secular dress, lived as a " Family " with the boarders, but observed the Rule of the Dominican Order. A charge against them of erecting a monastery in defiance of the laws of the land broke down in public court. In 1723 they acquired " ye little house," adjoining the convent, for the accommodation of parlour boarders, among whom were the Duchess of

[1] Concannon, *Poor Clares in Ireland*, 84–94.

Tyrconnell and her daughter, Lady Dillon, Lady Mount-garret, Lady Mountcashel, Lady Cahir, The Countess of Fingal, Lady Rice, Lady McDermott, Lady Bourke, etc.

Among the school-boarders, in 1725, were the daughters of Lord Mayo, Lord Reverstown, Lord Kenmare, Lord Dunsany, Viscount Netterville, Lord Trimbleston, Lady Cavan, and Lady Rice, as well as the Misses Butler, Keating, Fitzgerald, Dillon, Daly, Kelly, Bodkin, Aylmer, Lyster, and Reilly. Apparently, the young ladies came from every part of Ireland.

The *Annals* of the Convent provide interesting information on the devotions of the Dublin people at this time. In the very year, 1731, in which the Report of the Popish schools, convents, and chapels was drawn up by the Government, Pope Clement XII (26 April) granted a Plenary Indulgence to all the faithful who should visit the church of this monastery on the Feast of St. Joseph.[1] The convent chapel had been dedicated to "Jesus, Mary, and St. Joseph." Devotion to St. Joseph was long dear to Dubliners and he appeared to them as the head of the Holy Family, and as their shepherd in their long journey through the penal period. The Confraternity of the Most Holy Rosary of the B.V.M. was erected in the chapel by permission of Thomas Ripoli, General of the Order, 19th September, 1733, and was granted special Indulgences by Pope Benedict XIV in 1740.[2] It is thus not true to say that it was the Loreto Sisters who introduced the devotion into Dublin.

Notwithstanding the fine of £200 for the conviction of anyone who harboured a bishop, the Dominican sisters sheltered many. Colman O'Shaughnassey, bishop of Ossory, was consecrated there by Archbishop Linegar of Dublin, assisted by Dr. MacDonagh, bishop of Kilmore, and Dr. Stephen McEgan, bishop of Meath, in 1736, and, in 1747, Dr. Lawrence Richardson, bishop of Kilmore, was consecrated by Archbishop Linegar, assisted by Dr. S. MacEgan and Dr. Gallagher, bishop of Raphoe. On 14th October, 1744, Dr. Peter Kilkelly, bishop of Kilmacduagh, was consecrated there, and, in 1745, Bishop MacEgan, of Meath, was

---

[1] *Annals*, pp. 44–45.   [2] De Burgo, *Hib. Dom.*, 356–57.

being sheltered in one of their small houses in Channel-row,
" at his lodgings," for which he paid £10.[1] No doubt, the
other bishops mentioned had their lodgings there from time
to time.[2]

So lax had become the penal laws in Dublin, after 1745,
that the Dominican Sisters, rebuilt, in 1748, the former
Benedictine Royal Abbey from the very foundations. The
building cost £1,624. The convent and school were quite
prosperous, and the Catholic Ritual was carried out with
remarkable splendour, with choir and organ at High Mass.
So famous had the convent chapel become for high-class
music, then dear to the heart of every Dubliner,[3] that a
Protestant writer of the time mentions it as " a famous convent
in Channel Row, Dublin, where the celebrated Italian musicians help to make the voices of the holy sisters more
melodious, and many Protestants have been invited to take
their places in a convenient gallery to hear the performance."[4]
All this is a new light on conditions in Dublin where Catholic
Ritual and Music had apparently much to say to the breaking-
down of anti-Catholic prejudices. The climax to this better
understanding took place in 1789, in St. Nicholas's, on the
occasion of the recovery of George III.

The convent, however, suffered a marked decline from the
year 1780. " The financial losses of the nuns, about the year
1790, were beyond all hope of redress. All their funds had
been invested in loans made under bond or note to the Catholic
gentry, but the impoverishment of the latter by the unjust
enactments of the penal laws rendered them incapable of
discharging their obligations to the Dominican, nuns who
were thus placed in a condition of actual destitution."[5] In
1782 the debts due to the Community amounted to £955,
and 1792 to £1,836. Costs in lawsuits to recover their bonds
amounted to £838. To add to their distress, the bigoted son
of their former landlord refused in 1808 to grant them the
31 years' renewal of their lease, unless they paid double the

[1] Dominican Annals, 49.
[2] O'Connell, Dioc. of Kilmore, 483.
[3] A few years previously, Handel had popularised Oratorio with the " Messiah."
[4] Lecky, Hist. of Ir., I. 266.
[5] Annals, pp. 66 ff.

rent, and so they retired to St. Mary's, Vernon Avenue, Clontarf.

Many of the Catholic county families had their residences in the eighteenth century in the streets that have since become tenement quarters—the Dillons, Bellews, Dowdalls, Bryans, etc. They rubbed shoulders with the poor who lived in the alleys and lanes. They all assembled for Mass in the little chapel in Bull-lane, off Mary's-lane. The Bryans, for their exceptional interest in the building of the new church of St. Michan's in North-Anne-street had their family arms set up in the gallery entrance, where they still remain. The Dominican nuns had provided for the Catholic education of the daughters of these families in a difficult period.

The parish had no Catholic free school for girls. Mary Teresa Mulally supplied the want with the true zeal of an Apostle. She was born, October 1728, in Pill-lane (Chancery-street). Her father was a provision dealer on the north side of the lane. Retiring from business in 1735, he moved to a house on the west side of Phrapper-lane (Beresford-street).

When Father Mulcaile, S.J., took up active service in St. Michan's, in 1763, he found Mary Teresa a willing helper in the cause of the poor ignorant children of the parish. (In 1766, the parish contained 3,051 Catholic families ; there were 1,157 Protestant families ; the population would have been about 20,000). In June of that year, Father Mulcaile and Mary Teresa issued a joint appeal for funds to carry on their good work for the education of girls, but Mary Teresa had already, for a month, been carrying on a school for them in the top storey of a house at the corner of Bull Lane and Mary's Lane, opposite the old chapel. The " address to the Charitable of St. Michan's Parish " states that " she has under her care a certain number of the aforesaid poor girls, whom she instructs in their prayers and catechism, in reading and writing, knitting, quilting, mantua-making, plain work, etc. whereby they may be rendered useful to Society, and capable of earning honest bread for themselves." It was apparently a new idea in Ireland, to enable girls to earn " honest bread " by combining technical with primary education. Other industries carried on in Mary Teresa's school were lace and glove making. The articles were bought chiefly by the ladies of the parish. The proficiency of the girls in these industries is thus abundantly clear. It may be asked ; where did Mary Teresa acquire this extensive technical knowledge ? It would seem that she acquired it during her stay in Chester whilst on a visit to some friends or relatives. On her return to her native parish she lost no time in gathering round her the poor ignorant girls.

Her next great work was to erect a convent in George's-hill for herself and her two helpers (1789) and afterwards introduced to it the Presentation Sisters. Her work was the most outstanding and astonishing in the history of modern Dublin. She lived to see her schools prosperous and free. She died in 1803, and was buried in the vaults of the Convent Chapel ![1] Fr. Mulcaile had died, December, 1801, and was buried in the same vaults.

7. THE BEGINNINGS OF CATHOLIC LITERATURE IN DUBLIN.

Besides the effort, inadequate though it was, to provide education for hundreds of boys and girls of the city parishes, efforts were made by some priests and printers to supply the citizens with devotional and dogmatic works.

The pioneer of Catholic publications in Dublin was the Rev. Cornelius Nary, P.P., St. Michan's (1700–38). On his return to London from the University of Paris, he published, in 1699, in Antwerp and London, an *Account of the Chief Points in Controversy between the Roman Catholics and the Protestants.* It was a bold venture during the difficult years of William and Mary. After his release from prison in Dublin (1702), he contented himself with an edition of *Prayers and Meditations* (Dublin, 1705). It was out of the question, of course, to have his scholarly New Testament in English, with marginal notes, printed in Dublin, and so he had recourse to London (1705).

Under George the First (1714–27), when Catholics became more courageous, Dr. Nary at first contented himself with *Rules and Godly Instructions* (Dublin, 1716), and a *History of St. Patrick's Purgatory* (Dublin, 1718). Emboldened by the

[1] R. Burke-Savage, *A Valiant Dublin Woman,* 126–51.

reception of these publications, he entered again into the field of controversy. He faced Edward Synge, the Protestant Archbishop of Tuam, and replied to his *Charitable Address to all who are of the Communion of Rome*. By his replies he gave Dr. Synge no rest. His final great controversial work was *The Case of the Catholics of Ireland* (1724). It was bold writing in those difficult days, but he was a man of rare courage. His reputation for exceptional learning made him respected among his adversaries. It was fortunate that Catholic Dublin had such a champion, for it may be said that his influence had much to say to the mitigating of the penal laws in Dublin at that time.

As he lived until 1738 it may be presumed that the entry as to the "Weekly Conference" in the Report of 1731 applies to him. The entry states: "11 within a year & ½ last past vizt. 1 at ye Black Lyon in Pil Lane, 9 at ye King's Head on the Inns, 1 at Mrs. Cannons on Ormond's Quay." The Report also states that there was a Conference "held about a year & ½ ago" in St. Michael's parish, and "one held from 9 ber. 1730 to March following by one Lahy."[1]

Controversy was a feature of the period, 1714–1731, namely after the accession of George I. The "Weekly Conferences" were held at the principal taverns, because their rooms were sufficiently large for the audience, but perhaps also because of their friendly atmosphere and neutral ground.

Dr. Nary paved the way for other controversial writers. A translation of Bossuet's *History of the Variations of the Protestant Churches* was issued in two volumes in 1745 by Ignatius Kelly, at the Stationers' Arms, Mary's-lane. The year is important. This was bringing the religious fight into the enemy's camp in Dublin, in the vicinity of the Law Courts, Christ Church and Dublin Castle. Ignatius Kelly, in 1745, found it safe to print, and to sell to the intelligent Catholic reading people two volumes that set out abundantly the various and contradictory forms into which the so-called reformed religion had branched. It was the first time that Dublin Catholics saw in print such an attack on the Protestant position. They had been waiting for two hundred years to

[1] *Archiv. Hib.* IV, 131–32.

get this opportunity of putting the Catholic position in popular form, of justifying their fight for the Old Faith, and of claiming their right to be considered as good Christians as those who were protected by Dublin Castle.

Other controversial works were *The Impartial Examiner* by the Rev. John Jones, Popish priest (1746), and *The Case of the Roman Catholics of Ireland* (1755. P. Lord, Cook-street). The first had as its sub-title, " The faithful representer of the various misrepresentations imposed on the Roman Catholics of Ireland, in the several charges laid at their doors by the scribblers." The second had as an explanation of its title, " Wherein the Principles and Conduct of that party [Catholic] are fully explained and vindicated." A third work, somewhat of the same character, was *A Justification of the Tenets of the Roman Catholic Religion and a Refutation of the charges brought against the Clergy by Right Rev. Lord Bishop of Cloyne.* By Dr. James Butler.

The output of catechetical and religious books, chiefly between the years 1731 and 1786, is about the most remarkable feature of Catholic resurgence in Dublin before the Penal Laws were thoroughly abrogated. It would seem that when Dublin Catholics saw that the " Inquiry into the Further Growth of Popery " of 1731 was a mere inquiry and that they were not visited with any official interference in the number of their parochial clergy, their chapels, and their poor schools, they took courage to come out into the open and beard the lion in his den. Catholic printers, publishers, and booksellers were already flourishing in their trades, but, so far, they did not print openly Catholic literature. After 1731, their printing presses were busy turning out and their shop windows were displaying a new kind of literature. All this Catholic activity became possible through the zealous support of the merchants, traders, and craftsmen. Some of the publications preserve for us the names of the subscribers, and among them we find men of those various classes. These militant Catholics considered it as much a part of their duty as Catholics to purchase those publications, catechetical and devotional, as to subscribe to the support of the clergy, chapels and charities.

On the other hand, without the co-operation of the Catholic

clergy of Dublin, regular as well as secular, those publications could not have been translated or edited in Dublin. The majority of the secular clergy of Dublin of 1704 had received a continental education and they were quite familiar with the catechetical and devotional books that were popular in European countries. The regular clergy entirely received their education on the continent. The Dublin clergy suggested the works that would be useful to Dublin Catholics emerging from the Catacomb life, and advised the printers to lay the foundation of Dublin's wonderful resurgence of religious and intellectual life.

A work called *The Decalogue Explained* set forth that it was " very useful for all Pastors, Missioners, and Masters of Families " ; the editor and printer had in mind the needs of those different classes in their work for those under their charge. They provided a book of infinite value, for the pastor among his people, the missioner on his rounds in the country, and the father of a family for his children an l his dependents. Here a vital point is touched—the serious view that the educated well-to-do Dublin Catholic father of a family took of religion. He sought for the latest publications on religion and devotion, and read, or had them read, for his children in his home. His object was to raise up a defence against the Protestant tradition supported by the penal laws. The penal laws were almost a dead letter, but the defence of the Catholic faith against the ruling Protestants was a thing that was uppermost in his life—materially and spiritually it was his very life.

The most important of the early Catholic publications used in Dublin was the *Abridgement of Christian Doctrine*, or Douay Catechism (printed in London in 1732). It was the high-water mark of Catechetical instruction—for children of the fifth class. A minute in the SS. Michael and John's Register (26th October, 1828) states : " That the lads who receive catechistrical instruction in this Confraternity be not considered qualified to become teachers until they are fully instructed in the Large Abridgement and be otherwise particularly distinguished for their pious conduct."

Thomas-a-Kempis's *The Following* [*Imitation*] *of Christ*

(Dublin, 1733) was an early arrival in translations. The Dublin English translation was made from the Latin. We do not know the name of the translator—probably some Dublin priest who could not conveniently put his name to it.

It is interesting to note the streets where the Catholic printers and publishers had their printing presses and shops. The printers set up their establishments near the Catholic chapels : Thomas-street, Bridge-street, Winetavern-street, Cook-street, Church-street, and Mary's-lane—all adjacent to the 1749 chapels. It may be legitimate to conclude that the priests of those districts had much to say to the editions of the various works, and that the printers relied on them to help them in his important sphere of Catholic action.

Appended is a list of the principal publications of the period :

NOTE

The Real Principles of Catholicks, or a Catechism for the Adult. Explaining the principal points of the doctrine and ceremonies of the Catholick Church. By J. H. C. (John Joseph Horngold.) (Philip Bowes, Church Street. 1750.)

Historical Catechism. Containing a summary of the Sacred History and Christian Doctrine. Translated from the French of Abbé Fleury. (B. Gorman, Bridge-street. 1763.)

A Devout Paraphrase on the Seven Penitential Psalms. Or a Practical Guide to Repentance. By F. Blyth, Disc. Carm. (John Lamb, Winetavern-street. 1749.)

Defence of the Seven Sacraments against Martin Luther, by Henry VIII. Translated into English from the original Latin edition by T. W. Gent. (First Irish Edition printed by James Bryn at the corner of Kezar's Lane in Cook Street. 1766.)

The Sacraments Explained in Twenty Discourses, by John Joseph Horngold. (Richard Cross, Bridge-street. 1770.)

The Decalogue Explained in Thirty-two Discourses, by John Joseph Horngold. (Richard Cross, Bridge-street.)

The Decalogue Explained, and the Creed, Theological Virtues, seven Sacraments, etc. In Fifty-one excellent Moral Discourses. Very useful for all Pastors, Missioners, and Masters of Families. By Rev. Bernard Francis, O.S.F. (R. Cross, Bridge-street. 1778.)

Some Reflections upon the Prerogatives, Power and Protection of St. Joseph, Spouse of the Blessed and ever Immaculate Virgin Mary Mother of God. (Eleanor Kelly, Mary's-lane. 1755.)

The Spiritual Treasury of St. Augustine, compiled by Fr. White, O.S.A. (James Byrne, Thomas-street. 1755.)

A Guide to Heaven. Moral Reflections compiled partly out of the maxims of Holy Fathers and partly out of the sentences of ancient Philosophers. By John de Bond, O.Cist. English translation from Latin. (John Buck, Bridge-street. 1755.)

Practical Instructions on the Obligation and Manner of Keeping Lent. By a priest of the diocese of Kildare. (James Byrne, Cook-street. 1771.)

Life of Ven. Benedict Joseph Labré. (P. Wogan, Old Bridge. 1785.)

A Short Treatise on Prayer. Translated from the French by Father Field, P.P. of St. Michael's. (J. Meehan, Aungier-street. 1787.)

The Office of Holy Week. With explanation of the Ceremonies. (1772.)

The Sufferings of Our Lord Jesus Christ. Translated from the Portuguese of Father Thomas of Jesus, O.S.A. (Eleanor Kelly, Mary's-lane. 1754.)

The Devout Christian Instructed in the Life of Christ. From the written word.
(P. Wogan, Old Bridge. 1784.)
  Lives of the Saints. Translated from the Spanish of Fr. Ribadonira, S.J.
(B. Gorman, Bridge-street. 1763.)
  Lives of the Fathers,Martyrs, Saints. By Rev. A. Butler. (James Hoey, Parliament-street. 1766.)

8. Catholic Charity in Eighteenth Century Dublin

The care of foundlings became a problem of great magnitude in eighteenth century Dublin. In the early part of the century Catholics had neither the power nor the means of dealing with them. The State, by an Act passed in 1703, set up a workhouse, governed by a corporation appointed by it, in James's-street, 12th October, 1704, in which all vagrants found in the city were to be lodged. In this category destitute children were included, and they were to be kept in custody until the age of sixteen, when they were to be apprenticed to honest persons, " being Protestants." The Committee of Inquiry held by the Irish House of Commons, in 1758, as to the state and management of the Fund of the workhouse of the City of Dublin, declared that the establishing and supporting of a well-regulated Foundling Hospital in the city of Dublin would indeed be " an excellent charity highly beneficial to the Publick, and greatly promote the Protestant interest of this Kingdom."[1]

By 1729 the workhouse had become entirely a Foundling Hospital. In 1730, a cradle or turning wheel for taking in infants, and a bell, were provided at the gate for use by day or by night. Between 1750 and 1760, 7,781 infants were admitted into the institution, of whom 3,797 died, and 52 were wholly unaccounted for. In 1798, a Committee of the House of Commons found that, in the previous six years, out of 5,216 children sent into the Infirmary of the Foundling Hospital only three came out alive.[2] Between 1784 and 1796 out of 25,352 children entered on the books of the Foundling Hospital 17,253 died either in the Hospital itself or in the country where they had been put out to nurse. In London, at the end of the century, the deaths were one in six.[3] It

---

[1] Maxwell, op. cit., 130.
[2] King Moylan, *Dublin Hist. Rec.,* I, II, III, nos. 1, 2, 3.
[3] Maxwell, op. cit., 132–34.

was also found that "a great majority of the children were formerly abandoned as hopelessly afflicted with venereal disease. It is a singular fact that of 10,272 children sent to the infant infirmary in 21 years (1775–96) no less than 10,201 were stated as venereal."[1]

The Protestant Vestry Books of the North City throw useful light on the state of affairs in that district. "In St. Paul's books as well as in St. Michan's, there are pages of lists of these unfortunates, and there are numerous records of the burials of children found dead in various places. For example, in 1730 there were fifty-eight foundling children sent to the workhouse from St. Michan's Parish. From the whole of the city there were 265. St. Michan's had the largest number, St. Paul's had four, and St. Mary's four. . . . The money payable per annum to the workhouse by St. Michan's Parish was £516 18s. 10d.[2] There is a record of the numbers [from the Parish] in the workhouse, Oct. 5, 1730. . . . Out of a total of 349 there were 170 children. This indicates great poverty and crime in the parish."

The writer then continues : "The north side was then the most crowded part of the city. It was a place of many contrasts : there was wealth and fashion ; there were great houses of the nobility, and comfortable homes of merchants ; and there was much poverty, drink and crime ; there were narrow lanes and filthy alleys where crowds of the poor existed ; there was much gaiety and excitement, and there was much violence and crime and misery."[3]

The "multiplication of servants" in the fashionable houses, and the "immorality of a graver kind," mentioned by Lecky, were in great measure the cause of the preponderance of the foundlings in St. Michan's parish. In 1718 the number of houses in the parish was 1,051, whereas in the whole city the number was 10,004, that is, as 1 to 9. The foundlings in the parish in 1730 were 58, whereas in the whole city they were 265, that is, as 2 to 9. Thus there were twice as many foundlings from the parish, on the average of houses, as there were

---

[1] McGregor, *Picture of Dublin* (1821), pp. 249–50.

[2] It may be necessary to state that the Protestant Churchwardens controlled parochial affairs.

[3] Young, "St. Michan's Parish in 18th Century," *Dub. Hist. Rec.*, III, no. 1, pp. 6–7.

in any other parish. The fashionable houses were the majority in the parish, the poor being crowded into lanes and alleys, whereas in the south side of the city the houses were chiefly tenements.

The State Foundling Hospital held sway for at least 70 years—until after 1770. Meanwhile, Catholics could do nothing to oppose it, as the Act of Parliament of 1703 was still unmodified. There is nothing to show definitely when Catholics put up a fight against this Hospital ; it must have been, however, between 1770 and 1786, but it is probable that it was after the first Catholic Relief Act of 1783. The opposition to it came about in a casual way, and set Catholic Action for the first time on its steady and progressive way.

The appalling state of the Foundling Hospital disgusted one decent minded unmarried mother who left her child at the door of " Adam and Eve " chapel, off Cook-street. Some of the traders of the district combined to look after the foundling's welfare. The news spread abroad that Catholic foundlings were being taken charge of in Cook-street, and the deposited foundlings increased in numbers. The charitable Catholics, realising the advantage to the Church of the possession of the Catholic babes, began to deposit pennies for the foundlings in the poor box of ' Adam and Eve ' chapel. The pennies became so numerous that the Franciscan fathers formed a society for the protection of the foundlings, and called it the Patrician Orphan Society. It had for its motto : " Lend an Ear of Pity to the Melancholy Tale of the Poor, and pay with Cheerfulness the Debt of Charity."[1] The Franciscan Fathers, no longer content with the casual pennies dropped into the box, organised the parishioners of St. Michael's parish into a society the members of which should pay $6\frac{1}{2}$d.[2] a month to be collected on Sundays.

The monthly subscriptions also became inadequate for the support of the increased number of foundlings, and it was considered that an appeal should be made to the Catholic citizens of Dublin. The chapel for the appeal was, of course,

---

.[1] Kelly, *Dub. Hist. Rec.,* III, no. 1, p. 13.
[2] $6\frac{1}{2}$d. Irish money, 6d. English. Parochial Registers of the period show that he $6\frac{1}{2}$d. standard was in use.

the parish chapel, St. Michael's, Rosemary-lane, and Father
Austin, S.J. was to be the preacher. Apparently the news of
the sermon by the great Jesuit preacher had spread throughout
the city, and immediately Protestant opposition became
vehement against the "impudent Papists." Charity sermons
in Catholic churches were forbidden, and opposition to the
State Foundling Hospital was not to be tolerated. The
Archbishop, Dr. Carpenter, refused his consent for the sermon
saying that "it was probable, if they thus made themselves so
publicly known, their chapels might be thrown about the
streets." The incident occurred between 1770 and 1786,
the period during which Dr. Carpenter ruled the See, and
the worst period in the history of the Foundling Hospital.
Dr. Carpenter, however, gave his consent for the Charity
Sermon in the year following his refusal, and Father Austin
preached it, notwithstanding the threat of the fanatics to call
upon the Government to suppress it.[1] He was thus the
pioneer in the matter of charitable appeals. Here again,
special tribute must be paid to the zeal and generosity of the
merchants and traders, and to the charitable consideration
of the poor, ever ready to help a neighbour in distress.

Before the foundation of the Patrician Orphan Society for
foundlings the valiant woman, Mary Teresa Mulally, had
provided for orphans of another type on the north side of the
city. As well as being the pioneer of technical education, she
was the pioneer of the orphanage for Catholic girls. She
began by renting a small house in Mary's Lane in 1771, where
she housed, clothed and instructed five orphans. In 1783
the number had increased to 10, and by 1787, through the
contributions of charitable Catholics, she was able to purchase
the Glass House[2] plot on George's Hill for the necessary
accommodation. Her efforts for the welfare of the orphans
appealed so strongly to the charitable Catholics that by the
year 1794 she was able to erect on a portion of the Glass
House ground a new orphanage, at a cost of £804, for 20
children. Subscriptions and bequests for the support of the

[1] Battersby, *Jesuits in Dublin* (1854), p. 95–97.
[2] For an interesting description of the Glass manufacture see Maxwell, *Dublin Under the Georges.*

orphans continued to pour in up to the year of her death (1800), and these she wisely invested, so that 24 orphans were constantly maintained up to 1824. Between that year and 1800 the number increased to 40.[1] These were difficult years for the poor, as we shall see, especially after the Plague of 1832.

[1] Archives, Presentation Convent, George's Hill.

II

THE CAMPAIGN FOR CATHOLIC RELIEF

1. THE CATHOLIC COMMITTEE

IN 1760 a Catholic Committee was formed in Dublin to look after the interests of Catholics, especially in the matter of relief from penal disabilities. It was founded by John Curry, Charles O'Conor and Thomas Wyse, men of liberal education, some of whom had continental University education. They were of the type that the Catholic merchants and traders required to lead the Catholic movement. Little is known of the activities of this Committee for thirteen years—up to 1773. The Minute Book of the Catholic Committee, 1773–92,[1] contains important information as to its members and its activities.

Its early members were chiefly of the trading type. It was not until 25th June, 1778, that the Catholic temporal lords, Fingall, Kenmare, and Gormanstown, and the gentry, appear as members. It was in that year that the first Relief Act of Catholics was passed, and that the Archbishop of Dublin, Dr. Carpenter, attended in the King's Bench at the head of seventy of his clergy to take the Oath prescribed by the Act.

The first Catholic bishop, listed as a member of the Committee, was Dr. Troy, Archbishop of Dublin. His name appears on the Minutes, 26th December, 1787. He had been appointed to the See of Dublin, 3rd December, 1786. He attended many meetings of the Committee and his advice was welcomed on several occasions. Though a resolution had been passed in 1782 that every Catholic bishop should be considered a member of the Committee, yet it was not until after 1788 that a list of the Catholic bishops was entered in the Minutes (out of place). How many of them actually gave their names to the Committee we do not know. The only other bishop, besides Dr. Troy, who was present at any

[1] Dudley Edwards, *Archivium Hibernicum*, IX., 3–173.

of the meetings was Dr. Butler, Archbishop of Cashel, in 1791.

Owing to the timidity of Lord Kenmare and some of the Catholic gentry in pressing the Catholic claims in 1791, the Catholic Committee ceased to be dominated by the Catholic lords, and the influential Catholic merchants of Dublin took over its control. The chief of these merchants was Edward Byrne, the wealthiest in Ireland. He acquired Allen's Court in Mullinahack, off New Row and Bridge Street, the stately house of Lord Allen, in 1770, which became an unofficial meeting-place for the members of the first Catholic Committee. It was not until 1791, after the defection of some of the Catholic gentry, that Edward Byrne became the guiding spirit and practically the Chairman of the Committee. John Keogh, a Dublin silk merchant, came also to the fore at this time and became an ardent supporter of Byrne. The Minutes of the Committee conclude in 1792, with the adoption of Richard Burke, son of Edmund Burke, and Theobald Wolfe Tone as members and officials.

The official meeting-places of the Committee were the city taverns. Mention is made of the Elephant, Essex-street (east) ; King's Arms, Fownes-street (Ryan's) ; the Globe Coffee House, Derham's, Essex-street (apparently the Elephant) ; and Ryan's, Mary's-lane.

Though the Minutes might lead a superficial reader to infer that the Committee did little else than pass resolutions of loyalty to George III and present addresses to lords lieutenants on their coming into office and their departure from Ireland, yet the organisation of the Catholic householders of Dublin was the most important work it accomplished. These householders commanded the respect of the people in the back streets and influenced their opinion in political matters. They were the merchants and traders who had grown important in city life in spite of the penal laws. It was to their unstinted generosity, in financing every Catholic effort, in supporting priests, Catholic publications, chapels, orphanages, and the Catholic Committee, that was due the success of the Catholic claim against the iniquities of the penal laws.

Unfortunately the Minute Book of the Committee gives no

account of the subscriptions received. It is clear, however, that the Dublin householders had been contributing generously, for, in 1778, £1,500 was sent to the London agent of the Committee. A new collection for legal purposes was organised in Dublin and the country towns, but it may be taken that the country contribution at this time was small. The only reference in the Minutes to a city collection was, in 1779, when £38 7s. od. was handed in as part collection of St. Catherine's parish. That reference gives some idea of the subscription from the nine (civil) city parishes. It must have reached about a thousand pounds, as in the next year £210 was paid as fees to lawyers for preparing a plan for the further relief of the Catholics of Ireland, and £500 was sent to the Committee's London agent.

In the election to the general committee, for three years, in January, 1781, whilst representatives were elected from the nine Dublin civil parishes—four from each—only ten towns elected representatives. Archbishop Carpenter of Dublin had been asked to promote the city election. Apparently he did so, for in the election of 1784, the returns for seven city parishes were signed by the parish priests. Nineteen country towns elected representatives. For the 1791 election notices were sent to the parish priests of the cities and towns. Fifty-two towns nominated representatives. Thus, in ten years, the number of towns that joined the Committee had risen from ten to fifty-two, and the extraordinary increase was clearly due to the influence of the bishops and priests. It was, however, the spirited action of the Dublin merchants and traders, supported by the parish priests of Dublin and their Archbishop, which gave the lead to the rest of Ireland. It was at this time that the Committee was making its supreme effort for the passing of the Relief Bill, which took place in 1792. [1] Yet, it must be said that the Committee was very modest in putting forward only the four following objects : Admission to the profession and practice of the law, capacity to serve in county magistracies, a right to be summoned and to serve on grand and petty juries, the right of voting in counties for Protestant members of Parliament.

[1] Dudley Edwards, op. cit., 123–51.

Dr. Carpenter, Archbishop of Dublin (1770–86) is referred to in the Minutes of the Catholic Committee (1774) as the authority to decide the question of the profession of the civil principles of Irish Catholics proposed by the Committee. He found them orthodox. In 1778, he attended the King's Bench at the head of seventy of his priests to take the oath prescribed by the Relief Act just passed. His efforts in the political arena, from the year he became Archbishop, were "the first made by any priest or bishop in the direction of Catholic Emancipation."[1] He died in 1786, and was succeeded, 3rd December of that year, by Dr. Troy, who carried on his political work.

Thomas Troy was born in Porterstown, in the parish of Blanchardstown, Co. Dublin, 7th July, 1739. Whilst yet very young he wrote in his diary, "I was removed to Smith-field, and sent to school in Liffey-street [the school attached to the chapel]; I was received into the Order of the Most Holy Rosary [Dominican] at Dublin, 5th July, 1755; I was examined by the gentlemen of Bridge-street [Dominican Priory], Dublin, 5th July, 1755; I suppose I pleased them, though I must have made very little progress in study; I owed my success more to the care of friends than to the lessons I learned at school."

He was then sixteen years old, and, in the next year, he proceeded to the Dominican House of St. Clement's, Rome. Whatever his early attainments were, he became a distinguished student, professor of Theology and Canon Law, and prior of the Convent. He was nominated to the vacant See of Ossory in 1776 by the Stuart Pretender whose claim to Ireland was still recognised by the Holy See, and was appointed by the Pope, 1st December. This was the last occasion on which the Pretender used the privilege exercised by the Stuarts for nearly a hundred years of nominating Bishops to the Irish Sees.

Settled in his diocese, he set his face against all organised disturbances of the peace, and principally against the White Boy combination of 1779. Though he had been nominated for the See of Ossory by the Stuart Pretender, yet he was a

[1] Donnelly, *Dub. Par.*, II. 55–56.

confirmed supporter of the ruling authority, as were the Irish bishops in general.

Obedience to the laws, and loyalty to the king, with a view to a further relief from the penal laws, was the Catholic policy. On 2nd April, 1789, the Catholic Committee—Lord Kenmare in the chair, and Dr. Troy present—passed an address of the Roman Catholics of Ireland to the king on his "happy restoration to health and to the personal exercise of your royal authority." Dr. Troy followed up this resolution with a religious service in his metropolitan chapel of St. Nicholas, Francis-street, his three suffragan bishops attended —James Caulfield of Ferns, Daniel Delany of Kildare and Leighlin, and John Duane of Ossory. A remarkable musical performance, with orchestra, chorus, and soloists, preceded the *Te Deum* and Benediction, and concluded with "God Save the King." The church was crowded on the occasion. "The Band consisted of all the eminent Professors and a number of amateurs, among them several gentlemen of the Established Church, who evinced the liberality of their sentiments by the prompt alacrity with which they attended."[1]

2. THE DUBLIN CORPORATION OPPOSES CATHOLIC RELIEF

In 1778 came the first of the Relief Acts, and, in 1792, the Irish Parliament readmitted Papists to the practice of Law, and repealed the Acts against foreign education, the keeping of schools by Papists, foreign education of Papists, and the keeping of more than two apprentices by Papists. Irish Catholics were still not admitted to the Parliamentary franchise, or to civil and military office under the Crown.

Determined opposition against the granting of these further Reliefs came from the Protestant Dublin Corporation. Its members were supporters of the Protestant Independent Irish Parliament; they expected it to support "the Protestant Ascendancy in our happy Constitution." They registered, in 1791, that the sincere thanks of the Corporation be returned to their "faithful representatives," Lord Henry Fitzgerald and Henry Grattan, "for their indefatigable exertions in

[1] *Universal Magazine and Review*, 1789. (P. Byrne, Grafton-street, Dublin.)

parliament in support of the rights and privileges of the people."[1]

Yet, when there was question of granting the natural rights of the people to Catholics they immediately presented Addresses to the King and Irish Parliament to oppose the grant. The Address to the King, 20th January, 1792, prayed his majesty " to preserve the Protestant ascendancy in Ireland inviolate " and assured him that they were " firmly resolved to support it free from innovation and determined most zealously to oppose any attempt to overturn the same."

The King, in his reply, 7th February, 1792, to the Corporation, expressed " the satisfaction he derived from their determination on every occasion to support our excellent constitution in church and state."[2]   He did not refer to the Relief Acts.

The Address to the City's representatives in Parliament, Lord Henry Fitzgerald and Henry Grattan, entreated them to " oppose with all your influence and great abilities any alteration that may tend to shake the security of property in this kingdom or subvert the Protestant ascendancy in our happy constitution."[3]

The question at issue was the granting of the elective franchise to Catholics. The Corporation " resolved unanimously [5th March, 1792] that the thanks of this Assembly are justly due and are hereby most sincerely given to the majority, consisting of two hundred and ten members of the House of Commons, who by voting against extending the right of elective franchise to Roman Catholics, nobly stood forward the defenders of the Protestant ascendancy in Ireland upon the principles of the glorious revolution."[4]

The Corporation met, 11th September, 1792, " pursuant to a requisition for the purpose of taking into consideration a letter circulated throughout this city and kingdom, signed, ' Edward Byrne.' "   This was the Catholic merchant of Mullinahack, the Chairman of the Catholic Committee. A letter, addressed by the Corporation to the Protestants of

---

[1] Cal. Anc. Doc. Dub., XIV. 196.
[2] Ibid., 242.
[3] Ibid., 243.
[4] Ibid., 249.

Ireland,[1] states clearly the Protestant position of " No sur-render " :

" Countrymen and friends,

" The firm and manly support which we received from you, when we stood forward in defence of the Protestant ascendancy, deserves our warmest thanks. We hoped that the sense of the Protestants of Ireland declared upon that occasion would have convinced our Roman Catholic fellow subjects, that the pursuit of political power was for them a vain pursuit, for though the liberal and enlightened mind of the Protestant receives pleasure in seeing the Catholic exercise his religion with freedom, enjoy his property in security, and possess the highest degree of personal liberty, yet experience has taught us, that, without the ruin of the Protestant establishment, the Catholic cannot be allowed the smallest influence in the state.

" For more than ten years the press has teemed with various writings intended to prove that Roman Catholics have an equal claim with Protestants to a participation in the exercise of political power in this kingdom, that such a participation would not be injurious to Protestants. That prejudice only prevents Protestants from conceding this claim. . . .

" Session after session the restrictive laws were rapidly repealed, and the last session of parliament left the Roman Catholics in no wise different from their Protestant fellow subjects, save only in the exercise of political power. . . .

" Every Irish Protestant has an interest in the government of this kingdom, he is born a member of the state and with a capacity of filling its offices, this capacity he derives from that constitution which his ancestors acquired when they overthrew the Popish tyrant, it is guaranteed by that consti-tution, it is secured by the law, he is in possession of it, and we know of no power under heaven authorised to alienate this our most valuable inheritance. . . .

" And that no doubt may remain of what we under-stand by the words Protestant ascendancy, we have further

[1] *Cal. Anc. Doc. Dub.*, XIV. 267 ff.

resolved, that we consider the Protestant ascendancy to consist in—a Protestant king of Ireland—a Protestant parliament—a Protestant hierarchy—Protestant electors and government—the benches of justice—the army and the revenue—through all their branches and details Protestant.

" And this system supported by a connection with the Protestant realm of Britain."

In 1792 the vast majority of the people of Ireland were in favour of securing their natural rights by constitutional means, and, in the city of Dublin, the Catholic merchants and traders, who were the acknowledged leaders of the people in political matters, were definitely constitutional. They had long ago abandoned the Stuart cause, and Archbishop Troy, the last Irish bishop appointed through Stuart nomination, had already shown his loyalty to the British Crown. The Protestant Corporation conveniently made no reference to this loyalty at their very door, in the big commercial establishments and in the homes of the industrial workers. Their attitude was one of perverse intolerance, and they would allow " no power under heaven," King or Parliament, to alter the constitution which they were " resolved with our lives and fortunes to maintain."

The Protestant Dublin Corporation, the most powerful body, outside parliament, and the ruler of commercial and industrial life, would rule also political life.

3. Henry Grattan Supports the Catholics.

The Catholic Relief Bill of 1793, granting the elective franchise to Catholics, put an end, for the present, to the claim of the Dublin Corporation to dictate in political matters, but it left other Catholic grievances still urgent matters for redress. The Catholics in Dublin were content to work for their removal on constitutional lines.

In January, 1795, a new viceroy, Earl Fitzwilliam, a Whig, arrived in Dublin. He saw immediately that any attempt to postpone the discussion of Catholic grievances in parliament would be futile and would probably lead to an armed revolt in Ireland. He gave Grattan permission to prepare a Catholic

Relief Bill, which would give parliamentary representation to Catholics, but he received a positive order from Secretary Portland, 20th February, to withdraw all countenance from the Bill. A week afterwards (27th February), a meeting of the Catholic citizens of Dublin was held in Francis-street metropolitan chapel to signify their approval of the action of Fitzwilliam and Grattan and to point out the issues at stake. Archbishop Troy, the pastor of the parish, granted the use of the chapel for the occasion.

An address on behalf of the Catholics of the City of Dublin was presented to the Right Honourable Henry Grattan, which was signed by Thomas Braughall, chairman, and John Sweetman, secretary. Braughall was a Dublin silk merchant, was a member of the Catholic Committee during the years 1773-92, and was present at almost every meeting. He was a representative of St. Audoen's parish, Dublin, and of the towns of Drogheda, Dundalk, Naas and Carrick-on-Suir. It may be taken that his influence in those towns was due to his silk trade. John Sweetman was also a member of the Committee and a representative of St. Andrew's parish.

The address to Grattan stated : " We are instructed by the Catholics of Dublin to offer you their humble tribute of thanks and gratitude, as well for the eminent services which you have rendered to this kingdom on various occasions, as for your able and generous exertions in their cause. . . . As mover of the Catholic Bill you are endeavouring to inculcate the necessity of moderation and justice, where you before inspired courage. . . . Never before did Ireland speak with a voice so unanimous—Protestant and Catholic are at this moment united."

The Protestant Dublin Corporation opposed the Bill and, 13th March, drew up an address to the King stating that they upheld " the genuine [sic] principles of civil and religious liberty, and [were determined] to maintain the Protestant religion as established by law. And we consider that the present application of our Roman Catholic fellow subjects to obtain the repeal of all restrictive laws whatsoever would prove, if successful, highly dangerous to those great objects."[1]

---

[1] *Cal. Anc. Rec. Dub.*, XIV. 400.

The next day (14th March), the Catholic address was presented to Grattan who, in his reply, stated : " In supporting you, I support the Protestant. We have but one interest and one honour ; and whoever gives privileges to you gives vigour to all. . . . Your Emancipation will pass. Rely on it, your Emancipation must pass ; it may be the death to one Viceroy ; it will be the peace-offering of another. . . . Let me advise you by no means to postpone the consideration of your fortunes till after the war [Anglo-French] . . . My wish is that you should be free NOW. . . . On this principle I mean to introduce your Bill. . . . His Excellency Lord Fitzwilliam, may boast that he offered to the Empire the affections of millions."[1]

Within a month Fitzwilliam was recalled, and left Dublin, 25th March, much to the dismay of the Dublin merchants and traders, who closed their premises as his carriage, drawn by wealthy citizens, made its way to the port. His recall was disastrous as, it would seem, it was the prelude to the Irish Rebellion of 1798. Catholic hopes in the redress of their grievances by constitutional means were for the time being shattered ; belief in the good faith of the British Government was absolutely destroyed, and many regarded the only solution as one of an Independent Irish Republic. Yet, with their claims set aside, the Catholic people of Dublin were not in favour of revolutionary methods. They were content to continue on constitutional lines in the hope that by the very force of their importance the day must come when their influence would decide the issue. That is the note sounded in Archbishop Troy's Pastorals that profoundly influenced Dublin Catholics in their political opinions for more than half-a-century.

4. ARCHBISHOP TROY'S PASTORALS.

The Civic Fathers would admit no " principles of civil and religious liberty " as genuine which did not " maintain the Protestant religion as established by law." This " No

---

[1] A contemporary copy of the address and answer (Fitzpatrick, No. 2 Upper Ormond Quay), preserved in the Presbytery, Francis-street, was kindly presented to me by Canon Hayden, P.P. and deposited in the National Library.

Surrender" attitude was in great measure responsible for the advance of the United Irishmen movement in Dublin.

The most determined opponent of the movement was Archbishop Troy. In August, 1795 he issued a Pastoral Address in which he denounced "a plan devised by Roman Catholics in general to destroy the Established Government. We detest and abhor every proceeding of persons associated under the title of *Defenders* or of any others, tending to injure the property or person of any one ; or to disturb the public peace. . . . We declare that the Oaths of Association taken by those *Defenders*, instead of being in any manner binding, are only Bonds of Iniquity." [1]

In his Pastoral Address, 16th February, 1797, he denounced "the usurpers of the power in France. These impious demagogues [of the French Revolution] have destroyed every thing valuable and dear to man. They have torn up the very foundations of society and religion. They have reversed everything. Neither the hallowed altar nor an ancient throne occupied by a long succession of illustrious monarchs has escaped their sacrilegious and unrelenting fury. . . . To these detestable and destructive systems we are to ascribe the sophistical theory of abstract but impracticable rights of man, and the uniform silence on his *duties* to God studiously observed by the constitution framers and revolutionary dictators of France. . . . At present we earnestly beseech you, dearest Brethren, to reflect seriously on the situation of France, where the horrid consequences of systematick infidelity and licentiousness have been woefully realized, and on the melancholy fate of those countries into which the French arms have penetrated, with the most positive but vain assurances of friendship and protection to the deluded unfortunate inhabitants. This plain simple reflection alone should be sufficient to put you on your guard, and we trust it will, against any attempts to seduce you from your attachment to religion, or from that allegiance to his Majesty and duty towards Superiors of every description which it inspires and inculcates. Do not then approach the rotten tree of French Liberty, if you desire to live." [2]

[1] Moran, *Spic. Ossor,* III. 476.   [2] Ibid., 490.

Oliver Bond, in 1797, in his house in Bridge-street, was exceedingly active in administering the oath of the United Irishmen, and in arming men. At a provincial meeting in his house, 19th February, 1798, it was resolved : "That we will pay no attention to any measure which the Parliament of this Kingdom may adopt to divert the public mind from the grand object we have in view, as nothing short of the entire and complete regeneration of our country can satisfy us."

Archbishop Troy was ready with another Pastoral Letter (1798) to undermine the Irish Republican movement, and again he attacked the French Republic upon whose support so much depended :

"Neither can you expect freedom or security from French invaders, by the eventual success of their hostile designs in these kingdoms. Ask, enquire, observe whether and what kind of liberty and security is enjoyed in France. You will find, alas ! that unhappy country subject to the most tyrannic military despotism, a prey to infidelity, licentiousness and anarchy ; under the dominion of terror exercised by successive factions, gratifying their lust of power and of money by oppression and extortion, whereby the people in general are become slaves and beggars. I say nothing of the massacres, assassinations, emigrations, proscriptions and other countless evils, caused by the revolutionary maxims prevailing in France, which have barbarized a civilized people, and in a great degree banished literature, with religion, from that once Christian and learned nation ; the rulers of which, desirous to preserve their own usurped power by any other means, seem intent on subjugating all Europe. . . .

"Compare your present situation with the past. Twenty years ago the exercises of your religion was prohibited by law ; the ministers of it were proscribed ; it was penal to educate Catholic youth at home or abroad ; your property was insecure, at the mercy of an informer ; your industry was restrained by incapacity to realize the fruits of it. At present you are emancipated from these and other penalties and disabilities, under which your forefathers, and some amongst yourselves had labored. You are now at liberty to profess your religion openly, and to practise the duties of it ; the ministers of your religion exercise their sacred functions under the sanction of law, which authorises Catholic teachers ; a College for the education of your Clergy [Maynooth] has been erected at the recommendation of his Majesty ; it is supported and endowed with parliamentary munificence ; the restraints on your industry are removed, together with the incapacity to realize the fruits of it for the benefits of your posterity. What, let me ask you, has effected this favourable change—this great difference between your past and your present situation ? I answer : Your loyalty, your submission to the constituted authorities, your peaceable demeanour, your patience under long sufferings. It was this exemplary and meritorious conduct, invariably dictated by the principles of your religion which pleaded your just cause, and determined a gracious king and a wise parliament to reward it, by restoring you to many benefits of the Constitution.

"You will perhaps reply, that some legal disabilities still exclude the most loyal and peaceable Roman Catholic from a seat or vote in Parliament, from the privy council, from the higher and confidential civil and military departments of the State. I grant it. But is it by rebellion, insurrection, tumult, or seditious clamour on your part, these incapacities are to be removed ? Is it by adopting or countenancing the modern French principles of licentious liberty and anarchical equality that you are to recommend yourselves to our rulers ? Is it by encouraging French Republicans to invade this country that you are to expect a continuation of his Majesty's favour and protection ? Is it from the enemies and scoffers of revealed religion and of the Catholic faith in particular, or from the French philosophers, attempting to destroy the very remembrance of it, by abolishing the observance of the Sabbath, and substituting an infidel for the Christian calendar, that you are to be protected in the free exercise of the Catholic faith ? Is it by the pillagers of Brabant, of Holland, of Venice, of Rome, etc., etc., that your property will be secured ? Is it by resisting the power of the State, disobeying the laws by entering into illegal associations, by administering or taking combination oaths, equally offensive to God and our temporal rulers, that you can preserve and foster the benevolence of our most benevolent sovereign ? . . . Resist then, strenuously resist, every attempt of the rebellious or disaffected to alienate you from your loyal dispositions, and the obedience due to constituted authority : Deliver up your arms and weapons of every kind, to those appointed to receive them. Renounce for ever all connections with any prohibited association. Follow, my dearest Brethren, follow, I conjure you most earnestly, this seasonable advice. It flows from a heart warmed with the purest zeal for your temporal as well as your eternal interests. It is dictated by the tender love I cherish for you as your Spiritual Father and most sincere friend. Do not then, for Jesus' sake, do not despise my admonitions, and thereby expose yourselves to danger and misery in this life, and to endless torments in the next."[1]

The winter of 1797-98 had been spent in completing the preparations for the great Rising in Spring. On 30th March, 1798, five weeks after the declaration of the United Irishmen that " Nothing short of the entire and complete regeneration of our country can satisfy us," all Ireland was put under martial law, and proclaimed in a state of rebellion. By this proclamation the military were directed to use the most summary method of repressing all kinds of disturbances.

The " rebellion " gave Major Sirr his first golden opportunity to advance in power. Having arrested a committee of eleven at the tavern of the Widow Magrath on Rogerson's Quay, on the last Sunday in April, he went the next day to Harold's Cross Green, accompanied by a military guard, where he " found a May-pole erected, seditiously decorated with the *Cap of Liberty*, alias the Jacobean emblem, the *Bonnet Rouge*. The soldiers quickly prostrated this idol of political paganism, as we trust they will every object put in opposition to the true and saving principles."[2]

[1] Moran, *Spic. Ossor*, III, 552.
Hammond, " Major Sirr," *Dub. Hist. Rec.* IV, no. 1, p. 21.

This display of the symbols of the French Revolution, notwithstanding the Archbishop's Pastoral, is distinctly interesting. Dr. Troy had made St. Mary's, Liffey-street, his metropolitan parish in 1797 and left his residence in Francis-street for one in North King-street. It does not appear that there was as yet any chapel or resident priest in Harold's Cross, then in the parish of St. Nicholas, Francis-street.

" Majors Sirr and Swan, with their picked men, went from door to door rounding up suspected rebels and gathering the surrendered arms. The names of more than a thousand suspects in the Liberties were returned. Between the 23rd May and the 16th July, 1798, upwards of 700 prisoners were sent into the Provost Prison."[1]

The city and Liberties had a period of peace after Sirr's round-up of September, 1798, but, with the advent of Spring, Archbishop Troy, 4th March, 1799, thought it prudent to issue another Pastoral Address " to be read distinctly at each Mass, on Sunday next, the 10th instant." " If we seriously reflect," he wrote," " on the recent calamities with which it hath pleased the Almighty Ruler of the world to visit this Kingdom, we shall clearly perceive that they are so many manifestations of divine wrath excited by our transgressions of His holy law."

The Archbishop continued : " On Wednesday next, the 13th inst., the Holy Sacrifice of the Mass will be offered in every Parish of this Archdiocese, to recommend our most Gracious Sovereign and these Kingdoms, to the protection of Heaven ; and to preserve this our dear country in particular, from hostile invasion and anarchy."

5. ARCHBISHOP TROY AND EMMET'S RISING

On the next day, Sunday, after Emmet's Rising of the 23rd July, 1803, Dr. Troy sat down in his house in North King-street, to pen his famous pastoral :[2]

" Dear Christians. Our inexpressible concern at the rebellious outrages in this city during last night is only

---

[1] C.S.O.P., II., Record Tower, Dublin Castle, 512/52/11.
[2] The text is from an original printed copy.

equalled by our surprise and astonishment at their having taken place when we flattered ourselves that a returning sense of religious duties, and the sad recollection of similar calamities, would have effectually prevented a repetition of them.   You cannot forget our frequent exhortations to a loyal and peaceable demeanour, nor our repeated instructions on the religious obligation of allegiance to the King, obedience to the laws, and respect for all those constituted by Divine Providence to govern us, so forcibly enjoined by our Divine Redeemer and his Apostles. . . . To what principle, then, can be ascribed the horrid rebellious scenes of last night ?   It would be difficult to particularize it, if we were not acquainted with the too successful endeavours of modern French writers and legislators, usurping the title of Philosophers, which they disgrace, in mistaking the *rights*, and disregarding the *duties* of man, in their infidel and seditious publications. . . .

" Is it by them you hope to be protected ?   What greater reason have you to expect freedom from slaves than Holland, Switzerland, Belgium, Milan, Piedmont, Savoy, and other states, formerly enjoying the blessings of civilized society under their ancient established regular governments in peace and security, but now degraded to the condition of conquered provinces by the alluring and deceitful promises of France, and groaning under the evils of French fraternity ? Do not, dear Christians, be likewise deceived.   Be unanimous in resisting foreign invasion and aggression, from whatever enemy it may be attempted.   Preserve your honour by evincing that loyalty which our Holy religion inculcates. . . .

" The exercise of your religion, your persons, and property are protected by the laws.   Avoid, then, all combination, all associations, clubs or meetings tending to subvert or violate them. . . .

" Let the untimely fate of the wicked or deluded abettors of rebellion, and even of the many innocent who have suffered, and must unfortunately suffer during the progress of rebellion, deter you from associating with the seditious of any description, and much more from assisting or encouraging them in their rebellious practices and views, which, if successful, even for a day, would ruin your country."

Within three weeks of Emmet's execution, Dr. Troy issued another letter, 10th October, directed against the republicans of France. He ordered that " on Wednesday, next, 19th instant, the Holy Sacrifice will be offered in each Parish of this Archdiocese, to recommend our most gracious Sovereign and these Kingdoms to the protection of Heaven, and to preserve them—particularly this our dear country, from the designs of our common enemy, by whom we are menaced. . . . . The leaders and promoters of the French revolution declared it could not be effected without previously destroying, if possible, the Roman Catholic faith and worship in France. . . . The regicide, republican French have masked their progress to infidelity, and their hostility to revealed religion, by destroying seminaries instituted and endowed for the education of Catholic clerical youth."[1]

The Archbishop mentions that " the Irish seminaries on the continent, mostly founded by our own countrymen, did not escape their [French Republican] sacrilegious ravages. Seventeen of them, in which near five hundred scholars and masters, were maintained and educated, have ministered to their capacity. Of these some have been destroyed, others converted to profane purposes; all are rendered useless to us."

In his " Report of the State of the Diocese of Dublin to the Sacred Congregation of the Propaganda, in 1802,"[2] the Archbishop gives the following details : 2 houses in Paris, one for priests, another for clerics, containing 150 students ; in Nantes, 100 ; in Bordeaux, 40 ; in Douai, 40. In Belgium, at Louvain and Antwerp, 50 priests and secular clerics, besides about 80 Franciscans and Dominicans in their houses in Louvain. The Irish College in Rome, as we have said, was also closed by the French in 1798, as Ireland was in the British Empire.

Dr. Troy has been severely criticised for this pastoral letter,

[1] *Vindication of Most Rev. Dr. Troy*, against the charges by a Yeoman, by a R.C. of Dublin (2nd ed., 1804). App. V.
[2] Moran, *Spicilegium Ossoriense*, III. 632.

for his association with Dublin Castle, and for his letters to the Castle authorities asking for "favours for his relatives."

As to his pastoral letter, Lord Hardwicke, the Lord Lieutenant at that time, in a private letter to his brother, the Home Secretary,[1] says : "I think Dr. Troy's pastoral letter to the popish clergy of the Archdiocese of Dublin is the greatest piece of craft, dissimulation, and hypocrisy that I ever read. It has the appearance of having been written some time, and of being well weighed and considered. Nobody can give the least credit to his total ignorance of the conspiracy."

The pastoral simply reiterates much of what he had already written in former pastorals, already referred to. His arguments against disloyalty were already set in a definite formula. The Viceroy does not take notice of the former pastorals. As a matter of fact, the pastoral seems to have been written in a moment of intense irritation.

As to Dr. Troy's "craft, dissimulation, and hypocrisy"; he does not say in his pastoral that he was ignorant of the coming Rising. He confesses "our surprise and astonishment at their [rebellious outrages] having taken place, when we flattered ourselves that a returning sense of religious duties, and the sad recollection of similar calamities would have effectually prevented a repetition of them."

Among the Rebellion Papers, Record Tower, Dublin Castle, there are about thirty letters of Dr. Troy. Two of these ask for promotion of his nephew, a civil servant, for health and family reasons. The other letters were written in discharge of his duty as Archbishop of Dublin and Metropolitan of Leinster in behalf of prisoners whom he considered wrongly imprisoned, in behalf of prisoners about to die that they might have the consolations of Religion, for the protection of schools, colleges, and chapels against the Yeomanry and Military after '98 and 1803, and for the rebuilding throughout the province of Dublin of the chapels burned by the Yeomanry and Military during and after the Rebellion of '98. As late as 1803, he was writing to Dublin Castle to have those chapels rebuilt by the Government. So far he had succeeded in having the Authorities visit and estimate the damage done in

---

[1] MacDonagh, *The Viceroy's Post Bag*, 326.

45 out of 56 cases. Many of them had already been repaired. These facts have been hitherto unknown to historians and other writers.[1]

Archbishop Troy forwarded (9th September, 1804) to Dublin Castle a letter directed to him and signed by three Catholic prisoners in Kilmainham. The letter and the culpable delay in dealing with it is an eloquent expression of the gross disregard of the spiritual needs of the political prisoners which was characteristic of Dublin Castle. It states : " Several instances have occurred and come to our knowledge here, where the attendance of a Roman Catholick clergyman was absolutely necessary, and most earnestly solicited, but to no purpose. It must be allowed that, in close confinement men are more subject to various complaints, and more liable to sudden changes of health than when at liberty, and that, to be deprived of the benefit of the clergy in the event of any illness or precarious state of health, must be a privation unknown to any civilized country. The excuse given is that no such indulgence is allowed by Government to State prisoners, but we can not be persuaded that the Government have given any directions to the contrary. There is at this moment a man who lies dangerously ill of a fever. We have applied for the admission of a clergyman to him which was peremptorily refused. We trust your Lordship will immediately represent to the Government the severity and bad policy of such a system and that you will obtain a general order for the attendance of a clergyman at all times when required, which we take the liberty of soliciting in the names of all the Roman Catholick State prisoners confined here. We beg the favour of an immediate answer as the man we mention is in imminent danger of his life and calls loudly for a clergyman which will not be granted. . . . James Dixon, Bernard Reile, Thos. Cloney. Kilmainham Prison. Saturday morning. 8th August, 1804." This letter, written 8th August, was not delivered to Dr. Troy until 8th September, and, he states in his letter to Dublin Castle, " was handed to me at a late hour last night." (Rebellion Papers, Dublin Castle, 620/14/174.35). The Governor of Kilmainham had

---

[1] I hope to be able to publish Dr. Troy's correspondence later.

delayed the sending of this urgent letter for one month ; meanwhile, the man dangerously ill of the fever, and the other sick prisoners, had no priest to attend them. Some time afterwards, this barbarous state of affairs was remedied, and chaplains were appointed to the State Prisons, but the reform was due to this letter of three State prisoners forwarded by Dr. Troy to Dublin Castle.

III

THE YOUNG FAMILY

1. A Catholic Dublin Merchant

Watson's *Gentleman's and Citizen's Almanack* of 1781 has this entry : "Lynch and Young, Merchants, W. New Row, Wholesale Merchants." The 1783 edition has this extra piece of information—that the firm was " free of the 6 and 10 per cent. in the Custom-house, Dublin, as regulated by a late Act of Parliament." West New Row, between Thomas-street and Lower Bridge-street, was an important residential district and commercial centre.

Charles Young, one of the members of the firm, was born in St. John's parish, city of Limerick, of William Young and Mary Cahill, and was baptised, 10th March, 1746. His father was a prominent merchant, and his uncle John was Bishop of Limerick (19th June, 1796—22nd September, 1813). We do not know when he came to Dublin, but it was probably shortly after the repeal in 1779 of the prohibition Act against the woollen industry. The revival in Dublin apparently attracted him, and his partner, to the city. There is no reference to a Lynch or a Young among the merchants of Dublin before 1781 ; it would thus seem that, in the preceding year, the firm as wholesale merchants had been established. Charles Young was then 35 years of age, and his partner, Henry Lynch, 30 years.

Lynch and Young married two sisters ; Henry Lynch married Catherine Hevey, and Charles Young married Margaret Hevey. There is no entry of their marriage in the Registers of St. Catherine's. Where they were married we do not know, but this we know, that Mary, the first-born of Charles Young and Margaret Hevey, was baptised in 1783 in her father's house in the parish of St. Catherine's, and apparently in West New Row.

Charles Young and Margaret Hevey were blessed with a large family. Mary, the eldest child, was born 9th October,

1783 ; John, 19th December, 1784 ; Henry, 8th June, 1786 ;
Catherine, 28th August, 1789 ; Francis, 3rd February, 1791 ;
Johanna (c. 1792) ; Sylvester (c. 1793) ; Ann (1794) ; William
(1796) ; James (c. 1797) ; and Charles, 21st December, 1798.[1]

John apparently died before 1791 ; his name does not
appear on the tomb-slab of the family grave at Mulhuddart—
the first inscription is of the year 1796. Francis died in 1797,
aged 6 years, and Ann died in 1810, aged 16 years. The
remaining eight children survived their parents, and several
of them lived to a ripe old age.

Two tomb-slabs cover the burial places of the Lynch and
Young families. On one, a few yards outside the north wall
of the old church, is the following inscription :

" The Burial Ground of Messrs. Lynch & Young of
New Row, Dublin.
Here lie the mortal remains of

	Died		Aged
Mrs. Catherine Lynch	Decem.	1796	42
Francis Young	6 Jan.	1797	6
Ann Young	—	—	16
Mr. Henry Lynch	11 Decem.	1811	61
John Lynch son of said			
Henry and Catherine Lynch	2nd May	1819	—
Charles Lynch	5 Decem.	1819	32
Andrew Lynch	11 Nov.	1824	—
Jasper Lynch	5 July	1836	51

On the other tomb-stone is the inscription :

" The Burial Ground of Lynch and Young of New Row
Dublin.

Father Bernard Lynch
Mr. Henry Young
Mrs. Catherine Lynch.   Mr. John Lynch
Parents of said Bernard Lynch."

[1] The baptismal registers of St. Catherine's, Meath-street, are defective from
1792 to 1798.

It has been hitherto recorded that Charles Young and Margaret Hevey had eight children. Three others must be added to the number, John, Francis and Ann, who died young ; the Registers of St. Catherine's and the number one tomb-slab record the existence of Francis and Ann.

It would appear that three families were included in the firm Lynch and Young—Henry and Catherine Lynch, John and Catherine Lynch, and Charles and Margaret Young. With these were joined Mr. Henry Young, apparently a bachelor, and a brother of Charles. Though the business house was at 31 W. New Row, it would seem that the three families had their dwelling houses in the same street. Henry Lynch, the chief member of the firm, died in 1811, aged 61 (his wife had died 16 years previously, aged 42). From 1811 until 1821, Charles Young was the sole member of the firm.

As a wealthy merchant, Henry Young took his place beside the Catholic merchants of the city in the religious and charitable activities of the period. His name appears as subscriber to some of the Catholic publications. He was also a prominent member of the Catholic Committee, and at the 1791 election he and his partner were elected representatives. Charles Young was elected one of the three representatives of his native city of Limerick, and Henry Lynch one of the two representatives of Galway.[1] They became collectors of their native cities for the support of the Committee. They thus belonged to that " knot of high-spirited commercialmen " who early supported the small group of emancipators and, by their financial support, made possible the first attempts at organising Irish Catholics towards Emancipation. These men, said Wyse, were " the first collection of individual Catholics who dared to meet and consult on Catholic affairs " since 1690.

It was only natural that Lynch and Young should be brought into close contact with Archbishop Troy, who was parish priest of the metropolitan chapel in Francis-street from 1786 until 1797. His house, 50 Francis-street, a few doors from the chapel, still stands. It was only a few hundred yards from the important house of the firm of Lynch and

---

[1] *Minute Book,* p. 119 (Archiv. Hib. IX).

Young, which had an open door for the city clergy. Dr. Troy frequently partook of their afternoon dinner, about 3 o'clock, when most of the work of the day was generally regarded as completed. Here he met many of the principal Catholic laymen and discussed the important subjects of the day, religious, social, and political. He found Charles Young a staunch and liberal supporter of the Church.

Charles Young was a man of education and refinement, and of solid piety. His wife was in every way worthy of her excellent husband. Their home was a model one, and their children grew up models of youth. Henry, James, and William became priests of the diocese, Charles became a Jesuit, and Sylvester, who succeeded to the business, became a leader in Catholic social activities. Of the three daughters, Catherine became a Poor Clare in Harold's Cross, and Mary and Johanna Ursuline nuns in Cork.

2. HENRY YOUNG'S BOYHOOD

Henry Young was seven years of age when the most important Catholic Relief Act of 1793 was passed, and, no doubt, was beginning to take an intelligent interest in public affairs under the careful tuition of his constitutional father. No doubt, also, he met Dr. Troy and other ecclesiastics at the family gatherings. In the momentous year of 1798 he was twelve years of age and the eldest of seven children being reared in the big house in West New Row. He must have been aware of the visits of Majors Swann and Sirr to the district and of the rounding up of the republicans in the Liberties, the surrender of their arms and their imprisonment in the Provost's prison in the Marshalsea adjacent. He was old enough to appreciate the significance of the political situation, and, no doubt, his careful father explained it from the constitutional standpoint. Moreover, he would have heard read in the family circle Dr. Troy's pastorals. Henry never deviated from the constitutional view.

He earned from his brothers and sisters who were competent to appreciate his holiness the title of " The Saint." When they wished him to join them in their games they found him in the cellar praying or reading pious books by candle-light. No doubt, the family possessed a respectable library of the devotional and catechetical books printed in Dublin.

His eccentricity, his brothers and sisters thought, went beyond beyonds when he hoarded his weekly pocket-money, cakes and fruit, which they found he was distributing among the poor of the district. All these luxuries, they considered, were intended for their own personal pleasure, and not to be given to others. His unselfishness and sacrifice were unusual in one so young, and they were dominant features of his later years.

Though it was the recently reconstructed Augustinian chapel near his father's house that presumably he frequented for early morning Mass, yet the new parochial chapel in Meath-street must have been a special source of attraction to him. Over its High altar was a large altar-piece painting of Christ carrying His Cross which had been brought from Dirty-lane chapel. As devotion to Christ's sufferings appears later as a determining influence in his religious life, it is quite likely that it had its beginnings or was fostered as he gazed on this famous painting in his parish chapel. Here too, no doubt, he developed that devotion to the Blessed Sacrament for which he was so remarkable in his priestly life.

There is nothing to show where the children received their early education, but it is most probable that they received it at home from tutors. They excelled in music, history and literature. As the family was large and growing up, Henry's father apparently thought it wise to send him to a boarding school, and was, no doubt, influenced by the fact that he showed exceptional religious tendencies. The only available one near home was the classical school at Inch near Balbriggan. Thither he was sent about 1800. Apparently it was under ecclesiastical control, as, in 1808, among the subscribers to the edition of Father Barnaby Murphy's sermons was the Rev. Christopher Flinn, the principal of the Academy.

Unfortunately we have no information about the early history of this Academy. From later references we must conclude that it was a very important establishment, and, no doubt, patronised by the wealthy merchants of Dublin and by the gentry of Meath and North Co. Dublin.

In a letter to Father Peter Kenney, S.J., who was prospecting for a suitable house for a Jesuit College for boys, Dr. Plunkett, Bishop of Meath, mentions (25th January, 1813) that " Balbriggan, as to situation, would suit you better ; not however, without considerable expense. I mean the house at Inch. I saw it some years ago. No striking idea of it remains in my mind. A convenient extensive building would appear there to great advantage. To the price or rent asked for the ground I should not very much object : we pay higher for chosen spots of land."[1]

Apparently, the grounds of Inch were extensive, and the house respectable and fit to stand, but, for a new college, additional building would be required. For a small college it seems to have been ideal, but it ceased some time between 1808 and 1813—for what reason we do not know.

In this school Henry attracted to himself many young friends whom he formed into a society for good works, and whom he induced to join the Sodality of the Blessed Virgin. " The Sodality of the Blessed Virgin Mary was founded by a young Belgian Jesuit, Father John Leunis, professor of the Roman College, in the year 1563. It was meant primarily for the students attending lectures in that College. It spread gradually to other Jesuit colleges, and the spiritual advantages of it soon became so evident that the wish was expressed on all sides that its ranks should be thrown open to a wider circle of earnest Catholics. The first step in this direction was the canonical erection of the *Prima Primaria* [Parent Sodality] of the Roman College by Pope Gregory XIII " (5th Dec., 1584).[2]

When Father Henry Fitzsimon, S.J. arrived in Dublin, his native city, at the beginning of April, 1598, he made it his first work to found a Sodality of the Blessed Virgin in imitation of those sodalities whose beneficial effects he had observed abroad. He saw that if the faith was to be preserved and the practices of piety revived among the Catholic laity, at a time

[1] *Irish Jesuit Directory*, 1941, p. 200.
[2] MacErlean. *Sodality of B.V.M. in Ireland.* (*Irish Messenger* Office, 1928), p. 5.

when religion was oppressed, some kind of organised society was necessary. Accordingly, the General of the Jesuits was petitioned time and again to aggregate to the *Prima Primaria* such sodalities as were attached to Jesuit colleges, churches, and houses in Ireland. The difficulty about the aggregation was that permanent stations and residences of the Jesuits were almost impossible on account of the fierce persecution raging at that time. However, in 1617, the Holy See allowed the aggregation of the Sodality of the Blessed Virgin at Cashel, and the graces were declared available also for women. The Dublin Sodality was aggregated 27th May, 1628.

The part played by the Sodality in the preservation of the Catholic religion in Ireland was immense. " When it was first introduced, the people as a whole were firmly attached to the faith, but the ordinary practices of Catholic piety had in very many places fallen into desuetude ; deflections from the faith, external conformity to Protestantism and assistance at heretical services were not unknown, though nearly always insincere. The Jesuit Fathers, however, saw even greater dangers in the widespread moral corruption due to intercourse with heretics."

" Hence it was that the Jesuit Fathers were so urgent in their appeals to Rome to have the sodality aggregated to the *Prima Primaria*, for the sodality's first and most essential aim was the revival of piety and religious practices in the individual, by its rules, the monthly meetings, the instruction of the Director, and the frequentation of the Sacraments. . . . . Other Catholic practices, such as the family rosary, were also propagated."

" The works of Mercy and Charity prescribed by the rules were accurately carried out. The chief of these were : the training by good example of their families and dependents in virtue and the frequentation of the Sacraments, the fostering of piety and vocations in the young, the care of the sick, the relief of the poor, the instruction of the ignorant, the quiet and unobtrusive prevention of sins and scandals, the proposal and promotion of works of piety and religion, and the visitation of prisoners."[1]

[1] l.c.

At the beginning of the nineteenth century there was as much necessity for those works of piety and mercy as there was in the early seventeenth century. Henry Young's experience of the conditions obtaining in his own parish of St. Catherine inspired him to gather around him those who might become apostles when they left the Academy. Thus, as a boy of 16 years, he began his great work of Catholic Action, and it was on the lines of the Sodality of the Blessed Virgin that he constructed his own apostolate in later years and instructed the parochial Confraternities. His vision of the importance of the Sodality at this time is truly remarkable. Many of the boys that Henry induced to join the Sodality became priests and attributed the awakening of holy desires in their hearts to the " little apostle of Balbriggan," as they used to call him.

3. Vocation to the Priesthood

On leaving the Classical and Commercial Academy at Inch, when he was sixteen years of age, Henry Young was inclined to join the Cistercian Order, but his practical father considered he would be more useful as a priest in a Dublin parish, where zealous and holy priests were needed at this important turning-point in the religious life of the city.

The choice of a college for the young Levite was, no doubt, a matter of serious consideration for his parents. The recently endowed Royal College of Maynooth would have been an obvious choice, as the Irish colleges in France, Belgium, and Rome had been suppressed during the French Revolution. Yet revolutionary ideas had made their way into Maynooth College, and of its sixty-nine students in 1798, no fewer than eighteen were expelled for having taken the oath of the United Irishmen. [1]

The College was still under suspicion in 1799. In his letter, introducing the vice-president, Father Francis Power, to Dublin Castle to present his report, Dr. Troy states : " If upon enquiry it be found that any United Irishmen or

[1] *Cath. Encycl.* Maynooth College.

abetter of their irreligious and revolutionary system has been clandestinely introduced into the College, it is my wish, and that of every other Trustee that he be punished ; but if none such be discovered there, I hope you will vindicate the College from any aspersion or unfavourable suspicion which may be occasioned by the apprehension and confinement of Thos. Power, one of the scholars, by ordering his discharge and declaring the information against him unfounded."[1]

It is an interesting question as to whether the revolutionary ideas of the Maynooth students originated from the Society of the United Irishmen or from the students of the Irish colleges on the continent, especially in Paris. The students of the Irish College, Paris, were imbued with French revolutionary ideas, and, in 1793, they sent a declaration, signed by a large number, to the Pantheon Revolutionary Tribunal, charging the Superiors with being dangerous suspects, namely English loyalists, and counter-revolutionaries. The Superior was immediately placed under arrest. [2]

Shortly afterwards, on account of the French war with England, these students had to return to Ireland. The two Irish Colleges in Paris housed one hundred and fifty students. There were usually in Nantes one hundred, in Bordeaux forty, in Douai forty, in Louvain and Antwerp fifty. (Six houses in Rome had Irish students, and there were many Franciscan and Dominican students in Louvain.)[3] All had to return to their Irish homes. How many of these students found their way into Maynooth College there is no means of knowing.

Notwithstanding the Vice-President's report of 1799, the College was under suspicion for many years, and the Castle authorities were inclined to make an example of some of the priests ordained there by punishing them, but Archbishop Troy held their hand by asking them to name the disloyal priests, and, if any were found disloyal, he would punish them.

It would seem that on account of this suspicion about

---

[1] S.C.P. II. 31, Record Tower, Dublin Castle.
[2] Hayes, *Ireland and Irishmen in the French Revolution,* pp. 62–63.
[3] Moran, *Spic. Ossor.,* III. 632.

Maynooth College, Dr. Troy, as an intimate friend of the Young family, advised Charles to send his son Henry abroad for his education for the priesthood. Another notable prelate who would have been naturally consulted on the subject was Henry's uncle, John Young, Bishop of Limerick. Educated at Louvain, where he received his Doctorate in Divinity, he would have favoured a continental education for his nephew.

The international college of the Propaganda in Rome was the only continental college to which Henry could have been sent. Rome had just recovered from an upheaval much more serious and far-reaching than that which Henry had witnessed in Dublin in 1798. Napoleon had been selected by the Directory, in 1796, to lead the French troops into Italy. The Papal States did not escape ; Pope Pius VI had to submit to humiliating terms, and his city of Rome was threatened. The Directory was not satisfied with these severe terms, and ordered the complete destruction not only of the Temporal Power, but of all Papal authority. On a paltry excuse the French army entered the city and a Roman Republic was proclaimed (1797).

The wild excesses of the Paris mob were reproduced in Rome, and the Pope was taken prisoner and ultimately died in Valence, 22nd August, 1799. In 1802, his remains were brought back to Rome and laid in the Basilica of St. Peter. On the death of the Pope, in 1799, the Cardinals met in Venice, under the protection of Austria, and elected Pius VII. Austria, Spain, Naples, Sardinia and Russia, congratulated the new Pope, who made a triumphant entry into Rome, 1800. The Concordat between Napoleon and the Holy See was solemnly proclaimed in Paris and Rome, Easter Sunday, 1802.

Rome was thus at peace in the summer of 1802 when Henry returned from the Academy of Inch to his home in New Row and when the debate on his future college took place. It was decided to send him to the Propaganda College. His vocation, at the age of 16 years, must have been solidly founded when he was allowed to go so far for his priestly training.

4. Henry Young in Rome.

Students of the international Propaganda College had many advantages over students of national colleges. They had as companions youths from many nations, chiefly Eastern. Italian was the language of the college, but anyone with a flair for languages could become a fluent speaker of many languages. Moreover, one became acquainted, in the daily routine of life, with representatives of many nations and with the customs and religious life of many peoples. The Propaganda College was the Catholic Church in miniature. The students spoke freely of the work before them and of their difficulties in the Propagation of the Faith when they returned as priests to their native land.

All this was a source of tremendous enthusiasm for an Irish student who had to face many difficulties when he returned to his mission. Dublin had its own special problems in the conditions created by the Penal Laws.

" The young Irish student, whose life at home had been so pure and holy, found new incitements to sanctity in the scenes which now surrounded him. Every step he took, every day of the year as it came round, brought with it some sacred association—drew him nearer to God." [1] Every turn Henry took in the streets of Rome brought him into contact with the footprints of saints in churches and institutions. He visited those places and was inspired by the life and labours of those heroes of the Church Militant. He was enthralled by the magnificent celebration of their feast days. He saw in the Roman Catacombs the great evidence of the faith and steadfastness of the early Christians during the days of the persecution. He saw the churches that were built in the fourth century, immediately after the Constantine edict of the freedom of the Church (331), and he was inspired with great hopes that he might be a builder, in different circumstances, in his own city, that had likewise but recently emerged from the days of persecution.

It was, moreover, no small joy to him to see the Vicar of Christ pass once more in triumph through the streets of Rome after his great victory in maintaining the purity and integrity

---

[1] Fullerton, *Life of Father Henry Young*, p. 30.

of the Catholic Faith. Nowhere else in the world does the ecclesiastical student come under such salutary influences to mould his priestly character, and nowhere else does the student for the mission receive such powerful inspirations for his work in the mission field.

" It was there," said Lady Fullerton, " that began Father Henry's career of detachment from everything that the world considers desirable or attractive. We learn from one of his sisters, the Abbess of St. Clare's. who related it to a friend, that it was during his studies in Rome that, praying in one of those churches in which he spent every hour he could snatch from his studies, he felt an inspiration to lead a life of extraordinary austerity and self-denial. He seems to have considered this a special call, and he scrupulously followed it during the long course of years that he was to spend in the world—but not of the world."

He asked a young student, a great friend of his, who was dying, to pray in Heaven that he himself might never be occupied with aught but God and His service. The friend promised, and it would seem as if his prayer was heard, for Henry Young's indifference to all not connected with his religious duties amounted almost to unconsciousness.

His biographer continues :. " One of his fellow-students, who became afterwards a Roman prelate, told a Jesuit Father, many years ago, that, if he survived Father Henry Young, he thought it not unlikely that he would be called upon to testify that even at the College of the Propaganda he led a life of heroic sanctity."[1]

Henry had not finished his course in the Propaganda College when Rome was again invaded by French troops. Napoleon had commanded Pope Pius VII to expel all Russian and English subjects from the Papal States. The Pope rejected his demands, and Rome was taken by General Miollis in 1808. The Emperor's decree, abolishing the temporal sovereignty of the Pope, and annexing his territory, was published in Rome, 10th June, and the Papal flag was lowered from the Castle of St. Angelo, and the tricolour was hoisted over the Eternal City.

[1] Fullerton, *Life of Father Henry Young*, 31-32.

Brave men affixed to the doors of the Roman basilicas the Bull of Excommunication of Napoleon, and before the sun went down the Roman people rejoiced that the Pope had despised the imperial edict. Nevertheless, the Pope was brought a prisoner to Savona where he lay for three years. British subjects had to look to their own safety, and Henry had to seek refuge in the House of the Vincentian Fathers at Monte Celino. Here he was ordained, Pentecost Sunday, 1810, by Bishop Concannon, O.P., who had been Bishop of Kilmacduagh and Kilfenora (1798-1800).

Henry had the supreme delight of seeing a second triumph for the Vicar of Christ over his enemies, for, the year after his ordination, he witnessed the return of Pope Pius VII, after his three years of exile from Rome. He seems at this time to have had no desire to return to the missionary life of Dublin. The religious life of the Vincentian Fathers appealed to his ascetic mind, and, no doubt, the missions to the villagers outside Rome gave him scope for his apostolic zeal. Italian was then at least as easy to him as English, and he could preach to the country folk in their own dialect.

It has to be explained how Archbishop Troy should have left a student of the Dublin Diocese in Rome for several years after his ordination, and not have called him home for the work of the diocese. The only explanation is that Henry's education in Rome was paid for by his father, and that Henry was free to choose his own mission ; and it seems that notwithstanding the friendship between the Archbishop and the Young family, Henry triumphed in his desire to remain in the Vincentian Mission around Rome. He had become an ascetic.

At the Vincentian College of Monte Celino, Henry made on all who knew him the same impression as at the Propaganda. The Venerable Servant of God, Padre Roberti, was one of his fellow-students. Addressing the students of the Irish College, in 1832, one who had been well acquainted with him said that he would be ready, if he survived Henry, to bear witness on oath to his sanctity, and that he should not be surprised if the day came when their countryman would be placed on the altars of the church.[1]

[1] *Life*, 34.

It is to be regretted that we have not the names of the people who spoke so fervently of Henry's sanctity. His biographer, in 1874, five years after his death, was unfortunately not at liberty to disclose the names of her informants. As to the genuinity of the opinions there can be no doubt.

Henry would have remained on the Vincentian mission in and around Rome were his own wishes alone consulted. It was on those missions that he acquired that ease in preaching which was to be so useful to him afterwards in the parishes of old Dublin. He was no orator, but he preached the word of God in the same unvarnished style to the people of Dublin as he had preached to the country folk in the villages on the hilltops outside Rome.

Providence decided that he should not remain on the Vincentian Mission in Rome, but that he should return to the mission field in Dublin. A question of great importance arose at this time in Ireland. It was the celebrated question of the Veto—as to how far the British Government could have a deciding voice in the appointment of the Irish Bishops. Archbishop Troy sent to Rome, in 1814, his coadjutor, Archbishop Murray, and Dr. Blake, P.P. of SS. Michael and John's, to state the case of the Irish bishops.

Dublin was in need of pious and zealous priests to undo the effects of the recent political disturbances in the religious life of the people. Ignorance, misery, and degradation were present to an alarming degree. The housing of the poor, the badly lighted and filthy lanes and alleys, the want of proper schools, and the inadequacy of accommodation in the penal-time chapels made the condition of the Catholics deplorable and difficult.

Dr. Murray was informed by the Vincentian Fathers of the merits and missionary zeal of Father Young, and he insisted that he should leave the cloister and take his place as a missionary in his native city. Missionaries, apostles, were the priests who toiled in Dublin during the early nineteenth century, and Henry Young became an outstanding figure.

After four years of missionary life in and around Rome, Henry, obedient to his Archbishop, left the Eternal City, on the long journey to his native city. He crossed from Holyhead on Christmas eve in a coal brig, and, having arrived in Dublin early on Christmas morning, he set out at once for the Augustinian chapel in John's Lane, where he worshipped as a boy. Here he said his three Masses and poured forth his soul in long thanksgiving. Only when he had finished the duty he owed to the Almighty did he think of visiting his parents and of snatching a little repose.

5. FATHER YOUNG IN ST. MICHAN'S

Father Young's first appointment in the diocese was as curate under Father Wall, P.P., in 1814, in the old chapel in Mary's-lane. He said the 11 o'clock Mass on week-days, and after that visited the parish priest to get instructions as to the parochial affairs he was required to look after. He took his duties seriously, and, after his eleven years in Rome speaking Italian, he considered that his English was not of the best and set himself the task of acquiring a respectable knowledge of it. It must be remembered that he left Dublin when he was 16 years of age, and that whatever acquaintance he had had with religious literature in English had been well nigh lost.

When he was satisfied that he had a respectable knowledge of the subject he devoted his spare time to writing sermons. Yet, he would not dare set out on the duty of instructing others unless he had the approbation of the Vicar-General, Dr. Hamill, for his discourses. At this time the people who frequented the old chapel in Mary's lane were of a very mixed kind. The old streets sheltered the rich as well as the poor, and rich and poor rubbed shoulder to shoulder, but the parish was rather of the fashionable type. No wonder then that Father Young, in the pulpit, was overawed, and sought the best advice for his sermons.

He had a room in Mary's-lane where he wrote and slept. His pious mother, wishing to see her son decently housed, had his room comfortably carpeted and furnished. Calling a few days afterwards to see him, and hoping to find him working in the midst of a comfortable room, she found that the furniture had disappeared with the exception of the wooden

portion of the bedstead, one chair, and a stool. The carpet
had completely disappeared from the floor. It was the winter
of 1814, and excessively cold weather. She found him sitting
on the stool, cutting the carpet into pieces and hanging them
on the chair. He explained to her that the poor women of
the parish were badly off and needed the carpet for petticoats.
As for the chair, he kept it for the Archbishop when he desired
to call, and, as to the bed, it would serve him as a very good
seat as well as a place to sleep on. [1]

Nothing could weaken his determination to lead an ascetic
life. Neither the kindness of his mother nor the entreaties
of his sister, Catherine, the nun in the Convent of Poor
Clares, Harold's Cross, could move him from his fixed rule
of life. To Catherine he wrote, 12th January, 1815 : " I
would willingly comply with your desire that I should
celebrate some morning this week in your chapel ; but, dear
sister, my situation and fixed hour in Mary's lane chapel forbid
me to acquiesce in your request. Let us offer up to the Lord
this mortification of our will, which He will bountifully
accept as a pleasing holocaust, and will impart to us more
abundant graces. You know that if I asked leave of my
Superior, he might perhaps give it to me ; but still it would
be an infringement on the rules of the chapel, a subversion
of order which should not take place, except through necessity.
Therefore, let us sacrifice our private gratification to public
order and the common good. Moreover, I should have to
substitute another priest to say my eleven o'clock Mass, which
I would not like to do." In another letter he says : " When
in Mary's-lane, I refused even to say Mass for my mother "—
apparently in the home in New Row.

These letters reveal his spirit of sacrifice and his unfailing
attention to his duties, especially the confessional, which was
to be characteristic of him all through his long life on the
mission.

On beginning his missionary career in St. Michan's he
preached and promoted the First Friday devotion, with
special prayers and Benediction after Mass, and also the
devotion of the First Saturday in honour of the Immaculate

[1] *Life*, 42.

Heart of Mary. He gave new life to the devotion to the Sacred Heart of Jesus, new life to Mary's-lane chapel. It was remarked afterwards that he never officiated in any church without placing in it an image or picture of the Sacred Heart. To make Him known and loved was the passion of his life. His manifold labours show the holy restlessness of his desire. In the church, the street, his little room, every hour of the day was marked by something done with that intention. He became known as the great promoter of the devotion throughout the diocese. He would have acquired it in the Vincentian House in Rome.

As to the devotion to the Immaculate Heart of Mary on the first Saturday of each month for the conversion of sinners, he was also one of its great promoters, indeed its pioneer, in the diocese. His great object in life was to raise his devoted poor people out of their misery, material and spiritual. He trusted to the devotions to the Sacred Heart of Jesus and the Immaculate Heart of Mary to warm their hearts with love of Jesus and Mary and to convert them from their evil or careless ways.

Although his voice was unmelodious, even harsh, he read aloud in a way that irresistibly impressed his hearers. *The Imitation of Christ* and Challoner's *Meditations* were his favourite books. People noticed that those harsh tones of his became sweet when he uttered words in praise of Jesus and Mary, especially when he read those words in *The Imitation of Christ*, which were the keynote, so to speak, of all his teachings : " To be with Jesus is a sweet Paradise ; to be without Jesus is a grievous Hell." The same change of accent was likewise noticed when after having spoken of the Blessed Virgin as God's Mother, he always added the words, " and our Mother also."

A short sentence uttered in his characteristic style was as good as a sermon. One evening he was preaching, and became so absorbed in contemplation that he lost the thread of his discourse and was at a loss how to proceed. After a pause, he said in a broken voice, " Our Blessed Lord fell under the Cross," and he descended abruptly from the pulpit.

His complexion in youth was fair and pale, but neither

sickly nor sallow. He had regular features, a straight long
nose, brown hair and eyes of a bluish grey. He often smiled
but never laughed. He was rather small of stature, and, in
his old age, his shrunken form became diminutive in the
extreme. He was scrupulously neat and orderly in all that
he did. There was nothing commanding in his exterior,
and yet how humbly and how reverently did many a knee
bend and many a head bow down to receive a blessing from
him whose delight it was to look poor and insignificant.

There is scarcely a virtue of which we do not find evidence
in Father Henry's life. In charity, in mortification, in the
love of poverty, he equalled some of the most devoted and
austere saints. In these respects, he was compared during his
life to the Curé d'Ars, and with St. Peter of Alcantara.
Whenever he spoke of himself, it was with the most unmis-
takable contempt. A few years before his death, he attended
a course of sermons delivered in John's Lane church by the
celebrated Dr. Gentili. Someone remarked in his hearing
that these discourses were effecting a remarkable work of
conversion in the neighbourhood, whereupon he said, with
great earnestness, "I am sure it is so, for I feel that even I
myself am being converted."

His oldest and most intimate clerical friends spoke and wrote
in glowing terms of his humility—of his sincere and entire
contempt of himself. Popular veneration of him increased
with the years.

His stay in St. Michan's was short and the Registers contain
only one entry made by him over his signature, namely of
the baptism of an illegitimate child. He and his brothers, as
we shall see, were devoted benefactors of poor sinners and
orphans.

6. Father Young at Harold's Cross

Father Young was transferred to the parish of St. Nicholas
late in 1815. The church was considered " an old but very
firm building ; and though one of the largest chapels in
Dublin, it is too small for the congregation that constantly
resorts to it. There is a large and convenient house lately
erected, adjoining the chapel for the residence of the curates.

The clergy consist of a parish priest (Dean of Dublin) and eight curates."[1]

As this description was written in 1821, it must be presumed that the new presbytery for the curates "lately erected" did not exist during Father Young's residence in Francis-street ; apparently, he had his lodgings in the "dormitory of the Friars," from 1815 to 1817. One of his brothers came to see him at the "dormitory" and said to him : "How very inhospitable you are, Henry ! You have never asked any of us to dine with you." He replied : "Well, if you like to come to-morrow and share what I have, you will be welcome." Accordingly, at the appointed hour his brother made his appearance. Father Young laid the cloth, and the servant carried in two large plates of stirabout, or oatmeal boiled in water. "Is this all you are going to give me?" exclaimed his brother. "Is it not plenty?" he replied. "If I had anything better, you may be sure I would give it to other friends of mine who badly want it." He had a keen sense of humour and enjoyed playing practical jokes. His favourite dish—in fact, his only meal of the day—was stir-about, except when preaching during his mission period, when he allowed himself a cup of tea and dry bread.

Parochial work in St. Nicholas's was not easy in those days considering the enormous district, reaching to the Dodder, and the density of the population in the city portion, which was about twice what it is to-day. Father Young relates in a letter :[2] "In the years 1815–17, when I was a curate in St. Nicholas, Francis-street, I used, in my turn, on Sundays to celebrate Mass [at 9 o'clock] in Harold's Cross chapel, and then, a second Mass [at 11 o'clock] in Milltown, returning home by the fields." On one of his sick calls he caught a fever that so reduced his vitality that he was sent to take charge of the chapel at Harold's Cross (1818). Here he began his real mission.

The chapel was a miserable building, a cottage converted into a chapel, on Harold's Cross Green (near the present Mount Jerome, and afterwards a school). Opposite the Poor

[1] McGregor, *Picturesque Dublin* (1821), p. 150.
[2] *Life*, 55.

Clares' Convent was his own cottage, of which he occupied one room on the front.

There must have been at the time a considerable population on the sides of the Green. Rocque's map of 1765 shows many houses and mills in the vicinity. In fifty years, with the great industrial progress, the village on the Green must have grown considerably. There were mills at Kimmage and Harold's Cross. The mill-workers lived on the Green, and difficult people they were to deal with.

Father Young's arrival at Harold's Cross reminds one of the entrance of the famous Curé d'Ars into his parish. He had the mill-workers to convert, and he had to prevent the faction fights then prevalent on the Green between the men of the Dublin mountains and the people of the Coombe.

One day at Harold's Cross he was accosted by a man who told him a lamentable story of his distress. He listened with his usual kindness, and promised him help. The man poured forth profuse thanks and walked away. Shortly afterwards, Father Young found that his old silver watch had disappeared, whereupon those who were walking with him were loud in their indignation. Smiling he remarked : " I cannot imagine how he took it. Don't you think he was very ingenious ? "

The mills drew many undesirable characters from the city streets, and when the Maypole and other festivities were held on the Green, drinking, fighting, and loose conduct were the order of the evening. His remedy against this lawlessness was the Daily Mass. In order that his flock might attend Mass before the mills opened he said Mass at 5 o'clock. He put up a notice in the window of his room facing the Green that confessions were heard at all hours. Little by little he won the hearts of the people and won them to the frequentation of the Sacraments.

In the confessional he impressed on the penitent that it was with the Father in Heaven he was dealing, of whom he himself was the representative. In order to inspire the penitent with a sense of God's presence, he used, when hearing Confessions in the little sacristy behind the altar, to accompany each penitent, as he left, to the front of the altar, and kneel there for a moment before returning to his confessional.

Father Henry Young's Ciborium (Milltown Chapel).

FATHER CHARLES YOUNG, S.J.
(Painting in Belvedere College).

He gave himself no rest, and he did not allow anyone to rest in his sins. One by one he visited the mill-workers, exhorting, persuading, and even threatening each one to come to the chapel and confessional. Every evening he rang the bell on the Green for night prayers, and walked through the village urging them to attend.

The ignorance of the people was one of the greatest obstacles to their reform, and schools should be founded if lasting good was to be effected. He induced the Brothers of Clondalkin in 1821 to send him a few men to teach and set up a school in his house.

The story of the founding of the monastery and schools of St. Joseph's, Clondalkin, is one of exceptional interest. In 1795 a few pious men of different trades formed themselves into a society and started a fund to which each subscribed a small weekly sum and a portion of which was applied for various pious purposes. After mature deliberation they resolved to found a monastery. In 1807 they formed a community and, by their united industry, realised a considerable sum of money with which they purchased land and began the building of the monastery, the first stone of which was laid by the Rev. Mr. Cahill, 2nd February, 1813. The undertaking had the approval of Archbishop Troy. They next founded a large free school in which nearly 200 boys were educated, some of them fed and clothed, and many were afterwards apprenticed to trades. Some of the community worked at their trades, whilst others taught in the schools. They were allowed to have an Annual Sermon, and subscriptions were collected by a lay committee in Dublin, who arranged all the business connected with the school. After their first Charity Sermon in 1815, they proceeded to clothe 105 poor boys. In 1826 they commenced to build a chapel, the stone of which was laid, 26th April, by Lord Cloncurry, who patronised the institution from the beginning.

The little community at Harold's Cross had the sanction of Archbishop Murray. What Rule the Communities at Clondalkin and Harold's Cross followed does not appear. At all events Father Young rejoiced in living with a community that appeared to him to revive, even in a humble way, some of the glories of the monasteries suppressed by Henry VIII.

At Harold's Cross as at Clondalkin, besides the free school there was what was called a " Mercantile Academy " which was supported by the profits from the articles made by the pupils under the direction of the members of the community. In other words, Father Young started technical education for boys, similar to Mary Teresa Mullaly's system in Mary's-lane for girls. Thus, side by side, with the technical work of the mill-workers, he added important education in business methods. His schools must have added considerably to the efficiency of the mill-workers, as well as bringing in increased wages to the homes of the villagers of the Green. In the few years he spent with them he revolutionised moral and material life for them. Those years must be regarded as the most intensive of his long laborious life. He was then a young man, still in his thirties, full of energy and zeal, and single handed he succeeded in the reformation of the district.

Milltown was also in need of reform. For the extensive district between the Calced Carmelite chapel in French-street[1] and Sandyford in the mountains there was no proper chapel. The mill-workers of Milltown had no chapel and no resident priest. The village was a favourite half-way house of the citizens on their excursions to the mountains. Revelling and drinking went on until the early hours of the morning in the dancing houses. Sometimes, Father Young, accompanied by a boy, would make his way late at night, across the fields and along the Milltown Path, and disperse the revellers. The districts of Rathmines and Ranelagh were then " in the fields."

Schools and a chapel were required to familiarise the inhabitants with the fundamentals of Christian belief and practises. A stable had served for a Mass-house. The stable belonged to a Mrs. Burke (whose son was afterwards Father Michael Burke, C.M.) who willingly gave it to Father Young for the erection of a chapel. The funds were soon provided and the

---

[1] On 25th October, 1825, Dr. Murray laid the foundation stone of their new church on the site of their pre-Reformation friary, in Whitefriars-street, and, in November, 1827, solemnly dedicated the church.

chapel was erected (1820) and still does duty for the villagers. [1]

He applied to the Franciscan Fathers on Merchant's-quay to found a school in the village. He mentions, in his *Catholic Directory* of 1821, that a "Franciscan Monastery, Mount Alverno, near Milltown, was founded in May, 1820, under the immediate direction of Rev. Mr. Dunne of Adam and Eve Convent. Mr. Owen Smyth, Superior ; Mr. Dillon, Local Director, and eight other Religious subjects. They govern a day, evening, and Sunday Free school for the poor male children of Milltown and the neighbouring villages." The Sunday school was for those mill-workers who could not attend day or evening school during the week.

Every Sunday and holiday Father Young walked across the fields from Harold's Cross and said his second Mass at 11 o'clock in Milltown. When someone spoke to him about the hardship of this journey and fasting, he said : " To tell you my feeling, I would rather lose a hundred pounds than forfeit my second Mass on Sunday." After Mass he would instruct the children in catechism and then, well after mid-day, he would take his plate of porridge.

For some years before the passing of Catholic Emancipation, Protestant preachers were very vehement in their denunciations of the Pope and the Catholic religion. Father Young, because of his intense zeal for the Faith, was particularly obnoxious to those ranters, and, on one occasion, was savagely attacked on the banks of the canal and would have lost his life were it not for the timely arrival of some boatmen.

A proselytising school at Milltown gave him much trouble, but he was determined that none of his flock should be caught. One day he appeared at the door of this school-room, and, seeing some of his flock there, he commanded them to leave. The master and his two sons, who carried on the school, flung him down the stairs, and afterwards brought an action for assault against him. He had no witnesses except the children, and it was not likely that a Court of Law at that time would give a favourable verdict to a priest. Fortunately, a friendly

---

[1] In recent years a nave was added to it by the late Canon Daniel Ryan, P.P., Cullenswood. It is one of the few pre-Emancipation chapels still existing.

solicitor took up his case and placed it in the hands of Daniel
O'Connell, who had the real attackers scouted out of court.

At Harold's Cross a school kept by one Darby Connor
must also have given him many anxious hours. Were it not
for a circular sent out by the St. Bonaventura Orphan Society
of Adam and Eve chapel we should not have known of the
existence of this school. The foundation of this society was
the occasion of the publication of one of the numerous
Protestant pamphlets of the period which tried by ridicule
to undermine Catholic Action and Catholic Emancipation.
It is entitled : "Plain Speaking or Broad Truths for
Poor Paddy. In a letter from Darby Connor, the School-
master, to his Roman Catholic neighbours in Harold's
Cross." (Goodwin, Printer, 40 New-street).[1] Darby Connor
was probably a Catholic orphan and was taken over
by a Protestant Society. To his school in Harold's Cross a
pupil one morning brought a ticket that had been handed
into the boy's house. Darby gives a fac-simile copy of it in
his pamphlet which is worth recording :

"Saint Bonaventura Charitable Institution.
　　Founded, Nov. 14, 1820, and held in Adam and Eve
　　　　Chapel.
　　"As a member of this infant establishment you are
earnestly solicited to pay your subscription regularly to the
weekly collector in order to carry into effect the laudable
intention of the Founders, whose direct object is to rescue
Catholic children from those schools which we consider
dangerous both to their Faith and Morals.

REV. J. B. KEANE, President.

MR. O'REILLY, Vice-President."

Then Darby pours forth a scurrilous attack of eight pages
on Catholic Action. Portion of it is interesting as showing
the activities that excited his venom : "Poor unfortunate and
simple-minded Catholics ! How many tricks are practised
on your purse, and your patience in the shape of Mary
Magdalene Societies, Purgatorian Societies, Franciscan Institu-

[1] T.C.D., Gall. H. 6.48. No. 32.

tions, Bonaventura Institutions, Patrician Societies, Christian Doctrine Societies, all of which may be reduced into one and the same thing, namely, expedients for collecting money for the clergy. Some people have asked why these Catholic Societies never publish their cash accounts in the way that Protestant Societies usually do, so that everyone may see what is done with the money."

It is only necessary to repeat that those Catholic Charities were, in almost every case, founded by laymen, and were controlled, financially and otherwise, by them, and that their books were scrupulously kept and audited. The priest was the spiritual director and had nothing to do with finance or the general working of the societies. Darby, in saying that the schools the Bonaventure Society was out against were the Protestant Sunday Schools was guilty of a manifest desire to deceive. In the ticket, that he quotes, it is definitely stated that the Bonaventure Society was an " infant establishment " ; infants do not go to Sunday Schools. Protestants did not care how ridiculous they made themselves provided they poured ridicule on Catholics which would deter decent-minded Protestants from supporting the Catholic claim to equality in religious and social matters. This pamphlet of 1823 came at a time when the Catholic claim was being voiced by the Catholic Association, and when the ultra-Protestant party was leaving nothing undone to undermine Catholic influence.

Another case in which a Catholic school met with opposition from the Protestant church supporters in the matter of providing education for the poor was that of the Loreto Sisters of Rathfarnham. Six months after Mother Ball and her companions had taken up their permanent residence there (5th November, 1822), they decided, according to their Rule, to open a school for the poor (6th May, 1823). This was to be run on the up-to-date Lancastrian system, namely, by means of charts and blackboards. Ninety pupils, a large number indeed, attended on the opening day, and soon the attendance reached two hundred daily. In addition, a Sunday school was opened for the instruction of a large number of mill workers. On week-days the girls had special courses in knitting, needlework, and the manufacture of straw bonnets (quite the fashion for girls of the period). A midday substantial meal was provided for as many as seventy-two of the more destitute children, who were about one-third of the school-going children. All this was a noble effort on the part of Mother Ball, after six months' residence, considering the expense of fitting up the Mother-house, and that little revenue had been received from the boarding-school upon which all her hopes were centred. Yet the Loreto Sisters would have continued their poor-school were it not that more ample funds were forthcoming from Protestant sources to entice the Catholic children by important bribes from the Loreto school. To counteract the influence of the Loreto Sisters among the Catholic children of this definitely Catholic district, the wealthy members of the Established Church, with the immense power of the Establishment in patronage and influence, decided to open a Protestant school at Whitechurch. The winter was approaching, and the tempting offers of blankets and warm clothing, as well as the promises of good employment in Protestant houses, were held out, especially to the girls. The result was that the nuns were unable to compete against this sinister attraction. The Protestant school won, and the attendance at the Nuns' school fell away for a time, but, only for a time, for, as soon as the Boarding-school became a success, the Protestant school at Whitechurch ceased to attract Catholics to its walls. At this time, 1823, the struggle for existence was hard in city and vicinity.

7. FATHER YOUNG AND PRINCE HOHENLOHE.

Archbishop Murray, in a Pastoral Letter " To the Catholic Clergy and Laity of the Diocese of Dublin," 15th August, 1823, stated that it was his " delightful duty " to " proclaim to you a new and wonderful manifestation of the goodness of God," and he continued : " The account of this wonderful cure reached us officially on the 2nd inst. in a letter from Mrs. Mary Catherine Meade, Prioress of St. Joseph's Convent [Carmelite, Ranelagh], under date of the preceding evening.

This communication stated in substance that one of the religious Sisters of that community, by name Mary Stuart, had been afflicted with sickness for four years and about seven months ; that, during such period, she had frequent attacks of paralysis, each of which seemed to threaten her with immediate dissolution ; that the most powerful remedies had been applied without producing any other than partial and temporary relief ; that for several months past she had been confined to bed, wholly deprived of the power of assisting herself or of moving out of the position in which she was laid ; that, when moved by her attendants, how gentle soever, she not only suffered much pain but was also liable to considerable danger and to the temporary loss of speech, and that for the last five weeks she had entirely lost the power of articulation ; that up to the morning of the 1st instant she continued in this deplorable state, without any symptom of amendment, and apparently beyond the reach of human aid ; that, on a certain hour that morning, as had been settled by previous arrangement, she united her devotions (as did also her numerous friends) with the Holy Sacrifice of the Mass, which was to be offered by Alexander, Prince of Hohenlohe, in the hope of obtaining immediately from God that relief which no human means could afford ; that, with this view, she received, though with much difficulty, the Divine Communion at the Mass, which was celebrated at the same hour in her chamber for her recovery ; that, Mass being ended, and no cure as yet effected, she was in the act of resigning herself, with perfect submission, to the will of God, when instantly she felt a power of movement and a capability of speech ; that she exclaimed with an animated voice : ' Holy, Holy, Holy, Lord God of Hosts ! '—raised herself without assistance to offer, on bended knees, the tribute of her gratitude to heaven ; called for her attire, left that bed to which she had been for so many months, as it were, fastened, walked to the Convent Chapel with a firm step, and there, in the presence of the Community and Congregation, joined her religious Sisters in the solemn thanksgiving which was offered up to God for this wonderful interposition of his goodness.

" As soon as this statement reached us, we felt it a sacred duty to examine the grounds on which it was made, that, if it originated in mistake, we might endeavour to dispel the delusion, but if, founded on fact, we might proclaim the glory of God. We hastened, therefore, to the spot, to investigate the circumstances of this astonishing cure. We found the late invalid seated in the parlour, surrounded by her friends ; she rose, she knelt, she resumed her seat, she detailed the history of her sufferings and her cure, as they have been just related, and as they will be found in her sworn attestation which we subjoin. Her companions and attendants who had assisted her in her infirmity, and watched so long over her bed of languishing, confirmed this account in all its details, with a degree of candour and simplicity which could not fail, even then, to produce on our mind the clearest conviction, that the restoration of the said Mary Stuart to the state of health in which we saw her, was beyond the reach of human power."

Archbishop Murray returned to the convent after several days to subject, as he says, " all the circumstances of this extraordinary case to a new and rigid inquiry," and, he adds, " we called in to our aid the wisdom and intelligence of our Reverend Brethren, the Roman Catholic Clergy of this city, and we have the consolation of knowing that our judgment is supported by their unanimous opinion when we declare, as we do hereby declare, on what appears to us the most unquestionable evidence—that the cure which was effected in the person of the said Mary Stuart, on the 1st of August, instant, is the effect of a supernatural agency, an effect which we cannot contemplate without feeling in our inmost soul an irresistible conviction ' that this is the finger of God.' " [1]

So far we have the authoritative declaration of the Archbishop of Dublin, 1823, but Lady Georgiana Fullerton (*Life of Father Henry Young*) gives us important information as to the prayers that were offered for the recovery of Sister Mary Frances. She states that " it was chiefly from Father Young

[1] *Notices of the Life and Character of His Grace, Most Rev. Daniel Murray*, Late Archbishop of Dublin, by Rev. William Meagher, P.P., Rathmines, 1853, pp. 144–48.

that the nuns heard of Prince Hohenlohe, and of his wonderful answers vouchsafed to his prayers." Father Young was then in charge of Harold's Cross and Milltown chapels, and of the district in which the Convent of Ranelagh lay. How he heard of the name and fame of Prince Hohenlohe we do not know; it may have been through some of his friends in Rome.

Alexander Leopold Hohenlohe-Waldenburg-Schillingefurst was born 17th August, 1794, at Kupflrzell in Wurtemberg, and was ordained priest 16th September, 1815. He did parochial work at Stuttgart and Munich, and went to Rome in October, 1816, to justify himself against accusations that he was using German in the administration of the Sacraments. He had no difficulty in putting his accusers to shame. He returned to Munich in 1817 and was made canon of Bamberg in 1821. About this time began the numerous cures that are said to have been effected through his prayers.

His belief in the efficacy of prayer for the cure of corporal ailments was greatly strengthened by the immediate cure in himself of a throat affection through the prayers of a devout peasant named Martin Michael. The news of this cure spread abroad, and, when the Princess Mattilda von Schwarzenberg, who had been a paralytic for eight years, heard of it she appealed to Hohenlohe and Martin Michael for their prayers. Her cure was effected.

Hohenlohe then appealed to Rome to be informed if he might be permitted to attempt similar public cures in future, but he was told that he might continue them in private. On account of this permission, Hohenlohe was inundated with requests from all parts of the world for his prayers and those of the peasant Martin Michael. His practice was to specify a certain day on which he and Martin Michael began their prayers for the particular request. So numerous were the letters for their prayers that Hohenlohe employed as his secretary and disciple, the Rev. Joseph Forster. It will be useful to state here that Hohenlohe became titular bishop of Sardica, in 1844, was the author of four volumes of sermons and ascetical treatises, and died, 14th November, 1849. His

friend and disciple, Father Joseph Forster, pastor of Hutten-
heim, died in 1875.[1]

To return to our story. In a letter of the year 1823, Father
Young wrote to the Rev. Mother of Ranelagh :[2]

"Dear Reverend Mother,—In answer to your kind note,
I give you the address of the Rev. Mr. Forster, as stated by
his Grace Dr. Murray. The address to his Serene Highness
I send you as it was sent to me in the last package I received :
à Son Altesse le Prince Alexandre de Hohenlohe, Chanoine
Titulaire de l'Eglise Cathédrale de Bamberg à Bamberg."

This letter was presumably written before 11th May as,
on that day, Dr. Murray succeeded Dr. Troy as Archbishop
of Dublin. Father Young does not call Dr. Murray Archbishop of Dublin but " his Grace," then Coadjutor. A few
months before that date, Father Young, as he stated in this
letter, had written a letter to his Serene Highness. How long
before that date he was in correspondence with Prince
Hohenlohe on spiritual matters we do not know.

In this same letter he asks the Rev. Mother who was
writing to the Prince to pray for Sister Mary Stuart :
" Recommend to him myself, my spiritual wants, and the
spiritual and temporal welfare of those committed to my
trust, and also the prosperity and good success of my last
charitable establishment for the glory of God and the salvation
of our neighbours. The whole weight of this triple charity,
as expressed in the circular letter enclosed, falls on my shoulders.
I have to provide for tender infant children rescued from
misery, and I must unwillingly refuse many suchlike applications for other distressed orphans. May the Lord God supply
in their behalf the deficiency of our weakness and misery,
and may He relieve the widow, the orphan and the poor."

Though it is a digression from our subject, we must take
note of this " triple charity." Apparently, Father Young
had set up a society in Harold's Cross for widows and orphans,
for which he was solely responsible, and had sent out " circular
letters " for funds. This is the only reference we have to this
society, and were it not for this letter on the subject of the

---

[1] *Catholic Encyclopaedia,* Hohenlohe.   [2] *Life,* pp. 77–78.

illness of Sister Mary Frances, we should have known nothing about it. Yet, in the busy industrial centre of Harold's Cross, his Widows' and Orphans' Society must have been a crying want, and, as he stated, he was unable to cope with "other distressed orphans."

Concluding this famous letter, Father Young says : " I hope your application will be favourable and wonderful towards the relief and health of your afflicted religious sister." The application for the prayers of the Prince Priest was indeed " favourable and wonderful," and the cure was complete and permanent.

Sister Mary Stuart lived for many years in good health, and was chosen to establish a new convent of the Order at Blanchardstown, and afterwards another at Fir House, Tallaght. On the 1st August, every year since this event, there is Benediction of the Most Holy Sacrament at St. Joseph's Convent, Ranelagh, in thanksgiving for the favour conferred on Sister Mary Stuart.

Before the news of the cure had reached the Prince Priest, he wrote a letter, by his secretary, the Rev. J. Forster, dated 10th August, at Bamberg, to Father Esmonde, Rector of the Jesuit College of Tullabeg.[1] This letter seems to have been enclosed in a letter to Father Young, who forwarded it to Father Esmonde on the 18th November. The Prince, through his secretary, wrote :

" On the 1st of October at 9 o'cl. I shall offer my prayers for your cure, according to your request. Unite your prayers, at the same hour, after having confessed and Communicated, with the evangelical fervour and whole-hearted and persevering confidence that we must show in our Redeemer, Jesus Christ. Enkindle in the depths of your heart the divine virtues of a true repentance, Christian Charity, infinite faith for a favourable hearing, and an unshakeable resolution to lead an exemplary life, so as to keep you in the state of grace.

" Some devotion of a day in honour of the Holy Name or the Holy Cross of Jesus.

[1] Archives, Tullabeg College.

"M. Michael will join his prayers also.

In the name of the Prince,

J. FORSTER, Curé.

To Dom Esmonde,

(for the whole college and students, 4 October).

Repeat, on the 9th October, at 9 o'cl."

Apparently, Father Young, in his correspondence with Father Esmonde, in connection with his edition of the *Catholic Directory*, had mentioned the desirability of having the Prince Priest pray for " his cure." Father Young, in his letter to the Rector (18th November), gives details of general interest :

"I have the pleasure to inform you that our holy very Rev. Prince de Hohenlohe has promised to offer up his prayers and sacrifices, united with Mr. Martin Michael, on the 1st day of Decr., Jany., and Feby., for all petitioners in general, conformable to my request made him when I informed him of the great good done in Ireland preparing for the First of August and Sept.

"He moreover promised in a letter to Dr. Murray to pray for all the inhabitants of Ireland, England, and Scotland on the 15 of each month. The following are the words of the Rev. Mr. Forster. 'Son Altesse et M. Michel sont invités par moi 'unir ses prieres en faveur de tous les inhabitants en Irlande, Angleterre, et Ecosse le 15 de chaque mois a 9 heures '—9 o'clock is the hour of sacrifice and prayer also on the 1st Decr., Jany., and Feby. You will please to announce the above.

Your truly devoted,

H. YOUNG."

It will be useful to tabulate the points of Father Young's letter. He had been for some time corresponding with the Prince Priest. He had announced to the people of Ireland, probably in his *Catholic Directory* of 1822 or 1823,[1] that the Prince would pray for them at his Mass on the 1st August

---

[1] Unfortunately the only copy extant, so far as we know, of the *Directory* is of the year 1821.

and 1st September. Apparently, the people had joined in this Crusade of Prayer for Ireland, and " great good was done."

Archbishop Murray, apparently informed by Father Young about the holiness of the Prince, also wrote to him, " for all the inhabitants of Ireland, England and Scotland." It is interesting to note how he, like Archbishop Troy, grouped the " Three Kingdoms " together.

Finally, Father Young asked the Rector of Tullabeg to announce to the Fathers and Students the Prince's promises to pray for all.

Father Young was on intimate terms, and in constant correspondence with Prince Hohenlohe for years after the cure of 1823. In 1829, he informed the Christian Doctrine Confraternity of SS. Michael and John's that he had three original pictures, presented to him by Prince Hohenlohe, of the Redeemer, the Blessed Virgin and St. Mary Magdalen, and he wished that copies of these subjects, of which he had the plates, should be distributed as premiums to the children attending the Christian Doctrine classes in SS. Michael and John's. The Confraternity gladly accepted his offer of purchase and reproduced them for teachers and children by the thousand. Father Young was not to profit by the purchase : he had given the pictures and plates to a Mrs. Collier, Harold's Cross, who was apparently in need at the time, and she left the price to the Confraternity. It is another instance of how Father Young exercised his charity ; he bestowed the pictures unobtrusively, and he negotiated the sale for the benefit of the widow, and probably of orphans also.

From all this it is clear that his ten years as curate of Harold's Cross were years of intense application not only for the people of the district in his remedies for their reform, but in the apostolate of the pen, and in the spiritual reformation of the people of Ireland through the prayers of Prince Hohenlohe. Such a combination of spiritual interest was unique in the early nineteenth century in Dublin. Yet this unobtrusive, energetic, spiritual curate of an outlying district of a city parish was able to carry it out, in his own quiet way. Were it not for the Tullabeg archives we should have known nothing about his efforts for national regeneration.

8. DEATH OF FATHER YOUNG'S PARENTS.

" Stern as he sometimes appeared," says his biographer,[1] " there could not be a more affectionate heart than Father Henry's. His apparent coldness towards his relatives was the result of a spirit of penance which pervaded his whole life. What he denied to them and to himself of pleasant intercourse, familiar exchange of thoughts, and expressions of mutual affection, was supplied by an intense solicitude for their spiritual welfare, an ardent desire that in the next world, not one of them should miss the blessedness which alone seemed to him worth a care or thought. He seldom conversed with them ; but in his secret hours of converse with God they were never forgotten."

It excited some surprise that when his mother was on her death-bed, in 1824, he was seldom seen by her side. " Those hours," says his biographer, " which an ordinary filial affection would have led a son to spend gazing on the beloved face which he was so soon to behold no more, Henry Young employed in going from one poor home to another, where, for her sake, or for his own, grateful hearts and pious lips would breathe forth prayers at his request, collecting those spiritual alms, those suffrages which smooth the last passage of a soul through the gates of death, and ascend with it to the God of the poor ; from one church to another, where communicants were kneeling ; wherever help was to be sued for and obtained, for the loved and parting spirit, even then nearing eternity."

This was Father Young's way of filial affection. A year afterwards his father died. Two letters written by him about this event are happily preserved.[2]

They were addressed to his sisters, Ursulines in Cork.

" J.M.J.

12th January, 1825.

" Dear Sisters,—Among the many letters you will receive announcing the precious death of our dear father, I hope my few words will not be superfluous. I had written to

---

[1] *Life*, p. 79.   [2] *Life*, 80–84.

you yesterday of the immediate expectation of his death,
so your tender hearts are already prepared to receive the
melancholy but happy tidings of his holy edifying death.
He was during his whole illness perfectly composed and
resigned, and seemed without pain, though tortured most
acutely by the blisters applied to him. Whenever we asked
him " was he in pain," he always answered, " no." In
this composed state he passed the night. He attended to
our prayers and ejaculations around his bed, and moved
his lips in silence whilst his blessed soul was absorbed in
God. This morning I announced to St. Clare's Religious
the immediate expectation of his death, and said Mass for
him. They were each morning very solicitous, especially
our good Sister Catherine. I gave him, on my return from
Harold's Cross, the Absolution and Plenary Indulgence
in articulo mortis, and read the prayers for the departing soul.
We suggested to him frequently the sacred name of *Jesus*,
which was his last word ; and while in prayer, this holy
servant of God expired in most perfect tranquility at two
o'clock in the day, January 12, 1825, twelve hours before
the anniversary of our dear mother. Instead of grief and
tears we should rather rejoice at the consideration of such
a holy, edifying death. 'Precious in the sight of the
Lord is the death of His saints.' As for my part, dear
sisters, I am so overjoyed that I cannot express the exultation
of my heart. I am rejoiced at the good tidings that are
said to us, ' we are to enter into the house of the Lord, we
are to possess the blissful mansions of eternal glory, the
true land of the living, where we shall be inebriated with
the plentitude of God's house, and where we shall drink
with delight at the torrent of pleasure ; where we shall
see God face to face, and in this beatific vision be transformed into the Divinity, according to the word of the
prophet. *I say ye are Gods and sons of the Most High.* Should
we not therefore rejoice at this glorious departure of our
dear parent into immortal bliss, and should we not strain
every effort to arrive thither ourselves to meet the embraces
of our blessed parents in the land of the living, where we
shall be never more separated. We are now, dear sisters,

truly orphans, but Christ has promised not to leave us long orphans, for He will send down His Divine Spirit, the Paraclete, to be our comforter and He will come Himself in person to be our father and mother, and to be our best of parents. He will visit us Himself daily in the Eucharistic food, and by His Divine graces and blessing He will protect us under the shelter of His wings all the days of our lives, till that happy day arrives when He will call us with those sweet words of the spouse : *Come, My beloved, come from Mount Lebanon, come to be crowned with wreaths of immortal glory.* Amen.

Your loving brother,

HENRY YOUNG."

In this beautiful letter written by Father Young when the mortal remains of his father were scarcely yet cold, we see not only the tender brother and devoted son but the confirmed mystic viewing all earthly ties and affections in the light of the Eternal Truths.

His next precious letter was written to his Ursuline sisters on his return from the graveyard :

" J.M.J.

14th January, 1825.

" Dear Sisters,—Just arrived from the internment of our dear father, I take the pen to give you the concluding particulars. His children were dining together at Sylvester's on the day of his death. Notices were sent to almost every chapel to offer the Masses of the week for his happy repose. The corpse was laid out at midnight, when William and I and Mr. O'Mealy recited the Office for the Dead. The following day and night, Offices, Rosaries, and Prayers were continually recited in his bed-chamber, so that we have endeavoured to fulfil every filial duty. This morning we have celebrated three Masses for our deceased father previous to the funeral. Eleven carriages followed the hearse, filled with friends and relations whom I am unacquainted with. I did not say a word to any one. We five brothers were mourners in one carriage, and from the carriage went to our mother's remains where we recited the Rosary of Jesus while the procession went around the churchyard. The Rev. Mr. Russell officiated. We then recited alone the Rosary of the Seven Dolours of the Blessed Virgin Mary, and like Magdalen, were the last to quit the sepulchre. As we were fully convinced that our father's blessed soul arrived at its centre, God, as soon as his corpse reached its centre, the earth, we recited the Glorious Mysteries of the Rosary of Jesus and Mary on our return from Mulhuddart to Gardiner-street, where we just now took a cup of tea.

I hope, my dear sisters, you have received all the letters I have written from time to time since Mary's charge to me, and that you are satisfied with my details of the edifying death of our dear parent. Having fulfilled this pleasing duty, I do not believe I shall have occasion to write to you any more. I therefore conclude with wishing you every joy and happiness, which I truly experience instead of sorrow and sadness.—I am, dear sisters, your loving brother,

HENRY YOUNG."

It is interesting to note that Father Young did not know his relatives who attended the funeral and did not even exchange a word with them. Earthly ties meant little to him, and he was assisting at the passing to the Throne of God of a servant of God. It is also interesting to note that he intended to write no more letters to his sisters in Cork. Now that their parents were gone to their eternal reward he was free from family ties and was concerned only with his missionary work. It is an extraordinary fact that the names of his parents do not appear on either of the Lynch and Young tombstones. Apparently such outward show did not appeal to him. Their souls were with God, and that was all that mattered.

The Mulhuddart graveyard was popular not only among the people of North Co. Dublin but amongst the citizens of Dublin, and many imposing tombstones still testify to their importance. The Dominican nuns of Channel-row, who had buried their dead in St. James's graveyard, Dublin, between 1717 and 1777, secured a community burial-ground in Mulhuddart, and the Augustinians of John's-lane had a plot with tombstone near the Young tomb.

It must have been shortly after 1786 that the Lynch and Young firm acquired the burial plots in Mulhuddart—it was the period of Catholic Relief when Dublin Catholics were no longer content to abide by the restrictions still in force as to Catholic burials. That those restrictions did not exist in Mulhuddart cemetery is abundantly clear from the religious service performed by the Fathers Young over the grave of their parents. It was this freedom to perform the Catholic burial service that made Mulhuddart a popular graveyard for the citizens of Dublin. In this respect Mulhuddart was exceptional.

When the Catholic churches and cemeteries were confiscated during the so-called Reformation they were closed in general to Catholic worship and burial. By the early eighteenth century the Protestant rectors allowed Catholics to be buried in the ancient graveyards on payment of a fee and on condition that no Catholic service should be held. It happened, however, that there were no Protestants in Mulhuddart, and both church and cemetery were in ruins in 1630,[1] and the Protestant rector made no claim to the property. The Catholics fastened on to them, and held the annual pattern at the ancient holy well adjacent, on the 8th September, with a great concourse of people and with abundance of tents for the refreshment of the people.[2] That was how Isaac Butler described it about 1740; apparently the festival was held with due decorum. Before 1781 a " Dublin convent " covered the Holy Well with a building that still exists—this convent was apparently that of the Dominican Sisters of Channel-row. Thus, Catholics had perfect freedom for their devotions and burials in Mulhuddart.

The old restrictions against the Catholic burial service in

[1] For a short history of Mulhuddart see Ronan, *Journ. Roy. Soc. Antiq.*, Dec. 1940, pp. 182–193.
[2] *Journ. Roy. Soc. Antiq.*, 1893, p. 13.

the city graveyards continued, however, well into the nine-teenth century. The burial of a Mr. D'Arcy, an esteemed Dublin Catholic, in the ancient graveyard of St. Kevin's, Camden-row, where Archbishop Dermot O'Hurley and Father Betagh, S.J., were buried, brought the question to a crisis, in 1823. A priest attended to read the Catholic burial service over D'Arcy but was prevented by the sexton who asserted that he was acting according to the instructions of Dr. Magee, Protestant Archbishop of Dublin.[1]

Dr. Blake, P.P. of SS. Michael and John's, in a public letter, charged Dr. Magee as being responsible for this bigoted proceeding. A reply was soon forthcoming.[2] It is entitled : *Remarks on the present conduct of several of the Roman Clergy in Ireland : being a reply to the late seditious letter of Rev. M. Blake P.P. by a Friend to Liberty.* (Dublin : for Ann Watson, Capel-street. 1823.) In this pamphlet the " Friend to Liberty " tries to institute a comparison between the condi-tions of Catholics in Ireland with those of Protestants in the Catholic countries on the continent, deliberately ignoring the fact that it was the minority in Ireland who were imposing their will on the majority. In order to relieve Dr. Magee of any responsibility for the prohibition of the priest's presence in St. Kevin's graveyard he simply stated : " Regulation pertained to the general duties of every church minister and church officer."[3] That was the fact, but it did not absolve Dr. Magee as an accessory to the fact or, according to the sexton, as a continuator of a custom of the penal code which decent-minded people of the period should have regarded as obsolete. The Catholic Church was doing its best to foster loyalty to the Government but the Protestant Church was still showing intolerance.

The writer stated that O'Connell had advised the people to conduct their burial service and pay no attention to any order to the contrary. Apparently, the people followed his instruction. The writer mentioned a case that occurred at

---

[1] *Life of Edmund Rice,* p. 298.

[2] The number of pamphlets, about this year, 1823, printed by Protestants, against the pretensions of Catholics is truly phenomenal. As many were anonymous, one must assume that they were inspired from higher quarters.

[3] *Pamphlets,* Gall. H. 6 48, no. 26, T.C.D.

Castledermot when the priest, with surplice and holy water, conducted a burial service in the old graveyard. The regulations for Catholic burials in and around Dublin were so strictly carried out afterwards that the indignation of Catholics and liberal minded Protestants was roused. Mainly through the exertions of O'Connell and the Catholic Association, the ground now known as " Golden Bridge Catholic Cemetary " was purchased in 1828, and was opened the next year for all religious denominations who might bury their dead with their own funeral rites without interference.

The demands for plots became so numerous that another site had to be acquired. Nine acres were purchased, at the junction of the roads leading to Glasnevin and Finglas. Two toll-gates barred the way to these roads. To avoid payment of the tax upon carriages, it was decided, on the advice of O'Connell, to cut a new avenue into the plot between the two roads. Prospect Avenue, or Cemetery Road, was the result of this bold stroke, and, through it, all funerals went until the present Finglas Road was constructed. The cemetery was consecrated in 1832. Similar Catholic cemeteries were opened throughout the country.

9. Father Young's Brothers and Sisters.

It will be useful to review here, briefly, the position of the members of the Young family at this time.

Mary, the eldest child, had been sent as a boarder, while still very young, probably about her fourteenth year (1797), to the Ursuline Convent, Douglas-street, Cork, where she showed an inclination to gaiety and pleasure. After some years she returned home, and remained there for a few years. She told her father she wished to become an Ursuline nun, but, as her health was delicate, he thought it a whim. She had her way, and returned to the Ursuline Convent, 27th July, 1803, four days after the Emmet Rising. The nuns were shocked at her delicate appearance, and did not believe that such a frail creature could carry out the arduous work of an Ursuline. Again, she had her way, and, in spite of ill-health, received the habit, 26th October, 1803, and was professed, 7th November, 1805.

She then began her long vocation of educator. She " had the charge of teaching writing to the different classes of a crowded school for fourteen years and took care of their shoes for nearly so long a period." She was an excellent organist and was mistress of the choir, copying the music books with her own hand. She also learnt and taught fancy-work and painting. She translated and got printed the Ursuline *Constitutions* and *Novices' Directory*. In 1824 she negotiated the printing of the Ursuline *Manual*, compiled by Mother Mary Borgia McCarthy.

Like her brothers, Fathers Henry, William and James, she could translate, compile and write original work. Like her brother William, she had a flair for history, and produced three books on Irish and English history which were considered at the time not only original in design, but corrective of previous histories. The most famous of these books was *A Catechism of Irish History* (47 pages), printed in Cork in 1815. Along with Cobett's *Reformation* it was in use in the first school of the Christian Brothers in Dublin, in Hanover-street, off City-quay, and occasioned the Commissioners of Education an immense amount of anxiety.

The Ursuline *Annals* (unpublished) tell of the State opposition to this epoch-making book because it fearlessly told the truth about Irish History. They state that " an Abridgement of Irish History was drawn up in the form of an historical Catechism, by one of the young people of the monastery, to give our children the rare acquirement of some knowledge of the history of their own Emerald Isle. But the little cup of bitter truth was so revolting to the taste of the times that it was dashed from the lips of the generality, though it was eagerly swallowed by the few friends of sincerity and of Ireland. In a word, it was mentioned in Parliament in such hostile terms that the Superiors of this monastery judged it more prudent rather to yield to the temper of the times than to attract the notice and ill-will of those who were, from ignorance at least, too well disposed to misinterpret the proceedings of Convents. Accordingly the little Catechism was suppressed in our schools by the Superiors of the monastery ; and in a short time it was out of print, so rapidly had the first edition been bought up."[1]

This *Catechism* is obviously the " Sketch of Irish History compiled by way of question and answer for the use of schools"[2] which was denounced by William Magee, Protestant Dean of Cork (1813–1819) and afterwards Archbishop of Dublin, as " a monstrous book " and " injurious to the young mind." A periodical called *The Protestant* (1822) calls it " a work pregnant with treason and falsehood and inculcating the most inveterate hatred to the British Government." The Commissioners of Education (30th May, 1825) reported in similar terms : " It appears to be a work of the most objectionable nature, and calculated to keep alive every feeling of religious hostility to Protestants, and political hatred to England." Accordingly, as we have seen, it was mentioned in the British Parliament in " hostile terms," and its use in the Christian Brothers' Schools was regarded by the Commissioners of Education as undesirable. A modern authority on educational matters, however, says of it : " It was quite apart from the ordinary colourless historical primer which will be found in use even now. Throughout the text the attention of the teacher and scholar is focussed on ideas and policies. . . . Perhaps no such writer of English, firm in texture and direct in expression, ever composed a primer of history for poor schools, before or since 1815."[3]

This is high praise from the learned Jesuit professor of Education in University College, Dublin. The *Sketch* was a pioneer work in expounding national history for our schools, but the truth was bitter to the Protestants of the day.

Sister Ursula's next book was *A History of the United Kingdom of Great Britain and Ireland from the Earliest Ages to the Treaty of Amiens in* 1802. " Compiled from various Authors and intended chiefly for the Young Ladies education at the Ursuline Convents." It was in two volumes, comprising about 700 pages. The dedication to the Bishops of Cork and

---

[1] O'Rahilly, Alfred, *An Ursuline Writer in Irish History*. (Cork Hist. & Arch. Soc., XLVII, no. 166, July–Dec., 1942), pp. 77–86.
[2] Halliday Collection, R.I.A., Vol. 1075.
[3] Corcoran, *State Policy in Irish Education*, 212–222.

Cloyne was signed M.U.Y. (Mary Ursula Young). In it she states that she wrote the book to give the young ladies of whom she had charge in the historical department " a thorough knowledge of our national history and that of the country with which it is intimately connected." She found the books she consulted so full of " religious or national prejudices " that to correct them for her pupils was out of the question, and that a new compilation was necessary " wherein truth and simplicity have been my only guides," and which she undertook " in obedience to the commands of my superiors."

A third publication, of the same year (1815), was *Questions on the History of the United Kingdoms of Great Britain and Ireland*. It was also chiefly intended for the young ladies of the Ursuline Convents, and was written by " a member of the Ursuline Community in Cork." It had the approbation of the Diocesan authorities, and a copy was presented by the community to Pope Pius VII ; the book was afterwards translated into Italian in Rome.

Sister Ursula's teaching methods were so successful in the poor schools and the young ladies' schools of the Ursuline Sisters in Cork that she was sent to Ursuline Convent, Thurles, at the request of the Archbishop, 1818, to introduce her educational improvements there. She remained at the work for two years, and returned to Cork where she received the additional task of Mistress of Novices (1823).

The Ursuline Archives state that " it was a mystery of the Community how this delicate sister could accomplish so much ; all her strength was in her mind and will. . . . Her health broke down under the constant strain—knowing her frail constitution, she wished to accomplish much in the shortest time. She died a saintly sister, beloved by all who knew her, 25th July, 1830, at the age of 47 years." She wrote on her obituary card : " I promise to remember specially before the Throne of God all those who will pray for me."

Her publications created a great stir at the time. Nothing like them had been introduced into poor or boarding schools. In them she was practical like her brother, Father Henry, and, like her brother, Father William, showed an intense admiration for the glories of ancient Ireland. Her Irish history was written from the Catholic view-point but it conformed to the prevalent political ideas of the time. Her success as an author, and her ideas, must have had.considerable influence on Fathers Henry and William. In 1815, the year of her publications, Father Henry returned from Rome, but, in a few years, he took up his pen, in the cause of Catholic Action.

It is interesting to observe that, although she wished her books to be correctives to the bigoted histories (full of " religious or national prejudices ") which were accepted even in the Catholic schools of the time, she had no hesitation in using the title " History of the United Kingdoms of Great Britain and Ireland " ; and, though she wished to impart " a thorough knowledge of our national history " she wished to do the same for the history of Great Britain for the reason that Ireland was " intimately connected " with that country. All this is further proof, if proof were needed, that the Young household was brought up on strictly constitutional lines and that its members adhered to that policy in their writings and public activities.

Mary Ursula's sister Johanna, was also a nun in the Ursuline convent of Cork. She was born about 1792 (nine years younger than Mary) and had been a boarder, like Mary, at the convent. She (as Mary Louisa) entered the convent as a Sister in 1816 (thirteen years after Mary), two years after Father Henry returned from Rome, and died in 1858, at the age of 66 years.

Their father died possessed of considerable property. The business house he left to Sylvester, and to his sons in the priesthood he bequeathed large sums. He did not forget the convents in which his daughters were professed. The Ursuline *Annals* of Cork relate that " Mr. Young, father to our two dear sisters, left £200 which is deposited in the French Funds, for the purpose of contributing by the interest to clothe the poor children instructed here." The gift is indicative of the charitable disposition of the great father of the saintly family. The *Annals* of the Poor Clares, Harold's Cross, always bear witness to it and record that he and Charles Lynch, the brother of his partner, were among the chief benefactors to the Orphanage at Harold's Cross in 1805.

Mary Teresa Mullaly, of George's Hill was also a contributor.[1]

The third surviving sister, Catherine (*b.* 1789), entered the Poor Clares Convent, Harold's Cross, 30th April, 1811, took the habit, 19th November, 1811, was professed, 16th November, 1813, by Dr. Murray, and died 15th March, 1858. She was Mother Abbess for twelve years before she died.

As to the boys of the family, the career of Henry is well marked, but that of William and James is not so easy to follow. In the Records of Maynooth College William is entered, 1st October, 1817, as assigned to the Humanity Class. He was then aged 21. It may be that he had spent some years at his father's business, and was influenced by his brother Father Henry, then a few years on the Dublin mission, to study for the priesthood. He was ordained in Maynooth on the Saturday within the Octave of Pentecost, 1822, having received Minor and Major Orders within the week. James (*b.* 1797) entered Maynooth College, 25th August, 1815, and was assigned to the logic class, but there is no further reference to him in the College Records. We have no information as to where he was ordained and where he spent the first years of his priesthood. It is probable that he joined some Religious Order of which he was still a member at his father's death in 1825, but which he left between that year and 1831. When William became parish priest of Baldoyle, 1831, James was appointed C.C. of Howth (in the same parish).

Sylvester was in charge of the business, and Charles was, apparently, an assistant. Charles, the youngest child (*b.* 1798) was in London in 1815, when his brother Henry wrote to him from his lodgings in St. Michan's, where he was curate. He was then on his way to Oscott College, where he spent several years, and then wandered for some years throughout Spain where he became proficient in Spanish language and literature, and an ardent lover of both. Here he acquired his great charm of manner and attractive voice and expression. All these made him an outstanding personality in after years. Meanwhile, he was, apparently, undecided as to whether he should become a Jesuit or return to help his brother Sylvester

[1] Concannon, *Poor Clares in Ireland*, 123-27

in the business, as his father was now growing old. His father seems to have retired from the business in 1823, as, in the *Directory* of 1824, Sylvester Young is entered as the proprietor of the Woollen Warehouse, 31 New-row, with his residence as 5 Lower Gardiner-street. Why Sylvester retired to Lower Gardiner-street during the life-time of his father we do not know.

Such were the surviving members of this outstanding Dublin merchant family—unique in the records of old Dublin. All were wonderful workers, each in his own sphere, in the social and religious life, yet the most remarkable member of the family was Henry. It is clear that all regarded him as such from his earliest years, and particularly when he returned to the Dublin mission from Rome.

IV

FATHER YOUNG AND PAROCHIAL ORGANISATIONS

1. St. Michan's Parish

(a) Christian Doctrine Confraternity

It is difficult to estimate exactly Father Young's part in the work of parochial organisations. As he had been attached at one time or another to six parishes, and as from his first appointment he set out to be an apostle of the people, it must be taken that his work for the organisations was a whole-time occupation. He has told us himself that he had no time for anything else except his priestly work. Fortunately, we have a few precious documents that throw the necessary light on his work in some parishes. As he began his career in St. Michan's it will be useful to begin our review with the organisations in that parish.

The earliest Confraternity register in St. Michan's Archives is entitled " Confraternity of the Blessed Sacrament and Christian Doctrine Established in Mary's Lane, Nov. 1798." For the years 1799 and 1800 the teachers were all women. In 1799 the names of 70 are given ; in 1800 only 26 are given ; in 1801, 21 are entered ; the number remains around 21 in after years. The usual monthly subscription of a member was 6½d. which was paid by most members. The names of male members of the confraternity do not appear until January, 1801, when there were 19. The Rev. N. Wade and the Rev. Michl. Blake head the list.

Father Wade, P.P., and his energetic curate, Father Michael Blake, took over, in 1801, the Christian Doctrine teaching in the parish, and put it on organised lines, with separate branches for boys and girls. The male branch drew up elaborate Rules for members and pupils, which shows what a serious view it took of its duties, and what an important part the teaching of Christian Doctrine in the churches on Sundays played in Catholic life in those days.

Pasted on the inside of the cover of the Register is a printed text (11 in. x 7 in.), with elaborate border, of " St. Michan's Christian Doctrine Rules," of " Nth. Anne-street chapel and under the patronage of St. Michan." (Warren, Printer, High-street) There are at least nineteen rules (the document is torn) most of which deal with the duties of the teachers and the obligations of the children—most detailed, showing how seriously the members took . their religious task of instructing the young. Some of them are worthy of special note.

" 11. That the children be divided into different classes according to the following order : 1st. Class, Prayers, including the Acts of Faith, Hope and Charity. 2nd Class—Small Catechism. 3rd. Class—Abridgment of the General Catechism. 4th Class—General Catechism. 5th Class—Fleury's Historical Catechism. But to this last class no one is to be admitted but such as shall be declared fit by some priest of the Chapel."

" 15. That the Members do recite each day some one of the following devotions, viz :—The Office of the Blessed Sacrament, or the Pange Lingua . . ." (document torn).

There is a reference to a Brief of the Holy See as to the Indulgences granted to members of the Christian Doctrine Confraternity, and the prescribed conditions, one of which seems to have been Holy Communion on the third Sunday of each calendar month.

The last Rule seems to deal with Masses for deceased Members within one calendar month from the day of death.

The success of the well organised Christian Doctrine Confraternity in such troubled times drew from Archbishop Troy a well-merited recognition of important Catholic Action, the education of the young in Catholic doctrine and practices. The poor schools of the time were not qualified or had not the time to impart the special instruction. It was reserved for the educated parishioners to give Sunday after Sunday to a systematic instruction of the children of the district. The children responded nobly, no doubt ordered by their conscientious parents, and the little chapel of St. Michan's in

Bull-lane was thronged with several hundred children. The following document records Dr. Troy's appreciation : [1]

" His Grace, Most Reverend Doctor Troy, wishing always to promote the glory of God, and to furnish his beloved flock with means of Salvation was pleased, some years ago, to give leave to Mary's Lane Parish to have the Benediction of the most Holy Sacrament every third Sunday of the month, on account of the charitable instructions, which were given every Sunday in that Parish ; that leave did not concern this Chapel [Presentation Convent]. But His Grace, considering that this Religious Institution was founded particularly for that purpose, and that, nowhere, that duty is performed with more zeal, regularity and edification, than in this house, and by the Religious and respectable ladies who compose it, and who, consecrating themselves to God at the foot of this Altar, make a particular vow of it, His Grace, I say, upon these considerations, has been pleased to grant to this Chapel the same benefit. So, my dear Brethren, every third Sunday of the month, there will be in this Chapel the Benediction of the most Holy Sacrament, and for not to disturb the Parishioners from the Parish Chapel, it will not begin here before two. Let us, my dear Brethren, let us reunite in praises, and in thanks to God, for the temporal and spiritual blessings, which His merciful hand bestows every day on us ; let us, according to the Precept of Our Saviour, edify one another, by works of charity, in order that our fellow Christians may see them, and glorify Our Father, Who is in Heaven, and who, after this World will reward with an eternal glory our fidelity in the accomplishment of our christian duties. May Almighty God the Father, the Son, and the Holy Ghost, make us worthy of it, and grant it to us."

This concession to have Benediction of the most Holy Sacrament, every third Sunday of the month, in St. Michan's was indeed a unique privilege. The date of the grant does not appear, but it was probably a few years after 1798, when Dr. Troy was anxious to encourage religious societies to undermine the influence of French Republican principles. He found a ready response in the people of St. Michan's.

[1] Archives, Presentation Convent, George's Hill.

(b). Devotion to the Sacred Heart

It has been already observed that the Devotion to the Sacred Heart was begun in the diocese in the chapel in Bull-lane by Fr. Mulcaile, S.J., an assistant in the parish. About ten years after his death, "The Confraternity of the Most Sacred Heart was established in George's Hill" (3rd May, 1809); "among the duties of the Association was the making of the Holy Hour on one day each year; each associate chose the day on which duty should be done. This is one of the earliest examples of the practice of the Holy Hour in Ireland."[1]

The "Register of the Associates of the Sacred Heart of Jesus enrolled in the Presentation Convent, George's Hill, 1809" is still preserved in the convent. The names of the Presentation Community are first given, with the day and hour chosen for their Adoration. A list of nine clergymen is next given with the day and hour of their Adoration. The list of the lay associates follows, beginning at 15th September, 1809. The names are chiefly of women, but a few men had enrolled themselves. In the first year (September, 1809 to September, 1810) eighty-two were enrolled, and the days and hours of their Adoration are given. Up to September, 1839, a period of 30 years, 4,590 had performed their hour of Adoration.

The first of the Regulations of this Sodality states: "Pope Pius VII, by a brief, dated January 25th, 1803, had empowered the priests of the Congregation of St. Paul [St. Vincent de Paul, i.e. Vincentians], to aggregate to the Sodality of the Most Sacred Heart of Jesus, erected by them in the city of Rome, all the Sodalities throughout the world, erected or to be erected according to their Association, and to communicate to them the Indulgences, which has been granted to the Sodality itself in Rome."

Father Young was, as we have seen, a missionary at the Vincentian House, Rome, between 1810 and 1814, and was, therefore, aware of the wonderful spread of the Devotion

---

[1] Burke-Savage, A Valiant Dublin Woman, 227-30.

to the Sacred Heart throughout the world. He was thus well equipped to spread the devotion in St. Michan's and elsewhere. In 1814, the year in which he came as curate to St. Michan's, a book of the *Devotion and Office of the Sacred Heart of Our Lord Jesus Christ*, was published by P. Blenkinson, 129 Capel-street. Unfortunately we have been unable to discover a copy of it, but we have seen the 8th edition, printed in 1840, entitled : " The Pious Sodality of the Most Sacred Heart of Jesus, universally propagated throughout the Christian world, containing the Novena and Daily Devotions. ' I have loved thee with everlasting love.' Jer. xxxi. 3. Eighth Edition. With the Approbation of the Most Rev. Dr. Murray, A.D. Dublin : Printed for the Catholic Book Society, 5, Essex-Bridge, 1840. (From the Hollybrook water-press, Golden-Bridge)."

It states that " The Novena of the Sacred Heart of Jesus may be practised on every Friday during the Novena, or nine Days previous to the feast of the Sacred Heart, within its Octave and at any other time devotion may suggest." The Act of Reparation of the " Nine Fridays " is included in the prayers of the Novena and is practically, word for word, as we have it to-day. It was recited : " For the innumerable irreverences and grievious offences, by which we and others, had insulted the Heart of Jesus." Then follow the Litany and the Rosary of the Most Sacred Heart of Jesus.

Though it cannot be said that Father Young had any hand in the first publication of this book, yet it would seem that he was in touch with its subsequent editions. Along with the plates of pictures he had received from Prince Hohenlohe (to which we have already referred) he had a plate of a picture of the Sacred Heart (the Heart encircled by thorns and surmounted by flames) which was considered (1829) useless for the production of pictures. This was apparently the plate used by the printer of the book on the Devotion to the Sacred Heart for the picture which served as a frontispiece.

It may be mentioned here that the Divine Office and Mass of the Most Sacred Heart of Jesus was granted to the clergy of the diocese of Dublin shortly before 1821.

Appended is a note on some religious books published

shortly before Father Young came to St. Michan's and whilst he ministered there. *Think Well On't* was a favourite premium in the Catechism classes.

NOTE.

Elevation of the Soul to God, translated from the French of l'Abbé B. By R.P. 4th edition, 1811. (P. Wogan, 15 Lr. Ormond Quay.)

Instructions and Meditations for every day in Advent. By Rev. Oliver Flock, 1813. (G. Walsh, Wood-Quay).

The Sincere Catholic's Treasure. Texts with Notes from Douay Bible, 1815. (Hibernia Press Office, No. 1, Temple-lane).

Think Well On't, or Reflections on the Great Truths of the Christian Religion for every day in the month. By R. Challoner, D.D. 41st ed., corrected, 1815. (P. Wogan, 15 Lr. Ormond Quay.)

(c.) *Classical and Mercantile Academy*

After the death of Father Mulcaile the education of boys seems to have been entirely in the hands of the secular clergy. Three Jesuits returned to Dublin in 1811 and set up their residence in Father Mulcaile's house, No. 3, George's-hill— these were Fathers Peter Kenney, Gahan, and Dinan. This event took place three years before the ceremony of the restoration of the Society by Pius VII in the church of the Gesú, Rome, at which Dr. Murray and Dr. Blake were present, and presumably Father Henry Young. The Jesuit Fathers remained in George's Hill until 1816 when they took over the chapel and premises of Rev. Dr. McMahon in Hardwicke-street, who died in that year. So far, we have no evidence that they were engaged in educating the boys of the parish, but it is only reasonable to presume that they did assist the parochial clergy therein. They were in the parish when Father Young was an assistant C.C., and, no doubt, they received from him many requests for the exercise of their zeal.

Higher education for Catholic boys, in this period, was a matter of supreme importance. The Saul's-court type was no longer attractive. More pretentious schools, called academies, were the order of the day for Protestant and Catholic boys. For the latter it was imperative that they should have up-to-date commercial training. St. Michan's Classical and Mercantile Academy led the way for them. Unexpected light is thrown on it by a rare book entitled " *A Complete Treatise on*

FATHER MURPHY'S ACADEMY (NORTH ANNE STREET).

Newgate Prison (Green Street).

the Geography of Ireland; adapted to the Merchant, the Gentleman, the Politician, the Antiquarian, the Naturalist, the Scholar and the Artist. By Paul Deighan. Sold by the Author at his School-book and Stationery warehouse, no. 5, Swift's Row, 1st Sept., 1812."

This is the second edition of this remarkable work; the first edition appeared in 1803. It contains copies of letters from the heads of schools and academies all over the country praising this timely publication. We are thus provided with the names of the academies and their principals. Among them is the Classical and Mercantile Academy of North Anne-street, with Father Barnaby Murphy as principal.

It will be interesting to see the new style of building provided by Father Murphy for his academy. Two detailed estimates for wood and plaster work, made out for him in 1810, came my way recently.[1] They refer to the old house and the new one, and show the ornate style of the period. When Father Murphy acquired the old house we do not know, but apparently the new house was built about 1810. Both houses still exist, Nos. 38 and 39 North Anne-street, and are now called the Brewery house, opposite St. Michan's church. They are as staunch to-day as they were in 1810, and they show not only an artistic taste but a fine conception of space for the class-hall. The academy seems to have been of exceptional importance, and of all its contemporaries it seems to be the sole survivor.

As well as being a successful principal of a classical and commercial academy, Father Murphy was a learned and popular preacher. The people of those days expected and got a sermon at the last Mass of about an hour's duration. The sanctification of the Sunday was taken seriously by the Catholics of pre-Emancipation days. Father Murphy's sermons could not have been preached in less than an hour. Eight of his charity sermons, in various city churches, brought in over £1,700. The contributions received on those occasions speak well for his popularity as a preacher and for the interest of the people in the poor schools of their parish. The list of contributors to his edition of his sermons surpasses anything

[1] Supplied by V. Rev. Canon McGuirk, P.P., Rathfarnham.

of the time. It occupies over 50 pages and numbers over 1,900 subscribers from all parts of Ireland. His sermons were published in 1808. As he reconstructed his academy in 1810, it seems legitimate to conclude that the proceeds of his volumes were spent on it.

(d.) The New Church.

The old chapel in Bull-lane, as we have said, was still doing duty during Father Young's curacy in the parish, but during that time, building operations were going on in the new parish church in North Anne-street. Fortunately, the parish had many rich and influential Catholics. The district was then considered one of the healthiest parts of the city, and was inhabited by many of the aristocracy. The Baptismal records reveal the names of the Catholics. Captain George Bryan, of Jenkinstown, Co. Kilkenny, lived at No. 12 Henrietta-street, and was the prime-mover for the erection of the new church. There were also the Dowdalls, the Dillons, the Bellews, etc., Catholic families that had survived the restrictions of the Penal Laws on their estates. With their town houses in St. Michan's parish, they rejoiced at the resurgence of Catholic activity and especially at the emergence of the penal-time chapel of Bull-lane into the elegant church in the fashionable North Anne-street.

When Father Christopher Wall became parish priest in 1807, the parishioners were determined on building a new church to meet the requirements of rich and poor alike. Captain Bryan and Messrs. Doyle and Coyle were appointed collectors, and they went round to every house in the parish to collect the money for the site. The only available site was between North Anne-street and Halston-street, on the ancient St. Mary's Abbey Green, and it was purchased. Captain Bryan gave the handsome sum of £300, and £100 a year until the church was completed. The church was begun in 1812 and was finished in 1817; Father Young must have rejoiced to see the building soar aloft and to witness one of the first attempts in the city at modern church building in place of the penal time chapels. Before it was finished he was moved to another and more fruitful sphere of activity. Yet, we must describe the church as completed.

The granite front in Anne-street was in the Gothic style, and the interior was richly decorated with stucco and sculpture. Over the high altar was a full-length in *alto relievo* of our Saviour beneath a canopy by Smith, the sculptor of the figures on the Custom House. At the back of the high altar was the presbytery that faced on Halston-street and which was built about 1820.[1] As a token of gratitude to Captain Bryan the committee had his family arms emblazoned in the gallery porch in North Anne Street where the monument still exists.

2. Dr. Blake at SS. Michael and John's

In the midst of his intense labour in his mission at Harold's Cross and Milltown, Father Young found time to devote his pen to the apostolate. To this Apostolate he was called by his friend Dr. Blake, P.P., SS. Michael and John's. As Father Young was to be associated with him in many pioneer works in that parish, it will be useful to see firstly what manner of man Dr. Blake was and how he developed the parish and made possible those works of their combined efforts.

Michael Blake, son of George Blake, a native of Nobber, Co. Meath, was born in Dublin, 16th July, 1775. He was educated by Dr. Betagh in his seminary in Saul's-court, and entered the old Irish College, Rome, May, 1792. He was one of the last group of students to leave Rome at the break-up of the college during the French occupation in 1798. On the 26th July, that year, he was ordained by Archbishop Troy in Liffey-street chapel, and was appointed C.C. to his native parish of St. Paul's. In March, 1802, he appears as C.C. in

---

[1] In 1861 the present presbytery was built. The church was to be extended to Halston-street, but this work was not carried out until 1891 when Father Conlan had a chancel, two side chapels, a tower and a belfry turret built. The chancel window, in perpendicular Gothic, is one of the most imposing windows in the city. The figure of our Saviour was removed to another part of the church where it is still suitably honoured. The immense black marble holy-water font that did service in the Bull-lane chapel since 1704 was set up in the new porch in Halston-street. The chapel in Bull-lane was advertised for sale. An advertisement appears in *Freeman's Journal* (10th Jan., 1818) to the following effect : "To be sold by Auction on the Premises on Monday, the 26th of January, 1818, the old Chapel of St. Michan's, Mary's Lane." The sale was evidently not effected, as the building was used for some years afterwards as a school.

St. Michan's and disappears after January, 1806. Apparently
he was transferred in that year to SS. Michael and John's
to assist his former teacher Dr. Betagh, who resigned four
years later (1810). He then became parish priest of that
church and continued the work of his master in the old
Classical and Grammar school in Saul's-court.

Dr. Betagh "at his residence, 80, Cook-street, died on
Saturday night, February 16th, about 12 o'clock, in the 74th
year of his age," and was interred temporarily in the vaults
of the Presentation Convent, George's Hill, 19th February,
1811. On that day, Tuesday, the funeral from Cook-street
was attended by "groups of persons of every religious persuasion, who knew his virtues and respected them . . . the
procession proceeded in the following order : The charity
children of Rosemary-lane chapel, two and two ; next the
hearse containing the body of the deceased, drawn by six
horses ; next, near three thousand respectable citizens on foot
in scarfs and hat bands, two and two, followed by upwards
of 150 private carriages. The rear was composed of an
immense multitude, the whole forming an aggregate of
upwards of 20,000 persons. . . . The utmost respect and
veneration for the memory of the lamented deceased were
evinced throughout the whole of the ceremony, and especially
marked by the citizens shutting their shops in the different
streets through which the procession passed."[1]

The reconstructed stable-chapel of 1700 had done duty
for 110 years, but Dr. Betagh, for many years before he died,
had been looking out for a site for a more impressive church.
Fortunately, a suitable site came in the way of Dr. Blake.
James Farrell, 4, Merrion-square, East, the owner of an
extensive brewery in Black-pits, purchased, in 1790, the old
Smock-alley Theatre which he converted into a warehouse
for the storage of whiskey etc. As the building was fast
falling into decay he handed it over to Dr. Blake for the new
parochial church, 8 July, 1811, for £1,600. SS. Michael and
John's was opened in 1815 with its double granite fronts in
Smock-alley and Lr. Exchange-street. It is the first church
on record in Dublin in which the penny-a-week contribution

---

[1] Walker's *Hibernian Magazine*, Feb., 1811.

of the poor was mainly responsible for the building. It is interesting to note that the present vaults were originally the pit of the old theatre, and that the first to find rest there was Dr. Betagh whose remains were transferred from George's Hill. A memorial tablet was erected to him, with elaborate inscription, by the parishioners, on the epistle side of the church, which has been recently transferred to the gallery stairs. Surely, the name and fame of Dr. Betagh deserve a better fate.

In defiance of the penal code Dr. Blake set up a bell to call the people to Mass and to toll the Angelus—the first bell set up in any Catholic place of worship in Ireland for nearly three hundred years. " This audacious proceeding aroused the fury of the Orange bigots, then all-powerful in Dublin, and Alderman Carleton instituted proceedings in the King's Bench against the offending parish priest. The latter was fortunate to secure the advocacy of Daniel O'Connell and when the alderman learned this fact, he quietly climbed down and no more was heard of the matter. It was the last kick of the Penal laws."[1]

Unfortunately, it was not the " last kick." Father Young's experience (already related) occurred a few years afterwards, and other examples were to follow.

In 1815, Dr. Blake was selected by the Irish Bishops to accompany Archbishop Murray and Bishop Murphy (Cork) on their mission to Rome on the Veto Question. Though SS. Michael and John's was opened in 1815, it remained unplastered and unpainted for three years. Immediately after his return from Rome, Dr. Blake set about to collect the funds for the necessary improvements. He hit on the happy idea of having a Church Concert which would bring in several hundred pounds in one day. As this Church Concert was a pioneer effort of its kind, and as, fortunately, its details are preserved—quite an exceptional piece of fortune for the period—we have no hesitation in describing this interesting event.

Dublin in those days was, as we have seen, a lover of high-class music ; the influence of the Music Hall in Fishamble-

[1] Donnelly, *Dub. Par.* II, 197.

street was still felt, and the visits of the Italian Opera Singers were particularly welcome. The great occasion for elaborate church music would be the dedication of a new church. Up to 1819 there were only two great churches built, SS. Michael and John's, and St. Michan's; St. Mary's, Marlborough-street was not yet completed. The music on those occasions was confined to an elaborate " High Mass," usually Mozart's " Grand Mass." Another occasion would be the " reopening " of a church after repairs and decoration. The year 1819 saw at least three city chapels repaired and decorated, namely, the Capuchin Church, Church-street, the Dominican Church, Denmark-street, and SS. Michael and John's. Grand concerts of Sacred Music, Vocal and Instrumental, were held in them—in August, September, and October respectively to pay for the improvements. Advertisements were inserted in the *Freeman's Journal* on several days before the concerts.

In the case of the Denmark-street concert the performers were Dublin artistes, and the musical items were drawn from the works of Handel and Haydn. The most imposing programme was that provided at the concert in SS. Michael and John's which was held on Sunday, 10th October, and was made to synchronise with the presence in Dublin of the Italian singers who were performing Grand Opera in the Theatre Royal.

The building of SS. Michael and John's new church had taxed the resources of the parishioners. In 1819, the parochial collectors got busy again, and, in five months, June to November, they gathered £463 from private subscribers and from the penny-a-week of the poor. Dr. Blake, P.P., gave the handsome subscription of £50. The collection was £22 per week—as large a sum as the best suburban parish of to-day would contribute, but three times more valuable.

An interesting volume[1] to hand entitled : " Painting this chapel, emproving the entrance to the Gallery and making other necessary repairs and alterations therein," shows the subscriptions and the payments for the improvements.

Dr. Blake received weekly sums of £30 and £40 from the

---

[1] This MS., the property of Rev. Dr. Blake, P.P. (afterwards Bishop of Dromore) was kindly presented to me by the late Most Rev. Dr. Mulhern, Bishop of Dromore.

treasurer to pay the carpenters, plasterers, painters, carriers, etc.   He was his own clerk of works.

The entries for the concert and the preparations for it are unique.   The tickets of admission were registered in special account books, and were sealed with sealing-wax that cost 26s.   The printer of the tickets was paid £5 3s. 9d., and the cost of advertising was £2 19s. 7d., namely, 10s. 10d. to the *Freeman's Journal* (for 4 insertions), 10s. 10d. to the *Evening Post*, and £1 17s. 11d. to the *Morning Post*.   " Placard Men " were employed for tramping through the principal streets for six days before the concert at a cost of 23s. 2d.   A carpenter and his assistant were each paid 13s. for the day, and an assistant labourer 5s., " for putting up Orchester."   " Ropes to tie Scaffold for erecting Orchester " cost 5s.   It would seem that the choir and orchestra were set up on the gallery. An interesting item deals with the hinges and bolts for the security of the conductor's chair on the sloping gallery.   There was a practice, Saturday, 9th October, the day before the concert, for choir and orchestra, as there is an entry in the Account Book of 2s. 6d. " for carrying Musical Instruments." A piano was apparently used for the practice, as 2s. 2d. was paid to " Chairmen [Sedan] for carrying Piano home."   A " Mr. Barrett, Musical Professor," was paid 15s. 0d., probably for putting the choir and orchestra through their items.

The advertisements in the *Freeman's Journal*, during the week preceding the concert, supply interesting information. The first insertion (2nd October) states : " The Public are respectfully informed that to gratify the admirers of Sacred Music, the Celebrated Italians now in this city, have been engaged, and will perform in the above-mentioned chapel, on Sunday, 10th inst."   The Italian Opera Season had opened in the Theatre Royal, 27th September, Don Giovanni being the favourite opera, with Signor Ambrogetti in the title role.

The insertion in the *Freeman's Journal*, 7th October, supplies all the information we require about the artistes and the programme.   It reads thus :

" Grand Concert of Vocal and Instrumental Music in St. Michael and St. John's Chapel, Exchange-street, on Sunday, the 10th October, 1819, for liquidating the Debts incurred for building the Organ and improving the chapel. The Concert will commence at two o'clock.

Principal Vocal Performers, Signor Begrez, Signor Romero, and Signor Ambrogetti. Leader of the Band, Mr. Mori (from the Italian Opera House, London). Conductor, Mr. Panormo.

Part First.

Grand Overture	Cherubini.
Hymn, ' O Gran Dio,' Sig. Ambrogetti .	Haydn.
Quartetto. ' Miserere ' (of the Vatican) Messrs. Cassidy, Begrez, Romero and Ambrogetti	Bincini.
Duetto. ' By thee with bliss,' Messrs Cassidy and Morrison	Haydn.
Concerto ' Violino,' Sig. Mori . . .	Mori.
Recitativo ed Aria, ' And God said . . .,' ' In Native worth,' Sig. Bcgrcs . .	Haydn.
Motteto, ' Panis Angelicus,' Sigrs. Ambrogetti and Romero	Janaccioni.

Part Second.

Concerto, ' Organ,' Mr. Panormo . .	Steibelt.
Aria, ' Ave Maria,' Signor Begrez . .	Borghi.
Terzetto, ' Iste Confessor,' Signors Begrez, Ambrogetti, and Romero . . .	Baini.
Solo, ' Violoncello,' Mr. Pigott . . .	Beethoven.
Selection from the ' Gloria in Excelsis,' Sig. Romero	Terziani.
Air, ' With Verdure Clad,' Signor Begrez .	Haydn.
Grand Chorus, ' Haleluiah ' (from the Mount of Olives)	Beethoven.

Tickets 5s. each."

The payments to the performers are given in Dr. Blake's Account : To Signor Ambrogetti, £13 13s. od. ; to Signor Romero, £11 7s. 6d. ; to Signor Begrez, £11 7s. 6d. ; to Signor Mori, £5 13s. 9d., and to Signor Panormo, £5 13s. 9d.

The rate of payment is interesting. Ambrogetti, as the principal tenor of the Italian Opera Company, received an enhanced fee. The other two Italian vocalists received double what the principal violinist and conductor received. The sum, £5 13s. 9d., as the basic fee, seems strange ; it is probably computed on the relative value of Irish and English money. The English shilling was ordinarily regarded, in the early nineteenth century, as equal to 1s. 1d. Irish, but, in the above rates of payment, the Irish equivalent seems to have been about 1s. 1½d. in 1819. Yet the rate of payment for advertisements, 10s. 10d. and £1 17s. 11d., is built on the 1s. 1d. basis.

The "Instrumental performers" were paid £12 10s. 11d., and the Choristers, £9 1s. 0d. Two of the choristers, Messrs. Cassidy and Morrison, were paid an additional fee of £1 each for their part in special items of the programme. No doubt, the Italian performers were entertained in the presbytery, but the choristers were not forgotten, as an entry of 5s. for "lemon cakes etc. for Choristers" shows. The conductor, Signor Panormo, seems to have been an organist in one of the city chapels. At the Grand Concert of Sacred Music, in Denmark-street chapel, Sunday, 22nd August, 1819, he was the solo piano. At SS. Michael and John's Concert he was the solo organist and conductor.

The "reopening," on the 10th October, seems to have been initiated with a High Mass, probably at 11 o'clock, as there is an entry "for breakfast at reopening" and another entry for work "in kitchens, Chapel House," apparently to cope with the increased demand on the kitchen range. The total cost of "reopening," including the cost of the Concert, was £72 5s. 3d. The receipts were not less than £500. An entry of 8d. for "5 sheets of large paper for Balance sheets" is given, but the sheets have been lost ; they would have given valuable information. No doubt, there was seating accommodation for the gentry and the merchants who paid a large subscription, but the rest of the audience had to stand.

Besides the attraction to the Catholic people of Dublin to hear the Italian Opera singers in Sacred Music, there was the great spirit of loyalty and generosity of the parishioners towards their parish church—their payment for admission they would regard as a contribution to the great work of beautifying God's House. For three years they had worshipped in this great new building, but the unfinished interior was a reproach to them. Most of them had worshipped in the penal time chapel in Rosemary-lane for many years. Their joy at the " reopening " and at hearing the grand music that the Catholic church could provide, interpreted by the greatest singers and instrumentalists of the day, can only be imagined. No doubt, it was the first time that most of them heard an organ in church. The organ in SS. Michael and John's was built on the most modern principles, and the first of its kind in a Dublin Catholic church. There is an item in the accounts for £168 for the erection of the organ, but it is scarcely probable that this included the cost of the instrument. To Dr. Blake the honour, and glory, not only of the exceptional concert but of the erection of the grand organ, must be given. He was not only a man of culture, but a very practical parish priest, and the most distinguished priest of the diocese.

3. FATHER YOUNG AND THE PURGATORIAN SOCIETY

To Dr. Blake may be traced the organisation and expansion of lay parochial societies ; for this work he called upon Father Young to assist him with his pen. SS. Michael and John's became the parent and the great exemplar of many of those societies.

In 1817, Dr. Blake founded the most important society in the diocese, that of St. John the Evangelist, " for promoting Spiritual and Corporal Works of Mercy." Its object, as Father Young states in his *Catholic Directory* (1821), was " to instruct the ignorant, to administer comfort to dying persons, and to relieve the suffering souls in Purgatory."

Though parochial day and evening schools were already in working order in the parish, yet there were many boys and girls engaged in factories who could not attend either school. Their only means of instruction was the Sunday Free School in Smock-alley, taught by the brothers of the St. John Society and some pious ladies, and there they learned to read and write and cast accounts to help them in their daily work.

The second object, "to administer comfort to dying persons," was the real work of Mercy of the society. Dr. Blake's noble design of forming this society was to put down effectually abuses at wakes by deputing a number of edifying young men to read pious books, and recite the office for the dead on those occasions. Those, in a short time, formed rules for their government. They attended the sick and dying, prepared them under the directions of the clergy for the last Sacraments, and performed other offices of mercy.

The Brothers did incalculable good. Pecuniary and medical aid was also daily administered, towards which small weekly contributions were given by the members of the society, and by the public. Whilst these works of charity were performed towards the sick, dying and dead, the members according to rule, attended to their own sanctification by assembling in the church on the first Monday in each month, by assisting at the Holy Sacrifice on that day—offered for the repose of the souls of the faithful departed, and particularly of the deceased members, parents, relatives and friends—by approaching the Holy Communion for the same intention, making a preparation for death, and by reciting in the evening of the said day the office for the dead. They also assisted at the Solemn Office and High Mass, for the deceased members, celebrated on appointed days in the beginning of the four seasons of the year.[1]

The benefits derived from the society in a few years were so great that, in 1820, Dr. Blake, with Rev. H. Young, presented a memorial to his Holiness Pope Pius VII for the sanction and privileges of the Holy See. Archbishop Troy forwarded his special approbation of the Society to the Pope, and joined in requesting the communication of all the privileges and indulgences annexed to the pious sodalities of the Sacred Heart of Jesus, etc. Father Young, at the end of his *Evening Office Book*, gives the Indulgences granted to the Purgatorian Society of SS. Michael and John's Parish, in the City of Dublin, and to other confraternities united to, and incorporated with the Society.

"Since that period [1817] the parent Society in Smock-

---

[1] Battersby, *Irish Catholic Directory* (1836), p. 93.

alley has been extending its works of mercy, piety, and religion, by branch societies, by a library of some thousand volumes lent to members and persons recommended by them ; by a Sunday school for the instruction of poor children [distinct from the Christian Doctrine Confraternity], by religious reading, and by administering comfort, spiritual and temporal, to the sick and dying. There is another branch of St. John's Society in St. Michan's parish, No. 176, North King-street."[1]

Father Young, in his *Catholic Directory* (1821), states that a Purgatorian Society was "lately established in Dunleary where forty pious members meet three times a week to say the Office of the Dead, and assemble every evening to recite the Rosary and other devotions." Dunleary had also a Confraternity of Christian Doctrine, and "twenty pious members teach the children the Catechism in the Chapel after Mass." All this was due to the example set by SS. Michael and John's.

Having obtained the grant of Indulgences for the Society, the next thing was to issue a booklet explaining the nature of the Society and giving its Rules.

The title, "Society of St. Patrick," was then given to all Purgatorian Societies "for promoting the Exercise of the Spiritual and Corporal Works of Mercy." Under this title the booklet (of 8 pages) was printed by J. Coyne, 74, Cook-street, price two pence, 1821, sanctioned by his Grace, The Most Rev. Dr. Troy. This booklet was from the pen of Fr. Young.

A few extracts from it will be useful. "Religious confraternities—conducive to the salvation of every member—afford a holy union and society of pious brethren—aid and assist the Clergyman in the discharge of his duties by instructing the ignorant, reclaiming the sinner, affording comfort to the sick and distressed, and by relieving the suffering souls in Purgatory."

Every member was to pay 6d. a month to promote the pious purposes of the society.

Saturday before 1st Sunday of every month a Mass was to be offered for the subscribers.

[1] l.c.

Every Sunday the Office for the Dead was recited by the Society for the souls in Purgatory and for the members of Society.

Every member was entitled to 3 Masses at death, and a Mass was said every quarter of the year for the members. and their parents, friends and relatives.

" Every member of this Confraternity must be ready and willing to read the Office of the Dead at wakes, in order if possible to abolish these unchristian and diabolical practices which are alas ! but too common at wakes ; and are disgraceful and insulting to our holy Religion."

" The order to be observed is this. The friend of the deceased is to give the earliest notice to the officiating Priest, who is supposed to know whether the deceased died of a contagious disease or not, and also whether the deceased died in peace with God and the Church or at least with a desire to do so. If the priest judges it expedient to have the office read at the wake, he is then to send a printed order to the Vice President or Secretary, who are to have a list of all the Members. The Vice President or Secretary is immediately to choose out and give notice to nine of the reading Members to assist each night, until the body is interred. All the members are to take their turn by rotation at every successive wake. The nine Members shall attend accordingly at the house of deceased, for such time as may be allotted to them, and there read the office of the dead, and some pages of chapters in a religious book, with which the Superior shall furnish them. Any member that neglects his duty in this point shall be reported to the President from whom he shall receive a public reprimand in presence of the Choir on the next office day. He shall also pay a fine of five pence for such neglect unless he can give a very satisfactory apology for his absence. If the deceased be a Member, eighteen are to be appointed to read the office at the wake, and all Members are recommended to attend. The Parishioners shall be advised and encouraged to give notice as above mentioned. So that it will be considered as an invitation to the Members to attend.

" XII. Some of the Members who are most capable are to be appointed by the President to teach Catechism in the

Chapel on Sundays. And all of them are recommended to instruct the ignorant poor in their own houses and immediate neighbourhood, if opportunity serves.

" XIII. Fines for absence from weekly office and catechism.

" XIV. Every Member of the Society shall attend their duty monthly and show by example the respect in which they hold the Society.

" XV. All Members of this Society shall say the Rosary on all the days of lent and advent, on every Sunday and holiday in the year, and on feasts of the Blessed Virgin. The rosary is to be said in part or in the whole, in public or private, according as the President shall direct. The Members of the confraternity are also recommended to induce their friends and families to join in family prayers every day.

" XVI. If a member of this Society be sick or in a distressed situation, the Committee is immediately to meet and order him such pecuniary relief as the funds will permit. If the funds will not be sufficient to afford him the necessary relief, the Committee is immediately to call on all the Members of the confraternity for an extraordinary subscription according to each ones means and circumstances.

" XVII. No Member of this Society shall sit down in a public house in the parish, on a Sunday or pay-day,[1] without leave of the President, under the penalty of 10d., and if any Member be seen drunk, he must pay 2s. 6d. for the first offence, and 5s. for the second, if he be drunk the third time, he shall be expelled from the Society, and his name erased from the books.

" XVIII. As ours is a Society of a spiritual nature, every Member of it is strictly enjoined not to meddle or interfere in political matters, nor to enter into or engage in secret combinations of any kind, or for any purpose whatever, under pain of expulsion. [Library attached to each Society.]

" XX. Every Postulant must be introduced to the President by two members.

" XXI. Every new Member must purchase a copy of these rules and office book, if he can read. If he cannot read ; he may perform his duty by listening attentively to the rest."

[1] See p. 263.

Though the name of the compiler is not given, it may be taken that it was Father Young who compiled the booklet at the request of Dr. Blake. The whole tone of the rules is distinctly his. He was one of the pioneers of Temperance. Dr. Blake and he, knowing city life so well, apparently agreed, in 1817, that one of the remedies against Intemperance was to abolish drinking at wakes by providing prayers and religious reading. Hence arose St. John's Society. It is perfectly clear that Father Young constructed the Rules and Practices of this Society on those of the Sodality of the Blessed Virgin which the Jesuit Fathers had introduced into Ireland and which he had established when a boarder in Inch Academy, Balbriggan.

It is significant that Father Young's name is coupled with Dr. Blake's in the petition for the Indulgences for the Purgatorian Society, which is as follows :

" Most Holy Father,

" In order to promote the pious dispositions of the faithful of this city, and to render them more charitable to the poor sick, and more zealous to relieve, by their suffrages, the souls in Purgatory, a pious Society, under the patronage of St. John the Evangelist, has been established here, with the permission of our Most Rev. Archbishop, whereof the members, according to rule, attend the sick and dying, prepare them for the last sacraments, under direction of the pastor, and after death recite the Office for the Dead before interment for the happy repose of their souls. Moreover, they assemble in Church on the first Monday of each month at the august Sacrifice of the Mass offered for the souls in purgatory, and approach the Holy Communion for the same intention ; and, in the evening of the said day, to recite in choir the Office of the Dead for the same purpose. Finally, for the greater comfort of those suffering souls, they assist at the solemn Office and High Mass for the Dead, which are celebrated on appointed days in the beginning of the four seasons of the year.

" To perpetuate these devout practices, and to increase the zeal and charity of all the members of this congregation towards the dying and deceased faithful ; we, prostrate at the foot of Your Holiness, do humbly petition you to grant us perpetual plenary Indulgences—1st. on the day of enrolment into this Society—2nd. on the first Monday of every month—3rd. on the appointed days of the quarterly Office and Mass, provided the members approach to the holy Communion, and fulfil the other requisite conditions. Finally, we do also humbly petition the grant of a partial Indulgence of seven years and seven quarantines each time they perform any of the offices and respective duties, prescribed by rule. We earnestly beseech the Almighty to grant Your Holiness a long and a happy life, for the good of his Church, and humbly begging your apostolic benediction,

> We profess ourselves,
> Your Holiness'
> Most devoted and
> Most obliged Servants,
> Michael Blake, P.P. of
> SS. Michael and John's,
> and Henry Young, Chaplain
> to St. Clare's Nunnery.

To give greater credit to this petition, we have requested and obtained the recommendation of our Most Reverend Prelate.

APPROBATION OF THE MOST REV. DR. TROY.

I approve of the aforesaid Purgatorian Society, of St. John the Evangelist, and request His Holiness to grant to the members thereof the Indulgences petitioned for, and also a communication of all the Privileges and Indulgences, which are annexed to the pious sodalities of the Sacred Heart of Jesus, under the direction of the secular Clergy of St. Paul in Rome, and erected in the Archdiocese of Dublin.

> Fr. John Thomas Troy,
> Archbishop of Dublin."

" From the audience of His Holiness, held on the 4th June, 1820.

" Having considered the petitions of this memorial, and the request of the Most Reverend Archbishop of Dublin ; His Holiness, Pope Pius VII, through me undersigned, Secretary of the Sacred Congregation of Propaganda Fide, has graciously consented to grant all the indulgences petitioned by the members of the Purgatorian Society of St. John the Evangelist, and has extended to them also those privileges and indulgences which are granted to the pious sodalities of the Sacred Heart of Jesus, under the direction of the secular Clergy of St. Paul, provided they fulfil the pious works enjoined to obtain them.

" Dated in Rome, from the House of said Congregation, the day and year as above marked. Grants given, without any kind of payment.
instead of seal X

C. M. Pedicini, Secretary.

This agrees with the original copy.

Fr. John Thos. Troy.

" To the greater honour and glory of God, in praise and veneration of the Blessed Virgin Mary, and of all the Angels and Saints, for the conversion and salvation of our neighbour, and for the speedy deliverance and happy repose of all the souls in Purgatory.
Amen."

Father Young, in his booklet, adds : " Other Pious Practices of Devotion, mentioned in the title page, which may be very desirable to the pious reader ; wherefore he promises to print them separately in a small book, as a Supplement to the Evening Office. This Supplement will contain the following prayers in Latin and English :

" The Litanies of the most sacred name of Jesus, and of the Blessed Virgin Mary.—The Hymn of the most blessed Sacrament for Benediction.—Several fragments of Hymns to be sung at benediction,—some devout Anthems sung at or after benediction.—Divers proses, verses, anthems, and prayers, for the conclusion of benediction. Also the following hymns and proses in Latin and English :—Puer nobis nascitur,—Adeste fideles,—O filii et filiae,—Victimae Paschali,—Veni, Creator,—and Veni, Sancte Spiritus, with the Prayers.—A shorter Invocation of the Divine Spirit.—The Te Deum, or Hymn of Thanksgiving, with its Prayer.—The Lauda Sion Salvatorem.—Adora te devote.—Jesu dulcis memoria.—The Stabat mater.—The Miserere Psalm and Prayer.—The De profundis and prayer.

"To this Supplement will be added, Morning and Evening Prayers, Some brief Meditations or Reflections, Prayers before and after Sacramental Confession and Communion, and other devout practices. The Supplement will be published, with the Lord's assistance, at Easter, 1824, if not beforehand."

Father Young finally observes that "*The Laity's Directory*, for the use and correct recital of this Evening Office, will be annually published in the month of December."

If Father Young had written nothing else but this booklet of the Purgatorian Society he would have been remembered in the Annals of the Diocese for heroic, pioneer work. His conception of the helps for the devotion of the people was not only practical, but liturgical. His Roman training runs through all his apostolate of the pen, and he had the vision, exceptional at the time, to apply that training to the peculiar needs of Dublin. Dr. Blake saw the advantage of that training, and of his heroic sanctity, for his work of reform in the city of Dublin. What Father Young had accomplished in Harold's Cross, Dr. Blake was anxious to have carried out in SS. Michael and John's.

The Heroic Act of Charity in favour of the holy souls in Purgatory was one of Father Young's favourite themes. In his letters to relatives and friends he reminded them "of the great indulgences granted to those who make the whole oblation of their Masses, Communions, prayers, good works, and respective occupations in favour of those suffering souls."

With all his austerity Father Henry had a keen sense of humour and was never at a loss for an answer. On one occasion, about this time, Dr. Blake preached a charity sermon in one of the city churches to a large congregation. A Quaker gentleman, who had come to hear him, made himself conspicuous by keeping his hat on, in accordance with his religious practice. When Dr. Blake retired to the sacristy after the sermon he declared that he would not give Benediction of the Most Holy Sacrament if that Quaker was allowed to keep his hat on. Nobody wished to reprimand the Quaker who was a good employer and a charitable man. " Leave it to me," said Father Henry, who was present in the sacristy, as he rubbed his hands with delight. He took a collection plate, approached the Quaker most courteously, and said : " Sir, the clergy would consider it a great kindness on your part if you would on this occasion act as our collector." Pleased with the compliment, the Quaker followed Father Henry to the door of the church to collect the alms of the people as they went out, and carried out successfully his injunction to make them subscribe liberally. Dr. Blake often quoted this incident as an example of Father Henry's shrewdness and presence of mind.

4. The " Catholic Directory " and " Evening Office."

It is certain that Father Young was the author of other publications besides the Rules of the Purgatorian Society, but he modestly refrained from adding his name to them. In 1821 he published the *Catholic Directory for the Diocese of Ireland*. It would seem that having been so successful in his first publication, he was commissioned by Dr. Blake, with the approval of Archbishop Troy, to edit this important work for the priests of Ireland. It was not the first of its kind ; Father Bernard MacMahon had edited it for some years before his death in 1816.

Father MacMahon was born in Castlering, Co. Louth, about 1736, was educated in Antwerp, and returned to Louth about 1774. About 1780 he came into prominence as an editor of publications, devotional and mathematical. He was affiliated with the Dublin diocese in 1787. The next year, and for three years, he was accommodated with rooms at the Pigeon House by the Lord Lieutenant to observe the

" Tides of High Water," and put together a system of tide-tables which was adopted by the Commissioners of the Custom-house and of the Coast-office " to the great advantage of the public at large." It would seem that he was the editor of the *Missale Romanum* of 1787 and 1795 (copies in the National Library), and of the New Testament of 1783 and 1803. In the eighth edition of the New Testament, 1810, Dr. Troy mentions him in his approbation. The Holy Bible of 1791, with similar approbation, is attributed to him. Perhaps his most important religious work was his edition of Butler's *Lives of the Saints*. This second edition was printed in Dublin as early as 1780, namely, within six years after he returned from Antwerp. He seems to have edited the *Directorium* for the Recitation of the Office and the Celebration of Mass for the " secular clergy of the Kingdom of Ireland," from 1792 to 1816. According to the *Orthodox Journal* (November, 1816), he undertook the *Directorium* at the express injunction of the Archbishop, and " though attempts have been made by other clergymen in Cork, Limerick, and Waterford, to publish works, yet the Doctor's annual production has been always preferred."

When the Poor Clares removed, in 1804, from Drum-condra-lane (Lr. Dorset-street), to which they had removed from North King-street in 1752, to Harold's Cross, Father MacMahon took over the house and chapel, rearranged the nuns' cells into a living room and utilised the chapel as a chapel-of-ease to Liffey-street chapel. Here he lived until his death in 1816.[1]

In 1821, Father Young compiled his great work, the *Evening Office Book*. He compiled a booklet on the Rules of the Evening Office Confraternity, and was asked to compile a booklet for the Jubilee of 1826. We have not been able to trace the latter booklet. Though it may not have been published, it may be taken, as we shall see later, that he compiled the prayers to be recited by the priests and people of SS. Michael and John's parish on their Jubilee visits to the churches named in the arrangement.

[1] O Cásaide, *Co. Louth Arch. Soc.*, 1940, pp. 257-79.

It would seem that he was appealed to from many quarters to prepare for press spiritual works. It was a great tribute to him, and apparently there was no one else in the diocese to undertake this work. In 1822 he published an edition of M. l'Abbé Claude Arvisenet's *Memoriale Vitae Sacerdotalis*. He had at heart the ordering of the priest's life, and he gave the example in his own life. The work was more than once reprinted in Dublin. He had at heart also the spread of Temperance. It may be said that he was the pioneer in the diocese, twenty years before Father Mathew preached in Dublin. He published, in 1823, a popular treatise against drunkenness, written in his own quaint, earnest and simple manner, for the poor and ignorant. As ascetic, a busy city curate, a preacher, and a writer, Father Young was outstanding in the early years of the nineteenth century. His apostolate of the pen was carried out mainly during his busy missionary period at Harold's Cross and Milltown.

As to the *Catholic Directory*, we find in the Index Catalogue of the National Library under " Young, Father Henry," " *Catholic Directory*, Dedicated to St. Patrick, of the Dioceses of Ireland, 1821. printed by John Coyne, 74, Cook-street. Printer and Bookseller to the General Confraternity of the Christian Doctrine."

The *Directory* contained information useful to the whole Church in Ireland, but was particularly concerned with Catholic activities in Dublin. It set the format for *Battersby's Directory* of 1836, and after. Unfortunately the *Directory* for the year 1821 is the only one that we have been able to discover of his editions, yet he seems to have edited it in subsequent years, but for how many we do not know. A letter [1] of his to the Rector of Tullabeg College is as follows :

" J.M.J.

18th Nov.

" Dear Rev. Sir,

" I send you at present the enclosed three half sheets, but promise in about 10 days hence to send you the remainder to the end of Dec.

---

[1] Archives, Tullabeg College ; through the courtesy of Rev. R. Burke-Savage S.J.

" Some unforeseen occurrences caused a great delay in my Directory this year, but there are now two compositors on this work to hurry it off, and my compilation of Ms. copy is prepared for the press.

" You may be assured that the expense of your 25 copies will be about half the former costs."

The remainder of the letter deals with " Our Holy very Rev. Prince de Hohenlohe," to whom we have already referred, and places the year as 1823.

The important points, for our present purpose, are that Father Young was still editing the *Directory* for its fourth year in 1823, that he was collaborating with the Rector of Tullabeg, and that the Jesuit Fathers required 25 copies for their various houses. It is also important to stress the fact that, during his intense activity in Harold's Cross, he was able to carry out this laborious task for several years. As Battersby's first edition of the *Irish Catholic Directory* was issued in 1836, it seems legitimate to conclude that Father Young's *Directory* continued up to that year. If that be so, then Father Young, in the midst of his missionary work, in the country parts of the diocese, must have continued his apostolate of the pen, during the years 1827–36, side by side with his preaching in the churches and his visiting of the homes of the poor.

The next important work of the apostolate of the pen, which Dr. Blake called upon him to undertake, was an edition of the Evening Office Book. The title of the book is as follows : " Vespers and Complin, or the Evening Office of the Church, according to the Roman Breviary, in Latin and English, for the use of the Members of Pious Confraternities, and of other devout Laity in Ireland and England. To which are added, the Office of the B.V.Mary, the Office of the Dead, and other Pious Practices of Devotion : Sanctioned and Recommended by the Most Rev. Dr. Troy, Most Rev. Dr. Murray, Very Rev. Dr. Hamill, V.G., Very Rev. Dr. Blake, V.G.

May our evening prayer ascend to thee, O Lord ; and may Thy mercy descend upon us.

Dublin : Printed at the Hibernian Press Office, Temple-lane, for the Confraternity of St. Michael and St. John's Chapel, and for other Pious Confraternities and Devout Laity : Sold at Richard White's, 25, Lower Exchange St., opposite said Chapel, and by all the Booksellers, 1822."

In the " Dedicatory Prayer to Our Lord and Saviour, Jesus Christ," Father Young states : " The Divine Office of the Church is, next to the august sacrifice of the Altar, the most acceptable tribute of praise and honour to You, dear Lord, and the most profitable devotion, and efficacious prayer for us to recite, in order to obtain your divine graces for the sanctification of our souls. . . . We most Humbly beg, dear Lord, that you will bless us all, by imparting your celestial graces on us, and all Christians, who practise these evening devotions to your divine honour. Grant that we may begin the day by assisting devoutly at Mass, and when our daily occupations are over, we may assemble again in your Sacred Temples, and there pay you the tribute of Evening praise and sacrifice. May we continue faithfully in these sacred occupations to the end of our lives, and may we be admitted, after our mortal pilgrimage, into the realms of Celestial Bliss, in the happy company of all the Angels and Saints, where we will continually sing forth your praises, and contemplate your Divinity for an endless Eternity. Amen, dear Jesus, Amen."

The Evening Office for the year comprises 500 pages. A Table of Moveable Feasts (1822–1870) and a Calendar of Saints (for the dioceses of Ireland and of England) take up 42 pages. Three pages are devoted to " Directions for Reciting the Evening Office." " The Members of Confraternities being assembled in choir at the appointed hour every evening : the Hebdomatory, or President for the week, at the head, or principal place before the altar ; the two Antiphonarians at each side ; and the other members in parallel lines before him beginning by seniority."

Besides the " Little Office of the B.V.M." the whole " Office of the B.V.M." is given, occupying 100 pages. Matins, Lauds, and Vespers of the " Office of the Dead " occupy 66 pages. The whole book consists of 722 pages.

In the last paragraph of the Evening Office Book Father Young reveals himself unmistakeably. In the whole Office Book his name appears only once, namely in the petition of Indulgences for the Purgatorian Society, coupled with the name of the Dr. Blake, P.P. of SS. Michael and John's. At the end of this huge volume he asks for " the kind indulgence of pious readers for Omissions and errors," and petitions all and sundry " to pray to the Lord for his and their eternal salvation." That is characteristic of him ; whilst he laboured for others whose salvation he had ever at heart, he wished it to be remembered that he himself had a soul to save and asked for their prayers that he might be faithful unto death. His work on those publications, during the years 1819–22, was colossal.

We are indebted to the Minute Book of the Evening Office Confraternity for precise information on the compiling of this Office Book. The project began as early as 1819, for, in that year (25th April), a meeting was held in the Library Rooms, Derby Square, of the Superiors of the Chapels of St. Michael and John's, Francis-street and Liffey-street, and Treasurers were appointed for those Chapels, and for " Saint Anne [sic] Street Chapel," to receive subscriptions for the Evening Office Book. Three members of SS. Michael and John's Confraternity, Henry Southwell, Levins Moore, and Joseph Berry, were appointed (30th May) to assist the Rev. Dr. Blake in revising the Evening Office Book and preparing it for press.

From all this it appears that Father Young, having recovered from his fever, and having been appointed to the charge of Harold's Cross Chapel, began, in 1819, his compilation of the Evening Office Book. So, that, in the midst of his labours to stop faction fights, and induce the mill-workers to attend daily Mass, to attend night prayers, and to come to confession, he was burning the midnight candle putting together this huge work and others.

The Minute Book shows how his labours were appreciated. At a general meeting of the chief officers (" Superiors ") of the various confraternities of the Evening Office of the city (15th May, 1823), Dr. Blake presiding, it was resolved :

"That considering the great religious advantages which have been derived and are derivable from the practice of reciting the Evening Office by the laity we hail it as a blessing to our country that a new and more correct edition of that work had been lately given to the public by the Revd. Henry Young, sold at Wm. Battersby's, 33 Winetavern St., from which copies can be easily supplied to any part of the United Kingdom, and we are determined to do our utmost to increase the number of the Evening Office Societies and to circulate copies as widely as possible.

"That the Rev. Henry Young to whose labours and piety we are indebted for that excellent edition of the Evening Office is entitled to our most grateful thanks and that the same be presented to him by our chairman.

"That our thanks are also due to St. John's Society [of SS. Michael & John's] for having assisted and forwarded that Edition by applying thereto as a loan a considerable portion of its funds, and that we are determined to use every exertion that what has been advanced by that Society shall with as little delay as possible be refunded."

Father Henry Young was also asked to draw up the Rules of the Evening Office Confraternities. These rules were revised, amended, and adopted by the Society (13th March, 1825). The booklet went into several editions. We quote from the edition of 1868. The booklet is entitled : "Rules of the Confraternity established for reciting the Evening Office of the Church, according to the Irish Calendar, in the Parish Church of St. Michael and St. John, Dublin. P. Ward, printer, 20 Christchurch Place, Dublin, 1868." The Preface is a splendid example of Father Young's zeal for the liturgy, and a sample of his literary ability. Of itself it is worthy of being quoted fully, and as it is practically impossible to obtain a copy of the booklet, the preface may be suitably inserted here :

" PREFACE

" In the name of the Most Holy Trinity.   Amen.

" The design of this Confraternity is to promote true piety and solid devotion in the souls of those whose zeal for their eternal salvation shall induce them to spend a few moments in its practice, by rendering familiar to them those sacred prayers, consecrated for so many ages by the use of the holy Catholic Church.

" To correspond with those gracious designs should be the object of every pious Christian, and in what manner can we do so more effectually, than by uniting with her to celebrate from day to day, the memory of those eminent servants of God, who, after adoring her with the lustre of their virtues on earth, shine now in heaven more glorious than the stars in the firmament. And as it is presumed that such, and such alone, are the motives of all those who have already begun this pious practice, it is hoped it will be performed by them in a manner pleasing to God, and edifying to each other.

" And as a love for one another has always been the characteristic of the saints, and the principal tie by which the children of the Church are united as joint members in the mystic body of Jesus Christ, who teaches us to consider mankind as one family, of which Almighty God is the common Father, and enjoins us to pray for each other's corporal and spiritual necessities as if they were our own ; for this purpose, appropriate prayers are prescribed by the rules, to be said for any of the members or their relatives who may be visited by sickness or any heavy affliction, and for the spiritual and temporal necessities of all, particularly the conversion of such as are in the state of mortal sin.

" In like manner, as our charity should not be confined to this life, but piercing to the dreary mansions of purgatory, we should supplicate relief for our brethren there detained, the rules also prescribe the Office of the Dead to be said for all deceased members and relatives on the day of their death, monthly and anniversary days. Thus can each soul, associated in the practice of this devotion, increase not only his own spiritual good, but also that of his brethren and friends.

" Such are the designs and intents of this Society. Let it therefore be concluded by submitting to all who practise this devotion, two serious reflections, namely—the making a good or bad use of it. The first is, that engaging in its practice, we have chosen the saint in heaven for our patrons

and protectors, and that if we join to the veneration of their
memory the emulation of their actions, we shall correspond
to the full design of the Church in celebrating their feasts,
and shall certainly experience the happiest effects of their
patronage during our tedious journey through this vale of
tears ; but more especially when approaching death points
out the term of our existence, the final completion of our
mortal pilgrimage, the crisis when the insidious arts of the
great enemy of our salvation are rendered doubly acute by
increased malice and despair, we shall behold those illustrious
heroes of virtue descend from on high to shelter and sustain
us at that awful moment, to inflame with the fire of charity
our departing souls, to pour into them the balm of consolation,
to soften the bitter pang of separation, and cheer our hopes
at the prospect of eternity. In a word, by sheltering us with
the mercy of the Most High, they will preserve in our souls,
amidst the dissolution of our agonising frame, the fire of
faith, of hope, and of love. Thus bearing us victorious over
the power of Satan, they will conduct us in triumph to the
bosom of our God, where the beneficent Creator, recognising
in us features similar to theirs, will give us his paternal benediction, and appointing us seats with them in glory, shall settle
us in everlasting bliss.

" But, on the contrary, if we neglect the emulation of their
actions, and, careless of our salvation, make their celebration
but a mere matter of form, without deriving therefrom any
solid good, we will render ourselves unworthy of their protection either in this life or the next, and insulting the mercy
of God by the contempt or neglect of such helps to salvation
(which may heaven forbid), will make this very devotion
instrumental to our own misery and woe, for whilst we recite
the praise of God in his saints, our actions dishonour both the
one and the other ; we will become objects of horror in his
sight, and at our departing moments, instead of intercessors ;
and in the awful hour of trial, will behold those saints, whom
we have invoked here, rise up in judgment against us, and
bless ten thousand times the equity of that sentence which
would for ever seal our eternal reprobation.

" May that GOD, who is the bountiful giver of all grace

and sanctity, avert from us this worst of evils ; and let us remain ignorant of his saints, than know them thus to our eternal misery ! May He, who is the source of virtue, and glory of his saints enable us at once respectfully to venerate, and faithfully to imitate them, that whilst we are employed in the praises of each one he may interiorly address us in these, his own divine words: ' Observe him and hear his voice ' ; that whilst we speak to God by his saints, He may speak to us by them, and upon this sacred communication may our souls receive daily increase of virtue, as we daily celebrate fresh examples of it ; and through their patronage, may his supreme benediction descend upon this devotion, and all those who practise it, to the glory of his name, the honor of his saints, and our own eternal salvation. Amen."

There are 25 rules. A few important ones may be quoted here :

" That the persons who compose this Confraternity shall be of unblemished character, edifying morals, and devoted to prayer, to spiritual exercises, and charitable offices towards their neighbours, and punctual in the observance of these rules ; no person can become a member who belongs to any society condemned by the Church." They assembled every night in the church at 9 o'clock.

" That if the Blessed Sacrament be kept in the church where the divine office is recited, each member coming in and going out shall adore on his knees in these words : ' I adore you, O Lord Jesus Christ, in the Most Holy Sacrament of the Altar.' And before the office, the short invocation of the Holy Spirit shall be recited, and a commemoration of the Most Holy Sacrament be made."

" That in honor of our Blessed Lord's Passion, the solemn office of Tenebrae be recited in holy week."

" That on each Wednesday evening the office of the Blessed Virgin be solemnly recited in the church according to the instructions laid down in the office book of the Blessed Virgin."

" That the acting president, on receiving notice of the illness of a member, will specially offer the five Paters and Aves in honour of the five adorable wounds of our Lord, for the spiritual comfort and recovery or happy death of the sick member ; and when it is known that he is near death, the prayers of the dying shall then be recited ; and when he has departed this life, the members will recite the office of the dead. And on the seventh day after death, the Holy Sacrifice of the Mass shall be offered for the happy repose of his soul ; also on the thirtieth and anniversary days ; and that the office of the dead be recited on the same evenings."

" That on the death of a relative of a member, within the degree of uncle or aunt, the office of the dead shall be said on the day of decease, thirtieth and anniversary days."

" That the Holy Sacrifice of the Mass be offered on the second Sunday of each month for the Spiritual and temporal welfare of the members, also for the repose of the souls of the deceased members ; and that the office of the dead be recited on the second Monday of each month for the repose of the souls of the departed members and relatives, and that the above intention be annually entered on the altar list of the dead."

" That it shall be the duty of the members to attend in the church of SS. Michael & John's at the 8 o'clock Mass on the 2nd Sunday of each month, to receive Holy Communion."

The Confraternity felt itself so indebted to Father Young that it passed a resolution (13th June, 1824) that " a subscription be entered into to testify our gratitude to him for his part services to us." The testimonial was presented to him, 18th September, 1825, when the Minutes record that " Rev. H. Young returned thanks for the donation." It may be taken that his retention of the donation was as brief as his reply, and that he gave the money in charity soon after he left the meeting-room. Such gifts he invariably bestowed upon the poor, who followed him wherever he went.

5. The Evening Office Confraternities

The foundation of SS. Michael and John's Evening Office Confraternity was laid in Derby square under Rev. Dr. Betagh, S.J., when parish priest. The inspiration came from Peter Kenney, a former pupil in Dr. Betagh's school in

Saul's-court. Peter used to assist his master in the Derby square evening school and gather some of the boys to recite Vespers there. He was then at business and about 21 years of age. The Minute books of the Confraternity state (11th March, 1832) that " the institution [Confraternity] was founded nearly 40 years ago by the Revd. Petr. Kenny, S.J., under the auspices of the late venerable and very Revd. Doctor Betagh from whom it received every support." A framed list of the " Regulators of the Choir, Rectors and Superiors " mentions that the Confraternity was founded in 1799. Peter Kenny's name appears among the " Regulators," " Rectors " and " Superiors." The list must have been made out between 1799 and 1802, as in the latter year Dr. Betagh sent Peter to Carlow College for his higher studies.

In the list of the Deceased Members special mention is made of " The Rev. Dr. Peter Kenny, Founder of the Evening Office Society. Died at Rome, 19 Nov. 1841, in the 63 year of his age. Three offices to be recited namely one on the 9th Dec., one on the 16th to be a Public Office at which all the branch societies and the several confraternities are invited to assist, and one on the 20 Dec. 1841, and an anniversary officc to which the branch societies shall also be invited. The Proper Prayer to be recited each night from the first Office to the 30th day (but one office for a priest or monk ; the Revd. Dr. Kenny being the founder forms an exception)."[1]

The List includes the years from 1821 to 1853, and shows that the members were entitled to offices on the day of death, the 7th day, the 30th day and the anniversary.

As to the newly organised confraternity, whose Minute Book we happily possess, it came into being immediately after the building of SS. Michael and John's church in Smock-alley, under the new pastor, Rev. Dr. Blake. Unfortunately the first volume of the Minutes has been lost owing to the zeal of the president about fifty years ago, who took the volume to write up the history of the Confraternity for a new edition of Father Young's Evening Office under the direction of V. Rev. Dr. Tynan, P.P. of SS. Michael and John's. The

[1] For an interesting account of Father Kenney see *Irish Jesuit Directory* (1941), pp. 193–216.

volume was never restored to the Confraternity archives. The present volume begins at 1819. The loss of the first volume is deplorable as it would have shown the beginnings and struggles of the society. The present volume shows the society as well established and in perfect working order.

In the early period the Confraternity's chief concern was to have an edition of the Evening Office for every day in the year—it met every evening for the recitation of Vespers and Complin. It was intent on the proper liturgical recitation of the Evening Office.

For laymen it was somewhat difficult to understand the liturgical arrangement of Vespers for every day in the year. The parent branch mastered it under the tuition of Father Henry Young, and it was ready to instruct the members of the other branches. Apparently the Evening Office originally consisted in the recitation of the Vespers of the Sunday, but, on the publication of Father Young's Office Book, the Vespers would be of the feast of the day. The parent branch proposed (8th June, 1823) " that a deputation of two members wait on the Gentlemen [clergy] of James's St. Chapel to know will it be agreeable to have the young men of the Confraternity instructed to recite the Evening Office of the Church."

The Rules for the " recitation " of the Office were drawn up by Father Young, and were transcribed by Mr. Ambrose Sullivan to whom the thanks of the Council were offered for their " grand style." The manuscript copy that we have is certainly copied in " grand style " and is probably the one referred to. Father Young's " Preface to the Rules " was a matter of great importance for the proper recitation of the Office, and the Council ordered it to be printed (11th June, 1826). It was sold at 2d. per copy, and the printer, Mr. Sheerin, was a member of the Confraternity. The Rules were read on the fourth Sunday in each month by the Acting President at the recitation of the Office.

In an address of SS. Michael and John's Confraternity to their new pastor,[1] Rev. Andrew O'Connell, (11th March, 1832) the objects of the Confraternity are set out :

[1] Rev. Dr. Blake had been transferred to St. Andrew's for the purpose of building a new church.

" The above Society has for its object the Glory of Almighty God and the sanctification of its members by the recital of these inspired psalms and anthems so calculated to elevate the soul and inflame it with the love of Him to whose honour they are recited. Revd. Sir, May we request of you to patronize our humble efforts, and enable us to continue this religious exercise so pleasing to the Divine Majesty, and may that God, whose minister you are, long preserve to the church a name dear to our religion and our country to distil the waters of life from the Sacred Volumes and to break the bread of Angels to the little ones."

The meeting-place of the Society had been, up to 9th March, 1823, in Father Betagh's old school-house, 4 Derby-square, where the members recited the Evening Office. It would appear that a few months afterwards the Evening Office Confraternity was accommodated in the church. A resolution (8th June) states : " that the appointed President, Antiphonaries and Assistants, if they cannot attend constantly during their week, they are requested to send notice to the chapel to that effect in order to keep up that regularity so essential in religious societies."

The Society soon began to provide furnishings in the chapel for their requirements. They " commenced using our new Candlesticks on 25 Dec. 1823," " got our new desk in Jan. 1824," and ordered " that in order to keep our little things that we have for the use of the office safe, a new lock and three keys be purchased for the press in the chapel." On 14th March, 1824, it agreed " that if it meet the approbation of the Very Rev. Dr. Blake that we all assemble at the chapel at 3 o'cl. on Easter Sunday morning to recite the office of the Blessed Virgin Mary." The permission was granted, and the recitation of the Office on Christmas morning as well as at Easter was carried out on a grand scale in subsequent years. The Office of the Blessed Virgin was usually recited at 2 a.m. and the Office of the Day at 3 o'clock, and two dozen wax candles were lighted.

The elaborate arrangement for the recitation and singing of the Office on Christmas morning (1832) deserves to be quoted in full :

" First Cantata.   Gloria in Excelsis.

Second, the Veni Creator, or the invocation of the Divine
Spirit.

Third, the O Sacrum, at the Commemoration of the
Blessed Sacrament.

Fourth, at the end of the Office of the Alma, the Litany
of Blessed Virgin Mary, and conclude with the Adeste
Fedeles.

May everlasting Praise, Honour, Power, Glory, Benedic-
tion, and Adoration be ever given to our Adorable
Lord and Saviour Jesus Christ in the Most Holy and
Adorable Sacrament of the Altar."

As to the candlesticks and the desk already mentioned, the
Council passed a vote of thanks to all members concerned
(March, 1824) :

" Thanks to John J. Ennis for his gift of our elegant new
and superb desk and for his zealous exertions to promote the
welfare of this society.   That the label engraved at his expense
and presented by John Kelly be put on the desk.

" Thanks to Mr. James McEvoy for his gratuitous labour
in making the new wooden candlesticks and cross.

" Thanks to Mr. John Cullen for his gratuitous labour in
turning the same.

" Thanks to Mr. John Lennon for his gratuitous labour in
painting the candlesticks and cross.

" Thanks to Mr. Kelly for his gift of our new Japaned
sconces.

" Thanks to Mr. Luke Sheridan for his gratuitous labour
in printing the very appropriate summonses."

Thus, besides merchants and shopkeepers, the Society
included craftsmen such as carpenters, turners, metal-workers,
painters and printers.   They were all united in a great
apostolate—the sacrifice of prayer and good example for the
spiritual welfare of the parish.

The sacrifice of these men who gathered night after night
in the church, after their day's work, for the recitation of the
Office was, no doubt, a subject of conversation among the
parishioners, and their good example must have had a salutary

and spiritualising influence among them. These men rightly considered themselves lay apostles. Father Young had already, in his writings, emphasised the merit of this sacrifice.

The Society regarded itself as a " Religious Society," and the recitation of the Office as a sacred duty on the part of the members. The elaborate Rules and Preface, drawn up by Father Young and printed for the various confraternities show all this clearly. Every half-year six presidents (Superiors) and twelve antiphonaries (Rectors) were elected for the ensuing six months to conduct the recitation of the Office. The members were arranged in two choirs, on Epistle and Gospel side of the church, and each severally had his numbered position. In 1837 there were 43 on each side, and as late as 1859 the same number was present. The members came from various parts of the city. If the officers appointed for the month were unable to attend during the week they were obliged to send due notice so as " to keep up that regularity so essential in religious societies." The acting president of the week was " obliged to devote at least half an hour to the Instruction of the Members to enable them to go through the office in an edifying manner."

Besides the apostolate of self-sacrifice and prayer, the Society engaged in activities that were more directly of a charitable nature. The first of these was provision of Masses for deceased members. This practice seems, as far as we know, to have originated with the Purgatorian, Evening Office, and Christian Doctrine Societies.

One of the original rules of the Confraternity was that seven Masses should be provided for each deceased member. A resolution (3rd November., 1828) ordered that four of the seven Masses should be celebrated immediately before death, when it is ascertained that such person is in danger of death by the will or visitation of God, for the spiritual comfort and happy death of such member." (The honorarium for each Mass was 2s.)

The Council ordered (15th March, 1835) that " the novena of St. Joseph be recited in the Office every year from the 11th to the 19th March ; that the novena of the Sacred Heart of Jesus be recited in the Office every year beginning on the eve of Corpus Christi, the day appointed by the Church ; and the Votive Office of the Blessed Sacrament, on the first vacant Thursday in the month of September, for reparation for any irreverences committed by the members in presence of the Blessed Sacrament in the course of the year."

6. The Christian Doctrine Confraternity

(a). Protestant Opposition

Having spent about two years on the Missions in West Wicklow (see VI.) Father Young returned to the city as assistant-priest in SS. Michael and John's. It was Dr. Blake who was responsible for his recall. We have seen how an entry in the Evening Office Minute Book of that parish stated that he "sailed for Rome from Kingstown Harbour, Tuesday, August 17, 1824." When he had renovated his parish church, in 1819, he started a movement to have his *Alma Mater*, the Irish College at Rome, reopened after its suppression by the French revolutionaries in 1798, gathered a considerable sum of money for burses, and urged the Irish Bishops to support the project. He left Ireland to negotiate the opening of the College, and, after much opposition in Rome, he succeeded, 24th February, 1826, in taking formal possession of the Umbrian College. It was a great disappointment to him that he was appointed its first rector when he wished to return to his parish and superintend its many activities at a difficult time. When he had the College in full working order, Archbishop Murray acceded to his wishes and recalled him to his parish, to which he returned, January, 1829. Shortly afterwards he asked for the co-operation of Father Young for the purpose of putting new life into the various societies of the parish.

Here we must pause awhile to review the education of Catholic children in this important parish, which was the principal centre for the south city. Father Betagh, S.J., parish priest of old St. Michael's, and Vicar-General, was responsible for the Catholic poor schools of the parish. The chief evening school was, as we have seen, in Derby Square, off Werburgh-street, many years before he died in 1811. There was another evening school at the back of the houses on Skinners-row (Christchurch-place) which acquired great notoriety. Archbishop Troy, 23 August, 1803, shortly after the Emmet Rising, informed the Castle Authorities about this school " where the ignorant journeymen, apprentices and labourers are instructed after their work. I mention this lest, from any misapprehension of its design, it should be disturbed or molested by the Police Officers or others."[1]

In the Derby Square school, under Dr. Blake, eighty boys were educated and clothed, twenty-two got breakfast, and sixteen were educated, clothed and fed. To provide for the hundreds of others who received no instruction, he erected the new Christian Doctrine Confraternity in 1818, and had the classes held in the new church in Smock-alley. During his five years in Rome the Catholic position in Dublin had become difficult. These were the years preceding Catholic Emancipation.

The situation is set out in an address of Rev. Dr. Yore, his administrator in SS. Michael and John's (22nd October, 1826), to his Christian Doctrine Confraternity. The Minute Book of the Confraternity has this entry :

" The Rev. Mr. Yore said : It gives always great pleasure in seeing you, and would attend every Sunday, but from circumstances preventing him—Recommends perseverance in Religious instruction, as the best means of Insuring these Children a good life and a happy death—As a proof of the necessity of such instruction he mentioned a circumstance of a dying person whom he attended the day before, who was so immersed in Ignorance that he did not even know what the Rites of the Church were—but this poor unfortunate individual had seen the days of Persecution in this country— he was in his boyhood when the Penal Laws were inflicted with rigour—when these useful institutions were restricted and forbidden, and he partook of the Ignorance and misfortune that was the necessary consequence.

" Remarks that above all things we should attend to order, and obedience to Superiors, that this is a great

[1] *Rebellion Papers*, Record Tower, Dublin Castle, 620/11/160.14.

Characteristic in Catholicity, whereas the reverse is the strongest feature in Heresy, and in it is found the Latent seeds of every mischief—in Union consists your strength—with it every thing can be effected. The Rev. Gentleman then recommended great moderation in our speech and conduct, and said that notwithstanding these observations he felt happy in being able to congratulate himself and them on the good order that prevailed."

In another address (25th February, 1827) he is reported as having said :

"Never was there a period in which our exertions were more required—every thing should be done to promote the knowledge of our Holy Religion—never was such exertion made by our opponents—it is our duty to guard the children of the Fold against the rapacity of these wolves —it appears as if now they were making their last effort, for which reason it behoves us to be more on the alert, as the sting of a dying animal [sic] is the most bitter of all.

"Heretofore many were Catholics by instinct, they did not take the pains to examine, nor to inform themselves of their Religion, they had no solidity—and whilst the ranks of the establishment are filling up with dupes and fanatics, ours are filled from Conviction and Sincerity—during the present time, preparation for Confirmation should be attended to, with these children, who are qualified —hopes that fresh opportunities will occur that he can give us more of his attention, and by our joint exertions, we will be able to marr the efforts of our adversaries."

The Council were rigid in the carrying out of their elaborate rules. The members of the Confraternity were reminded by the President of " the necessity of attending early at the Hour of Catechism, and of being in waiting for the children, in order to impress on them by example the importance of being regular and attentive." He told them that their " duties " were those of " members of a Religious Society—enforcing his arguments with some well selected citations from the Fathers." (25th February, 1827.)

The members, however, were not content with " being in

waiting for the children " ; they went out into the bye-ways of the parish on Sunday mornings to collect the boys playing in the streets, and, if they suspected a boy of giving the wrong address of his parents—as sometimes happened to avoid the labour of learning Catechism—they marched the boy to his home, and were often rewarded by the Catholic mother's consent to take him to the Catechism class.

An interesting resolution of the Council (26th November, 1826) states : " That the duty of seeking after those children (and which has been followed up by volunteers from this Confraternity) be suspended until further notice in consequence of the Prevalence of Fever, Thro' the poorer districts of the City." This was the " Plague " of 1826.

The impoverishment of the Catholic citizens, due to the " Plague," gave the rich Protestant Societies an opportunity of tempting the poverty-stricken Catholics to come to their meeting-houses for food and provide them with anti-Catholic spiritual food. Father Yore, as we have seen, referred to the resurgence of the anti-Catholic spirit. The Christian Doctrine Confraternity of SS. Michael and John's was on the alert and sent out its members into the slums to collect information on the conditions of the impoverished Catholics.

A Report (25th March, 1827) states : " Dr. Duffy visited a number of places and witnessed the most frightful scenes of misery ; recommends that something may be done to afford partial relief to some of those Creatures in extreme cases—in order to rescue them from those temptations with which the enemies of their Religion are constantly assailing them— states that himself and his colleague Mr. Kelly brought in a great number of children, and many more would have attended but in consequence of their wretched condition. Mr. Kelly recommends that particular attention should be paid to Ship-street as there are great numbers of boys there who don't attend Catechism in any Chapel."

" Resolved that a certain Sum be put in the hands of the Volunteers [Visitors] each Month for the use of the poor. The President earnestly recommended that each Member of the Confraternity do exert themselves to procure subscriptions for this purpose."

A member reported (22nd July, 1827) that " he observed several Catholic children brought promiscuously with Protestant children to the church of St. Bridget [Bride-street], and having made inquiry finds it has been going on for some time."

An entry, 23rd December, 1827, in the Minute Books, gives further information. It states that two members reported that they " took the name and residence of thirty-five boys, collected from some of the most deserted and impoverished places in the city, and who are totally ignorant of all idea of Religion—the greater part of whom they gave up to the President—they also succeeded in dissuading the mother of a girl who had hitherto went to the Methodist school in George's-street, to take her away and send her to Catechism in this chapel."   As in the case of St. Michan's, Catholic ladies taught girls in SS. Michael and John's on Sundays.   The arrangement in modern times that the girls should occupy the gallery, and the boys the body of the church, apparently came down from 1818.

Brothers and Sisters of the Christian Doctrine Confraternity were making a determined stand against the wiles of the proselytisers.   The opposition to their efforts was increasing with every move of O'Connell and the Catholic Association towards Emancipation.   The parish of SS. Michael and John's was a strong supporter of the Catholic Association and collected the Catholic rent for its support at the church doors.

The Christian Doctrine Confraternity of SS. Michael and John's considered it a duty to be of assistance to the parochial clergy wherever called upon.   The church required painting, and the Confraternity, 20th August, 1826, voted £5.   New vestments were required, and the Confraternity undertook to collect the money to buy them at a cost of £100.   The members asked the several Christian Doctrine Confraternities in the city to subscribe.   They collected £75, and Father Yore paid the balance " out of his own pocket," 27th January, 1828.

Up to the year 1826 the collectors at the church doors would appear to have been appointed by the clergy—no doubt, from among the principal gentlemen of the parish.   It would seem that the Christian Doctrine Confraternity of SS. Michael and John's was the first to put the matter on a permanent basis. It was resolved (22nd October, 1826) " that this Confraternity do take upon them the Entire Collection for the Clergymen of this Chapel." Thirty-three members gave their names to attend to the collection in turn.

The Council was generous, according to its limited means, in subscribing to various good works. One of the most interesting entries of its subscriptions referred to the Christian Brothers. An entry (28th December, 1828) recited that a letter was received " from the Monks engaged in educating the poor of Ireland asking a portion of the funds to assist them in building a training school in Richmond Place." An entry of 25th January, 1829 refers to the new foundation of the Christian Brothers in North Richmond-street : " Resolved. That two pounds be given to the monks engaged in building a training school at Richmond Place for the Education of the Poor."

Though concise, the resolution contains important points. To appreciate the implications it is necessary to review the situation before the erection of the O'Connell Schools.

Archbishop Murray had applied to Brother Rice to found a school in his mensal parish of St. Mary's. There was in the extensive and populous parish only one wretched and elementary school, in Liffey-street, under a secular master, with a small and irregular attendance. Brother Rice readily accepted the invitation, and, through the help of the parochial clergy and the charitable laity, the house No. 42 Jervis-street, was fitted up as a school and residence, and opened, June, 1827.

There was already a remarkable classical and commercial school in No. 64 Jervis-street, conducted by Father Meagher (afterwards P.P. of Rathmines). Many youths who entered the Sacred Ministry received their early education in this classical school, among them the patriot historian, Father Meehan, to whose brilliant talents and untiring labours Irish literature and history are deeply indebted, and Father Matthew Collier, afterwards P.P. of St. Agatha's. Brother James Hoare was educated in this school, and afterwards taught in the Christian Brothers' School in No. 42 Jervis-street, and subsequently became the third Superior-General of the Congregation. Brother Anthony Maxwell, who became the fourth Superior-General, was likewise educated in No. 64.

The Christian Brothers' school in 42 Jervis-street, was intended as a temporary one, and a new site was purchased by Mr. Bryan Bolger, an architect, off the North-Circular road. The purchase was carried out with the greatest reticence so as to avoid all opposition from bigots and property holders. In 1828, when Catholic Emancipation was a foregone conclusion, Protestant opposition, especially Orange, became daily more manifest. The intention was to drive Catholics into open rebellion and thus defeat the efforts of the Government. The Minutes of the Catholic Association of 1828 show how the Association defeated the Orange plan and succeeded in securing tranquillity throughout the country.

The system of education of the Kildare Place Society by its proselytising practices, had been denounced by the clergy and had been renounced by the Catholic children. O'Connell urged the necessity of a Central Model School for the training of Catholic teachers and recommended that this training school should be connected with the school about to be built by the Brothers. The Catholic Association agreed with the suggestion and voted £1,500 towards the erection of the school. Apparently, the Brothers sent out an appeal to the charitable and religious societies of the city, and the Christian Doctrine Confraternity of SS. Michael and John's accordingly subscribed.

The important point in all this is that the SS. Michael and John's Christian Doctrine Confraternity and the Catholic Association, as voiced by Daniel O'Connell, were immediately concerned with the training school of the Christian Brothers who were to carry out the education of the poor in the parishes of Dublin. They had in view the necessity of more up-to-date education in the parochial schools, and the training of teachers under the guidance of the Christian Brothers at Richmond Place, to defeat the Kildare Place Society system.

In 1821, that portion of the Circular-road between Russell-street and Richmond-street was well built on.[1] Behind a

---

[1] McGregor's, *Picture of Dublin* : see Map.

group of houses on the Circular-road were waste spaces running down Richmond-street that had been merely cut out for building purposes. Mr. Bolger acquired one of those vacant plots for 980 years, 25th March, 1828, for which he paid £210. The foundation of the Catholic Model School was laid by Daniel O'Connell, 9th June, and the school became popularly known as O'Connell school. O'Connell was surrounded by thousands of citizens who had accompanied him in procession from the headquarters of the Catholic Association, the Corn Exchange, Burgh-quay. In his address he stated : " In this national seminary there would be perfect fair play for every class and creed."

Six months after the passing of the Emancipation Act, namely, 8th December, 1829, Mr. Bolger resigned his lease of the Richmond-street school to Brother Rice and two other Brothers. (By his will, 14th December, 1834, he bequeathed all he possessed for the continuation of the good work.) On 23rd June, 1831, the Founder, his two Assistants, one professed Brother, and four novices came from Hanover-street and became the first occupants of the monastery.

The schools were opened, Monday, 4th July, for registration purposes, and 500 applied. On 11th July, 600 boys were marshalled at 42 Jervis-street and marched in processional order to Richmond-street to assist at the blessing and formal opening of the schools.

(b). Sweep-Boys

Another class of child that was a source of anxiety to Dr. Blake was the sweep-boy. On the general subject of sweep-boys a contemporary writer[1] states : " We think the existence of such a trade is a reproach to the policy of any state where it is permitted, but we think the only effective remedy would be to remove the cause . . . the condition of a young sweep is but little improved because he knows how to read and write." The horrible cruelty of a master-sweep to his apprentice, for which he was brought into court, excited the public sympathy and led to the establishment of

[1] Warburton, etc., II, 858.

the Sunday School Society, in 1816, of which the Lord Mayor was a member. " At their first meeting various enormities were reported from the best evidence. Several instances of murder, the constant practice of employing them [the young sweeps] to rob or steal by night ; procuring young females, and using them as boys ; in effect, such a system, cruelty, indecency, and moral depravity, was displayed as degraded the present state of these wretched children far below the level of humanity."

Many of those children were employed by the masters without the usual indenture between master and apprentice, and were thus outside the jurisdiction of the law. It was considered that such a state of affairs should be ended. Moreover, as those children " cannot pursue their trade . . . when they attain too large a stature, and as few can become masters, the great majority, at an adult age, must be thrown upon society without knowledge, principle, or employment. To counteract the present influence, and to qualify them for something better hereafter, a school was established to instruct them in reading, writing, and arithmetic. The trustee of Kellett's bequest[1] readily granted the large rooms of that school for the purpose. Here they assemble every Sunday, a breakfast is provided by the subscriber ; and they are supplied with shirts, cloaks, caps, shoes ; premiums of soap, combs, and money are given to excite a sense of decency and a feeling of cleanliness. . . . About forty attend every Sunday and some of them evince a great desire to learn."

The same writer continues : " We are concerned, however, to state that the charity is for the present [1818] suspended by the interference of their own clergy of the Roman Catholic persuasion, who suspect an intention of proselytising the children. Now, besides the usual precaution of using the Bible and other books of instruction without note or commentary, care is taken here, that no Protestant visitor shall even hold the book out of which the child is instructed, lest he might be suspected of supplying an oral commentary to a book that had none, and instil any doctrine inimical to the Roman Catholic Church . . . we trust these forlorn outcasts will

[1] Kellett's Protestant school in Drumcondra Lane (Lr. Dorset-street).

not be deprived of the new-born sensations of comfort, cleanliness, and wholesome food, by an unfounded suspicion."

Between 1816 and 1818, " a machine for sweeping chimneys was sometime since invented by an ingenious man of the name of Robinson, which was approved of, and recommended, by the [Royal] Dublin Society, to whose examination it was submitted ; it consists of brushes fixed to flexible joints, so as to adapt themselves to the size of the chimney. This machine has been used with much success in Dublin, but it fails where the flues of the chimney are intricate or circuitous.[1] Would it not be possible for the legislature [1818], which taxes hearths, and regulates the size of bricks, to oblige chimneys to be built so as to be accommodated to such a machine, and for the public to supersede the necessity of employing sweeps by encouraging it."

It was Dr. Blake who interfered with the Kellett arrangement and founded the Sweep Department in Derby Square in 1818 ; the Sweep Boys came from the vicinity, namely, Bride-street and Chancery-lane. It had been a long walk for them to Kellett's School, but the inducements were substantial. Because of many examples of proselytism in that period the efforts of the Kellett School were open to grave objections and were not above suspicion.

The members of the Christian Doctrine Confraternity made great efforts to induce them to attend Sunday School at Derby Square where they were taught the rudiments of learning, besides their prayers and catechism. In its early period the school was attended by 61 boys. A decline in the attendance seems to have set in during the absence of Dr. Blake between August, 1824, and January, 1829. He was in Rome during that period, as we have seen, in charge of the Irish College. The first notice of the decline is in a Report of the Derby Square Branch, 24th September, 1826,[2] which states that " the average number of children is from 40–50, including 10 new ones from the last month. The number of teachers

---

[1] The sweep boys could overcome any angles in their ascent in the chimneys until they became of " too large stature."

[2] The Minute Book of the Confraternity which has been preserved begins in August, 1826. No doubt, there was a Minute Book for 1818–1826, but it has been apparently lost.

is now six. Two of their Teachers have last month given in
their resignation . . . it is necessary to fill up their places as
these Sweep children require greater attention than any other,
being entirely destitute of any other mode of instruction."

The Sweep branch went from bad to worse, and the Council
ordered the " Sweep Department " to submit a monthly
report. Mr. Battersby furnished a report, 23rd September,
1827 : " Attendance of Teachers and children very indifferent
—is of opinion that unless they obtain a fresh supply of
Teachers, the assistance of that Branch of the Confraternity
will cease altogether." Apparently this " Department " fell
through, as, at a council meeting, 20th July, 1828, the President
remarked that before assisting other confraternities by supplying teachers they should " re-establish the school for the
instruction of the Sweeps." A few months afterwards, 25th
January, 1829, Dr. Blake, lately returned from Rome, stated
at a council meeting that " he would take the liberty of
recommending the poor little sweeps as one of the greatest
objects of charity. There are at present (said he) about
twenty of those objects attending the School of St. John's
Society and not more than two or three gentlemen to instruct
that number ; if any gentleman would have the goodness
to give me his name that would be disposed to instruct those
poor little ones I shall feel obliged."

It was about this time that Dr. Blake had Father Young
recalled from the Wicklow Missions to SS. Michael and
John's to look after the Catechism Classes, and apparently
the " Sweep Department." At all events, for a whole year
there is no complaint registered in the Minute Books about
the department. It may be taken then that during that year
it was a success, thanks to the efforts of Father Young. Unfortunately, in September, 1829, a difference of opinion arose
between him and the Confraternity Council as to the length
of time he preached to the Catechism classes in the church,
the Council considering that his lengthy discourse left them
not sufficient time for teaching Catechism. Dr. Blake said
that he would settle the matter, but, apparently, Father
Young considered his missionary efforts of more importance
than preaching at Catechism classes, and it would seem that

he considered the time had come for him to continue missionary work. He went to North Co. Dublin towards the end of 1929.

It is significant that the " Sweep Department " soon registered a decline. The first report for a whole year, 28th March, 1830, states : " This branch was for want of teachers on the verge of dissolution ; they wanted members to second the efforts of the members engaged in the school. At a former period some of the members got 61 of these forlorn and destitute children to attend the Sunday school where they were afforded religious instruction—and many of them taught to read and write and keep accounts—and it was edifying to see the improvement in their habits and morals in a short time notwithstanding their low and degraded state. The work was going on since 1818."

The " Sweep Department " was reorganised ; an entry two months afterwards (16th May, 1830) states that there were four members appointed to assist the two members in charge of the Department every Sunday during the hours of instruction and that they were to be changed monthly. The Council went further, and decided that a director of the Sweep Department should be appointed every six months. The work had been set on practical lines, but unfortunately its subsequent history is unknown as the Minutes terminated shortly afterwards. The efforts of Dr. Blake and Father Young were at last bearing fruit.

(c). Christian Doctrine Classes

The Council of the Confraternity met in the parochial house at 12 o'clock once a month on Sunday. The members taught catechism from 1 to 2 o'clock. The recitation of the Acts of Faith, Hope, and Charity, according to the Rule, concluded the catechising.

Examinations were held quarterly and premiums were distributed among the deserving boys. An interesting list of the book premiums is given (15th October, 1826) : Lessons for Lent ; New Testament ; Virtuous Scholar ; Poor Man's Manual ; Think Well On't ; Burning Lamp ; Fifty Reasons ;

Defence of Catholic Principles ; Explanation of Mass ; True Wisdom ; Prayer Books ; Lover of Christ ; Spiritual Combat ; Shield of Catholic Faith ; Life of Christ ; Ardent Lover ; Hidden Treasure ; England's Book ; Letter to a Protestant Friend ; P. of Love of God ; Forty Maxims ; Net for the Fishers of Men ; Method of Conversing with God; Hayes's Sermons. Other premium books (October, 1830) were : Vespers and Evening Office ; Imitation of Christ ; Old and New Testament ; Shortest Way ; Catholic Piety ; History of New Testament ; Love of Jesus.

In February, 1829, the numbers in the five classes were 40 (Prayer), 200 (First Size Catechism), 191 (Second Size), 45 (Historical), and 19 (Abridgement), namely, 495 in all, taught by 64 members. It was about this time that Father Young was appointed to superintend the classes. He considered that it was his duty to preach to the children and that twenty minutes out of the hour for Catechism was not too long a time for his sermons.

The Council were annoyed at his breach of their Rules, and they entered in their Minute Book (20th September, 1829) that the " Rev. Mr. Young now preaches for 20 minutes to children instead of the Acts [of Faith, Hope, and Charity] ; only half an hour was then available for instruction. Dr. Blake, communicated with, said he would speak to Father Young not to interfere with the Rules. The Confraternity praise the pious and laudable exertions of Father Young to promote the Instruction of the Children and asked him to attend their Council meetings. He replied that his parochial duties did not allow him time."

We have already seen how Father Young had received from Prince Hohenlohe three pictures, of the Redeemer, the Blessed Virgin, and St. Mary Magdalen. He had copper plate engravings made from them, the plates of which cost nine guineas, and he had presented the engravings to the widow Collier of Harold's Cross to support herself by their sale. He had also a copper plate engraving made of a picture of the Sacred Heart. He put the plates before the Confraternity, 18th October, 1829.

The Confraternity reported (25th October, 1829) that the

plates were worth about 23s., but were worth more to them
for premiums. Three of the plates would give 2,000 im-
pressions, but the fourth (of the Sacred Heart) was of no
value. They offered £1 6s. 0d. to Mrs. Collier.

The Council decided (17th January, 1830) on using the
plates as follows : 500 copies were to be made of the three
pictures ; 200 of each plate were to be given to the teachers ;
50 of each were to be given as premiums to the boys, with
the inscription : " Obtained as a Premium from the Christian
Doctrine Confraternity of SS. Michael and John's, Dublin."
The pictures for the teachers were on " proof paper " and
cost 4s. per 100, and those for the boys, on plain paper, cost
3s. 3d. per 100.

The Confraternities were assisted very materially by the
Catholic Book and Tract Society, 5 Essex-Bridge, Parliament-
street, whose title states that it was " for the diffusion of useful
knowledge throughout Ireland." The Society was set up by
the Bishops of Ireland, 9th March, 1827. Its objects were :
(1) to furnish to the people of Ireland in the cheapest and
most convenient manner useful information on the truths
and duties of the Christian religion ; (2) to supply to all
classes of persons satisfactory refutations of the prevailing
errors and heresies of the present age ; (3) to assist in supplying
to schools throughout Ireland the most approved books of
elementary instruction.

The Council of the Confraternity voted a subscription of
£1 for the year to the Catholic Tract Society, and they
purchased books and premiums from the Society. The
Council paid to the Society 6s. for 24 of Fleury's Historical
Catechism, and ordered copies of Vespers in English and Latin
published by St. John's Society. It is desirable, they stated,
that the Vesper book should be in the hands of the children
of all confraternities. They were initiating the young into
a love for the Liturgy in the hope that they would become
members of the Evening Office Confraternity.

At a meeting of the Catholic Association at the Corn
Exchange, Burgh Quay, 23rd October, 1828, a resolution
was proposed to grant £300 to the Catholic Book and Tract
Society. O'Connell supported the grant and gave notice that

on an early day he would apply for a grant of £200 more. He did so not only to assist the good work of the Society, but as a protest against the Kildare Place Society. " The regulations of the Kildare Place Society," he said " are a living lie. They have the stamp and brand of falsehood upon · them."[1]

At this time the principal members of the Tract Society were the V. Rev. Dr. Coleman, P.P., V.G., St. Michan's ; the V. Rev. Dean Lube, P.P., St. James's ; the V. Rev. Dr. Glynn, Adm., St. Mary's, and the V. Rev. Father Flanagan, P.P., St. Nicholas's. In support for their appeal for a grant from the Catholic Association they stated that they had in the press works amounting to 61,000 copies. They were selling at a cheap rate to poor schools thousands of spelling books, tablets, copy books, slates, pencils and quills, and reams of paper. They " printed and disseminated " in the year " about half a million Books, Tracts, and Catechisms . . . at a saving of full of one third of former prices to the public." An objection by one of the members of the Catholic Association was to the effect that this was unfair competition against the ordinary printers and publishers. O'Connell replied : " A grievance of this kind is created by all similar improvement, and although a few persons may be injured by the reduced prices of the Society's books, it is their duty to give education to the people on as cheap terms as possible." [2] It is interesting to add that the annual outlay of the Society was at this time about £7,200. It will be useful to add here that, during the next nine years, it had printed and published " five million books that would have been circulated at one-half or one-third the price, saving the public a half million of money," and, it was claimed that " it has produced a spirit of enlightened piety, and a readable habit so essential to improve the character of the people at large."[3]

Between 1827 and 1835 the poverty of the people in the country districts seems to have increased, and their purchasing power, even of the cheap tracts and books of the Catholic

[1] *Minutes of the Catholic Association* (in my possession.
[2] l.c. See *Catholic Rent of 1828*, *I.E.R.*, Nov., 1942.
[3] Battersby, *Catholic Directory*, 1836 (introduction).

Tract Society, diminished. In 1835, the Archbishops and Bishops of Ireland established the "Catholic Society for Ireland" to "collect means to circulate the books already printed, or hereafter printed gratuitously where they cannot otherwise be purchased even at the present low rate of the Catholic Book Society—a valuable auxiliary to the Catholic Book Society." It aimed at "the gratuitous distribution of religious books and for promoting the Catholic Religion at home and abroad." The Catholic emigrants in England and Australia were to be provided for, and the Society was in touch with the priests in those missions. Furthermore, it had as its object " to assist the clergy with books in Irish and English, to promote the formation of parochial libraries, to supply Catholic soldiers, sailors, convicts, inmates of institutions with prayer books and other works, and circulate tracts against Drunkenness."

The Christian Doctrine Confraternity spread its tentacles in many directions. Newgate Prison in Green-street was an object of its mercy. The prison was begun in 1773 to take the place of the old Newgate prison at Cornmarket, and was opened for prisoners in 1781 at a cost of £16,000. Here were imprisoned several of the United Irishmen of 1798, followers of Robert Emmet, 1803, and Mitchell and others of the Young Ireland Party, 1848. Beside it was erected the Green-street courthouse in 1797 where all the State trials of 1798, 1803, 1848, and 1867, were held. The Sheriff's Prison was built in 1794 to prevent the abuses of private prisons, or of "Sponging Houses," where persons arrested for debt exceeding £10 were usually lodged (the prison is now the Gárda Barracks). The abuses in this Department were appalling, and ceased only in 1864. Newgate Prison ceased in 1863, and became a fruit market. It was finally demolished in 1893, and the site was converted into a public park.

The deplorable condition of the inmates of Newgate appealed to the members of SS. Michael and John's Confraternity as a work of mercy, and the Council (November, 1826) wrote to the Rev. Mr. Archbold, apparently the Catholic chaplain of the prison, inquiring as to the hours at which the members might attend and the time that might be allowed them for their instruction to the prisoners. Father Archbold replied from 37 Eccles-street that 12 o'clock (if that suited) on Sunday would be a convenient time and that he would attend to introduce them.   Accordingly seven members volunteered to assist at teaching in Newgate, among them being Mr. McWeeney and Mr. Battersby.

A report of those members stated " that several of those gentlemen who volunteered for the service went there re- peatedly without being able to obtain an introduction, or to see the Rev. Mr. Archbold ; at length they succeeded in seeing him, upon which he informed them that in consequence of some Political feeling existing among the officers of the Prison, he had at present an objection to their being intro- duced. (NOTE : it appeared that something or other had befallen a great church and state champion, and those other heroes think it wise to look to their own safety). . . . The Rev. Mr. Archbold said he felt himself greatly indebted to the Gentlemen of the Confraternity for their kindness and attention."

Apparently the " great church and state champion " was Archbishop Murray ; the title was intended to be compli- mentary to him as a great Churchman and a loyal supporter of the Constitution, but he had disappointed the members of the Confraternity in giving way to the objections of the officers of the prison.

As the parent or foster-parent of many Confraternities, SS. Michael and John's was much concerned with their wel- fare. The first reference in its Minute Books to the Meath- street branch is of 15th October, 1826 : "Resolved that from the Reports received from time to time this Committee is fully convinced that thro' the instrumentality of four members deputed by this Confraternity to assist in the Con- fraternity of Meath-street chapel great advantages have accrued to that Confraternity, it being remodelled for the greater part on the principal of our own they having adopted at the suggestion of these deputies the recital of the office of the Blessed Sacrament—Removal of abuses—augmenting their council to 12—procuring Forms [benches]—classification of the children—monthly meetings—cheque [check] lists—Masses for deceased Members, and the Establishment of the Evening Office (thro' which the members of their Confraternity had been greatly increased)."

During Dr. Blake's absence in Rome his place was taken as administrator by Father Yore, who was also spiritual director of the Confraternity. On the return of Dr. Blake, Father Yore was appointed parish priest of St. Paul's, and an address to him was voted by the Council (18th May, 1828) which was read to him the following Sunday. Two months afterwards (20th July) Father Yore requested the Council to co-operate with him in establishing Catechetical Instruction in his new parish and in reviving the Confraternity. The Council sent two of its members to carry out the work. It was reported (26th July, 1829) that the Arran-quay Confraternity and catechism classes were then on a proper basis, that the children numbered 200 and the teachers 28. Four members of SS. Michael and John's Confraternity were at that time assisting in St. Paul's.

An address was drawn up by St. Paul's Confraternity to that of SS. Michael and John's on the subject of the loan of the four members, whom they praised for their valuable assistance.

It will be useful to consider now the Catholic publications that had been printed in Dublin since 1815, when Father Young began his priestly labours in St. Michan's. As a supplement to the list of books given as premiums they will show what spiritual helps were being provided by the clergy for their Catholic people, young and old.

NOTE

The Primer, or Office of the Blessed Virgin Mary. 1818. (Wm. Pickering, 8 Great Strand Street.)

Society of St. Patrick for promoting the exercise of the Spiritual and Corporal Works of Mercy. 1821. (Coyne, 74 Cook-street. Price 2d.)

Two Sermons, Palm Sunday, 1811, Death of Dr. Betagh, and 4th Nov., 1821, on Religious Education. By V. Rev. Michael Blake, D.D. 1821. (Coyne, 4 Capel-street.)

Key of Heaven, Manual of Prayer, 21st edition. Revised by Rev. M. B. Keogh, P.P., Howth. 1823. (R. Grace, 3 Mary Street.)

Prince Hohenlohe's Prayer Book, or the Christian praying in the spirit of the Catholic Church, translated from the German. 1823. (R. Grace, 3 Mary Street.)

Memorial of a Christian Life. Four books from the Spanish of Rev. Father Lewis de Granada, O.P. 5th ed., revised. By Rev. Father J. L'Estrange, O.C.D. 1824.

Explanation of Prayers and Ceremonies of the Holy Sacrifice of the Mass. Printed for the Christian Doctrine Confraternities of Ireland. 1825.

Key of Paradise, opening the gate to Eternal Salvation. New edition. 1827. (Coyne.)

Observations on the Laws and Ordinances which exist in Foreign States, Relative to the Religious Concerns of their Roman Catholic Subjects. By Rev. John Lingard. 1817. (Coyne, 16 Parliament-street.)

Shield of the Catholic Faith, or Tertullian's Prescriptions, translated from the Latin. A General Answer to all Traducers of the Roman Catholic Church. 1823. (Coyne, 74 Cooke-street.)

Defence of Catholic Principles in a Letter to a Protestant Minister in America. By Demetrius Gallitozin, Priest. 3rd ed. Originally printed in America, 1823. (Wogan, 28 Merchant's Quay.)

Abridgment of Christian Doctrine. By H.T. Revised by Jas. Doyle, D.D. 1827. (Coyne, 4 Capel-street.)

Manual of Controversies clearly demonstrating the truth of the Catholic Religion. By H.T. (Dublin, 1821.)

Rules for the Direction of Christian Doctrine and Purgatorian Societies in country parishes. 1832. (Warren, Dublin. 2s. 6d.)

Grounds of the Catholic Doctrine contained in the Profession of Faith, published by Pope Pius IV, for the reception of converts into the church, by way of question and answer. 1832. (Warren, Dublin.)

(d). *Christian Doctrine Branches*

SS. Michael and John's Christian Doctrine Confraternity founded branches and supplied members to assist them in various parishes. Of the nine parishes in the city proper five were still working with the 1749 chapels, with their lack of proper accommodation for Sunday Catechism classes. In fact, it was not until after the Emancipation year, 1829, that any further move was made in building modern churches, the first being in the case of St. Andrew's, Westland Row, in 1831.

Though the chapels were small the religious urge was vigorous. This urge was being fostered by the parochial societies of SS. Michael and John's, under the inspiration of Dr. Blake and Father Young. The Christian Doctrine Confraternity, especially felt a sense of parental responsibility and made heroic efforts for the education of adults and children in Christian Doctrine in many parishes. One of its most beneficent efforts was in connection with the Mendicity Institute in Moira House,[1] Usher's Island, in 1826.

[1] " Of those which have ' come down in the world,' probably the most striking instance is that of Moira House, the once palatial residence of Lord Moira, afterwards Marquess of Hastings, a determined upholder of Irish rights. . . . one of the most magnificent palaces in Europe. It had then three storeys, the uppermost of which has been removed, and the drawing-rooms on the second floor extended the full

The history of this Institute is of supreme interest and importance and the work of SS. Michael and John's Confraternity in Moira House was outstanding in charity and zeal. The Institute was founded, 26th January, 1818, for the relief of distress and to suppress street begging, and took over the premises of the Dublin Society in Hawkins-street when that body purchased Leinster House. It was founded during the worst epidemic of fever, 1817–1819, for a hundred years. It was one of typhus, which began in September, 1817, and brought famine in its wake. A Sub-Committee of Health was set up to report on the progress of the epidemic. Its first report showed that about 1,400 patients were being received per month in the two Fever Hospitals, Cork-street and Hardwicke (N. Circular-road and Lr. Dorset-street). The numbers per month went on increasing until, 26th September, 1818, the date of the Fifth Report, when the numbers admitted were reported as over 2,400 per month, and "many were rejected for want of accommodation and thrown back upon the healthy population of Dublin." The Report further states that " 22,000 patients were received in the last 13 months (i.e. since September, 1817) into the Fever Hospitals, of whom 1,000 have died." Thus, one in twenty-two of those admitted in that period died. As evidence that the disease, in the first year, increased with the months, 8,000 were reported as having been admitted between September, 1817 and February, 1818, whilst between February and September, 1818 15,000 patients were admitted.[1]

It is calculated that, in the whole period of the fever, 1817–19, about 42,000 people were admitted to the Fever Hospitals, and that one in eighty of the total population died, either at home or in the hospitals,[2] namely about 2,250. As the number of deaths for the first thirteen months was given as

length of the house. The 'octagon room' with a window the sides of which were inlaid with mother-of-pearl, John Wesley in 1775 'was surprised to observe, though not more grand, yet a far more elegant room than any he had seen in England.' Here Pamela, wife of Lord Edward Fitzgerald, was the guest of the Dowager-Countess, when her husband was arrested at No. 151 Thomas Street." (Fitzpatrick, *Dublin* (1907), pp. 261, 314.)

[1] *Typhus Fever Epidemic,* Record Tower, Dublin Castle, C.S., O.P., II., 565/474.
[2] Maxwell, *Dublin Under the Georges,* 120.

1,000, the decline in the death-rate was considerable for the remaining months of 1818, and the months of 1819. Organisation and care, no doubt, improved with the experience of doctors and nurses, who devoted themselves whole-heartedly to the enormous burden placed upon them. The letters of the eminent doctors of the period, preserved in Dublin Castle, show their zeal in the cause of the poor.

" In 1817 the outbreak of typhus seems to have been caused by unemployment and poverty after the war [Napoleonic], a scarcity of provisions, and deterioration in the quality of food, following a bad harvest ; and once it set in in the over-crowded state of the houses, together with insanitary practices such as the sleeping of several in a bed and infrequent changes of clothing among the poorer classes, rapidly spread the infection. It was the opinion of Dr. Whitley Stokes, who was well acquainted with the condition of the Dublin poor at the time, that sickness among them was due chiefly to dirt and to want of ventilation in their houses."[1]

As prevention is better than cure, the Sub-Committee of Health, in their reports were much concerned with it. They stated in their Fifth Report that they " had formerly recommended the establishment of dispensaries for the relief of general disease, and the adoption of measures for the suppression of contagious fever, but these measures were not adopted, and consequently the public health of the city has been endangered and injured, and the mendicants augmented."[2]

On the relation between disease and poverty the First Report used strong language : " In Dublin there did not exist a more prolific source of pauperism, wretchedness and mendicity than disease. . . . Few are aware of the numbers reduced by it from a state of comparative independence and comfort to one of utter destitution. . . . Of 588 mendicants supported by the Mendicity Association, 225 were reduced to that state by Fever in the family, 223 by general disease, and 140 by various misfortunes. . . . The great majority of the applicants to the Association consist of persons discharged from the Fever Hospitals. . . . Portion of the funds of the

[1] l.c.   [2] Warburton, *Hist. of Dub.* 737–40.

Mendicity Association could not be better spent than in the prevention of disease." The Mendicity Institute in Hawkins-street had erected a dispensary and cleansing-house nearby—in Poolbeg-street—four months before the date of the Report, and many months before the Public Authorities had made up their minds about the recommendations of the Report.[1]

Dr. Whitley Stokes, whose name is prominent in the Castle correspondence of the time, adds interesting details, and confirms the Fifth Report, on this subject : " Sickness was a dreadful aggravation of the distress of the poor " for when it "seizes on any two or three efficient persons of the family the rest are obliged to pawn their clothes and contract debts which they cannot pay for a long time after. When they recover they may relapse for want of covering or be obliged to stay from work for the same reason. . . . The same cause often prevents them from sending their children to school, and having them taught some method of earning their bread."[2]

It was all a great vicious circle—unemployment and poverty and dirt, disease, and still more poverty etc.—whilst the Public Authorities were perusing a huge correspondence and doing little else, and the charitable public were active, especially in the Mendicity Institute. The Institute had already adopted its plan of relief :

" The paupers are divided into seven classes : 1st. Those who are able to work at productive employments, such as spinners, knitters, straw-plaiters, and rug-makers, to whom wages are paid for work done, at its full value, as rated by the committee. Secondly, Paupers who are able and willing to work, but whose earnings are not adequate to their support, as street-sweepers, pickers of oakum, clothes-menders, etc., these are paid wages also, but at a medium low rate. Thirdly, Such as are unable to perform full work, who receive barely sufficient to support life. Fourthly, The infirm, who are fed, lodged and clothed. Fifthly, Children over six years, who are educated and instructed in useful employments. To these one meal a day is given with a portion of their earnings.

[1] Record Tower, Dublin Castle, C.S. 565/474.
[2] Maxwell, op. cit., 121.

Sixthly, Children under six years, who are fed and taken care of whilst the parents are earning their bread, and Seventhly, the sick and maimed, who are sent to appropriate hospitals, or receive medical attendance at their own habitations."

The Institute soon started technical education for the children of the mendicants, more or less on the lines laid down by Teresa Mullaly in St. Michan's parish. It acquired nearby "a large house in Fleet-street, where they have established school and work-rooms for the children. Of the children employed in straw-plaiting, forty-two have been taken into the employment of different shop-keepers, and twenty-four have gone into service. Twenty-four children employed in the spinning-school, have been provided for elsewhere, and are now in a fair way of bettering their condition. The lace-school is in a very flourishing state, and nearly all the children have been enabled to clothe themselves during the winter by depositing their earnings in a savings-bank. The adults, who are able to work, are employed in the manufacture of woollen nets and hair quilts, making up clothes for the poor, picking oakum, pulverising oyster-shells, spinning flax and tow, etc. The disbursements for the year 1819 amounted to near £10,000, whereas the expenditure of the last (year 1820) did not exceed £5,182 (including the various expenses incurred by the removal to Copper-Alley) which is the strongest proof that can be given of the efficacy of the plan, and the energy with which it has been followed up. The number of poor under the care of the Institution on the 2nd April, 1819, was 2,096, now [1821] it is reduced to 961 ; the remainder have left the city, returned to habits of industry, or, if they beg, it is by stealth." The chief reason was, however, that those affected by the fever of 1817–19 had gone back to work.

Among "the benefits that have already resulted from the establishment of this Association. . . . It has supplied not only the bodily but the spiritual wants of those who had seldom heard the name of their God, unless joined with imprecations ; the paupers attend public worship within the walls of the Institution, and Sunday Schools are also maintained, where adults as well as children receive religious instruction from competent persons of their own persuasions. . . . The Association is under the patronage of the Lord Lieutenant, and its officers are a President, who is the Lord Mayor, twelve Vice-Presidents, a Treasurer, Secretary, and a managing committee of sixty."[1]

The Institute soon realised that Hawkins-street was not the proper centre of its activity ; it should remove westwards ; and it removed to Saul's-court (Copper-Alley) off Fishamble-street, in 1820. It would be interesting to know if it took over Fr. Betagh's old seminary, as about this time, Rev. Dr. Doyle moved it to Castle-street. The Institute once more realised that westwards was its call—adjacent to the poverty-stricken district of the Liberties, the once most industrious part of the city. Fortunately, the palatial residence of Lord Moira was thrown on the market and the Governors wisely purchased it (1821) and the Institute became one of the most influential in the cause of charity for all creeds. Its object was entirely different from that of the Roomkeepers' Society that brought relief in an unostentatious manner to what may be called the better class poor. The poor who flocked to the Mendicity Institute on Sundays made no secret of their poverty—they were down-and-outs, and had little or no education. The need of the apostolic labours of Catholic and Protestant social workers was abundant, and the poor of all creeds were treated alike. Thus, a head-line was set which unfortunately, was not copied by other Institutes that catered for all creeds.

The first reference in the Minute Books of SS. Michael and John's Christian Doctrine Confraternity to its branch in the Mendicity Institute is an entry, 27th August, 1826, where is included a report from the branch stating that the number of their teachers who attend there were about ten or twelve whose attendance was most regular and satisfactory ; the number of children instructed was about 40 or 50, who were well supplied with books, and a priest attended once a week. The Confraternity subscribed to the support of the branch and supplied 1st., 2nd. and 3rd. size Catechisms. That there were children there who were fit for 3rd. size

---

[1] McGregor, *New Picture of Dublin.* (Archer, Dame-street, 1821) pp. 241-45

Catechism shows that their early education had not been neglected.

The branch had its own president but, apparently (28th January, 1827) it was not in a satisfactory condition as only three teachers attended regularly to teach " 40 or 50 children besides Hundreds of Adults who are totally ignorant of religion, and in a wretched condition for want of instruction." It was resolved that a Committee be appointed for that Institution, and that letters be sent to the various Confraternities asking them to attend a meeting on Palm Sunday at 11 o'clock, 1827, at Moira House, to put the branch on a proper basis. The following Confraternities were written to : Metropolitan, James's-street, Townsend-street, Bridge-street, French-street, John-street, Church-street, Arran-quay, Francis-street, Clarendon-street, Anne-street, Hardwicke-street, and Denmark-street.

Only seven presidents of the thirteen written to attended at Moira House, namely, Metropolitan, Denmark-street, SS. Michael and John's, James's-street, Arran-quay, John-street and Anne-street. These seven promised that "three persons from each Confraternity with one or two exceptions should attend to teach the Adults every Sunday."

That was a noble promise for, notwithstanding the precautions taken in 1818, fever again broke out in the city in 1826, and the Liberties were again the most infected area. A doctor in the Meath Hospital reported[1] that " sheds were built, canvas tents were erected, their floors covered with hay, on which the crowds of patients conveyed to the hospital in carts were literally spilled out. . . . In fact so immense was the number of sufferers that it became impossible to bestow medical care upon them all, indeed a large number of them got no medicine whatever, but all received reasonable care and comfort."

" The greater part of the Liberty," says another writer[2] " now presents (1821) a most wretched appearance ; and in times of public scarcity, or sickness, the situation of the lower classes of its inhabitants has been appalling to humanity."

[1] Maxwell, op. cit., 121.
[2] Record Tower, Dublin Castle, C.S., O.P., II., 565/474.

It was this fresh outbreak of fever that deterred many of the Christian Doctrine Confraternities from coming into this infected area. Yet, the other Confraternities were prepared to face the ordeal. They promised that about 21 teachers from the seven parishes would attend the adults, and that the " confraternities of St. James's and St. Michael and John's should each supply the Mendicant children with seven teachers" (15th April, 1827). In January (27), 1828, there were 120 children and about 12 teachers and, in May, it was reported that most of the children were going to Confession and Communion. The numbers increased in December to 160 boys with 22 teachers (seven from SS. Michael and John's).

Here again we see the increase of mendicity due to disease and unemployment. The normal number of Catholic children relieved by the Institute was about 50, but, in January, 1828, it was 120, and in December it was 160. Though the fever epidemic of 1826-27 was nothing like that of 1817-19, yet its evil effects as to mendicity seem to have been more prolonged ; that is to say, unemployment continued for a whole year after the fever had ceased and was on the increase at the end of the year.

The various Confraternities severally subscribed to the support of the Mendicity Branch 12/- per annum, Irish. Curiously, this sum was changed, 26th July, 1829, after the Emancipation, into 12/- British (13/- Irish).

A report from the Moira branch, 25th October, 1829, states that " the clergyman attending Moira House had re-marked that the conduct and morals of the children were much improved during the last year which are attributed in a great degree to the Instructions they received on Sundays." It appears (August, 1830) that there was a chapel in Moira House in which the children met for instruction, but the Rev. Mr. Dempsey and Miss Regan were of the opinion that " no ornaments are required on the altar in future." Apparently they considered that the ornaments, whatever they were, suggested by the confraternities were undesirable in such a chapel.

It was further reported that 8 out of 21 members attended, four of whom were from SS. Michael and John's; that " there was no Mass there this last month on account of the Archbishop's indispositions, and of the clergymen being called to other duties." This is the last report in the Minutes of this volume about this branch.

Fr. Dempsey was apparently a chaplain who was also deputed to say a second Mass in Moira House on Sundays and supervise the Catechism classes. His name does not figure among the Curates of the South City at this time. The Moira Branch seems to have returned to normal conditions in the year 1830; eight Confraternity members were considered to be sufficient, and the number of children mendicants had dropped from 160 to about 60. The conduct and morals of the neglected children of the Liberties had much improved owing to the Brothers of the City Confraternities, and, above all, to the zeal of those of SS. Michael and John's.

7. THE TEMPERANCE MOVEMENT

One of the most amazing features of Catholic activities at this period was the growth of the Temperance Movement. The seeds of the movement were sown by Dr. Blake and Father Young when they founded the St. John's Purgatorian Society, in 1818, one of whose objects was to abolish drinking at wakes. The evils of intemperance were a constant theme in Fr. Young's sermons and he laboured in his own way to counteract them. His brothers, Fathers James and William were also ardent promoters of Temperance.

Other priests in the city parishes took up the cause warmly, but it was not until about 1838 that Temperance Societies were established. The "Temperance Society" of St. Nicholas's could boast that it was founded by Rev. M. Flanagan, Francis-street, "before Father Mathew preached Total Abstinence." The "National Total Abstinence Association," under the V. Rev. Dr. Spratt, O.C.C., was founded in 1838. The "Metropolitan Total Abstinence Society" of SS. Michael and John's was founded by V. Rev. A. O'Connell, P.P., in 1839, and "St. Paul's Temperance Society" was founded by the Very Rev. Dr. Yore, P.P. in the same year. St. Audoen's also had its parochial Temperance

Association at this time.   Outside the city there were three Temperance Societies, at Blanchardstown under Rev. M. Dungan, at Palmerstown (Chapelizod) under Rev. Eugene Clarke, and at Sandyford under V. Rev. J. Smith, P.P. These priests had already enrolled between 30,000 and 40,000 before Father Mathew visited Dublin.

The social side of the movement was not overlooked.   On Sunday, 23rd August, 1840, the members of the National Total Abstinence Association held their second anniversary dinner in the parochial school-rooms, Mary's-lane, at which the Rev. Dr. Doyle presided.

On his first visit to Dublin, 1840, Father Mathew is said to have enrolled 75,000.   He preached at Sandyford, S. Co. Dublin, Sunday and Monday, 30th and 31st August (1840) and gave the pledge to 20,000. The collection for the parochial Temperance Society amounted to £100.   His second visit to the city was held on Sunday, 27th September, when he preached in the Pro-Cathedral on behalf of the Widow's House, Clarendon-street. The next morning a platform was erected at the entrance to the Custom-house from which he addressed the assembly and gave the pledge to 25,000 in batches of 5,000.   On Tuesday morning he gave the pledge to 40,000, also in batches of 5,000.   Thus, in his two visits to Dublin, he is said to have given the pledge to 140,000.   In all Ireland, at this time, it is said that $2\frac{1}{2}$ millions had joined the Temperance Movement.   Father Mathew paid his third visit to Dublin, 16th–18th November, and gave the pledge to 33,000, making in all 173,000 for Dublin.   How many, however, took the pledge twice and three times we do not know.

These visits of Father Mathew put great heart into the people of Dublin and strengthened the local societies.   Apparently the movement was not confined to the working class, for the *Catholic Luminary* reported that " Wednesday, 30 Nov. 1840, a splendid Temperance meeting, ball, and supper took place at the Rotunda.   Daniel O'Connell, Esq., M.P. in the chair, and the V. Rev. Dr. Spratt spoke."   The *Teetotal World*, a Temperance weekly Journal, was issued, price 1d.

The movement was likewise a spiritual one. The V. Rev. A. O'Connell, P.P., SS. Michael and John's, the worthy successor of Dr. Blake, celebrated the first anniversary of his Metropolitan Total Abstinence Society, 29th November, 1840, and conducted the spiritual exercises every evening for ten days previously in the church, gave Holy Communion to 1,000 members, and preached the closing sermon on the Sunday.

Father O'Connell was the recognised head of the Temperance Movement in Dublin. His word was law, and it was eminently practical. He linked up the movement with an industrial revival. The *Catholic Luminary* thus describes the occasion : " Grand Festival of the Irish National Temperance Association took place on Monday evening (last November, 1840) in the large room, French-street, Dublin, formerly the old chapel. V. Rev. Dr. Spratt took the chair." Father William Young (Father Henry's Brother) was on the platform. Dr. Yore, writing from 65 Queen-street, apologised for absence. Father A. O'Connell, P.P. of SS. Michael and John's, wrote : " Do tell your friends that we are determined on their amelioration, and that, in return for their fidelity to the pledge they have taken, we give them our pledge to use nothing but of their manufacture ; and thus do we hope to carry out the regeneration of our dear, dear country . . . may I beg of you to guard your friends against frequenting those places called teetotal shops, where gambling has been introduced." The *Luminary* continues : " There were several beautiful banners, on which were inscribed a number of admirable devices—in praise of Temperance, Union and Industry. Tea and coffee were served whilst the excellent Teetotal band played a number of delightful airs as ' Patrick's Day,' ' Garryowen,' ' God save the Queen ' . . . The Queen and Prince Albert were toasted with great cheering."

Bands were attached to practically all the local Temperance Societies, and had, doubtless, acquired considerable proficiency during their two years of practice. " God save the Queen " (Victoria) was regularly contributed by them, and the toast of the Queen and her Consort was regularly proposed and received with cheering.

When Father Mathew returned to Cork after his second visit to Dublin he brought back with him a rosy account of the enthusiasm of the Dublin people for Temperance, and read them a letter from Archbishop Murray which throws important light on the practical working of the movement in the metropolis.

Father Mathew, at Cove-street, Cork, 26th November, 1840, told the people assembled at the great Bazaar, that Archbishop Murray of Dublin, in a letter to him, said " that, while vast benefits had been produced by the pledge, the publicans sustained little injury. They re-opened their shops for the sale of cloths, Irish manufactures, and other such articles, and one business supplied the place of the other. The largest prison in Dublin was closed for want of prisoners." He hoped that " the spirit which burned so brightly in Dublin would extend itself to us—that the stigma of backwardness would be washed away from Cork—and that they should ere long have 40,000 instead of 20,000 teetotalers in this great city."

The Temperance Societies in and around Dublin had determined on a great show of strength and they chose St. Patrick's Day as the day for their public procession. The first meeting for its organisation was held, Monday, 8th February, 1841, by the Junior Total Abstinence Society in their hall in French-street. The V. Rev. Dr. Spratt, O.C.C., who presided, stated that " in or near the metropolis about 200,000 men and women are pledged," and that the entire number in Ireland was nearly four millions. The population of Ireland was then about eight millions.

The Rev. A. O'Connell wrote from Exchange-street enclosing a letter from N. H. MacDonald on behalf of the Lord Lieutenant, asking " that no banners or other symbols calculated to give offence or be a subject of misrepresentation to others " be used at the coming St. Patrick's Day Procession of Teetotallers. Father O'Connell agreed with this request, and added : " Our scarfs and ribbons we can, of course, wear with the appended medals. May I take this occasion to say that we have resolved upon the use of Irish Manufacture in the scarfs and ribbons to be worn on Saint Patrick's Day."

Saint Paul's Temperance Association members met " in the

large room of the theatre, Fishamble-street, to make suitable arrangements for the great procession. On the same day the members of Sandyford met, and agreed to walk in the procession. The Rev. J. Smith, P.P. (Sandyford) presided."

On the same day the National Total Abstinence Society, under Dr. Spratt, met in the large room, French-street. In the evening the Temperance Society of Blanchardstown (President : Rev. M. Dungan) had a tea and coffee entertainment. "The old chapel was splendidly decorated with laurel wreaths, and transparencies with appropriate devices. . . . The gentry of the neighbourhood . . . seconded their pious pastor in his exertions."

The great St. Patrick's Day Total Abstinence Procession of 1841 was held in the Fifteen Acres, Phoenix Park, and about a quarter of a million people were present. "The marines headed the procession to the strains of 'Royal Charlie' on Scottish bagpipes. Then followed Fr. Mathew's band, twenty musicians, dressed in blue and gold, playing 'Garryowen,' with men four abreast, the line extending from Mary's Abbey to Bloody Bridge. . . . Then came the T. A. Society of St. Paul's with its band on a lorry drawn by six horses. What of 'Smock Alley ?' No longer associated with 'your heroes of the sock and buskin.' 'West Essex-street' had replaced your venerable name. Here's a Cavalcade . . . the Metropolitan Temperance Society. The President, Rev. A. O'Connell, Catholic Pastor of SS. Michael & John's Parish, is seated in a splendid carriage, drawn by four white steeds, driven by postillions and proceeded by couriers, dressed in buff breeches, blue spencers and scull-caps, shaded profusely with tassels of gold. Beside the Rev. Gentleman are his Curates, Rev. Messrs. Smyth and Farrell."

"Next comes the 'Temperance Society,' founded by Rev. M. Flanagan, Francis-street, before Fr. Mathew preached 'Total Abstinence.'

"Who so glitter, with dew or sunshine upon their Irish Manufactured badges of white and gold ? The Very Rev. J. Spratt leads them on. This is the National Total Abstinence Society, pledged to use Irish Manufacture. . . . Times were in which Catholic and Protestant Irishmen met one another at drawn daggers round the ill-omened statue in College Green. They meet so no more. The pious Pastors have smoothed away the acerbities of sectarian rancour, and had such change been effected half-a-century since, their palace of legislature would not now be a mart for moneychangers. However, the evolution of the countryship goes bravely on . . . we will soon fly."[1]

Father Young was at this time attached to St. Paul's and must have thrown himself into the movement with great enthusiasm. He must have rejoiced to see the Sandyford Temperance Association take part in the great demonstration, at the head of which was his great friend, Father Smyth, whom he had assisted in founding this Association.

The St. Patrick's Day demonstration was the beginning of a round of festivities organised by the local societies to keep up the enthusiasm of the members, to provide them with counter-attractions to drinking saloons, and to entertain them in healthy surroundings. The first of the festivities was a great Temperance festival held in the Rotunda, Wednesday, 14th April, 1841, at which Daniel O'Connell presided, and V. Rev. Dr. Spratt was present.

On Sunday, 26th July a " grand Temperance Promenade and Tea and coffee party took place in Mr. Madden's fields, Cullen's Wood, near Ranelagh. Rev. A. O'Connell was in the chair ; thousands attended, and a number of excellent speeches were delivered. . . . The Metropolitan Total Abstinence Society, of which the Rev. A. O'Connell, P.P. of St. Michael & John's, is President now numbers upwards of 15,000 members. There is no room in the parish sufficiently large to accommodate them, and it is contemplated when sufficient funds can be procured, to erect a Temperance Hall for their use, adjoining the School-room in Essex-street West. Such a building is not only desirable, but absolutely necessary to enable the members of these societies, by having a place of their cwn to resort to, where they may have mental recreation, successfully to resist the allurements of those who would fain draw them back to their old haunts of wickedness."

St. Paul's Temperance Society, numbering 18,000 members,

[1] *Catholic Luminary* (1841), 502-503.

held a " splendid Temperance Tea Party, Sunday, 9th August, in the immense area opposite St. Paul's church which was covered with marquees. There were five immense rows of tables, each holding 400 or 500, and the band was in the centre. On some of the banners were the devices : ' God save the Queen,' and ' Long live Prince Albert.' The Rev. Dr. Yore, P.P., took the chair at 6 p.m. and proposed the toast of the ' Health of her Majesty and Prince Albert,' and of the ' Duchess of Kent,' whereupon the band played ' God save the Queen.' ' His Excellency the Lord Lieutenant ' was next proposed, and the band played ' Patrick's Day,' and ' Here's a health to all good lasses.' The final toast was ' St. Paul's Temperance Society,' and the band played ' Rory O'Moore.' "

It was announced that the weekly receipts of this Society amounted to £20, and that a sick fund in connection with it granted relief to the needy. The balance in hands was £358 4s. 6d., after about two year's existence.

Loan-Benefit branches were attached to some of the Temperance Societies and were " doing great good for the poor of the country." St. Augustine's Temperance Society, founded by V. Rev. Stuart, John-street church, had a Benefit and Burial Society attached to it.

The *Catholic Luminary* of 1840–41, from which the material for this chapter has been mainly drawn, concludes its splendid accounts of the Temperance Societies' activities with a few words about the " Support of Irish Manufacture, which, originated with a priest [Father A. O'Connell, P.P.], and generally responded to by all classes, will soon place Ireland in the highest possible scale of industry, and we trust, ere long, in permanent prosperity, as Temperance and Religion have already established her virtue, piety and peace."

8. DR. YORE AT ST. PAUL'S

Father Young was transferred from St. Audoen's to St. Paul's about the end of 1840. It is most probable that his services were required in connection with the Temperance Society, and that Dr. Yore, P.P. had asked Archbishop Murray to send him to St. Paul's.

In 1814, a Refuge founded some time previously in Ashe-street by Mrs. John O'Brien for unprotected young girls of good character, was transferred to the old Manor House of Grangegorman[1] in Stanhope-street. In 1819, at the request of Coadjutor Archbishop Murray, the Irish Sisters of Charity, under Mother Aikenhead, took charge of it. Dr. Murray undertook to raise funds for a convent and chapel, and said the first Mass in the chapel, 2nd February, 1819.

In the matter of higher Catholic education the parish was fortunate when, in 1823, the Rev. Dr. Michael Doyle trans-ferred his Classical, Mathematical, and Mercantile Seminary from Castle-street to No. 23 Arran's Quay. He did so, appa-rently, because he considered that he had a better field for his Seminary in the more important district of Oxmantown. It would seem that the Seminary in Castle-street had been the up-to-date successor of the Saul's Court Seminary. As a youth Michael Doyle had been president of the Christian Doctrine Confraternity in St. Catherine's parish. He entered Maynooth College, about 1805, and, after his ordination, was appointed to SS. Michael and John's in 1814. Shortly afterwards he established his seminary in Castle-street. On one of its account-forms which contained the expenses of one of the pupils for a term appeared the following elaborate announcement :

"Classical, Mathematical & Mercantile Seminary, Temple Court, 45, Castle Street, under the Patronage of the most Revd. Dr. Troy, the Most Revd. Dr. Murray, & The Very Revd. Dr. Hamill. Revd. Michael Doyle, Principal.

"The System of Education comprises the Latin, Greek, French, Italian and English Languages, Mathematics, Book-keeping, Arithmetic, Writing, History, Geography & the use of the Globes.

"Revd. M. Doyle delivers Lectures on Journalizing, Posting, and Closing Accounts, by double entry, at a fixed hour each day. He is anxious to submit to public inspection

[1] The Manor of Grangegorman belonged to Christ Church before the Anglo-Norman Invasion. As a home-farm its buildings and village of the fourteenth century are set out in the *Account Roll* by James Mills (*R.S.A.I.*). At the so-called Reformation this manor, like the other manors of the Regular Canons of Christ Church, was devoted to Protestant purposes.

his mode of instruction, and trusts that his system of Book-keeping will be found particularly worthy the attention of young merchants.

"In order to render his establishment both useful to the Public and honourable to himself, he is determined that the most Competent and Respectable Professors shall be employed in each Department.

"Revd. M. Doyle confidently hopes that attention to morals and instruction of youth committed to his care will recommend him to a share of Public Patronage.

"Terms : Writing, Arithmetic, Mathematics, History, Geography, use of Globes, etc., £1 14s. 1½d. p. quarter. Latin, Greek, French and Italian, 11s. 4½d. p. quarter. Entrance One Guinea.

"Chapel House, St. Michael & John's, Lowr. Exchange Street."

A somewhat similar but less expensive school was " The Clarendon St. Chapel Classical and Mercantile Academy."[1]

Father Doyle's Seminary was moved, shortly before November, 1823, to the more genteel quarter of Arran Quay, and was called the " Seminary of St. Patrick." A premium plate in a volume of Parnell's Poems has this inscription : "Praemia Laudi Sti. Patricii. Praemium hoc Literarium dederunt Praeses ac Professores Seminarii Sti. Patricii, no. 23, Arran Quay (1825). Seminarii moderatores. M. Doyle. J. O'Grady."[2]

From about 1814 to 1835, Dr. Doyle, besides being the principal of the Seminary, was curate in SS. Michael and John's. He was, therefore, a fellow-worker with Father Henry Young (1829) and lived in the same house with him. " During those twenty-one years, Dr. Doyle had given the blessing of a classical, moral, and religious education to many hundreds who now fill most influential situations. By close application, and a peculiar spirit of saving, he was enabled to realize from £12,000 to £15,000, but it should be ever borne in mind that instead of spending this on himself, or hoarding

[1] Kelly, *Dubl. Hist. Rec.*, III. no. 1., pp. 12-13.
[2] Dr. O'Grady preached at Dundrum, Sunday, 5th July, 1840, in support of the schools of that parish.

it as a miser, he at once devoted it to the great and important purpose of rearing up young men duly recommended to the ecclesiastical state, by establishing burses, or free places in various colleges, particularly in the Irish College at Rome." (namely in the Irish College, and in the Propaganda College for the support of Irish students).

" A letter has been written by his Eminence Cardinal Franzoni, Prefect of the College of Propaganda [c. October, 1840], to the Very Rev. Michael Doyle, of St. Michael's & John's, Dublin, presenting him with the thanks of the Sacred Congregation for his munificent grant of 500l. for the support of another burse in favour of the Irish Mission. This is, we believe, the third or fourth grant of the kind which this esteemed and venerable ecclesiastic has given for this truly noble purpose."[1] These were called the " Doyle Burses " that Dublin students still enjoy.

He was called by Cardinal Franzoni, in 1840, a " venerable ecclesiastic," though apparently he was ordained shortly before 1814. He must, therefore, have been in his late twenties when he entered Maynooth about 1805. This would seem to support Battersby's statement that he was " the principal of a seminary in Dublin " before he entered Maynooth. He would have been born then about 1780, and was 60 years old in 1840, and considered " venerable " at that time. Though only a Curate he was Archdeacon of Glendalough and chaplain to O'Connell during his Mayoralty, 1843–44. He died in 1844 (28th July), and was buried in the vaults of SS. Michael and John's, in " a singular stone coffin which he had made for himself during his life-time."[2] In this he was somewhat like Father Henry Young, who had his three coffins made for him, and paid for, for the reception of his remains in the vaults of St. Mary's, Marlborough-street.

Returning to the parochial church ; the appointment of Dr. Yore as parish priest, in 1828, put new life into the parish. A native of the parish (b. 22nd May, 1781), he received his early education in Father Betagh's Seminary in Saul's-court, was ordained in Carlow College, 1809, and was appointed

[1] *Catholic Registry* (1845), p. 433.
[2] Donnelly, *Dub. Par.*, II, 198.

curate in St. James's parish and chaplain to Kilmainham, where he attended about 40 executions. He became administrator of SS. Michael and John's in 1824, when Dr. Blake, P.P. went to Rome, and, in 1828, became P.P. of St. Paul's.

We have seen how immediately he requested the Christian Doctrine Society of SS. Michael and John's to reorganise the decadent Society of St. Paul's and how it became a flourishing body in the old chapel in the courtyard off Arran's Quay. The next work in his parish was the opening of the Catholic Cemetery at Glasnevin, which he blessed, February 1832, attended by about 30 priests, who rejoiced in this public defiance of the Protestant Rectors of the old city burial places inaugurated by Daniel O'Connell.

The old chapel off Arran Quay was no longer able to accommodate the people at the Masses on Sundays, and a new church was an absolute necessity. The difficulty was to secure a suitable site. Luckily the Police Court at the corner of Lincoln-lane was removed to Capel-street, and the site was acquired in 1835. Archbishop Murray laid the foundation on St. Patrick's Day of that year, and, on the 30th June, 1837, solemnly dedicated the elegant new church. Over £8,000 was subscribed, but Dr. Yore himself contributed the balance of about £1,000 to free the church of all debt. In a short time he provided the portico, tower, and cupola, and furnished it with a peal of bells—the first in any Catholic church in Ireland since the so-called Reformation.

It was to minister in this splendid edifice that Father Young was sent towards the end of 1840. He was, no doubt, an assistant at Dr. Yore's magnificent First Communion services for children. A contemporary says : " I have never witnessed anything equal to it for order, instruction, and edification— except upon the Continent—where everything combines to render it so touching and so irresistible."[1] For three months previous to the Communion Day " the most complete, pre- cise, and continuous practical instructions were given on two days each week, and again on Sundays, by one of the clergy- men, repeated by the Very Rev. Dr. Yore."

On the Communion Day several hundred boys and girls

[1] *Catholic Luminary* (1840–41), p. 285.

assembled at 9 a.m., attended by their teachers—one for every 20 children—the *Veni Creator* was sung by a special choir (which also sang during the Mass), and Dr. Yore gave a short address before Mass and another immediately before the Children's Holy Communion.

The children were conducted two by two to the altar by the teachers. A third short discourse from Dr. Yore followed, and Benediction of the Most Holy Sacrament was given after Mass. The whole service lasted two hours, and at 11 o'clock the children sat down to an excellent breakfast, at which Dr. Yore presided, assisted by the clergy and many respectable citizens.

A chapel-of-ease to St. Paul's was built, in 1823, at the junction of the Cabra and North Circular roads, at Phibsborough, and was dedicated to St. Peter. It was a Gothic structure, 18 ft. long and 37 ft. wide, but scarcely sufficient for the increasing congregation. Old Phibsborough consisted of clusters of mud cabins and whitewashed cottages. Part of the old village still exists at the back of Phibsborough and Circular Roads (south side)—it is an interesting relic. The village was at the junction of four parishes, and, up to 1823, was equally remote from the respective parish churches.

As to the education of poor children, the proselytiser had a promising field for his activities. Up to 1820, there was no Catholic school in the vicinity. The bait offered to them was Kellett's school in Lower Dorset-street, near the Canal (St. Xavier's Catholic schools now occupy the site). "This school was founded in 1811 on a liberal bequest of £5,000 left by Miss A. Kellet, of Fordstown, county of Meath, for that purpose. It is situated in Drumcondra, at the northern extremity of the city, a site judiciously selected, not only as being airy and healthy, but as affording means of education to the poor of this remote part of the city, who are too distant to avail themselves òf any other. The building is constructed in the most permanent manner. . . . The seminary consists of two apartments . . . the lower prepared to accommodate 350 boys, and the upper as many girls. . . . The girls are taught needle-work half the day, and receive the produce of their labour in articles of clothing, as an incentive to their industry.

Pupils pay three halfpence per week during the summer months, which is remitted in the winter to those who have been regular in their attendance.   Annexed to the school is a house and garden for the accommodation of four teachers, a master, head monitor, and two mistresses.   The whole cost £1,740, and is built on a lease from Lord Mountjoy, for 1,999 years.   The expenditure of the school is, Rent £17, 10, 0, Salaries, £130.   Since its commencement 590 boys and 457 girls have been admitted, and are now in the school."[1]

The cost of this school was £147 10s. od. p. a., and was paid out of the interest on the capital £5,000.   It is not stated who paid the £1,740, the cost of the building.   No doubt, it was provided by the Protestant Church directly or indirectly.

The important question is who were the poor of this district —" this remote part of the city ? "   It is most improbable that they were Protestants ; the hamlets of mud cabins and tiny cottages were inhabited chiefly by Catholics.   We may discard the Protestant interest in " airy and healthy " surroundings for schools—there was no catering for city children but for children who were already living in " airy and healthy " surroundings, at Phibsborough, " who were too distant to avail themselves of any other."   The chief interest of the founders of this school was to entice the children of Phibsborough and the other near districts to this modern and attractive school.   It was a great attraction, and, between 1811 and 1820, no doubt, many Catholic parents availed themselves of the opportunities for the education of their children, especially of the technical education for girls.

In 1820 the Catholics of Phibsborough thought it high time to provide schools of their own for the increasing population of the village.   Father William Meagher (afterwards P.P. Rathmines), lately ordained in Maynooth, undertook the education of the poor boys, and continued the work for about three years, when he opened the Classical and Commercial

---

[1] Warburton, etc. *Hist of Dubl.*, 858–59.   This statement is misleading.   It is scarcely possible that the 1047 children admitted between 1811 and 1818 were in the school in the latter year.

Academy at 64 Jervis-street (1824). The basement of the 1823 chapel was used as a school for fifteen years.

Dr. Yore, P.P., had between 1828 and 1835 expended about £4,000 in making the chapel a truly up-to-date church, and had received half of that sum from the weekly pennies of the poorer classes. Father William Young had been called, soon after his ordination, to assist in the building of this church. Over the sacristy were four neat rooms that served as the residence of the two curates. A lending and sale library, chiefly for the poor, was installed, modelled on the library of SS. Michael and John's, and a Purgatorian Society was founded which recited the Office of the Dead every Monday evening at 8 o'clock in the chapel and over the remains of every deceased member. The members paid 6d. at entrance into the Society, and 1d. per week. Provision for Masses for deceased members was the same as in another similar Society. An interesting feature of this church, at this time, was that the devotion of the Stations of the Cross was held every Friday evening.[1]

It was Dr. Yore's intention to enlarge St. Peter's still further by adding 50 ft. in front, and to provide it with a handsome steeple, but Archbishop Murray considered that he had sufficient work on hands in building St. Paul's and providing it with portico and belfry. Thus, the Archbishop and parish priest agreed that St. Peter's should be handed over to the new community founded on the Rule of St. Vincent de Paul. This community was Dublin-born, and had its origin among Dublin students in Maynooth College who wished to live under Rule ; they chose that of the Congregation of the Mission founded by St. Vincent de Paul. After their ordination, they opened a secondary school at 34 Usher's-quay, and, in a few years (1835), they purchased the residence at Castle-knock for the purpose of educating students for the diocese of Dublin. In 1838, they took over St. Peter's, Phibsborough.

This was the beginning of a most fruitful Irish Catholic activity. A wave of missionary enthusiasm and enterprise was spreading over the country to provide for Catholic ministration to the exiles in the British Colonies and the

[1] Battersby, *Ir. Cath. Dir.*, 1836.

United States. The number of emigrants to the States alone, 1820–1841, was over 300,000. Bishop John England, Charlestown, U.S.A. and Dr. Ullathorne, Vicar-General for Australia, came to Ireland, 1832–37, to obtain students and priests to meet the demands of their churches. Maynooth College was set on fire with enthusiasm by Dr. Ullathorne in 1837. He also preached to the charitable Dublin people (January, 1838), in SS. Michael and John's, on the "Horrors of Transportation," on behalf of his missions. All this was spasmodic ; and Irish organisation was necessary to deal with the requirements of the Irish exiles.

Fortunately, in 1837, Ireland was a subscriber to a new international Catholic Association, founded at Lyons, in France, in 1822, called the "Society for the Propagation of the Faith." A Father O'Toole came over from Paris, 1838, to establish the Association in Ireland. Archbishop Murray received him most cordially, and convened a meeting of the clergy of the city and suburbs, 18th September, 1838, at the presbytery of SS. Michael and John's to establish the Society. He was the first to hand in his subscription. It may be mentioned here that, between 1838 and 1852 (year of Archbishop Murray's death) £70,000 was subscribed from Ireland, more than a third of which was contributed by the diocese of Dublin.[1] This meant that about £5,000 a year was subscribed by Ireland during those fourteen years. It was the *Annals* of the Association, translated into English, welcomed by almost every household in Dublin, and read with deep interest, which spread the enthusiasm for the Association and the missions. The Catholic Book Society also lent a helping hand.

At this time, as we have said, the little band of secular priests in the Academy of Usher's Island had taken over, at the request of Archbishop Murray and Dr. Yore, P.P., the charge of St. Peter's, Phibsborough. The missionary spirit of St. Vincent de Paul, whose Rule they adopted without any formal initiation, urged them to welcome this new Society of the Propagation of the Faith, and they set up a branch in Phibsborough. Among the brethren of

---

[1] Meagher, *Archbishop Murray*, 145–46.

Phibsborough was Father Hand, who had taught at Usher's Quay ; he was transferred thither by Archbishop Murray, not as one of the community but as a secular priest of the diocese, and was appointed assistant to Father MacNamara, the superior of St. Peter's. Even when the little community linked up with the Congregation of the Mission, Paris, in 1839, he remained a secular priest.

On 18th September, 1839, Archbishop Murray held the first anniversary of the foundation of the Irish Society for the Propagation of the Faith in the Metropolitan church, Marlborough-street, and celebrated Pontifical High Mass. His Grace had thrown himself whole-heartedly into the work of the Society. He appointed the energetic parish priest of SS. Michael and John's secretary. Subscriptions poured in— two of £403 and £405 being anonymous. Between January and August, 1840, he received £3,800 which was sent to the Vicars Apostolic in the Colonies. The British colonies were considered at this time the most suitable objects for the Society's contributions. So far the central organisation for all countries had not been established and, apparently, each country was at liberty to send its contributions to whatever missionary field it considered most suitable.[1]

Father Hand in Phibsborough also threw himself into the work of the branch of the Society in St. Peter's, and " witnessing the generosity and zeal of the faithful " for the promotion of the Association " caught up the idea that a college for the Foreign Missions would be sure of success." Archbishop Murray favoured the idea.

A suitable house for the College was acquired in Upper Drumcondra on land that had in pre-Reformation days belonged to the Priory of All Hallows, which stood where Dublin University was afterwards erected. To preserve the historical continuity, Archbishop Murray ordered that the new College should be called All Hallows. Father Hand left Phibsborough, 17th October, 1842, and took up residence in his college as the first president.[2]

---

[1] See Purcell, " Father Hand," *I.E.R.*, Nov. and Dec., 1942. Rev. Dr. Doyle subscribed £500 for one free place, and Rev. Dr. Yore donated £100 and his library.
[2] *Catholic Luminary*, pp. 72, 120, 144, 192.

In a few years the little community of Vincentians at St. Peter's partially carried out Dr. Yore's plans, provided a large and well proportioned church, and removed the schools from the basement to more suitable quarters. It was at this time that Father Young came on a special mission to St. Paul's, and remained for about six months. After his daily work in the parish his evening recreation was to pay a visit to St. Peter's church and spend hours there in spiritual communion with the work of the Vincentians.   No doubt, he recalled the profitable days he had spent with the Community at Monte Celino, Rome, when, as a priest, he laboured with them in the villages adjoining the city. He was still a missionary priest, in the city and countryside of Dublin, after 25 years, and felt he could still draw inspiration from the work of the Vincentian Fathers. It is a singular fact that these fathers were to be his successors in the missionary field in Ireland. His missions were the inspiration of his own soul ; future missions were to be the well thought-out work of a community. He must be acclaimed the pioneer of Irish missions.

V

FATHER YOUNG'S MISSIONARY WORK

1. The Jubilee of 1826

IN 1815, the foundation stone of the Church of the Conception, St. Mary's, Marlborough-street, which was to take the place of the old building at the rere of the houses in Upper Liffey-street, was laid by Archbishop Troy. Dr. Troy did not live to see the completion of his greatest work for the diocese, the first great modern Catholic Church in Ireland on really architectural lines.[1]

The old building continued to do duty for the parishioners for a further ten years. The delay in the transfer of divine services to the Church of the Conception was due to the fact that the vaults under it had been leased for a term as a store for alcoholic liquors for the purpose of acquiring revenue for the building of the church.

It was not until 1824 that the Commissioners of Inland Revenue cleared the liquors out of the vaults. But before the vaults became a cemetery the church had to be blessed and dedicated.[2]

This ceremony took place, 14th November, 1825, the feast of the renowned patron of the diocese, St. Laurence O'Toole. Dr. Murray, the new Archbishop, sang the Mass, and the famous J.K.L., Bishop Doyle of Leighlin, preached the sermon. The music was in keeping with the great occasion, and " Mozart's Grand Mass " was sung by an augmented choir. Sovereigns were freely laid on the collection plate for admission. As on all such occasions, in those days, the church celebration had to have its counterpart in a tea or

---

[1] His remains, laid in the vaults of the Presentation Convent, George's Hill, on 11th May, 1823, were removed to the vaults of the Church of the Conception on 12th June, 1827.

[2] The receipts from burials in the vaults were an important contribution to the building fund ; for the years 1827–37 they were £3,744. The building fund was not closed until 1st January, 1844, and showed a cost of about £45,000. The porticoes were completed in 1840. It was considered a remarkable achievement that in 1844, 41 years after the beginning of the project, the church should have been free from debt. It meant that more than £1,000 a year had been collected to pay off capital and interest ; the weekly pennies of the poor lightened the burden.

dinner gathering. On this occasion a public dinner was the only fitting conclusion, and, though the organisers visualised, at first, that the presbytery would accommodate the applicants for tickets, it was found necessary to transfer the venue to Morrison's Hotel, Dawson-street.

A few months after the dedication, St. Mary's was the scene of an unprecedented exhibition of Catholic faith and fervour in Ireland. The occasion was the opening of the Jubilee of 1826. The Jubilee, held in Rome in 1825, was in the following year extended to the whole Catholic world. In the organisation of its devotions for the city parishes Father Young took a most important part. He was then in Harold's Cross but still in touch with the activities of SS. Michael and John's, the most influential parish in the city.

The Jubilee in Dublin was opened, 8th March, 1826, in St. Mary's by Archbishop Murray, who delivered a beautiful homily on the graces and Indulgences of the devotion. The Papal Bull was read by the Rev. Andrew O'Connell, who acted as deacon. The public devotions, consisting of prayers and instructions, commenced each morning at 7 o'clock and were repeated at midday and in the evening. Apparently the Jubilee devotions lasted for one week. Father Kenny, S.J., preached frequently during the week and at the closing ceremony of the renewal of baptismal vows. Unprecedented multitudes approached the Sacraments of Confession and Holy Communion.

"During the entire period of the Jubilee," says Dr. Murray's biographer, "which had to be extended again and again, for the purpose of enabling the numberless applicants to gratify their pious anxieties, like scenes of excited devotion were continually witnessed, in almost every parochial and every conventual church within the city, and in several throughout the rural districts. The Archbishop renewed, in person, the same imposing ceremonies, in each church, as those with which he opened the holy times in his Cathedral, and everywhere with similar corresponding fruits. It has been already remarked, that these fruits were not more conspicuous than they have proved enduring. The attachment of the Metropolitan Catholics to the observance of their religious duties had been, in fact, for a long time, anything but edifying. In later years owing to several concurrent circumstances consoling progress for the better was discernible, but to the fidelity with which the graces of the " holy year " were husbanded is due, in a chief degree, the amazingly increased frequentation of the Sacraments, which has now for so long a time, so happily distinguished the faithful of our city."[1]

On the other hand, a eulogistic account of the daily life of the Catholic people is given by a contemporary (1821) :

" In each of the parish chapels and friaries there is a regular succession of Masses, generally from 6 o'cl., in the morning until 11 o'cl. in the day of Sundays and Holidays ; and from 7 until 11 o'cl., and in some chapels, until 12 o'cl., on every other day. On the Sundays and Holidays all these Masses are attended by crowded congregations. In the parish chapels and friaries, sermons are preached on the evenings of every Sunday and Holiday during the winter season, and immediately after last Mass in the summer and autumn months ; and generally in the evenings of every day during the penitential times of lent and advent. On these occasions the chapels are crowded to excess."[2]

The Jubilee celebrations in the city parishes were, whichever statement we accept, providential, and awakened the citizens to the necessity of personal sanctification. The various parish societies had been doing heroic work to effect it, but it required the call from Rome and from the Archbishop of Dublin to make the people realise the meaning and the grandeur of their faith, and that they were an important portion of the Catholic Church spread throughout the world. It was a new vision to the people of the city and of the Liberties that they meant anything beyond their own struggle for existence in difficult times and in squalid surroundings. Most of the penal-time chapels were still in use; the lack of proper accommodation had, no doubt, something to say to their neglect of the sacraments. It was the first time the people were called upon for nearly three hundred years to proclaim that Catholic

[1] Rev. W. Meagher, *Life and Character of His Grace Most Rev. Daniel Murray* (1853), 102-107.
[2] McGregor, *Picture of Dublin* (1821), p. 148.

Dublin was still, in spite of those centuries of oppression, a living part of the Church of Christ.

The arrangements for the Jubilee devotions in SS. Michael and John's are set out in the Minutes of the Evening Office Society of 12th and 19th March, 1826 :

" Resolved that two members wait on the Rev. H. Young to ask his advice on our entering into a Unity to perform the prayers necessary to be recited to gain the Indulgence of the Jubilee and also to ask him what particular prayers are most recommended on the occasion."

" Resolved that we meet on Sunday next at 1 o'clock to hear from the deputation Mr. Young's Opinion on the above subjects."

The deputation reported that " the Rev. Mr. Young highly approved of our intention if we found it practicable. It was resolved that as many as find it convenient to join in the above unity will commence on Sunday next and to continue the Devotion for the fourteen succeeding Sundays."

" Resolved that the four following chapels are the ones to be visited by the above persons, the Metropolitan, Bridge St., Adam and Eve, and St. Michael & John's."

" It was announced that the Rev. Mr. Young was to have for sale the following week a little book which will contain some prayers and instructions on the Jubilee."[1]

Here again, it was Father Young's Roman training and experience that were relied upon by the priests and confraternities of Dublin to help them to carry out the Jubilee devotions in a manner befitting the great occasion. Once again, in the midst of his busy parochial work in Harold's Cross, he had to wield his pen and burn the midnight oil and see the booklet through the printers' hands within a week. We have not, unfortunately, seen a copy of the booklet.

As to the " Unity " mentioned above, the idea of SS. Michael and John's Confraternity was that the parishioners should meet at the church on the fourteen Sundays and proceed in processional order with the banners of their various

[1] Official publications of the Jubilee were printed by Coyne, 4 Capel-street, under the direction of Archbishop Murray : *Extensio Universalis Jubilei in Urbe Celebrato*, 1825 ; English Translation of the Bull (20th Feb., 1826) ; and *Pastoral Instructions of the Archbishops and Bishops of Ireland on the subject of the General Jubilee.*

societies to the four churches. Father Young approved of the "Unity." Those processions must have been enormous considering the density of the population in those days and considering that it was the first time that such processions were held in the city since the Guild processions of pre-Reformation days. It is easy then to imagine the enthusiasm and fervour of the priests and people as they marched singing their hymns through the streets and rejoicing in this opportunity of showing the fervour and force of Dublin Catholicism.

What a joy it must have been to Father Young to put that booklet together and to have had a hand in this great demonstration. But his greater joy must have been in the contemplation of the spiritual reform the Jubilee Devotions were working in the lives of the people. To bring about similar results among his own parishioners he organised the Jubilee Devotions in Harold's Cross. The district was outside the city arrangement, and he was at liberty to settle his own devotions. A great procession of the people was an essential, and he considered that it should be held in the midst of the beauties of nature as well as on the roadside. Accordingly, he asked a Catholic parishioner who had extensive grounds to allow the procession to proceed through them, but the owner refused as he feared that the trees and shrubs might be injured by the sightseers. The objection was very probably a valid one considering the conditions of the period, but, it is related, that shortly afterwards all the trees on the demesne were blown down in a storm. It is also related that, in connection with these Jubilee celebrations, Father Young's labours were incredible. "He seemed endowed with supernatural strength in preaching, confessing, and exhorting, and brought thousands within the grace of that great privilege."[1]

2. FATHER YOUNG'S MISSIONS

(a). County Wicklow

In May, 1827, began the most remarkable period of Father Young's life; he was then forty-one years of age. He set out to conduct Missions, inside and outside the diocese, which

[1] *Life*, p. 84.

lasted, with some short interruptions, for about thirteen years. It may be taken that he was chosen specially by Archbishop Murray to conduct those Missions. In the Vincentian Mission House at Monte Celino, Rome, in 1814, he had been visited by the Archbishop and induced by him to return to Dublin. The Archbishop knew the work of the young priest on the missions in the villages near Rome. But a few years Archbishop of Dublin, and in the full flush of the unexampled resurgence of Catholic faith and practice through the Jubilee of 1825–26, among the people of Dublin, he thought it opportune that the same facilities should be given to the people of the country districts. The parish priests of those districts had not only asked for the extension of the Jubilee to them but had asked for the extension of the blessings of the Forty Hours' Adoration.

The extension of those privileges seemed easy enough on paper, but was there the urge on the part of the country people to benefit by them ? Was there sufficient parochial organisation to induce the people of a parish to tramp miles of the road to come to the devotions in the church ? Churches were many miles apart ; and was it to be expected that people would walk several miles to and from the church to take part in evening devotions ? We do not know what was the response of the country people to the exhortations of the pastors to attend the Jubilee devotions, but, if we are to infer from the episcopal appointment of Father Young to conduct Missions in the West County Wicklow, it may be presumed that the appeals of the parish priests had fallen mostly on deaf ears.

Archbishop Murray requested the only priest of his diocese, Father Young, capable of conducting missions, to visit the country parishes and preach and teach what he had been carrying out in the city parishes. In those days, in the city, as we have seen, there was decided slackness in the frequentation of the Sacraments. It may be presumed that the same was true of country districts. The relief from the penal code had induced a certain ebullition among the young people which was not always in keeping with Catholic tradition. Indeed, in every parish, this exuberance of spirit was a force or tendency to be guarded against. The parochial clergy were sufficiently occupied in the essentials of parochial duties to leave them little time to look after the important details of personal sanctification. It was to provide the people with the means for this personal sanctification, hitherto little practised, that Father Young was appointed to begin his Missions in West County Wicklow.

A Mission was indeed a novelty, and the people warmly responded to the invitation and tramped the miles of road to listen to this little priest from Dublin, who was by no means eloquent, but who possessed, what was better for their purpose, the fire of Divine Love, which he knew how to enkindle in their hearts. His sincerity and enthusiasm won their attention and admiration.

Of all the devotions with which his name is associated that of the Rosary stands out pre-eminent. We have seen how he and his brothers recited it at the graveside of their parents and on the return journey to their brother's house. It was his constant practice to continue reciting the Rosary when travelling. It was his great devotion during his Missions— to re-establish the family Rosary, as he had sought to do in SS. Michael and John's, and to recommend the recitation to country people whilst travelling the roads on foot or by car. He saw in the devotion the elements of most other devotions. If he succeeded in winning back the people to that devotion he would have gone very far in familiarising them with the devotions to the Sacred Heart of Jesus, the Immaculate Heart of Mary, and the Passion of Our Lord. The devotion to the Holy Souls in Purgatory was next in importance, in his preachings, to that of the Rosary. He would have the people make the Heroic Offering of their good works for the relief of the Suffering Souls. No doubt, for the villagers and townspeople the daily Mass and the visits to the Blessed Sacrament were earnestly exhorted, and he gave them the opportunity of attending early Mass, and the example of visits to the Blessed Sacrament, for every minute he could afford from his outdoor missionary work was spent in the church before the Blessed Sacrament or in the Confessional.

His Missions were not of the weekly or fortnightly type— he spent weeks or months in a parish. His stay depended on the work to be done, the district to be traversed, for his idea of a mission was that of a personal visitation to every family in the parish. Until he had accomplished the family visitation he did not regard his mission as complete.

Besides his desire to renew devotional practices among the country people, he saw, as in SS. Michael and John's, that he had to lay the axe to the root of many abuses, the chief of which was the ancient custom of wakes. In the city, the Brothers of his Society could, within a few hundred yards, undermine the old custom of supplying alcoholic drinks, but in the country it was difficult to stop the visits of relatives and friends from miles around to the house of the dead and the consequent carousal. It was difficult to break down a tradition that had been rather fostered because of penal laws. Moreover, wakes were not only an outlet for profuse conviviality but for an exuberance of animal spirits out of keeping with the proper respect for the dead. Bishops and priests, even in penal times, had done their best to put an end to this irreligious demonstration, and had failed. Here was the work for an apostle—an outsider who came with new weapons to cut down the weeds in the Lord's vineyard.

The most poisonous weed in this field of the apostolate was the presence of the professional rhymer, who not only sang the virtues of the corpse, but stimulated the young by scurrility. Many attempts were made to stop the visits of the rhymer to the wakes, but they failed because of this craze for excitement during a period of suppression. It was Father Young's great objective in his Missions to stop this waking and to instil into the minds of the people that a soul had passed to its Judgment during those hours and that religious practices for its eternal welfare were to be fostered instead of the mawkish, and sinful, sentimentality that was customary and supported by the people. In the matter of Temperance, which was one of the planks of his reform, Father Young must have achieved remarkable results during his Missions.

Fairs, like wakes, were notable occasions for disorderly conduct. Fairs in villages and towns were more or less the same everywhere. An eye-witness[1] of the Rathfarnham Fair

[1] Dr. G. A. Little, *Malachi Horan Remembers*. Dub. Hist. Rec. IV. 4, p. 128.

(10th June) about the middle of the last century says of it :
" There were all kinds of side-shows in the streets. We would
have trick-o'-the-loop men, wrestlers, strong men, pipers,
ballad-singers, and the rest. But the cream of the milk was the
dancing. Lads, the best dancers in Ireland, would not fail to
attend. Every inn in the town would have a floor in its yard.
. . . There were all kinds of musicianers . . . we would be selling
all day and dancing all night."

No one could tell into what a Fair might not degenerate ;
faction fights were the things that were most to be feared.
In this regard, it may be useful to tell the part one man played
in helping to stop this deplorable exhibition of local rivalry
in West Wicklow. This man was the renowned Michael
Dwyer, and the place was the district of Father Young's
Missions, between Ballymore-Eustace and Baltinglass. In
the midst of all the striving of the people, after 1798, to clear
the yeomen and the militia out of the countryside, Irishmen
agreed to meet one another, with hurleys and sticks, and to
break one another's skulls.[1]

Michael Dwyer put, for the time being, at all events, an
end to that savage exhibition. Yet, the danger of its resurgence,
in days of freedom, was always present.

Father Young also played a man's part, about 30 years
afterwards, in showing the people the iniquity of all such
exhibitions in the field and at the fair. Whilst on his Missions,
he used to spend many hours, on fair days, walking through the
adjoining fields and gathering together the labourers in order
to exhort them not to take part in the riotous scenes at the
fair, but to join in the devotions in the church which were
held in reparation for the offences committed against God.

As he walked through the fair, his very appearance was
sufficient to put a stop, for a time, to sin and disorder. Sometimes he took more severe measures. It is related that, whilst
on the mission at Baltinglas, during fair days, he saw tight-rope
dancers displaying their talents in an improper manner.[2] This
exhibition was common at fairs. James Tissot's famous picture
of the " Tight-rope Dancer "[3] gives a good idea of the wanton

[1] Ronan-Cullen, '98 in Wicklow, p. 72.
[2] Life, p 101.   [3] James Laver, Vulgar Society

scene in London. The exhibitions in Ireland were, no doubt, English and tried to continue English manners and customs. Apparently, they were enjoyed by the people until Father Young intervened.

On the occasion in question, he tried to persuade the manager to stop the improper performance, but met with no success. " When, at last, a woman ascended the rope, and, disregarding his reproofs, exceeded her comrades in her unseemly evolutions, he took a summary means of terminating the exhibition by simply cutting the rope, which brought the lady to the ground, from no considerable height indeed, and without serious consequences to so agile an adept in the art of tumbling, but still unpleasantly enough to rouse her indignation."

The spectators, to their credit, listened to his call and followed him to the chapel to make reparation for the sins of the fair. He was summoned by the manager before the magistrate for damages, but read his Breviary in a corner during the trial. He was fined £5. He had already incurred the displeasure of certain bigoted gentry of the district for his zeal in removing Catholic children from Protestant schools.

The result of his interference was that the people of Baltinglas refused to visit the tent of the tight-rope dancing. The performance was continued, however, within the enclosure of the local gaol, and was patronised by the gentry. As to the fine of £5 against him, the difficulty was to decide who was to have the honour of paying it, as several people volunteered the money.

The parish register of Baltinglass contains the names of several Protestants received into the Church on this occasion. He erected in the church the Stations of the Cross, established the Purgatorian Society, and enrolled great numbers in the Brown Scapular of Our Lady of Mount Carmel. These three pious associations he endeavoured to erect in every parish that he visited. He likewise strove to have churches and schools rebuilt or repaired. Though it was illegal at this time—before Catholic Emancipation, 1829—to attach a bell to a " popish place of worship," yet he had a belfry and bell erected at Baltinglass.

Father Young continued his Missions in Blessington, Ballymore-Eustace, Kilbride and Eadestown, and drove up the mountains in severe winter weather to visit even the farthest cottage to preach to the inhabitants. His word was law and no one could resist his fervent exhortation.

Though his custom, during a great part of his life, was to partake of one very simple but hearty meal of stirabout each day, yet, during his Missions, he allowed himself a "collation." A servant in the house that gave him hospitality during a mission of four months in Stratford-on-Slaney, during the winter of 1828, states that "during his stay Father Young never took meat, eggs or butter. He had some bread and tea about 12 o'clock, and some gruel at night, on all days except Wednesday and Friday when his midday meal was a piece of bread with some water."

He is known to have reformed whole districts, not only by his fervent exhortations but by his personal piety. His wonderful devotion in saying Mass, his prolonged prayers in the church, and his zeal and charity, inspired a profound veneration in the people which stirred them to a change in their spiritual life.

During the patterns and fairs he used to erect booths in which he fitted up boilers and other vessels from which he served out coffee and buttermilk in order that thirst should furnish no excuse for entering the publichouse. He had notices of these provisions printed and circulated among the people of the pattern and the fair, but, unfortunately, his scheme was not an economic success.

He spent some months on the mission in Ballymore-Eustace. When he arrived in the town with his carpet bag he was directed to the house of two pious ladies, named Byrne, where he was to be lodged; there was no room for him in the parish priest's cottage. As soon as he put down his carpet bag in the Byrnes' kitchen he made his bargain for his board and lodging. He had no money, and he expected no stipend from the parish priest. He resorted to the following ingenious arrangement. When one of the Misses Byrne told him the price of the weekly lodging, he told her he would say Mass for her once a week—apparently half-a-crown was the price of the lodging. She agreed. His daily meal of porridge was not worth counting, so it was thrown into the price of the lodging. He enquired of the other Miss Byrne the cost of washing his linen and darning his socks, and he promised her another weekly Mass for her trouble. So, he had free board and lodging during the whole time of his mission in Ballymore-Eustace, but the pious ladies considered they were more than paid for their little hospitality by the Masses of the saintly missionary.

These facts were narrated to the author by a priest of the Dublin diocese who is a relative of the pious Misses Byrne, and who heard the name of Father Young passed on from one generation to another in Ballymore-Eustace as that of a saintly priest and hard working missionary.

(b). Garristown and Baldoyle

Father Young was recalled to the city mission in 1829, and took up duties in SS. Michael and John's at the request of Dr. Blake. We have already seen his work there. It would seem that he remained there until early in 1832, but conducted missions from time to time in North and South Co. Dublin.

During his mission in Garristown,[1] he lodged in Father Murray's cottage, the parlour of which was given over to him as a bedroom, but he preferred to sleep on the floor. No one knew when he rose, as he used to slip out noiselessly through the window, but he was always in the church long before 5 a.m., at which time he read aloud morning prayers for the congregation before saying Mass. Five o'clock was his usual hour of Mass, so that the people might get to their work in reasonable time.

Garristown, a place noted for brawls and ill-conduct, was completely reformed during his mission. For forty years, it is said, the parish had been given over to disorder. During Father Young's residence there, the farm-labourers were known to have neglected the spade in order to be present at his sermons in the church. He preached from the altar, and,

[1] *Life*, p. 102.

as he raised his emaciated hands, his hearers were reminded
of St. John the Baptist preaching in the wilderness : " Do
penance or you shall all perish alike." He felt he could
comfort the people by reminding them of the Beauty of
God and raise their hearts to recognise the Goodness and
Mercy of the great Creator who gave them the lovely countryside, and increased and multiplied the seed they sowed and
the cattle they tended. He appealed to the humble and holy
of heart.

He did not remain long in Garristown. He visited the
mountain district of Glencullen where his friend, Father
Patrick Smith, was parish priest. The chief object of his visit
seems to have been to instruct the children and prepare them
for the Sacraments, but the foundation of the Purgatorian
and Temperance societies was his great work for the people.
Father Smith, like Father Young, was a powerful advocate
of Temperance. The Glencullen Society was a credit to both
priests and cut a very respectable figure at the great Temperance Procession of 1841. Father Young seems to have
continued his missions from Glencullen as far as Bray, and
then returned to Dublin.

In 1831, his brother William was appointed parish priest
of Baldoyle (*Baile-Dubh-Ghaill*, Town of the Black Strangers,
i.e., the Danes) and Howth, and immediately erected schools
at Baldoyle for boys and girls. He was amongst the first to
benefit by the newly established National Education system,
and with the interest from a bequest (Keary) he was enabled
to maintain them. He next undertook the still heavier task
of building a new church at Baldoyle. The old chapel, humble
and primitive, was probably built in the reign of Charles II,
namely, shortly after Canon Begg became parish priest (1662).
Previous to that time the parishioners heard Mass in the
Grange of Baldoyle belonging to a Mr. Fitzsimon. The
Grange in pre-Reformation days belonged to All Hallows
Priory, Dublin, and, at the Suppression of Religious Houses,
became the property of the Dublin Corporation. The old
chapel of the Grange, the home farm of All Hallows, was
allowed to fall into ruins as there was no Protestant in the
locality to worship there, and no Catholic dare use it. Yet,

the Catholic family of Fitzsimon, the tenant of the Grange (1609), had Mass said in the house for the parishioners.

The old chapel of 1662 had done its work, and, in keeping with the modern ideas of church building in 1831, it had to have a successor. So, Father William laid the foundations of a respectable church, 84 x 40 ft., with suitable transepts. It was completed by his successors.

His next great work was the erection of a chapel in Kinsaley (*Cenn t-Saile*, the Head of the Brine or Estuary). A branch of the Plunkett family (of Loughcrew) of which Blessed Oliver was a member, had Mass said in their house, the Grange of Portmarnock, midway between Portmarnock and Malahide (now Grange House). Apparently, they had Mass said in the Grange during Elizabeth's reign.[1] The increase in the population of Portmarnock (*Port mo-Ernoc*) and Kinsaley made a new church imperative. For this work Father William desired the co-operation of his brother, Father Henry. Father James Young was then curate in Howth. Father William relied especially on Father Henry to help him in the erection of the church, the first stone of which was laid by him, at the request of Archbishop Murray, 5th March, 1832.

3. THE CHOLERA PLAGUE OF 1832

(a). *Dublin*

Father Henry was only a few weeks in residence at his brother's house at Baldoyle when he heard of the outbreak of cholera in the city (22nd March). When the occupants had gone to rest, he slipped out quietly and walked all the way to the Cholera Hospital in the city where he spent the night, and many other nights of the succeeding months.

Terror gripped the heart of Dublin when it was whispered around that some cases of cholera had been reported in the city, then in a deplorable condition of unpreparedness to ward off or cope with the menace through the woeful neglect of sanitation and through the congestion, poverty and squalor of the poorer quarters. It was well, indeed, that the charitable men and women of Dublin had during the preceding two

---

[1] Ronan, *Archiv. Hib.* VIII, 66–67.

decades banded themselves together in the cause of religion
and charity. It was well, also, that two Religious Orders of
Women, the Sisters of Charity (1819), and the Sisters of
Mercy (1831) had been already established.

Archbishop Murray sent a " Pastoral upon the first appearance of Cholera to the Roman Catholic Clergy and People
of the Diocese of Dublin," 25th April, 1832.[1] In it he says :

" The scourge which has fallen so heavily on a large
portion of Europe has, at length, reached our City. Several
of our Brethren have already been numbered among its
victims, and have passed, after the interval of a few short
hours of pain, from a state of perfect health to the grave. . . .

" Beloved Brethren, awake to your danger, and profit
by this admonition. You have disregarded the warnings
of the Word of God : He has sent a preacher to your
doors, to teach you by facts which force themselves on your
view that ' all flesh is grass, and all the glory thereof as the
flower of the field.' The grass is withered and the flower
is fallen because the Spirit of the Lord hath blown upon it.
Your sins have ascended to the throne of the Lord, and
demanded justice ; before that withering justice shall be
let loose against you, fall down in humble compunction
before Him ; turn away from those sins that have enkindled
His anger, and send up to Him the sacrifice of an humble
and contrite heart, through the merits of that atoning blood,
the spilling of which for our sins, we have so lately commemorated."

" It is ascertained beyond the possibility of a doubt, that
this great scourge marks out a large proportion of its victims
among the intemperate. . . . It is likewise ascertained, on
the authority of the most eminent physicians, that the
practice of waking the dead is most dangerous to the public
health, during the continuance of this destructive malady.
I admonish you, beloved children, with the affection—
and let me add, with the authority, of a parent—to abstain,
from the present altogether, from those meetings called
wakes ; and I caution the relatives of deceased persons
not to admit any stranger to enter unnecessarily under

[1] Meagher, *Archbishop Murray*, 154–56.

their roof, until after interment shall have taken place ; and I beseech them to procure interment with the least possible delay.

" Notwithstanding all the measures which have been taken to arrest the ravages of this awful visitation, we have to lament that it still continues the work of death. . . . I have heard from the clergy who attend the General Hospital the most consoling assurances, that nothing can exceed the zeal and humanity of the medical attendants, who there devote their labours with the most unremitting assiduity to the care of the Poor. The Priest is on the spot administer-- ing spiritual consolation to the sufferers ; the Sisters of Charity assist like Angels of Mercy round his sick bed ; every means that medical skill can devise is employed for his recovery . . . and should he unfortunately sink under the disease, the decencies of Christian burial are provided for—a spot for which, within the enclosure, has been duly consecrated, by my directions."

The Archbishop then refers to a matter that calls for some explanation. He says :

" With what grief, therefore, have I not learned that attempts have been made (yes, barbarously and inhumanly made) to prevent some of the afflicted Patients from receiving the benefit of medical attendance in this Hospital ! "

The public authorities, having converted Grangegorman Penitentiary into a temporary hospital, asked the Archbishop to allow the Sisters of Charity to visit daily. On hearing this, Mother Aikenhead at once nominated several of the Stanhope Street Community, including some of the novices, to take up the work. Mother Catherine, with two of her community, were brought over from Gardiner-street to help. The temporary hospital lay within about a hundred perches of the Stanhope-street Convent.[1]

Eight o'clock each morning saw the Sisters at their posts in the hospital where they remained until night-fall with the exception of an hour or so for dinner. The people, half crazy with terror, had been afraid to go to the hospital, but when

---

[1] *Life of Mary Aikenhead* (1928), 127.

the Archbishop issued his pastoral (25th April) they rapidly filled the hospital. The priests appointed to act as chaplains did their work with heroic devotedness. Among them was Father Henry Young, who spent nights in the hospital, consoling, absolving, and anointing the dying. Several priests died of the plague. The mortality among the nurses was particularly great. It often happened that everyone of them who had come in at night to attend the dying was carried out dead in the morning. Only one nun caught the contagion, but happily she recovered, and in a few days resumed her work at the hospital.

On the south side of the city a cholera hospital was opened in Townsend-street where Mother McAuley and her Sisters of Mercy, at the request of Archbishop Murray, came every day and nursed the afflicted patients. It was only a few months before (in January) that they had become a complete Religious Order. The zeal of Mother McAuley and her Sisters during the period of the plague was beyond all praise. Their chaplain, Father Carroll, never left the hospital and was assisted by several priests during their spare time. As in the case of the Sisters of Charity, it was remarkable that not one of the Mercy nuns fell a victim to the plague.

The cholera left hundreds of widows and orphans on Mother McAuley's hands ; the Orphanage and the House of Mercy in Baggot-street were crowded, and the yearly revenue which she had settled on the institution was insufficient for its wants. She made a bold stroke by writing to Princess Victoria through the Duchess of Kent.[1] " The Duchess returned a most gracious reply and, in a few days, a large assortment of fancy work executed by herself and her daughter was officially delivered at Baggot-street. The value of each article was enhanced by the autographs of the duchess and princess affixed. A bazaar was held in the house and thousands flocked to purchase the precious articles."

The Minute Book of the Evening Office Society of SS. Michael and John's shows how at least one Confraternity took the solemn word of the Archbishop to heart, for the Society also regarded the plague as a dispensation of Providence. A

[1] *Life of Mother McAuley*, 228.

Minute (15th January, 1833), tells of their spiritual activities during the period of the plague :

"The following prayers were said every evening after Office, beseeching the Almighty God to preserve the members of the E.O.S. and their relatives from the disease then raging which continued about seven months.

"First, seven paters and aves and Gloria patres in honour of the seven dolours and seven joys of Holy St. Joseph with an appropriate prayer taken from his feast of 19th March to be found 337 page of the Office Book, and concluded with the following :

"O Jesus, Divine Redeemer, be merciful to me and all the world. Amen.

"O Powerful God, O Immortal God, O Holy God, have mercy on us all that are in the world. Amen.

"Pardon and mercy, O My Jesus, during these present dangers, pour on us Thy Most Precious Blood. Amen.

"O Eternal Father, be merciful to us by the Blood of Jesus Christ, thy only Son, be merciful to us we beseech Thee. Amen.

"We were informed the origin of the above prayers was as follows.

J.M.J.

"Francis John Bartholomew, a Passionist monk at St. John and St. Paul's monastery at Rome. A most holy man and who had frequent revelations lately saying Mass, thought of the scourges about to fall on the world, wars, pestilence etc., when this prayer was revealed to him and he was told that whoever recited it with devotion should be preserved from the dangers with which the whole world will be visited.

"The Office of the Dead was said on every Thursday evening for those who died of the disease."

The Society resolved (15th January, 1833), that "the prayers after the Te Deum or Hymn of Thanksgiving be recited every evening after the Office in gratitude and thanksgiving to Almighty God for his Goodness in preserving the members of the Evening Office Society from the plague with which He has been pleased to visit the country called the Cholera Morbus."

The already existing Orphan Societies were called upon to make greater efforts, and new Orphan Societies were founded to cope with the immense number of orphans created by the Plague.

An Orphan Society, dedicated to St. Stephen, and founded in St. Paul's parish, 5th October, 1828, devoted itself principally to the new orphans. The committee met in the school-room, Queen-street, under Rev. Dr. Yore, P.P., as patron. The Orphan Society and Sunday Male School (St. James and St. Joseph), founded in St. James's parish, July, 1830, by V.Rev. Dean Lube, P.P., " to rescue from wretchedness and vice orphan children," rescued fifty destitute children, nineteen of whose parents died of cholera. Its society room was opposite the chapel in Watling-street. The County and City of Dublin Cholera Orphan Society was founded August, 1832, to rescue cholera orphans without religious distinction, and had its rooms in No. 12 Whitefriar-street. The Carmelites and secular clergy were its guardians. In two years 207 orphans were rescued and provided for. " The pennies of the poor were the principal means of support, collected weekly by charitable individuals." The Orphan's Friend Society, without religious discrimination, was revived, 1st October, 1832, in St. Andrew's, Westland Row. It supported, educated, and apprenticed the orphans to trade.[1]

Many families were deprived of their bread-earners, and unmarried men and women were left without support. For destitute Females the Franciscans founded a House of Refuge at 8 Coburg Place. Aged females were not forgotten in the already crowded programme of Catholic Action. A House of Reception was opened, in 1832, in St. Michan's parish, in 24, Upper Paradise-row (now Wellington-street), the first of its kind in Ireland. It was under the invocation of the Most Holy Trinity and had for its patrons the priests of the city parishes. H.R.H. the Duchess of Kent (mother of Queen Victoria) was a subscriber. It housed 18 women " of single

[1] Battersby, *Catholic Directory* (1836).

and exemplary lives." Men in their old age also found a happy home in which to end their days in a religious atmosphere ; the Augustinian Fathers of John's-lane founded St. Patrick's Asylum for men who had been " formerly well-off." The only instance of an asylum for men of a guild is that for aged printers, founded by the printers of Dublin on Crumlin-road in 1832. At this time much of the printing of Dublin was done in the vicinity of Crumlin. Other activities were the Burial Societies. One was founded by V. Rev. A. O'Connell, P.P. SS. Michael and John's, 25th October, 1835, under the invocation of St. Patrick, and had its meetings in the school-room Smock-alley. Another was the Andrew Christian Burial Society of which V. Rev. Dr. Meyler, V.G., was president. The object of these societies was to secure relief in sickness and Christian burial.

Considering the difficulties of the poor at the time, the Burial Societies were of the greatest assistance to the vast majority of the people. They were erected in almost every city parish, and the subscription was 1d. per week, with 6d. at entrance. They were definitely lay societies and had their own officers, and, besides providing a decent sum for the burial of the members of the associate's family, they granted a welcome bonus at Christmas. They continued into our own times as Burial or Tontine Societies.

A few words will not be out of place in reference to the two sisterhoods that did such heroic work during the Plague. They deserve special mention in an account of the Catholic Revival of the period.

Mary Aikenhead, the foundress of the Irish Sisters of Charity, was born in Cork, in 1787, of a Protestant father and a Catholic mother. Her father was a physician, and her mother belonged to the well-known family of the Stacpoles. About 1808, she was introduced to Father Daniel Murray, then curate in Liffey-street chapel, and confided to him her desire to join the religious state. Mary had had a glimpse of the submerged world of the erring and the stricken poor. She desired above all else to continue her service to the poor as a nun. An enclosed community could not serve the purpose she had in mind. She would have a " religious order that permitted her to continue her combat with poverty and pain on its own ground ; that would permit her to organise an army behind her in the same cause ; that would permit her to move freely about the streets. Finally, she wanted a Constitution so framed as to mould and support such an army of relief workers that they might not faint by the way."[1]

Father Murray became coadjutor-Archbishop in 1809, and, in 1812, introduced Mary and her companion to the Bar Convent, York, of the Rule of the Venerable Mary Ward which he considered the most suitable for Mary's purpose. In 1815, he decided to establish in Dublin a new Institute of Charity " specially adapted to the peculiar circumstances and needs of Ireland." Mary and her companion took over the Trinitarian orphanage with 14 orphans in North William-street, and Dr. Murray had the house enlarged and a chapel built at a cost of £2,000. Here was a complete novelty in Dublin—an order of nuns without enclosure. Another house was soon required as a noviceship, and the House of Refuge in Stanhope-street was acquired, and Mary became Mistress of Novices. Their orphanage was soon housing 100 children, but the mission to the sick was the great object of their charity. Their convent and schools in Upper Gardiner-street were opened in 1830.[2]

Catherine Elizabeth McAuley, the foundress of the Sisters of Mercy, was born, 29th September, 1787, at Stormanstown House, Ballymun, Co. Dublin. Having inherited £30,000 through the will of her benefactor, William Callahan of Coolock, in 1822, she was able to realise her early desire of founding an institution in which servants, and other women of good character, might when out of work find a temporary home. Dr. Blake was her chief spiritual adviser and found a site at the corner of Baggot-street and Herbert-street on which was laid the first stone of the new institution in July, 1824. Miss Anna Maria Doyle, sister to Father Michael Doyle of SS. Michael and John's, joined her and took charge of the house which was opened, 24th September, 1827. A Catherine Byrne took charge of the school and was assisted by Daniel

[1] A. Curtayne, *A Century of Service,* 1834-1934, pp. 17-18.
[2] *Life of Mary Aikenhead,* 36 seq.

O'Connell's daughters. None of the community of three thought of forming it into a Religious Order. At the suggestion of Dr. Blake, who had just returned from Rome (1829), Catherine, Miss Doyle, and Miss Harley entered George's Hill Presentation Convent, 8th September, 1830, to make their novitiate. They received the religious habit, 9th December, and were professed, 12th December, 1831, Dr. Murray performing the ceremony and Dr. Blake preaching the sermon. The other seven members of the community received the habit from Dr. Murray, 23rd January, 1832. The three objects specially mentioned in their Rule were " the education of the poor, the visitation of the sick, and the protection of distressed women of good character." As to the visitation of the sick, Catherine had, in 1828, broken down the barrier that kept a religious body from visiting any of the public hospitals then conducted by Protestant committees.

The cholera made its appearance, in the summer of 1833, in Ringsend and Irishtown. A Minute in the Register of the Evening Office Confraternity of SS. Michael and John's (15th August, 1833), states that it was resolved that, " in consequence of the return of the cholera, the prayers said on the former occasion be resumed." This Confraternity took a special interest in the parish and founded, in 1826, the Christian Doctrine Confraternity of St. Mary's, Irishtown, and had it supplied with books for the Catechism classes and two members as teachers. The old chapel stood in Chapel-avenue from penal times. From 1787 it was the parish chapel for Ringsend, Irishtown and Donnybrook. Irishtown chapel and priest's house were held from Lord Pembroke under an annual rent of £2 1s. 6d. which was returned to the parish priest.[1]

In his answers to the query sheet sent out by Archbishop Murray before holding Confirmation and Visitation in Irishtown, 1830, Dr. Flinn, P.P., mentions that " there are confraternities of the Christian Doctrine both in Donnybrook and Irishtown. . . . There is also a Purgatorian Society."[2] He calculated that there were about 3,000 Catholics in the Ringsend, Irishtown, and Sandymount district.

[1] Donnelly, *Dublin Par.* I, 21   [2] Ibid., p. 27.

Mrs. Verschoyle, wife of Richard Verschoyle, of Mount Merrion, agent to the Fitzwilliam estate, erected the poor school with £500 bequeathed for that purpose by Lord Fitzwilliam. A few years afterwards, she applied to Mother Aikenhead to send a few sisters to take charge of the girl's school, and she undertook to build a convent and to settle on it about £1,200, the interest of which was to sustain a chaplain. Mother Aikenhead and four sisters took possession of the convent, 16th June, 1831, the chapel of which was to be open to the public. Forty women and about the same number of men assembled at the convent in the evening for religious instruction. Sunday evening was devoted exclusively to the Irishtown sailors and fishermen. They had been careless about their religious duties, and many of the men were addicted to drink.

In a letter (7th August, 1833), Mother Aikenhead wrote from Sandymount : "We are in the midst of cholera. In Irishtown and Ringsend it is much worse than last year. By the aid of Sister Francis Teresa's brother [More O'Farrell] we got £20 from the Lord Lieutenant. I sent her and another to rent a house of the landlord's agent and we have obtained a store in Ringsend. With God's blessing we open our poor hospital this evening." A few weeks later she wrote : "Sisters M. Jerome and Francis Teresa are spending all their time in the poor little [cholera] hospital."[1] Fortunately, the plague raged only for five weeks with violence, according to Mother Aikenhead's report.

Consequent on the outbreak of cholera in Ringsend and Irishtown a Government Commission was appointed to enquire into the condition of the poor of the district (1833). The most important answers to the queries sent out were furnished by the parish priest, Dr. Flinn.[2]

As a result of the cholera the charitable societies of the city had many difficult problems to solve. It will be useful to review those societies and their work. The Minute Book of the Christian Doctrine Confraternity of SS. Michael and John's shows, in 1829, that there were 18 orphan children attending the Catechism classes in the church. This Orphan

---

[1] *Life of Mary Aikenhead*, 133.   [2] Donnelly, *Dub. Par.*, I, 30-36.

Society had been founded by Dr. Blake in 1816, immediately after the building of the new church, and Daniel O'Connell was its first president. Where the orphans were housed we do not know—very probably in lower Exchange-street, opposite the church, in the house afterwards used for other parochial purposes.

Catholic Charitable Societies increased considerably after the fever of 1817–19, and after the recurrence, 1827–28 ; but the urge was in favour of orphans, the resultant of the Fever. The poorer classes became more alive to the need of their help, and responded liberally to the appeal. Their penny-a-week subscriptions exceeded the total donations of the richer classes ; this is no reflection on the charity of the latter which was most generous. There was scarcely a Sunday on which there was not a charity sermon for one or other of those societies—on some Sundays there were at least two. Several of the secular clergy, such as Father A. O'Connell and Father Yore, were among the greatest preachers of the day and were called upon time and again to preach those sermons.

The Patrician Orphan Society of " Adam and Eve " was still doing heroic work. In 1836, 40 children—27 males and 13 females—were supported by it.[1]

The Metropolitan Male and Female Orphan Charity was founded, April, 1822, and had Sir Thomas Esmonde, Bart., as President. Up to 1836 it received 133 orphans. Its committee rooms were opposite to the Pro-Cathedral, in Elephant-lane[2] (Cathedral-street).

The Malichean Orphan Society, under the invocation of St. Malachy, was founded, 3rd November, 1822, and had for its president Rev. Dr. Murphy, Bridge-street chapel (St. Audoen's), and for its chaplain Rev. N. Coffey, Adam and Eve chapel. Its lay president was Mr. Ralph Walsh, 11 Essex Quay, the father of the great William J. Walsh, Archbishop of Dublin (1885–1920).

[1] Battersby, *Cath. Dir.*, 1836–37.
[2] This name is an example of how tradition can be obliterated. The original name was Mellifont-lane. Henry Moore, Earl of Drogheda, was the occupier of the Cistercian Abbey of Mellifont which had been granted to him by Henry VIII at the dissolution of the monasteries in 1540. His descendants had also property in Dublin and gave the names of the family title to Henry, Moore, Earl, and Drogheda (O'Connell) streets.

The Orphan Society of St. John of the Cross was founded February, 1825, and met in the Library room, Clarendon-street chapel.

An orphan Society of St. Vincent de Paul was founded in St. Michan's parish in 1826 with its committee-room in 3 Cuckoo-lane. In its first ten years it rescued 36 orphans. Another Society called the Mount Carmel Society for Destitute Orphans was founded, 13th April, 1828, which supported 45 orphans. Its committee met in 10 George's-hill. These two societies were apparently founded to rescue the orphans from the hands of the proselytisers and to hand them over to the parochial orphan societies.

An orphan society, without distinction of creed or parish owed its origin to the finding of a destitute child in St. Patrick's deanery. It was founded by lay men, March, 1827, and, within two years, it had ten orphans on its hands.

The Catholic societies had to deal also with the Magdalen problem. The Minute Book of SS. Michael and John's Christian Doctrine Confraternity, at 17th January, 1830, states that at least one of its members was engaged on Sundays in teaching Catechism in the Magdalen Asylum, 106 Mecklen-burgh-street (present Tyrone-street), which was founded by Rev. T. V. Holmes. Archbishop Murray was the patron and Rev. J. T. Laphen of the Pro-Cathedral was guardian. Father Holmes died a martyr to his zeal in the cause of the Magdalens. The asylum housed about thirty penitents and was controlled by a community of laymen who met every Friday evening in St. John's Library rooms, Smock-alley.[1]

On the subject of the Magdalens, it may be well to refer here to other activities in their behalf. A Magdalen asylum, under the patronage of the Archbishop, was founded, 1833, by Rev. John Smyth, C.C., SS. Michael and John's, in a house in Drumcondra-road. In a short time the house was found too small, and a large house and grounds were procured which housed twenty-eight penitents.

Father Young and his brother, Father William, took an active interest in the cause of the Magdalens. When Father Henry was in Harold's Cross, in 1825, and busy with the

[1] Ibid.

Societies of SS. Michael and John's, Father William founded the Female Penitent Asylum, Chancery-lane, which accommodated 45 penitents. In 1829, he removed it to James's-street, which was better suited for its laundry as a bleaching green was available there. In that year, Father William had to resign the presidency of the Asylum for twelve months in order to finish Phibsborough chapel. Meanwhile the house in James's-street became dilapidated, and, in 1831, he moved the asylum to 77 Marlborough-street as a temporary residence until the new laundry was built and a new house prepared. By 1836, 68 of the penitents who had been considered suitable for domestic service left the asylum to take up positions, and hundreds more had the happiness of returning to their homes. Father Henry was, in that year, and probably for some years previously, the spiritual guardian of the asylum, and his lay-brother, Sylvester, then living in 6 Mountjoy-place, off Mountjoy-square, was treasurer.

The famine and fever of 1818 had left many Catholic women widows. A house for them in John's-lane became too small for the numbers, and the establishment was removed to Archbold's-court, Cook-street. It supplied 34 destitute widows and other aged and distressed females, with food and raiment, and every other necessary. It was supported by subscriptions, and by a charity sermon on the third Sunday after Epiphany.

Another asylum for Catholic widows was set up about this time also (1818) in No. 8, Lower Liffey-street, " where seven houseless and friendless poor widows are supported by the charitable contributions of a few subscribers who are making exertions to establish a widow's house in St. Mary's parish, and to extend their protection and support to a great number of those destitute creatures."[1]

4. FATHER YOUNG AGAIN ON THE MISSION.

Whilst Father Henry was attending the cholera sufferers, his youngest brother Charles, entered the Society of Jesus, 2nd September, 1832. He was then 34 years of age,

[1] McGregor, *Dublin*, 272–73.

and resided at 5 Lr. Gardiner-street with his brother Sylvester, and was partner with him at 31 New-row. After eight years at the business he decided on entering the Society of Jesus and was sent to Namur and Rome, and, after his ordination, spent some years as Military Chaplain at Malta.

When the cholera had disappeared in the city towards the close of 1832, it is practically certain that Father Henry Young returned to Baldoyle to assist at the opening of the church at Kinsaley, dedicated to St. Nicholas of Myra (or Bari), the patron of sailors. Father Henry, having been curate in the parish of St. Nicholas, Francis-street, probably suggested to his brother the patron saint of the church. The first Mass was said in the church, 6th December, the feast of St. Nicholas. Shortly afterwards, Father William considered that he should make a pilgrimage to the shrine of St. Nicholas at Bari for the purpose, as he wrote to his parishioners, " of placing the Parish and its people under his holy protection. I offered up on the very tomb of the saint the Holy Sacrifice of the Mass on your behalf. I was blessed with the sight of his mortal remains and witnessed the prodigious miracle of the *Sudor*, or water called Manna, which exudes from his bones ; and which though distributed in quantities every day continues neverthe-less to issue forth fresh supplies. A portion of the Manna has been delivered to me sealed with the Bull of the venerable Prelate of the place, for the purpose of preserving under the altar of St. Nicholas at Kinsaley."[1]

During his absence he left the parish in charge of his brother, Father James, then curate in Howth. There was a curate, Father J. Tyrrell, in Baldoyle, and Father Henry took charge of Kinsaley. In his report to the Archbishop on the state of the parish, Father James stated that there were four Masses on Sundays and Festivals, two in Baldoyle, and one each in Howth and Kinsaley.

As soon as Father William returned from his pilgrimage to Bari, Father Henry considered that the parish was amply provided for, and decided to look for work elsewhere. Arch-bishop Murray found new missionary work for him—to go as an apostle from parish to parish and renew the faith and

[1] Donnelly, *Dub. Par.*, IV, 61.

enkindle the fervour of the people in the coastal parishes of North County Dublin.

In 1834, Father Henry gave missions in Swords, Rush and Skerries, and laid the foundation of a school on Lambay Island. Unfortunately, no details have come down to us about those missions, but it may be presumed that, according to this custom, he spent three or four months in each parish preparing the young for the Sacraments, preaching his mission sermons to the men and women, and founding religious societies to carry out his ideals. In 1835 he was curate in Blessington, according to the *Catholic Directory* of 1836, but ceased as such some time in that year.

The fame of his preaching had spread throughout the country ; its simplicity, fervour, and practical piety had won all hearts. Convents and colleges appealed to him to come amongst them and preach his simple sermons. Between 1836 and 1838 he seems to have made a tour of Ireland giving retreats to religious and students. No doubt, the Annals of those Houses still preserve important information, but we have no means of identifying those houses.

" The Ursulines of Cork," says his biographer,[1] " at whose convent he gave a retreat . . . still speak of the effect produced by his exhortations to penance. It seemed to them as if one of the Fathers of the Desert was speaking through his voice and calling them to follow in the narrow path which leads to life."

His sermons provoked smiles as well as making an impression on his hearers. During an eight-day retreat that he gave to a community of nuns, one of them gave his biographer a resumé of his opening instruction. " 'Tis a great work, sisters, a great work to climb up this hill of perfection in eight days. Well, Sisters, we must try. You remember reading when you were children the story of ' Jack and the Bean Stalk.' Well, Sisters, you must be like Jack. You must take the seven-leagued boots and climb up this high hill. But what are those boots, Sisters ? They are prayer and mortification. Yes, Sisters, if we put on those boots, they will assuredly bring us up to the top of the hill."

The popular veneration of Father Henry reached the

[1] *Life*, 108.

students in colleges and the brethren of Religious Houses. Students and religious knelt before him for his blessing whenever he visited their houses, but he always impressed on them the distinction between the sinfulness of man and the supernatural dignity and graces of the priest. He would have no respect shown to him as man but only as a priest of God.

Father James was imbued with the same missionary spirit as his brothers. He wrote to the Catholic Book Society of Ireland for a grant of books for his poor parishioners, and again he wrote from Howth, 29th July, 1836: " By your donation you will enable me not only to supply with books the fishermen who are able to read, but many also of the parishioners who are anxious for instruction."[1]

Father Young's lay-brother, Sylvester, was also engaged in charitable work. He was, in 1836, the treasurer of an " Orphan Society " of an unusual type. It was founded to aid the Sisters of Charity in Edinburgh to provide an asylum for destitute orphans of Irishmen who died in Edinburgh. It was called St. Patrick's Association, had for its patrons the Earl and Countess of Fingal, and held its meetings at 84 Damestreet. Here was a Missionary Society in Dublin, with Father Young's lay brother the moving spirit, before the Foreign Missions had been started in Dublin. Sylvester was at this time living in 6 Mountjoy-place, off Mountjoy-square, a fashionable residential quarter, and he had his woollen warehouse at 40 Lr. Bridge-street.

Father William was one of the patrons, in 1837, at the foundation of an asylum for aged single females at 6 Portlandrow. It is a curious coincidence that Father Henry was afterwards to be the chaplain to this asylum and to end his days there.

No doubt, it came as a shock to Father Henry, in 1838, when his brother, Father William, decided to relinquish his parish of Baldoyle and Howth and enter the Cistercian Monastery of Mount Melleray. He returned immediately to Howth to his brother, Father James, who decided that, in view of all the circumstances, and his own intensive work for many years, a continental holiday, chiefly in Rome, was due to him. So, Father James left Howth to Father Henry,

---

[1] *Life*, 108.

and Father William to his initiation into the Contemplative Order. In 1825, Father William had founded a Female Penitent Asylum, and removed it to 77 Marlborough-street in 1831. In 1838 he was succeeded as Guardian of the Asylum by his brother Father Henry, who had as treasurer his lay-brother, Sylvester.[1]

Father William remained only a short time with the Cistercians and took up missionary work in Cornwall in 1839. Father Henry continued as curate in Howth for the whole of that year during Father James's absence. He made a house to house visitation and discovered 800 persons, old and young, the blind and the infirm, who had not been confirmed. These he prepared for the Sacrament and presented them to Archbishop Murray. He established Purgatorian and Christian Doctrine Confraternities for the fishermen, which worked a thorough reform in their lives. He attended all the wakes and funerals in the parish and, by his very presence, turned them from scenes of dissipation into schools of devotion and respect for the dead. During Eastertide the crowd of penitents was so great that he often spent a whole night in the confessional. In this matter of instilling into the minds of the people the necessity of the frequent reception of the Sacraments and of giving them the means of carrying it out he was a pioneer. He wished to see abolished the custom of confessing and communicating but twice a year, at Easter and Christmas, which had established itself generally in city and country.

It is related that, during his mission in Howth, a Catholic gentleman fell seriously ill and refused to have a priest. Father Henry, having been asked to pray for him, replied : " I will say Mass for him on Friday next at 9 o'clock. When ordinary entreaties do not succeed, the Sacrifice of the Mass may avail." That morning, after the Mass, the dying man sent for the priest and died a sincere penitent.

House to house visitation was the great work of his missions. He felt that nothing less than that was of any use. His mission was not a mere series of Sermons, Confessions, and Communions. It was one of personal contact with every household,

---

[1] Battersby, *Catholic Directory* (1836).

and with every member of it. He learned their individual difficulties and he gave a personal exhortation in every case.

" Nothing," says his biographer,[1] " drew from him more severe words of reproof than the conduct of parents who allowed their children to leave home at improper hours, and who gave their daughters especially an amount of liberty incompatible with proper reserve and modesty of conduct. On that theme his eloquence was terrific. He used to paint their guilt in fearful colours, and denounce them as the authors of all the sin and sorrow which would one day result from their criminal neglect or indulgence.[2]   From house to house he used to go inquiring for the young ones of his flock ; inviting them to the sacraments, winning them by his affectionate words, amusing them by his droll sayings, laying traps to catch them if they eluded his summons. Full of holy wiles, he played innocent tricks in God's cause, and cheated the devil out of many a soul."

Up to the present day the name of Father Young is still remembered, and his fervent zeal for the spiritual reform of the parish is still spoken of among the people. " Sure, ma'am," said a poor old woman, shortly after his death, to a nun, " we had a saint one time in our parish ; his name was Father Henry Young ; he wore something made of bristles inside his waistcoat."[3]

5. FATHER YOUNG AND DEVOTION TO THE IMMACULATE HEART OF MARY

In 1840 Father Henry Young returned to Dublin as Curate or Assistant in the parish of St. Audoen and lived in the house adjoining the old chapel in the quadrangle off Lower Bridge-street.   About this time the religious exercises of the month

---

[1] *Life*, p. 112.

[2] The present Archbishop of Dublin, in his first Pastoral Letter to his people (Lent, 1941), treated of this subject as follows : " It is a grave error to believe that a school can ever hope to supplant the essential work of parents or can succeed in fully correcting the indiscipline that a parent's neglect has permitted to develop. If to-day, in the case of youth, a want of Christian self-restraint is sometimes to be deplored there is abundant reason to believe that the absence of virtue in the young can too often be traced to the lack of vigilance in the parents."

[3] *Life*, 107.

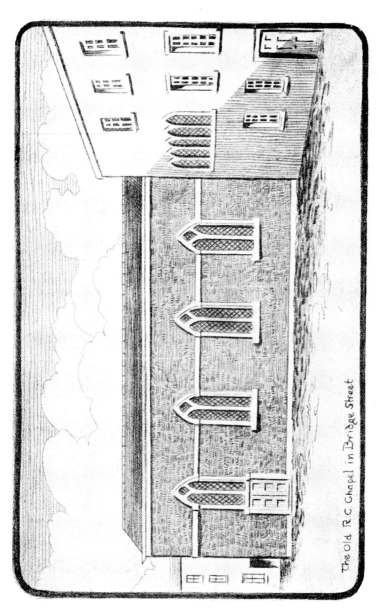

The old R.C. Chapel in Bridge Street

BRIDGE STREET CHAPEL.
(By kind permission of C.T.S.I.)

REGISTER AT ST. CATHERINE'S (FATHER HENRY YOUNG'S SIGNATURE).

of May were introduced into Ireland, at the wish of Archbishop Murray, with great solemnity by the Loreto Sisters at Rathfarnham.

It would seem that Father Young was recalled to Dublin and appointed to St. Audoen's by Archbishop Murray to preach and spread the devotion of the month of May. It was in the old chapel in Lower Bridge-street that the devotion was publicly inaugurated for the diocese. It would seem also that Father Young was responsible for the Dublin edition of a book on the Devotion entitled: *The new Month of Mary* or *Reflections for each day of the Month*, by V. Rev. P. R. Kenrick, Philadelphis, 1841. (R. Grace, 45, Capel Street.)

We have seen that during his first curacy in St. Michan's, he promoted the devotion to the Sacred Heart of Jesus and to the Immaculate Heart of Mary. During his missionary years throughout the diocese, the favourite devotion he wished to establish among the people was that of the Sacred Heart of Jesus. He was, indeed, the real apostle of this devotion throughout the diocese. It was not until he returned to the city, in 1840, that his other favourite devotion took practical shape. Meanwhile, the devotion of the "Miraculous Medal" (1830) had spread from France.

The devotion to the Heart of Mary, as in the case of the devotion to the Sacred Heart of Jesus,[1] is only a form of devotion to the Sacred Person, of which the heart is an expressive symbol and reminder. About the twelfth century there are indications in the sermons of St. Bernard of a regular devotion to the Heart of Mary. It was reserved for St. John Eudes (*d.* 1680) to propagate this devotion, and to have a Feast celebrated in its honour in France.[2] It was not until

---

[1] Article, "Heart of Mary" (*Catholic Encyclopaedia*).

[2] During all his life St. John Eudes was most insistent on the unity of Heart that existed between our Saviour and His Holy Mother. . . . Even though Father Eudes at all stages of his career emphasized this unity of hearts, his doctrines on the subject underwent a transformation as life advanced. The devotion to the Heart of Jesus seems to have blossomed out of the Devotion to the Heart of Mary until it became a separate devotion. In his early life it was the Heart of Mary that attracted his attention, and the first feast he established was in honour of that Heart. . . . But the last of the twelve volumes [of Father Eudes] is devoted completely to the Adorable Heart of Our Lord." Yet the title of its first chapter is: "The Divine Heart of Jesus is the crown of the glory of the most holy Heart of Mary."— (Quinlan. *History of Devotion to the Sacred Heart.*—St. John Eudes, *I.E.R.*, November, 1942, pp. 364–65.)

1799 that Papal sanction was given to the devotion. In that year Pope Pius VI, then in captivity at Florence, granted the Bishop of Palermo the feast of the Most Pure Heart of Mary for some of the churches of his diocese. In 1805, Pius VII made a new concession, and the feast was soon widely observed. Father Young was in Rome at this time and was in touch with the devotion at the Vincentian House. Such was the existing condition when a two-fold movement, started in Paris, gave fresh impetus to the devotion. The two factors of this movement were first of all the revelation of the "Miraculous Medal" in 1830, and all the prodigies that followed, and then the establishment at Notre-Dame-des-Victoires of the Archconfraternity of the Immaculate Heart of Mary, Refuge of Sinners, which spread rapidly throughout the world and was the source of numberless graces.

The devotion to the Sacred Heart of Mary for the Conversion of Sinners was begun in St. Audoen's, Bridge-street, August, 1840, by Father Monks, P.P., assisted by Dean Gaffney, Maynooth College. The Acts of Consecration and Reparation were recited on the "first Saturday of each month (a day particularly consecrated to the Sacred Heart of Mary) immediately before the Benediction of the Most Holy Sacrament."[1] A Sodality of the Sacred Heart of Mary was then established in the parish.

It would seem that Father Young's services were called upon for the promotion of the devotion. A booklet was published about this time by the Catholic Book Society, Dublin, entitled *Nature of the Devotion to the Sacred Heart of Mary for the month of August*, which, in its Introduction, shows all the characteristics of his writing. Like Father John Eudes, he was an apostle of the double devotion. The Introduction states that :

"The following little Tract, it is presumed, will be found profitable to all, especially the pious associates of the Sodality of the Sacred Heart of Mary ; for the great Feast of this Blessed Heart occurring on the Sunday after the Octave day of the Assumption, the reflection for every day, and which is derived from the sentiments of the Heart of

[1] *Catholic Luminary* (1841), p. 367.

Mary, considered in the various circumstances of her life, as well as the flowers and fruits, will dispose them for piously celebrating it ; and then the Blessed Mother will not fail to reward most liberally those who practice this little devotion. She will be their protectress in life, and at the dread hour of death hide them in her Sacred Heart, till the anger of her son have passed away, and they be able to stand with confidence before his throne, secure of a favourable sentence."

The booklet contains meditations for every day in the month of August, treatises on the Devotion, a Novena, and the Office of the Sacred Heart of Mary. It concludes with the " Rules of the Association of the Immaculate Heart of Mary for the conversion of sinners as established in St. Audoen's Parish church, Bridge-street." A Register containing the names of the members was kept, and a priest, appointed by the Archbishop, presided over the Association. The members should receive Holy Communion on the Second Sunday of each month. " This Association shall possess no pecuniary fund, its riches are the treasures of grace which God gives to those who devote themselves to him and to his Blessed Mother, and the indulgences which the Holy See has granted to it."

" The members shall meet on each Sunday evening, at 8 o'clock, in the parish chapel of St. Audoen's, Bridge-street, and shall say the Little Office and the Litany of the Sacred Heart of Mary, with the Acts of Reparation and Consecration, and the prayers to the Sacred Heart of Mary. They shall then read (or hear read) for fifteen minutes a spiritual lecture, generally from some book that treats of devotion of the Blessed Virgin, and conclude with five Paters and Aves—one for the Archbishop, Priests and Religious of the diocese ; one for union and perseverance among the members ; one for the conversion of sinners ; one for the increase of Catholicity in the Empire, and the progress of Temperance among all Christians, and one for the souls of the faithful departed, especially the deceased members of the Association."

This Association had become so popular that, in 1841, there were more than 2,000 members on the register, and a special Confraternity of 80 men was formed to recite the Office in the little chapel in Bridge-street. The Rules of the Confraternity were printed separately ; an edition of 1874 (to hand) was issued by Ward, 20 Christchurch-place.

The Sodality of the Sacred Heart of Mary became to the parish, and to the people of Dublin generally, what the Devotion to St. Anne in St. Audoen's had been in pre-Reformation days. Father Young had thus seen diocesan approval given to one of his earliest devotions, and, to-day, we see a wonderful devotion spring up in the city to the Immaculate Conception, but it is only a resurgence of the devotion promulgated by Father Young in St. Audoen's, a hundred years ago, to the Immaculate Heart of Mary.

There remains only to stress the fact that Father Young included in his Rules the advisability of prayers " for the progress of Temperance among all Christians." The inclusion of " all Christians " was characteristic of him. He was not limited in his spiritual outlook, and he asked the prayers of the Association " for the increase of Catholicity in the Empire." His religious outlook was not confined to Ireland ; his brother, Father William, was then on the mission in Cornwall. The appeal for prayers for the cause of Temperance was what one would have expected from him, and it coincided with the great Temperance Movement in which he and his brother, Father William, were taking such a prominent part.

Devotion to the Mother of God was not only the favourite devotion of Archbishop Murray, but, beyond all the Irish prelates of his time, he laboured to obtain, through the bounty of the Holy See, an extension to the Irish Church of the several festivals instituted in her honour. One of his first acts as Archbishop of Dublin (1823) was to have celebrated the festival and Office of the *Seven Dolours*, extended by Pius VII, in 1814, to the Universal Church but, from one cause or another, not introduced into Ireland until 1823. Other Offices of the Blessed Virgin he exhorted his priests to adopt instead of the Ferial Offices, and obtained permission for them to do so, as, for instance, the Office of the *Sacred Heart of*

Mary, her *Purity*, her *Maternity*, and that entitled *Auxilium Christianorum* which was the tribute of Pius VII in acknowledgment of his almost miraculous restoration to his Church and dominions.

The Diocese of Dublin was aggregated with the Archconfraternity at Paris of *The Immaculate Heart of Mary, Refuge of Sinners*, about 1840. It was this devotion at " Our Lady of Victories," Paris, which transformed that city from indifferentism to piety and good works. It is interesting to note that Archbishop Murray adopted this title of the Blessed Virgin for one of his new churches, namely at Rathmines.

The district of Rathmines was cut off from the ancient parish of St. Nicholas Without the Walls in 1823, but its new church was not completed until 1830 when, 15th August, Archbishop Murray dedicated it, the preacher being the famous Dr. Doyle, Bishop of Kildare and Leighlin. The dedication was to SS. Mary and Peter. · The structure, however, was faulty from the foundation, and a new one was begun, the foundation stone being laid by Archbishop Murray, " the 18th of August, the Festival of St. Joachim, in the year of Salvation 1850, under the Pontificate of Pius IX, and in the reign of Victoria I, Queen of Great Britain."[1]

The Living Rosary, or circle of fifteen persons, to make the devotion a living thing in the lives of the people, by meditation and prayer, had a real charm for the zealous Archbishop. His letter, 9th November, 1841, tells of the " rapid spread of the devotion . . . and the fruits of piety and virtue, which it has everywhere produced." An interesting item appears in this letter : " We are highly pleased with the design, and arrangement of *The Manual* intended for the use of members of the Sodality."[2]

About this time, Father Henry's brother, Father Charles Young, S.J., was one of the Jesuit Fathers engaged in

[1] It is interesting to note that whilst the founders, in 1850, commemorated the reign of Victoria in this solemn parchment scroll of dedication, deposited in a strong glass vessel in a chamber hollowed out of an immense granite block, they gave her only the title of Queen of Great Britain. They said nothing about Ireland. At the laying of the foundation stone of St. James's, in 1844, the parchment scroll styled per Queen of Great Britain and Ireland.—(Donnelly, II, 92–94.) After the definition of the Immaculate Conception, 1854, Archbishop Cullen added the word " Immaculate " to the title.

[2] Meagher, *Archbishop Murray*, 131–133.

introducing into Dublin another type of devotion for the sanctification of the people.

The commemoration of the ter-centenary of the Society of Jesus began in St. Francis Xavier's, Upper Gardiner-street, Friday, 23rd October, 1840, for it was in that month, three hundred years previously, that the Society was established by the authority of the Head of the Church. It was made the occasion of a nine days' retreat, the first of the kind held in that church, according to the exercise drawn up by the founder, Saint Ignatius. The exercises caused a spiritual sensation in Dublin ; they were announced from the pulpits of the city parishes, and booklets were scattered far and wide to explain their meaning and object. The best Jesuit preachers were employed : Fathers Kenney, Aylmer, Haly and Ferguson. Though the weather was inclement, and the distance to the church considerable for the people, yet, from the first Mass at 6.30 until 9 o'clock, the church was crowded. The interesting feature of the exercises, as regards the Young family, was that Father Charles Young, recently returned from Malta, was the selected reader of the prayers. After Mass at 7.30, the " Morning prayers were most audibly recited from the *Catholic Piety* by the Rev. C. Young, S.J., from the pulpit, in which all joined." Apparently, he was gifted with a similar penetrating and commanding voice to his brother, Father Henry, who read morning prayers for years for the people of the slum parishes. Father Charles recited from the pulpit, every evening during the exercises, the Rosary, *Miserere* and Night Prayers.

Father Charles spent only a short time in St. Xavier's, and spent the rest of his life, 56 years, between Tullabeg and Clongowes, where he was Spiritual Director. He took special delight in instructing the Spanish students from South America at Tullabeg in Spanish literature. Like his brother, Father Henry, he had solid and amiable qualities, cheerful, unaffected piety, simple gaiety, and yet profound understanding. Unlike him, he had grace of manner and elegance of bearing ; his Spanish education was different from the crude experiences of Father Henry in the villages outside Rome, and in the slums of Dublin and the Irish countryside.

To return to St. Audoen's : efforts were being made to
provide a more commodious church for the people and a more
fitting abode for the great Association of the Immaculate
Heart of Mary. Father Monks, the parish priest, on his
appointment in 1833, inaugurated the Penny Weekly Collection for the building of a new church. No doubt, he had
the wholehearted co-operation of Father Henry in the year
1840. By 1841, he had thus collected £5,436 and purchased
a site in High-street for £3,634. On Easter Monday, the first
parochial meeting for the building of the church was held and
was attended by Daniel O'Connell. The church cost £4,483,
and was dedicated, 13th September, 1846, by Archbishop
Murray. The old chapel, off Bridge-street, was abandoned
and was soon afterwards demolished but the chapel house was
let in tenements and was demolished only in recent years.

Whilst Father Henry was occupied with the promotion
of the Devotion to the Immaculate Heart of Mary in Bridge-
street chapel, and Father Charles was engaged in the Spiritual
Exercises of St. Ignatius in St. Francis Xavier's, Father William
was endeavouring to restore the Faith in the ancient Celtic
country of Cornwall.

6. Father William Young's Mission in Cornwall

(a). Missions

We have seen how Father William Young, having been
Parish Priest in Baldoyle and Howth, and having tried his
vocation as a Cistercian, decided to give the remaining years
of his life to the arduous mission in Cornwall.

The history of the Church in Cornwall resembles so much
that of Ireland that it is most probable that he was for that
reason attracted to the district. The people were Celts like
those of Wales, Brittany and Ireland, and the early Celtic
missionaries who lived and worked in Cornwall, or passed
through on their way from Ireland or Wales to Brittany, left
behind them many memories and legends enshrined in popular
memory, or in the dedications of churches and holy wells.
Moreover, the Cornish churches kept alive the traditional

life of their patron saints in Miracle Plays. These were written and performed in the Cornish language. Even to the end of the sixteenth century, when their Religious Houses were suppressed and an attempt was made to impose the Book of Common Prayer upon them, they continued their devotion to their Celtic dialect and recited " the Lord's Prayer, the Apostles Creed, and the ten Commandments " in no other language. Had they accepted the Book of Common Prayer in Cornish, the language might have been saved, but at the expense of their faith.[1]

Father William Young left Dublin for the Cornwall mission about the end of October, 1839. " On the 3rd November, he undertook the direction of the nuns at Lanherne, Cornwall, and of the congregation there." The Annals of the Convent give " the cost of his journey to Lanherne, £3 12s. 0d., and his washing and mending as 11s. 9d." " He was filled with grief at the state of religion around him, for only at Falmouth in Cornwall, was there a public church. In the ardour of his zeal he commenced on Ash-Wednesday [4th March], 1840, a course of public instructions in the neighbouring town of Columb, which he continued to deliver on Wednesdays and Fridays of Lent. On the 20th July, 1840,. he quitted the Convent to settle at Penzance, where he commenced to build a church in honour of the Immaculate Conception. The church was 90 feet long, 30 feet wide, and 54 feet high, with schoolrooms underneath." [2]

This church was a replica of the first church of St. Peter's, Phibsborough, the building of which Father William was, as we have seen, called upon to finish. He returned to Dublin in 1840 to collect funds for his Cornish church and mission. From the house of his brother, Sylvester, 6 Mountjoy-place, off Mountjoy-square, 2nd September, he addressed a letter [3] to the clergy and laity of the diocese in which he stated :

" That Cornwall was the last county in England to yield to the innovations which these latter centuries have made in religion in that country ; and that it is the last, also, in

[1] Rowse, *Tudor Cornwall*, 20–29.
[2] Extract from *Plymouth Diocesan Records*, which has kindly been supplied to me by the Diocesan Authorities.
[3] *Catholic Luminary* (1841), 164.

these days of religious regeneration, to make any sensible advance towards the re-establishment of the ancient faith.

" Since the period [of the Penal laws] there has been no Catholic house of worship in any town in Cornwall until, within some few years back, a small chapel had been erected in Falmouth for the strangers and foreigners coming into that port.

" That out of a population of nearly 400,000 inhabitants, which that duchy contains, there are scarcely two hundred resident Catholics. That those few are composed of English converts, a few scattered Irish, and some unsettled travellers and traders, a great portion of whom, in consequence of their want of religious instruction, and of opportunities of practising their religion, had been Catholics only in name, while their unhappy children were compelled in their school days to conform to a strange religion, to which, from the absence of any Catholic Chapel or Priest, they generally adhere in after life."

Father Young thus confirms the common opinion that the faith in Cornwall, and in Wales, was lost through the absence of priests. He says, however, that " there exists a laudable and universal spirit of religious inquiry everywhere abroad, which attracts crowds of auditors to Catholic sermons from many miles distant, whenever a priest has the charity and disinterestedness to announce the word of God in those neglected parts." He adds that there have been " conversions consequent on Catholic sermons, and the perusal of Catholic books."

He appeals to the Catholics of Dublin for his mission because of the motives

" which originally induced me to sacrifice my personal ease, comforts, and pecuniary considerations, to the service of such a destitute but promising mission. From my short experience of the mission to Cornwall, I am warranted in anticipating the most felicitous success. Far more than two-thirds of my hearers are Protestants of some grade or another. From several parts of the duchy I have received letters from individuals invoking my presence, and the assistance of my ministry, for their own spiritual wants, and for the reception of several converts into the Church. These urgent invitations I have been reluctantly compelled to postpone for the present, for the more permanent good of establishing missions and chapels for the use and accommodation of thousands.

"At present there is no house of Catholic worship in any part of my extensive mission. Penzance, at present, is my headquarters. The people of that rising town have declared, that if there were a commodious Catholic chapel there, it would be as numerously, as respectably attended as any house of worship in that town. The same may be said of any other principal towns of Cornwall. It is only kind in the Irish to patronize this mission. By Irishmen and by Irish Saints was the Gospel first preached in Cornwall.

"Let the renovation of religion in Cornwall become the work and the glory of the descendants of its original propagators. To effect this holy and glorious consummation, all I require is liberty from the venerable Parish Priests and clergy to fix up two small collection-boxes in each of their churches ; from the faithful, in general, I humbly solicit a donation of ONE SHILLING each, to be dropped, like the widow's mite, into the same."

He appeals especially to the Irish Teetotalers who have been admired "by every grade and caste of religion" in England for "the moral wonders—performed by the men and women of Ireland—in the Godlike march of temperance and virtue." He then continues :

"Our modern apostle of nations (for Father Matthew is respected almost to adoration, and his great principles are acted on in England, Belgium, and other countries of the earth) has commissioned me to extend branches of the Total Abstinence Society throughout Cornwall ; and already it has been established in two distinct portions of that duchy. Invitations and representations have been frequently made to me from various parts of that country to advocate publicly the cause of total abstinence, and preaching-houses of various sects have been rendered to my use for such occasions ; but as yet I have declined their pressing invitations. When I return, perhaps I shall comply.

"Temperance and faith, though not sister virtues, are fond and affectionate companions ; and religion never shines with a brighter lustre than when they go hand and hand together. It is this that lifts up Ireland, at the present moment, to a pinnacle of moral greatness which she never attained before, since those enviable primitive times when Ireland had been distinguished from all other nations of the earth, by the enviable appellation of ' Island of Saints.' How happy—how blessed—should we be if temperance and true religion were to salute and shake hands with each other in the ' sister Island ' ! "

The appeal had the approval of Archbishop Murray who was mentioned in it as one of those to whom contributions might be sent. A branch of the Temperance Association was at this time erected in the parish of St. Audoen, Bridge-street, under the patronage of the Catholic clergy, among whom was his brother, Father Henry, and Father William was invited to give a series of lectures to its members which began, Sunday, 6th September. " The zealous priest dwelt at great length on the powerful advantages of Temperance, and upon the glorious prospects for Ireland, under the mighty movement of Father Mathew, and the Catholic Pastors in each parish. He suggested the value of uniting all their force to prevent any relapse, of encouraging each other in the holy work, and of observing proper order and discipline in all their Societies." This " course of religious instructions and exercises, in Bridge-street Chapel, Dublin," was given " in order to advance the Catholic Missions in Cornwall."[1]

It is interesting to note how Father William Young hoped to combine the spread of the Faith with the spread of Temperance in Cornwall. His brother, Father Henry, had somewhat similar ideas for Dublin ; religious practices should go hand in hand with Temperance. Father William had delayed his complying with the requests of Protestants in Cornwall to preach the Temperance movement of Father Mathew in

---

[1] *Catholic Luminary* (1841), 166-68.

their conventicles. His object was, through the Dublin contributions, especially from the Temperance Associations, to build a Catholic church, worthy of ancient Catholic Cornwall, in which he could combine the preaching of the Catholic Faith and Temperance, not only for the benefit of the members of his flock, but for the conversion of non-Catholics.

The ancient glory of the Church in Cornwall was not forgotten, even in 1840, and, though the people had lost the faith, they saw in the place-names, the names of the Patron Saints of the parishes and churches, the folklore associated with those places and names, handed down in spite of change of religion, relics of what once they were. They were tenacious as to tradition, and they wished to know about those old Catholic practices. Hence, they welcomed a Celt amongst them, though not of their persuasion, yet one who was versed in their ancient history and who inherited the faith of their early Christian missionaries. Father William appeared to them almost the re-incarnation of an early Celtic Saint. The letters he received from non-Catholics all over the duchy on matters of Faith and Temperance show how he was regarded by them as one Heaven-sent.

He returned to his mission in Cornwall after his sermons in Bridge-street. He made another visit to Dublin in December, 1841, to collect for his Cornish mission, and he inserted in the *Freeman's Journal*, Saturday, 11th December, his "Apology for the Catholic Missions of Cornwall," which reads thus :

"The Rev. William Young apologises to the Catholic public and his correspondents for not having waited on them since his last return from the scene of his labours in Cornwall. The Church of the mission in Penzance is every day rapidly advancing ; but its funds are reduced to nothing. From Launceston, in East Cornwall, to the Lizard Point, in the south, and Landsend, in West Cornwall, the extent of the mission is more than eighty miles. It includes the Scilly Isles. Before the new mission was established there was no priest for twenty years.

"The children of Catholic parents have fallen away from

the faith which their fathers and forefathers for 1,400 years had professed because of the want of a foundation or provision for a mission, the want of a house of worship, and the want of maintenance of a clergyman."

Dublin Catholics responded liberally to his appeals, and he had the happiness of seeing his church at Penzance opened for public worship, 26th October, 1843, about three years after its inception. After a few years he felt, like the early Irish saints, the urge to wander for Christ (*peregrinare pro Christo*). He could have been very happy in his new church, which, no doubt, would have been frequented by many non-Catholics anxious to hear the word of God from a saintly Irishman, but he chose otherwise. He consigned his church and the Penzance mission to the Conceptionist Fathers, who had just arrived from Marseilles, and he " originated another mission at Bodmin, where he opened a church of Our Lady, on September 24th, 1846. The good missioner, placing Bodmin in the hands of Rev. Father Tieldell, went and laboured at Walsall, in Staffordshire, and at the new mission of Spitalfields, in London ; but, as Bodmin had been for some time vacant, he returned thither on the 1st May, 1852. Declining health, however, as his letter to Doctor Oliver, on 16th September, 1853, made known, compelled him finally to retire from Cornwall, on 20th July, 1854. He was with the Oblate Fathers of the Immaculate Conception at Sickling Hall, Yorkshire, in 1855, and at Cliffden Lodge, in the Hanwell Mission, London, with the Rev. Dr. Bonus, till he died on 1st December, 1859, aged 61."[1]

Father William was as amazing and as fruitful in his missionary zeal as Father Henry ; moreover he accomplished his great work within a few years. The Annals of Lanherne Convent state that " he built five churches and established schools," and " he presented to the Lanherne community the large statues of Our Lady and Child and St. Joseph, also the smaller ones of the Sacred Heart and Our Lady in the infirmary. The nuns hear Mass for him each year on the 1st December, the day of his death."

[1] *Plymouth Diocesan Records.*

Father William and Father Henry had many things in common—devotion to the Sacred Heart, the Immaculate Conception, and St. Joseph, and they were both ardent advocates of Total Abstinence. It is to be hoped that some day a worthy pen, at the other side of the Irish Sea, will do honour to the great apostle of Cornwall.

(b). Publications

It has already been shown that Father Henry and his sister Mary Ursula, the Ursuline nun, were writers and compilers of most important works of devotion and history respectively, and that they were pioneers in their own line. Father William was likewise a compiler, and a pioneer in his line. During his spare time on his mission in Cornwall he compiled two remarkable books. He brought the MS. of the first back with him on his visit to Dublin in September, 1840. This work—*The Voice of the Church*—was published in Dublin in the following year.[1]

In an " Address to the Reader " he thus describes its purpose. It is a debt " which he owes to the widely scattered members of his flock, to furnish them with motives to attach them, if possible, with still greater fidelity to the religion which an Augustin had planted, an Alfred defended, and a Bede illustrated."

Though ostensibly he wrote for the edification of the Catholics of Cornwall, and to make them loyal to and proud of their ancient inheritance, yet indirectly he wished to show to non-Catholics the evidences of the Catholic religion. Like his brother, Father Henry, he was qualified, with pen and erudition, to undertake the apostolate of the pen as well as that of the pulpit. Both were eminently practical—Father Henry in his work for the moral regeneration of Dublin, Father William for the Catholic revival in Cornwall.

[1] The title-page reads : " The Voice of the Church, from the Remotest Ages o Christianity. To which is added a Table of Scriptural References and Reasons which attach Catholics to their Religion. Compiled by The Rev. William Young, for the Use, and Benefit, of the Catholic Missions in Cornwall. Dublin : Published by James Duffy, 25 Anglesea-street. Sold at the Religious Library, 6, Essex-street. 1841."

The second work was a remarkable book, somewhat on the lines of the *Evening Office* of Father Henry. In a brilliant preface he states his object : " Although, by reason of their various necessary secular avocations, the laity are not bound, like the clergy, to its recital ; yet, that portion of it which includes the hymns and canticles, and which, besides the praises of God, contains solid principles of speculative and moral divinity, might, without interfering with their ordinary business, be frequently, if not daily, recited by them with great spiritual benefit and fruit." He added erudite notes for the information and edification of the readers on many important points of Catholic history and doctrine.

He called the book *The Catholic Choralist*,[1] and published it on the " Feast of the Assumption of Our Blessed Lady, 1842."

He calls it " this feeble production of my late sickly and ailing hours "—apparently his strenuous missionary labours in Cornwall had broken him down. He dedicated it to Father Theobald Mathew, the " Father and moral regenerator of his country . . . in the hopes that it may eventually serve the cause of temperance and religion, by supplying innocent, edifying, and agreeable occupation for those hours of recreation which an indulgent providence allows to weak and exhausted nature."

Though he, and his brothers, Fathers Henry and James, and other priests of the diocese, had been preaching and promoting temperance for twenty years before the Father Mathew Movement, yet he styles the Apostle of Temperance " the only pivot on which, and round which, the entire [machine] revolves." " Tariffs, poor-houses, prisons, and such like artificial expedients to remedy the evils which profligacy and misrule create, will gladly be forgotten ; and special commissions and party feuds, and starvation riots,

---

[1] " *The Catholic Choralist* for the use of the Choir, Drawing Room, Cloister and Cottage. Harmonized and arranged for the Voice, Band, Piano-Forte, and Organ. Interspersed with useful notes. Dedicated by Permission to the Very Rev. Theobald Mathew, O.S.F., Dublin : Published at the *Catholic Choralist* Office, 23, New Buildings, Essex Street (within two doors of Eustace Street), and at the Catholic Library, Penzance, Cornwall. M. J. Toomey, Agent, 1842." Like this brother, Father Henry, and his sister, Mary Ursula, he modestly refrained from putting his name on the title page of his publication.

will be remembered only to show forth, in higher and brighter relief, the superior happiness and blessings resulting from the one simple principle of Teetotalism.

"When we contemplate," he continues, "this mighty, unexpected, and sudden change in a WHOLE PEOPLE, from the one extreme of intemperance and degradation, to the opposite one of sobriety and total abstinence, our minds are insensibly carried up to contemplate the unscrutable councils of the Deity, and to adore that mysterious Providence which knows how to confound the pride of the human understanding, and to bring about the most glorious revolution the world ever witnessed, by means the most simple, and to all appearance, disproportionate."

Though it was all very well to preach the advantages and blessings of Temperance, and to form societies and organise monster tea-parties and amusements to divert the people from the frequentation of public-houses, yet Father William considered that something else was required for " the improvement of their hearts." It was sacred music ; to popularise it among adults and children. " With the helps and directions given in this volume," he says, " Clergymen may, without difficulty, form effective choirs in their respective parishes and be enabled, in a short time, to have appropriate pieces sung in their churches, both at Mass and Vespers. This will inspire emulation among their flocks ; and, while refining their tastes, will contribute, in a wonderful manner, to the improvement of their hearts."

Father William confines himself to the Vesper Hymns in this first edition of the *Choralist*. " To render these hymns," he says, " still more worthy of the dignity of divine worship, and to deck them out in all the attractive charms of sacred melody, they have been adapted, and arranged with considerable care, to the most exquisite airs—the compositions of the first masters. It is only necessary to mention the names of Haydn, Mozart, Pleyel, Webb, Beethoven, Sphor, Bach, Guynemer, Mazzinghi, Viotti, etc., as the authors from which selections have been made, in order to affix the stamp of merit on this little work, and to give it currency among the people. Yet it is not to these well-known authors the work is trusting.

On perusal it will be found to contain compositions rare, valuable, and novel in this country."

The sacred music of the masters was quite familiar to the Dublin people of the eighteenth century, as has been already mentioned, and adult choirs in the penal-time chapels sang it, especially the music of Handel, Haydn, and Mozart, on Sundays and Holidays. The Evening Office Confraternities had their own traditional Church chant for their various hymns, especially on the feasts of Christmas and Easter. Father William's object was to adapt the music of the masters to the liturgical and other hymns for the benefit of those assisting at Mass and evening devotions " for the improvement of their hearts." Realising the popularity of the music of these masters, he wished to use it in order to draw attention to the excellence of the hymns themselves from the doctrinal and devotional standpoint. He wished to make the Mass and Evening Devotions attractive in this manner, and he wished to have choirs established in every parish to turn the minds of the people from alcohol and through the attractive rendering of those hymns set to the music of the masters he would thus provide an antidote to intemperance. At all events, in promoting parochial choirs on those lines, apart from the Temperance motive, he was doing pioneer work.

His vision, however, went beyond adult choirs. He was concerned also with the singing of children in church ; this was another new departure, so far as we have been able to discover. He quotes Haydn for the importance of this new move. " The finest things," says Haydn, " that I ever heard in music did not approach the effect produced by the uniting of the voices of the children in the cathedral, and why are not these voices heard in every church and chapel in the land ? Why is not singing taught in our schools ? A better preservative to pure morals—a more delightful cheerful stimulant to all their exercises, whether of labour, study, or religion, can scarcely be divided. Nor would its effects be confined to the school-room or to childhood ; it would soon penetrate to the paternal feeling ; in another generation it would be natural to the land."

It is to be regretted that Father William did not make some

comment on this remarkable statement of the great master in order to emphasise the importance of the singing of children in church, which he had at heart. At all events, the words of the master are as worthy of attention to-day as they were in his time.

Though Father Henry had given an English translation of the hymns, with the Latin version, in his great work of the *Evening Office*, yet Father William in his edition of the Hymns, did not copy his brother's translation, but made a completely new one. When one remembers the busy life of these priests in their missionary rounds, one wonders how they were able to find time for the apostolate of the pen—it could only have been done by burning the midnight oil.

Father William gathered together over 250 hymns, of which 20 were on Temperance. It would seem that he was the composer of many of them. It is amazing that so many splendid pieces of Catholic poetry were in use in those days; to-day we could scarcely count 20 of which our people have any knowledge. All this is further proof of the great Catholic urge of those days and of the seriousness of the endeavours of priests and people. Catholicism was then deep, rooted in eternal principles, and ruled the daily life of the people. Life apart from it was unthinkable.

Though Father William had a respectable knowledge of music, as his sister Mary Ursula had, he employed another for the musical portion of his work. Part II of the *Catholic Choralist* deals with " a Selection of Sacred Music, adapted to the foregoing Hymns, and compiled from the most eminent masters. By B. Walsh, Teacher and Professor of Music, Baldoyle." According to an ancient of the parish of Baldoyle, B. Walsh was none other than the village schoolmaster. Father William, when parish priest of Baldoyle, must have had some arrangement with him about the compilation of this work, and it was only after he had been a few years on the Cornwall Mission that it was issued.

The Hymns occupy 166 pages, and the Music 136 pages. Mr. Walsh must have had a very extensive knowledge of the masters as well as a competent musical education. Besides adapting the hymns to the music of the masters, he lays down rules for singing, on the Solfeggio system, " as used by the Italian school to ensure the articulate pronunciation of the vowels, that the words or sense may accompany the sound." It is interesting to observe how the village schoolmaster of Baldoyle laid down a hundred years ago the rules for correct singing. It is interesting also to note the excellent printing of the music, by " William Holden, Music-Printer, 10, Abbey-street, Dublin." It is doubtful that such work could be done to-day in Dublin. The *Catholic Choralist* is then a precious reminder of a great age.

7. FATHERS JAMES AND HENRY AT FINGLAS

Father James Young, C.C., Howth, on his return from his year's continental holiday, was appointed parish priest of Finglas, June, 1841. Immediately he petitioned Archbishop Murray to allow him to have the services of his brother, Father Henry, then assistant in St. Paul's. He began a new parochial register[1] on the front page of which he wrote : " On Saturday, 5th June, 1841, I was inducted into this parish, in Finglas Chapel, by Rev. James Callanan, P.P., Clontarf, who was authorised by the Most Rev. Dr. Murray, A.B.D. The Rev. Henry Young officiated in Finglas, as my coadjutor, from the commencement of my Pastoral career till the middle of November, 1843." Father James lived in St. Margaret's, and Father Henry at Finglas. Father James intended his brother to be a missionary in the parish.

A Visitation Schedule, belonging to Father James, mentions, besides three chalices and ciboria, two monstrances ; the consoling rite of Benediction of the Blessed Sacrament had been promptly inaugurated by him in the two churches of his parish. It will be remembered that the custom of having Benediction on one Sunday in the month began in St. Michan's where Father Henry had been a curate. On one occasion he said that if the diocesan authorities allowed him he would have Benediction every day.

In the following November (9th) Archbishop Murray introduced into Ireland the Sodality of the Living Rosary. Father Henry was now well equipped with May Devotions

[1] Donnelly, *Dub. Pars,* IV, 171.

and Family Rosary as correctives to the pagan festivities of
the May-pole. When Major Sirr was called to Finglas in
1803 to quell a riot he found, as we have seen, that it was
" only a May-pole celebration " which had been held there
for over a hundred years.

Finglas May-pole was indeed the centre of riotous gathering.
Father Henry called it the " devil's potstick." Apparently,
booths were erected for side-shows and the sale of liquor,
and the concourse of people from adjacent districts was very
considerable. It was the people who were making a profit
out of this annual gathering who supported it. Father Henry
suppressed it, and had the Maypole cut down to light the fire
to cook the meal and potatoes for the poor. His communal
kitchen was again a failure.

The rioters were not yet defeated. When, according to
custom, they converged on Finglas, May-day, 1843, from all
sides of the country and found no booths wherein to quench
their thirst, they retired to the nearest public-house to carry
on their festivities. They did not reckon with Father Henry.
He appeared in the midst of them, men and women, and,
during their dancing, mentioned several of them by name as
disgracing the parish. The revellers fled, not wishing to be
identified by him. It is related that the instruments for the
amusement of the company received severe treatment from
him when the dancers had departed. The floor of the public-
house was littered with broken fiddles and bagpipes.

He was never merely destructive : he was, in fact, essentially
constructive. He had, in earlier years in the city, provided
remedies for one abuse or another. In Finglas, he preached
the devotion he had spread in St. Michan's and elsewhere—
the devotion to the Sacred Heart. By it he sought to make
atonement for all the offences against Temperance and
Chastity committed in the parish, and adorned the chapel of
Finglas with symbols of the Sacred Heart in statue and picture.

He was not pleased with the behaviour of the people during
Mass, especially the most solemn parts of it. Apparently,
it was their custom to stand, as there were few benches. The
penal time chapel, as we have seen, was devoid of seating
accommodation except on the galleries. He used to tell the

people, who did not kneel, to leave the church. He had no patience with them if they could not kneel during the solemn parts of the Mass ; it was his own custom to kneel for hours without support. He eventually succeeded in getting the people to kneel from the Sanctus to the Communion.

If we may use the term " free-lance," it will best express what Father Henry actually was. He was a missionary, and he was free to employ methods that the parochial clergy might not have considered prudent. A man of his calibre and status was required to abolish the abuses that had crept into Catholic life in city and country. In 1841 he was not satisfied that penal time customs should be continued.

During his stay at Finglas, he lived in a wretched little room over the sacristy. Though he was an early riser, usually about 5 o'clock, he depended upon the " priest's boy " to call him. The " boy " grew tired of this early rising, and, one night, put the small clock under his pillow in order not to see the time, and accordingly slept it out. Father Henry awoke to find that he had not been called, and pulled the bell-rope vehemently. The " boy " appeared, and asked an innocent question as to what Father Henry required. He was met with the stern question : " Why did you not call me, sir ? " The " boy " naively answered : " I did not know the time," which was quite true, but Father Henry illogically replied : " You lie, sir." Whereupon the " boy " resented the opprobrious term, and Father Henry repented. But, there was worse for the " boy." Father Henry ordered him to yoke the pony to the trap and drive him into town, as he must go to confession for his sin of reviling. The " boy " did as he was told, joined in the recitation of the Rosary several times going to and returning from the city, and served Father Henry's Mass when they returned.[1]

8. Father Young in St. Catherine's

After two-and-a-half years in Finglas, Father Henry was recalled by Archbishop Murray to the city, 15th November,

---

[1] This incident was narrated to me by William Cullen who was a friend of the " priest's boy " and a prominent member of the Evening Office Confraternity of SS. Michael and John's.

1843. He was appointed curate to his native parish of St. Catherine—to the scenes of his youth and to the people in whom his parents had taken a warm interest. His old home in W. New-row was only a few hundred yards away and was held by him in affectionate memory. He wrote : " I often looked up at the windows of the room where we were all born, and at those of the drawingroom where we were born again to God by Baptism." He took up residence in the substantial presbytery fronting Meath-street and almost hiding the quaint octagonal chapel where he had worshipped as a boy. He seems to have been very much at home in his new sphere of ministration, and, though he was then fifty-seven years of age, his energy seemed undiminished. As a man, and saintly priest, he emerges in unexpected fashion. He apparently had more scope here for his special zeal, and his experience as a missionary must have given him greater courage in dealing with difficult cases. He was held in great respect, and in great dread, by the people as he made his way through the slums shrouded in his simple cloak.

His mortification was the cause of much anxiety to his friends and relatives. Bread of fine flour was often baked for him but he gave it to the poor, and asked for shop-bread. A substantial dinner of meat and vegetables would be set before him, but, when the servant's back was turned, he threw up the window and lowered the meat to the beggars whom he had stationed outside the house, and dined on bread and potatoes.

Not only was he kind to the genuine poor, but he could not be harsh towards those who traded on his kindness. He was a good mark for the smart, unscrupulous beggar, and was sometimes deprived of his cloak or watch, and, on one occasion, of every stick of furniture in his room. A laundry-woman, calculating that, in his absent-mindedness, he would not miss his linen, pawned it. His charitable remark was : " But indeed I do not suspect the washerwoman."

He was pursued by beggars, who used to lie in wait for him outside the presbytery. He never refused an alms to a poor person, but when the number became overpowering he had his own little stratagem for getting rid of them. Unnoticed by them, he used to place some coppers on a window ledge or a doorstep, and, when confronted by the beggars farther on in the street, he told them to search number so-and-so house. During the rush of the beggars to the house he made his escape.

He enjoyed all these ways of the poor and his own devices for circumventing them, whether innocent or guilty. Both types were equally dear to him, and he hoped to convert the guilty ones by his charity and consideration.

Frequently destitute parents left their new-born children in his way, knowing full well that he would provide for them. When it was a question of a serious breach of morality he was ready for attack. Dance-houses were the occasion of much anxiety to the clergy and were not easily suppressed. A notorious house in the parish had baffled all his efforts to suppress it. At last, one night, having made himself acquainted with the pass-word and having disguised himself and provided himself with a heavy stick, he succeeded in reaching the dance-room. Dropping his cloak and brandishing his stick, he denounced them for their iniquities, and cleared the room. It was the death-blow of the dance-house.

A man who wheeled a collection of wax figures, by no means modest, from street to street, and exhibited them to bystanders on payment of their pennies, happened to hold his show in Meath-street one day when he was on his tour of the parish. When all persuasion failed to make the showman close down his exhibition, he overturned the board and scattered the figures in pieces about the street. The man complained that it was his only means of subsistence. " In that case," said he, " I shall allow you seven shillings a week as long as you live " ; he kept his promise faithfully.

His biographer gives authentic details as to his religious practices during his years in the parish. He frequently spent the whole night on the steps of the altar before the Blessed Sacrament. At other times he would enter the church at four o'clock in the morning and open the doors for the crowd of people already waiting for admission.

His confessional was the first sphere of his daily duty, and, having disposed of the penitents, he would kneel at a little table, upon which was a candle, and read out in a loud voice morning prayers in which the people joined. He familiarised them with the practice of meditation, read out the points, and gave them time to meditate upon them.

Death was one of his favourite subjects for meditation, and the death-bed was one of his favourite parochial visitations. It was his devotion to the Souls in Purgatory, which inspired him with the idea of founding St. John's Society for the purpose of reciting the Office of the Dead in the presence of the departed. He himself was faithful to its spirit and went constantly to pray over the dead in the tenements.

Of all his characteristics, Christian simplicity, that rare and perfect fruit of complete detachment from the world, was perhaps the most remarkable. He was as guileless as a child with the children of the world, God's poor, but he was singularly prudent with others when prudence was required. His letters to priests, nuns, and even to a bishop, show extraordinary wisdom and common sense.

This combination of what was regarded, in his time, as imprudence, in his dealings with the poor, and his prudence in his spiritual counsels, was not appreciated in his life-time. It was only after his death that the testimonials to his extraordinary prudence in spiritual matters came to light, and placed him on a plane quite different from that upon which he was placed while he lived. He was regarded as extremist, eccentric, even foolish. He was all things for Christ, like the Apostle Paul—he was foolish and he was wise—all things, so that he might win for Christ. He himself was nothing—the least of the Apostles—but he wished to preach Christ Crucified, in himself and his hearers. He set the example and preached that others might follow.

On the death of his father, he received a substantial sum of money which he immediately divided amongst various charities. He received more Mass Intentions than he could discharge, but the money went to the poor. As he could live on so little—bread and water, or occasionally tea, and porridge at night—he had no use either for his portion of the Sunday collections or for his Mass Intentions. He had always money to give away. His ecclesiastical superiors asked him to be less profuse in his donations to street-beggars. It went to his heart to say " No " to them, and, so, he contrived means to satisfy them.

Though by no means destitute of talent and culture, he cared little to cultivate what might attract the world and its honour. The Gospel precepts were his constant study. He never lost an opportunity of reproving persons of every condition for luxurious and extravagant display, especially when it took the form of lavish dinners to do him honour. Sometimes he walked out of the house, exclaiming : " This is no place for me : I will not stay to witness such useless extravagance." He considered such displays not only repugnant to the Christian spirit, but the fruitful source of debts and misery.

He was often seen carefully folding up in paper some old handkerchief, some broken rosary, some torn picture left in the church by the poor of his flock, and he never rested until he had found out the owner and restored the trifling, but possibly deeply valued property. Such minute acts of kindness, flowers on the roadside of life, show a habit of tenderness in the soul. Such a habit, especially when joined to sanctity, is irresistible in its influence. It was this combination of tenderness and sanctity which gave him his exceptional power over the sinful ones of his flock.

When he heard of the death of a child, he was wont to say, with a smile of joy, " Safe in Heaven." A young girl of great innocence and piety, whom he knew well, was found dead with her prayer-book in her hand. Beaming with delight, he preached on her happy death : " This young girl's death is a triumph. She fought well the battle of life, and died with the sword in her hand."

Though working strenuously on the mission, he lived ever on the brink of Eternity. To live in sight of Eternity seems to have been the key-note of all his work. " Eternity, Eternity ! " he constantly exclaimed. Nothing else mattered. He did not care whether his frugal meal once a day supported him until the morrow ; he thought only of Eternity. Yet, he was convinced that bread-and-water was the most wholesome meal that man could partake of. He boasted in his old age of his wisdom, in spite of the advice of his ecclesiastical superiors to look more to his food.

During missions, and for days before the principal festivals of the year, he seldom left the church. He used to fit up his confessional with a shelf for his few books and with a desk for writing ; he made it his sitting-room. When asked how he could endure the cold for so many hours, his reply was : " When I feel very cold, I have a fire at which to warm myself—the Blessed Sacrament."

After his first few years as a curate he ceased to write out his sermons. No doubt, he made a mental preparation. He preferred to allow himself be swayed by the subject of his discourse and by the thoughts that it evoked. Sometimes he became so wrapt up in them that he forgot the thread of his discourse, and would humbly ask : " Let us all recite five Paters and Aves that I may be enabled to remember what I was about to say." On one occasion, preaching before Archbishop Murray, he so forgot the thread of his sermon, in his inspiration of the moment, that he descended the pulpit and apologised afterwards to his Grace, saying : " You know, Your Grace, I am no preacher."

In his sermons to the people of the parish he was eminently practical and used familiar illustrations and parables. He dealt with the things of daily life which had a bearing on the social and religious welfare of the people. He warned the women against the familiar practice of having recourse to the pawnbroker's shop to get them out of their temporary difficulties. He was aware, however, that these difficulties were not always the result of their bad management. The fault in most cases could be attributed to the men, or rather to the system under which they worked.

Many masters made it a practice to pay their workmen on Saturday evenings at the public-house, or by an order or cheque for the amount due to twenty or thirty of them to be cashed at the public-house, with a deduction for drink to be consumed by them on the premises.

Against this practice Father Henry was adamant and vehement in the pulpit and elsewhere. He denounced it in a Temperance Treatise that he published in which he said :

" There was formerly a law enacted in favour of workmen, who could demand a second payment of their entire week's wages whenever their employer sent them to the public-houses to be paid. It would be desirable if this law could be nowadays put in force, for this double payment would soon bring employers to a sense of their duty and oblige them to pay their workmen in their own house, or in the workshop, or at a fixed, proper, and convenient place where no drink should be allowed.[1] It would also be desirable if employers could pay their men on Saturday mornings before they go to their breakfast instead of at evening, in order that their wives may have the whole Saturday before them to provide for Sunday and the following week."

All this goes to show how the spiritual-minded curate was able to descend to the smallest details of daily life, and to be a pioneer in reforming abuses that were legion in his time, and which, apparently, had escaped the notice or had not attracted the zeal of others.

It was one of his rules not to read the newspaper, but occasionally he glanced at the list of the dead and commended them the while to God's mercy.

It must have brought great joy to him when a branch of the St. Vincent de Paul Society was set up in St. Catherine's. He would now have an organisation to deal systematically with the distress of his beloved poor—an organisation of laymen who, after their business of the day, would devote their spare hours to the noble exercise of Christian Charity. In the next year (1846), when Ireland began to experience the ravages of famine, the French members of the Society gave a splendid proof of the universality of the bond of Christian Charity, by forwarding to their Brothers in Dublin about £7,000 for distribution among the starving poor.

The coming of the Sisters of Charity to Harold's Cross (1845) must have been an additional joy to him, especially when he learned that the relief of the sick poor—one of the objects of their Order—was to be undertaken by them in his

---

[1] Father Young was probably referring to a series of English statutes, extended to Ireland by a statute of 1817, and corresponding to the modern Truck Acts, 1831 to 1896.

district. Mother Aikenhead, in need of fresh air, had left St. Vincent's Hospital, where she had spent eleven years directing her various foundations from her bed of suffering. Having fitted up the house in Harold's Cross as the Mother House that had been removed from Stanhope-street, she turned a parlour into a school-room to which the girls working in the neighbouring factories resorted for secular and religious instruction. Father Young, twenty years previously, had made similar provision for the factory boys, and, no doubt, still took a lively interest in the welfare of this neighbouring district. Funds were low with the Sisters for the relief of the sick and poor of Francis-street and Meath-street parishes until Mr. Michael Sweetman, of Longtown, an old friend and benefactor of Mother Aikenhead, transferred to her £1,000 in stock, the interest of which was to be spent for this purpose.[1]

The Autumn of 1845 witnessed the total failure of the potato crop. The summer had been warm and fine until July, when the weather suddenly broke, and there was almost continuous rain during the weeks that followed. Half of the total population of Ireland subsisted at this time solely on potatoes. The Prime Minister, Robert Peel, sent two eminent scientists to Ireland, who reported that the year's crop could not be expected to be more than about three-eighths of the usual yield, and that in all probability the seed for future years would also be infected. He proposed a vote of credit of £100,000 to be placed at the disposal of the Lord Lieutenant for the purchase of food for the needy, but he did not find sufficient support. On his own account he ordered a very large purchase of Indian corn in the United States of America, which proved a material factor in the relief of distress.

"During the famine years Mother Aikenhead was indefatigable in trying to supply food and clothing for the crowds of half-famished people who flocked for help. Notwithstanding her own suffering state, she superintended the distribution of the food."[2]

The Christian Brothers in the district had a difficult task during those years of distress. Their original school in Mill-street was maintained up to 1846—for over thirty years—

---

[1] *Life of Mother Aikenhead*, 326.   [2] Ibid., 331.

as a most efficient school. In the Report of the Commission into the State of Education in Ireland (1837) the commissioner says of it: " I do not think we have one decidedly efficient school but that of the Christian Brothers, Mill-street, Dublin . . . quite equal to the Board's Model School in Marlborough Street."[1]

The building had however become so dilapidated that a new residence and class-rooms in Francis-street were erected by Father Flanagan, P.P., and the community took possession of them in 1846. Owing to the failure of the potato crop, people from the countryside maddened with hunger and despair flocked into the towns and cities. Dublin, more especially the Liberties, with its back streets and slums, became very soon overcrowded. To save the boys from the prosely-tising influence of the schools of the districts " the attendance at Francis-street schools was allowed to increase entirely beyond the accommodation. There were only two class-rooms, and the number of the attendance roll had risen to 700. Two Brothers only were available to take charge of this crowd of poor lads, so poor, indeed, that they were not able to purchase books or writing copies. The condition presented by the majority of these children was a sad and harrowing picture. . . . Nor were the Brothers able to relieve their sad need."[2]

This description was given by one of the Brothers who lived in Mill-street. Even the annual charity sermon, upon which the managers of those days chiefly relief for funds, met with a poor response. Though preached by the renowned orator, Dr. Miley, P.P. of Bray (January, 1848), yet its net result was only £28. In ordinary circumstances the collection would have reached two or three hundred pounds. Fortunately, a few months afterwards, two charitable laymen presented £150 to the superior.

In 1849 was a parish return of the cholera in the district which caused much uneasiness to the Sisters of Charity at Harold's Cross and to the St. Vincent de Paul Society. Mother Aikenhead wrote from Harold's Cross, 7th Sep-tember : " In these parts we continue to learn constantly

[1] *Life of Edmund Rice,* 337.   [2] Ibid., 206.

of some persons well known and many of large connections having been called out of life by cholera, and amongst the poor many deaths occur, in many parts of the city and suburbs."[1]

On 30th June, 1852, the day after his enthronement as Archbishop of Dublin, Dr. Cullen laid the foundation stone of the new church of St. Catherine, Meath-street. A house that stood between the street and the chapel was purchased, and, with the presbytery, was demolished. The new church, in perpendicular Gothic, was erected on the combined sites, and schools for boys and girls were built beside the church. The clergy had to retire to lodgings in the district.

Father Young got lodgings in the house of a pious woman who kept a bakery. Every Sunday he gave her his portion of the church collection to supply the poor with bread ; that was his practice also in SS. Michael and John's. It was the custom of the time to divide the Sunday church-door collection among the clergy immediately after last Mass.

9. FATHER YOUNG AND O'CONNELL

Father Young was a friend of Daniel O'Connell from his first days as a working curate in Dublin. His father had been, as we have seen, identified with the constitutional movement for the redress of the religious and civil disabilities of the Irish people, and it was probably in this way that Father Henry first came into contact with the Irish leader. He was a curate in St. Michan's, North Anne-street, when O'Connell held his first meeting—in the church—after the Catholic Association had been suppressed by Parliament (10th February, 1825). The meeting was held on 6th June, by permission of the Parish Priest, Dr. Wall, Dean of Dublin. He was closely associated with O'Connell during the days when Dr. Blake and himself founded the Purgatorian Society and the Confraternity of the Evening Office, of both of which O'Connell was a member. The patronage and purse of the Irish leader were important assets to the success of those societies.

Although the Rules of the Evening Office Confraternity,

[1] *Life of Mary Aikenhead*, 331.

drawn up by Father Young and Dr. Blake, forbade the members to belong to any political or secret organisation, they were not prevented from joining O'Connell's Catholic Association, the object of which was confined to securing Catholic Emancipation. The Minutes of the Association's proceedings for 23rd October, 1828, record that " Mr. John Ennis handed in £5 from the parish of St. Michael and St. John's." This sum represented the pennies of the people collected at the church doors by the " churchwardens " of the parish, with the consent of the clergy, who, no doubt, also subscribed.

When Father Young entered on his ministry in the parish early in 1829 O'Connell was in London working up support for the Catholic Emancipation Bill, introduced in the House of Commons by Peel on 5th March and enacted on 14th April.

It was while he was labouring with his brother, Father James, in Finglas, that those momentous and far-reaching events of November, 1841, occurred, events of which his friend and hero was the central figure. On 1st November, 1841, O'Connell was elected Lord Mayor of Dublin in the Assembly Rooms, South William-street. Almost for the first time in three hundred years—that is to say, except during the brief reigns of Mary and James II—Dublin had a Catholic Lord Mayor.

On the following Sunday, 7th November, O'Connell, garbed in his official robes, drove in the State coach to the Church of the Conception, Marlborough-street. A penal law still existed to the effect that no Irish official might attend Papist worship in his robes of office under pain of a penalty of £100 and deprivation of his office. O'Connell's " coach-and-four " was equal to the occasion. Laying his robe and cocked hat on a table at the entrance of the Church specially placed to receive them, he laughingly remarked, " The Lord Mayor may be a Catholic, but his robes are good Protestants." He was conducted to the throne in front of the High Altar. Archbishop Murray sang the Mass, and Dr. Miley preached the sermon, which occupied three columns of the *Freeman's Journal*. The ceremonies—with music, chiefly by Mozart, under the baton of Mr. Haydn Corri—lasted two-and-a-half hours.

It was the time of O'Connell's intensive movement for Repeal of the Act of Union. Monster meetings were held in various parts of Ireland during 1842–43, to which people flocked in thousands, demonstrating their solidarity in his cause. England, however, was equally solid against Repeal, and the first counter-stroke of repression was to deprive Repealers of the Commission of the Peace. O'Connell was dismissed from the Mayoralty, and more than thirty others from their magistracies, in May, 1843. Yet the movement continued. All previous monster meetings, great as they were, dwindled into insignificance when compared with the mighty gathering on the Hill of Tara, Tuesday, 15th August, 1843, a gathering in which Father Young took a worthy part.

The memorable scene is thus described : " Every district within sixty miles of Tara sent a contingent to the meeting. During the night crowds with banners were constantly arriving to the music of pipes and drums, fiddles and bagpipes. They bivouacked on the green hill, under the open sky. At the dawn of a lovely summer day, the place was black with human beings. To add to the solemnity of the spectacle, six altars were erected on the hillside and priests celebrated Mass after Mass for the multitudes, in a deep hush, nothing being heard but the low voices of the celebrants, the soft tinkling of the bells, and the fervid but subdued ejaculations of the myriads of worshippers kneeling on the green sward. The most perfect order prevailed."[1]

Father Young, then in Finglas, journeyed to Tara and offered his Mass before the assembled multitudes. It was the Feast of Mary's Assumption. The day selected for the meeting was symbolic, and one cannot doubt that it took on special significance in his mind.

An entry in the Minute Books of the Christian Doctrine Confraternity of SS. Michael and John's, Sunday, 21st July, 1844, states that " at a meeting of the Christian Doctrine Society convened for the purpose of testifying our gratitude to the Liberator of our country who now lies incarcerated

[1] MacDonagh, " O'Connell, the Tribune " (*Cath. Emancip. Cent. Rec.*, p. 69).

in Prison," a subscription was given towards purchasing a Gold Cross to be presented to him.

All Ireland offered a novena before the 8th September, the Feast of the Nativity of the Blessed Virgin, for the speedy release of the Repealers. The release took place on the Feast itself. The procession that conducted O'Connell (accompanied by his chaplain, Dr. Miley) and the other Repealers from Newgate prison to Merrion Square was six miles long and in it marched 200,000 men.

On the following Sunday, Archbishop Murray presided at High Mass and solemn *Te Deum* " in thanksgiving to Almighty God for the deliverance of the Beloved Liberator to his country, and his fellow-martyrs from unjust captivity." O'Connell and the other traversers sat in chairs of State beneath the pulpit. Dr. Miley, in his sermon, declared that " O'Connell has been released through the intercession of the Blessed Virgin."[1]

Father Young had been closely associated with the Liberator at many points in that great career. He had rejoiced in its successes, and had blessed its most spectacular triumph. He was destined now to fulfil a last, sad office in the human tragedy of its close.

In the midst of the desolation of the famine, O'Connell, broken in spirit and in body, undertook a pilgrimage to Rome, to receive the blessing of the Holy Father and restore, it was hoped, both mental and physical health. It was his last journey. The little party only reached as far as the Hotel Feder, Genoa, and there, on Saturday, 15th May, 1847, he died, in the presence of his son, Daniel, and his faithful chaplain, Father Miley, who administered the Last Sacraments.

The return of his body to Ireland is thus described : " The body was removed from Genoa . . . in July, and, on the journey homewards, city after city on the continent did homage to the remains. On August 1st, the *Duchess of Kent* left Liverpool for Dublin. . . . The ships of all nations in the port lowered their flags as the vessel steamed down the Mersey. Next evening, the steamer arrived in Dublin Bay, and was escorted up the Liffey by hundreds of vessels and smacks

[1] MacDonagh *Daniel O'Connell,* 307–310.

crowded with sorrowing Dublin citizens. . . . A plaintive wail went up from the immense crowd assembled at the Custom House Quay as the steamer approached."[1] Is it merely fanciful to suppose Father Young, at that time labouring in Meath-street, in the midst of that mournful gathering, watching the return of the last remains of his friend ?

The lying-in-state took place in the Church of the Conception, Marlborough-street. As O'Connell was a member of the Evening Office Confraternity of SS. Michael and John's—though exempt from attendance because of his busy life—the confraternities of the city recited the Requiem Office beside the remains on each of the three nights during which they lay in the church. Father Young, as an old friend, and as compiler of the Evening Office Book that gave new life to the confraternities, presided at the Offices.

An entry in the Minute Book of the Christian Doctrine Confraternity of SS. Michael and John's (made 29th August, 1847), states that it had been proposed at a meeting " that a sum of £1 be given towards a banner to be borne before the United Christian Doctrine Society of Dublin at the funeral of Mr. O'Connell on the 5th August, 1847, in testimony of their respect and veneration for that illustrious gentleman."

In the list of the Departed Members of the Evening Office Confraternity of the parish, contained in its Minute Book, is the following entry, surrounded by a frame of black lines : " The Liberator of Ireland, Daniel O'Connell, 15 May, 1847, 7th day, 20th day, 30th day, 15 June, and anniversary 22 May, 1848." On these days a special Office was recited by the Confraternity for the repose of his soul.

10. ARCHBISHOPS MURRAY AND CULLEN

Daniel Murray was born, 18th April, 1768, at Sheepwalk, Arklow. He was sent for higher education to Dr. Betagh's Seminary, Saul's-court, and afterwards proceeded to the Irish College of Salamanca, where he was ordained, 1790. His first appointment in the diocese was to St. Paul's, and he is mentioned in a document[2] of 3rd March, 1797, as a Governor

---

[1] MacDonagh, *Daniel O'Connell*, p. 375.
[2] C.S. *Official Papers*, Record Tower, Dublin Castle, II., 510/27/7.

of the House of Industry, Channel-row, in that parish. Shortly afterwards he was a curate in Arklow, and when, in 1798, his parish priest, Father Ryan, was shot dead by the yeomanry, he himself escaped through the fields and made his way to Dublin. Immediately he went to the lodgings of the rector of Arklow, Rev. Edward Bayley, 27th May, and took an oath that he was not a member of the United Irishmen and did not approve of their principles.[1] Furnished with a certificate for protection, he intended to return to Arklow, but Archbishop Troy appointed him curate to Liffey-street Chapel.

For ten years he was curate of St. Mary's and became an outstanding personality in the diocese. It was during those years he became acquainted with Mary Aikenhead and her programme for charitable activities which eventually culminated in the foundation of the Sisters of Charity. In 1809, at the request of Archbishop Troy, he was appointed Coadjutor-Archbishop of Dublin. They agreed on political and social problems, and Dr. Troy, grown old, was anxious to leave their development to the good sense of Dr. Murray. The question about the loyalty of the Maynooth students was, as we have seen, uppermost in Dr. Troy's mind. The president, Dr. Everard, resigned through ill-health, and, in his letter of resignation, he recommended, as his successor, Dr. Murray, so that the spirit of obedience of the students might continue under his care. Dr. Murray was appointed, 27th June, 1812.[2] The appointment of the Coadjutor-Archbishop of Dublin to the presidency of Maynooth was an extraordinary one. Nothing but a situation of the first magnitude could account for it. Dr. Everard considered that the only one capable of dealing with it was Dr. Murray. Apparently he succeeded, for, after the academic year, 13th November, 1813, he resigned the presidency, and returned to his religious and social activities for the diocese.

Attention has been called to his great work in the founding of the Sisters of Charity, Mercy and Loreto. His courteous and genial manner had more to do with their success than is

---

[1] *Rebellion Papers*, Dublin Castle, 620/38/181.
[2] *C.S. Official Papers*, Dublin Castle, II., 547/356/3.

generally supposed. The founders had confidence in his wise direction, and Archbishop Troy found in him an able coadjutor and entrusted him, during those fourteen years of coadjutorship, with the practical affairs of the diocese.

Though Dr. Murray was a welcome guest with Dr. Troy at Charles Young's table in West New-row, it is quite probable that he did not meet Father Young until his visit to Rome in 1814. Thenceforth, he and Dr. Blake were responsible for his many missionary activities. Father Young's veneration for these two great churchmen was beyond all words ; he translated it into constant endeavour to fulfil their expectations. During thirty-eight years he was rewarded with the fatherly solicitude of Dr. Murray. It was a great shock to him when he learned of the death, 26th February, 1852, of his great friend and spiritual father.

A writer in the *Freeman's Journal* of the day says of him : " He was a man pre-eminently fond of peace and quietness. . . . He was a man of a generous and a noble nature, raised far above everything low, vindictive and mean. No matter what was said or done against him, he never allowed any angry or revengeful feeling to obscure his clear intellect, or to warp his sound judgement, but pronounced on the matter in dispute solely on its merits, and delighted to do justice and show kindness to his opponents. The writer of these lines differed with him widely and frequently both in word and act, and nothwithstanding received early promotion and repeated proofs of kindness at his hands. A perfect gentleman, he was fitted to take his place in the palaces of kings as a true prince of the Catholic Church, and competent to meet the courtier on his own ground, not with the tinsel or frippery of mere worldly manners, but with the golden grace and solid dignity of true politeness, based upon an exquisite taste, a highly cultivated intellect, unbounded benevolence, unaffected purity, and pure religion. No man could say that he appeared in those high places for his own sake, for the purpose of ambition, or for the vanity of such distinction. All will admit that he went there because he thought it right and proper for the great Metropolitan of the mass of the people to be on friendly terms with the executive, to be in a position to act as their mediator, and to mitigate the severity of harsh laws in their regard. However the expediency of the course may be questioned, no one can doubt the purity of the motives of the benevolent and good Archbishop. . . . Posterity will affirm the judgement that a finer or purer character did not exist in his day.—*Sacerdos*."[1]

A kneeling marble effigy, erected soon after his death in St. Mary's, and executed by Farrell, is a speaking likeness of the saintly Archbishop. Dr. Donnelly says of him : " In appearance and bearing dignified and impressive ; in the celebration of Holy Mass, or in the solemn episcopal functions, he was a prince upon the altar ; while in meekness and moderation he strongly resembled the holy Bishop of Geneva [St. Francis de Sales], his favourite patron and model."[2]

As to church fabric in the diocese, it was computed that " 97 churches, great and small, have been erected in the archdiocese since the consecration of his Grace [1809] at an expense of little less than £700,000. In every parish, various new male and female schools have been built within the same period at a vast expenditure. So that, in the 48 parishes into which the diocese is portioned out, upwards of 220 clean, convenient, comfortable, and healthy places of instruction are at present in full operation. . . . An estimate made out with great care represents the amount of property moveable and immoveable acquired by religion in the Catholic Archbishopric of Dublin, during his incumbency, as exceeding considerably £1,200,000."[3]

After the death of Dr. Murray the diocese remained vacant for little more than two months, and was filled, 3rd May (Feast of the Finding of the Holy Cross), 1852, by Archbishop Paul Cullen who was transferred from Armagh by Pope Pius IX. Dr. Donnelly says of him : " The See of Dublin was now to possess for its Ruler an Ecclesiastic of great piety, exceptional learning, and unflagging zeal—a Churchman *par excellence*. A child of the Diocese—born [at Prospect] in the Parish of Narraghmore—he was sneeringly described in

---

[1] Meagher, *Dr. Murray*, 141–42. One may suspect Father Meagher to be the writer of the *Freeman's Journal* article.
[2] *Dub. Par.*, III, 106.
[3] Meagher, *Dr. Murray*, 146.

an issue of the *Dublin EveningMail* as ' the son of a half-hanged traitor,' because his father, a most respectable and peaceful subject, and in no way compromised in the events of the period, narrowly escaped the extreme penalties of the law in the lawless days that followed up the Rebellion of '98.[1] He received his ecclesiastical education in the Propaganda College, Rome. Whilst there, he distinguished himself by his simple, earnest piety and assiduous attention to studies. At the close of his theological course he was chosen to make the ' great act,' or public defence of all Theology, against all comers. This memorable event was honoured by the presence of the then reigning Pontiff, Leo XII, and was followed by the Degree of Doctor of Sacred Theology. Soon afterwards he was appointed Professor in the Propaganda, and, in 1833, when Dr. Boylan, on account of ill health, resigned the Rectorship of the Irish College, Dr. Cullen was appointed to succeed him. In this office he remained until December, 1849, when he was consecrated by Cardinal Franzoni, Archbishop of Armagh and Primate of all Ireland."[2]

His enthronement as Archbishop of Dublin took place in the Pro-Cathedral, 29th June (1852), in the presence of the Archbishops of Cashel and Tuam, thirteen bishops, Dr. J. H. Newman, Rector of the Catholic University, the Lord Mayor of Dublin, and many distinguished laymen.

In a Pastoral letter, 18th September, 1852, Archbishop Cullen announced that the Jubilee, granted to the Christian world by Pius IX in the previous year, would be solemnly opened in Dublin, Friday, 1st October, with Pontifical Mass in the Pro-Cathedral, and would include the Forty Hours Adoration, which would last until the following Sunday. The churches appointed for the visits in connection with the Jubilee were the Pro-Cathedral, St. Paul's, and St. Nicholas's. He issued a further Pastoral, 1st October, on the Forty Hours Adoration, as part of the Jubilee celebration, which was held

---

[1] As we have already pointed out, the military in the country parts of the diocese of Dublin, had taken the " law " into their own hands, and innocence did not protect man, woman or child from their savagery. Had the military had their way the See of Dublin would have been deprived of two of its most remarkable occupants, Drs. Murray and Cullen.

[2] Donnelly, *Dub. Par.*, III, 107, 108. See " Cullen," by Cardinal Moran, *Cath Encycl.*, IV, 546–66.

with great enthusiasm and fervour in all the city parishes. The Forty Hours Adoration was intended for the city and for the three days of the Jubilee. The country parishes did not see why they should be deprived of the graces of the Adoration, and they petitioned the Archbishop to have it extended to them. The petition was readily granted, and what was intended for a particular occasion became a regular annual event in every church and religious institute of the diocese, bringing innumerable blessings on priests and people. One of the first recorded celebrations of the devotion was held in SS. Michael and John's, 14th November, 1852, feast of St. Laurence O'Toole, and was styled " the most splendid ever seen."[1]

In 1854, Archbishop Cullen had the happiness of dedicating the church of St. James, the last successor of the penal-time chapels of Dublin. The quaintly irregular building erected on the north side of James-street, and at the east corner of Watling-street, about 1738, had done duty as a chapel for 116 years. In 1844, the site for the new church had been cleared on the south side of St. James's-street, and, 4th April, the foundation stone was laid by Daniel O'Connell, who gave a splendid donation on the occasion. The work on the church was begun immediately by Canon George Canavan, P.P., but was interrupted by the famine years of '47 and '48 ; he did not live to see it completed. It was finished under Father John Smyth, P.P. Rev. Dr. Manning (afterwards Cardinal) preached the sermon at the dedication. The church cost £14,000 ; built in pointed Gothic, " it is the purest and most effective in style of the many churches yet raised by our people."[2]

The clergy continued to occupy the chapel house at Watling-street for a few years, but, on the widening of the street, both chapel-house and chapel were demolished, and the priests had to obtain lodgings in the neighbourhood.

In 1854, Father Young was a curate in Meath-street and, no doubt, was present at the Dedication ceremony. One of the few occasions on which he accepted an invitation to

[1] Battersby, *Cath. Dir.*, 1853.
[2] Donnelly, *Dub. Par.*, II, 233.

dine out was in connection with the Mission given by the Oblate Fathers in the Augustinian Church, John's-lane. Father Robert Cooke, O.M.I., was commissioned by the founder of the Oblates of Mary Immaculate, Bishop de Mazenod of Marseilles, towards the end of 1855, to make another effort to establish the Congregation in Ireland. Having arrived in Dublin, he told the cabman to drive him to a suitable lodging, and was let down in Thomas-street. Next morning he said Mass in John's-lane chapel and was asked by the prior, Dr. Crane, to come with three other Oblates the following May (1856) to give a Mission in the chapel, which proved a tremendous success.

At a farewell interview with Archbishop Cullen, Father Cooke mentioned his desire to have a house of the Congregation in the diocese. His Grace told him to select his site, and after three days was informed that the site selected was at Inchicore, near the new railway works, where the workers and their families had no convenient church. His Grace granted the necessary authorisation. Father Cooke purchased for £2,150 a fairly spacious house and farm (18th June, 1856), and on the following Sunday (21st June) said Mass for the people in a room of the house.

Before the purchase of the house was completed—or more particularly when His Grace consented to the foundation of the Congregation in the diocese—Father Cooke apparently told Dr. Crane of his successful interview with the Archbishop, and the Augustinian prior invited the neighbouring priests to dinner. Father Young, a native and a curate of the parish, and a worshipper, as a boy, in the Augustinian chapel, was naturally one of the most esteemed guests. His 70 years, and his fame as a missionary, made his presence particularly desirable to the Augustinians. Most probably it was because of his early associations with their chapel that he broke his rule never to dine out.

The purpose of the dinner was not disclosed until the priests were seated at table, and then the word went round that the Oblate Fathers had been sanctioned for the diocese. When the news reached Father Young, he immediately clapped his hands, and shouted in raucous tones : " It is the

work of God, let us go to the church and sing the *Te Deum*."
Bishop O'Connor, O.S.A., thought it better to comply with
the command of the enthusiastic old priest, and rose from
table, to be followed by the whole company. It was Father
Young's devotion to the Immaculate Heart of Mary which
made him cry out that the establishment of her Order in
Dublin was "the work of God."

When the purchase of the house and farm at Inchicore had
been completed, the next thing was the erection of a chapel
for the railway workers. A young carpenter undertook to
have a large wooden chapel erected within a week, and
appealed to his fellow-workmen at the railway works. It
was an amazing feat; in a few days, 700 men, working from
6 p.m. to 9 p.m., after their day's work, in the month of June,
had their chapel ready for the accommodation of 800 people.
On Sunday, 29th June, 1856, Feast of SS. Peter and Paul, their
joy was complete when High Mass was sung by the Oblates
of Mary Immaculate. It is to be presumed that Father Young
was present on the occasion. The Oblate Fathers, in a few
years (8th December, 1858), had the foundation stone of their
present Retreat House laid by Bishop O'Connor, O.S.A.,
assisted by the Lord Mayor of Dublin.

To the Oblates was due the establishment of one of the
most important social institutions of the period. In 1858,
Parliament passed a law enabling Irish Catholics to establish
institutions for juvenile delinquents. For years previously,
judicial authorities had been most dissatisfied with the
methods of dealing with these juvenile offenders who were
herded in common prisons with hardened criminals during
their periods of punishment. The new law laid down a
maximum penalty of five years detention for juveniles. These
sentences could be much reduced by competent authorities
for good conduct.

A committee, under the chairmanship of Lord O'Hagan,
was founded in Dublin to attempt to take full advantage of
this new development. It was decided that such an important
work should be handed over to a Religious Congregation.
But to whom? In the name of the Committee, the newly
arrived Oblates of Mary Immaculate were asked to undertake

the work. The authorities of the Congregation agreed, and Rev. Father Lynch, O.M.I., was named first Superior of the work.

To this end was handed over to the Oblates in that year a derelict military barracks at Glencree, Co. Wicklow—some fourteen miles from Dublin. The building had been constructed at the end of the eighteenth century as a base of operations in the military hounding of Michael Dwyer and his Irish rebels. When the Congregation took it over it was a veritable wreck. Two rooms were barely habitable. By April, 1859, forty young boys were being cared for by twelve Oblate Lay Brothers: two years later the numbers had increased to more than three hundred. These boys were taught to read and write, and trades were given to them. A thorough religious training was specially provided. What a transformation within a few years for the juvenile delinquents!

VI

FATHER YOUNG'S LAST YEARS

1. FATHER YOUNG AT ST. JOSEPH'S, PORTLAND ROW

Up to the age of seventy years Father Young continued to work as a parochial curate and was still strong and active notwithstanding his austerities. He remained in St. Catherine's up to the year 1856, when he was appointed chaplain to St. Joseph's, 6 Portland Row.

This Asylum was founded in 1834 by Dr. Blake, recently appointed Bishop of Dromore. It was intended for respectable single women who were unable to earn their own bread. It consisted of three old rat-infested houses knocked together, was overcrowded soon after its foundation, and grew heavily in debt. Yet it was popularly compared with Lourdes because of its atmosphere of prayer, and the prayers of " the old ladies " were sought by priests and people. Father William Young was one of its patrons in 1837. It had fulfilled its purpose, though in crude fashion, for sixteen years, when the trustees and the inmates considered that better and more ample accommodation was needed. Adjoining property was available for expansion of the asylum, but there seemed no hope of obtaining the £1,200 purchase money. The inmates started the " seven Sundays " devotion to St. Joseph in 1850 and soon the money came flowing in, and the property was acquired, rent free for ever. The building of the chapel was next proceeded with in 1853, and, after a novena, again the money came flowing in.

To Dr. Blake may be chiefly attributed the success, such as it was, of the asylum in the first twenty-five years of its history. As most of the inmates were either Carmelite, Dominican, or Franciscan Tertiaries, he drew up for them a code of Rules which gave the asylum a quasi-religious character. Year after year he came to Dublin and preached the Charity sermon for it ; these sermons have been published His last sermon in Dublin (he died in 1860), was preached on St. Teresa's Day (13th October), 1856, at the opening of the newly constructed St. Joseph's Chapel and Infirmary. Such was the institution to which Father Young was appointed chaplain in 1856.

His appointment to St. Joseph's suited him well ; it relieved him of parochial responsibility, gave him more time for prayer, and more opportunity for continuous work in the confessional. The institution and its little chapel suited his ideas of poverty and humility. They were, he considered, to be a haven of peace to him in his declining years. He soon found, however, that the worshippers in the little chapel increased in numbers, attracted by his holiness and by his association with so many confraternities and religious activities in the city parishes. At his special request, a small room off the chapel, near the entrance, was fitted up for him. All this reminds us of the hermit of St. Doulough's, North Co. Dublin, in pre-Reformation days. In one of his letters he refers to his own cell : " My abode is under the sacred roof of this asylum church. My window is the church window, so near am I to the temple of the living God. My only excursions are to the churches of the Forty Hours' Adoration, when they are within the suburbs ; and on every Friday I go to Marlborough-street to confess to Canon Pope."

As long as he was able to walk, he used to attend the devotion of the Forty Hours in the churches of Dublin. During the procession of the Blessed Sacrament he was often seen to pass his hand over his face—a gesture that was familiar to St. Philip Neri, the great Apostle of Rome.

His daily life in St. Joseph's is attested by those who were his constant attendants from his arrival in 1856 until his death in 1869, except for the short time he was in the Clondalkin Monastery (of which later). He entered the chapel at 4 a.m. and remained there in prayer until 6 o'clock, when the doors were opened to the public. As in St. Catherine's, he went then to his confessional, read morning prayers and meditation, before the altar, said Mass, catechised children brought to him regularly for his inspection, interviewed people and advised them on many questions, and took his sole meal for the day at 2 o'clock. He laid his weary limbs at night in a small wretched box on the floor—which was popularly known as his coffin—with a bare wooden stool as his pillow.

He always recited the Divine Office on his knees before the Blessed Sacrament. This practice brought on an inward complaint, the first he ever experienced (1862). He had to submit to an operation under chloroform in his little cell. Speaking of his exceeding happiness at coming to the end of his mortal life, as he believed, he said : " All being so nicely arranged, it is time for me to go home." When he found that it was not yet time for him " to go home," he resumed his light-heartedness, in spite of his pain. As long as he was able to hear Mass in his cell and receive Holy Communion daily he was happy. He won through, but he was much perturbed when he found himself lying on a comfortable bed. " Who brought me here ? " he asked. " I must have my own bed." He was more distressed when he was placed under obedience to partake of whatever food was placed before him, especially when meat was included. He partook of it frugally and exclaimed : " God forgive them for what they make me do." What he felt most of all was the weeks of inactivity he had to submit to when he found himself gaining strength. Having recovered from his dangerous illness, he wrote to a relative of his :

" St. Joseph's, Friday.

" I am now, thank God, so perfectly recovered that Dr. McSwiney, of his own accord, has allowed me to celebrate on next Sunday, Patronage of St. Joseph, and on Monday to go off with James [his brother] to St. Margaret's [North Co. Dublin]. Many persons did judge that I would be in eternity before now, but the Lord God has graciously spared me to offer up more sacrifices to His honour and glory, beyond the fifty-two years since my ordination, on the 10th June, 1810, the festival day of Pentecost of that year. May I in future prove worthy of this honour to make amends for past defects, and may He crown us both with abundant graces here, the true seed of immortal glory hereafter—the ardent desire of your affectionate

HENRY YOUNG."

The feast of the Patronage of St. Joseph, to which he refers, was at this time celebrated on the third Sunday after Easter, and was styled the Solemnity of St. Joseph.

Apparently he was glad to go back to his brother James, P.P. of St. Margaret's and Finglas, and to renew his old associations with the parish.

Father James's " boy " narrates that, whenever Father Henry passed by the Glasnevin Cemetery on his journeys between Portland Row and Finglas, and looked at the Round Tower, erected in memory of O'Connell, he would laugh in scorn at this " ridiculous memorial " of the great Liberator. Apparently, he considered, with his Roman artistic ideas, that the symbol of protection from marauders—the Irish Round Towers were apparently for that purpose—was not a suitable one for the Liberator of the Irish people. A monument to represent for all time the resurgence of the Catholic life of the people from the penal code period was one that should have suggested itself to the Catholic leaders of the time. Instead of that, the people were given a symbol that was out of date by nearly a thousand years. His stay in Finglas was short—only a few months (June to September)—as, 17th September, 1862, Father James went to his reward. The tender parting of the two brothers, and the grief of Father Henry, who had so long schooled himself to self-restraint, showed the strong affection that was deep down in his heart. It was this affection that, notwithstanding his austerity and outward severity, inspired his friends and the poor to put their trust in him.

2. FATHER YOUNG AT ST. JOSEPH'S, CLONDALKIN

Father Young, finding himself fit again, desired active work in his 77th year, and the diocesan authorities, with a view to his health, appointed him chaplain to the Carmelite Brothers at Clondalkin. As a chaplain to a community he had to be up with the brethren at an early hour to celebrate Mass ; this for a man of his years was a tremendous task. Yet he carried it out faithfully—as long as he had an ounce of strength left he would be up at 5 o'clock to prepare for his Mass.

He had always a great regard for the Carmelite Order. In the city, and on his missions in the country, he had always promoted the Association of the Brown Scapular, and at Harold's Cross, he had gathered around him in his house a few of the Brothers of Clondalkin to teach the school he founded there, and lived their community life. He was glad, in his 77th year, to be with them once more living that life and taking his part in the education of youth.

An advertisement of the school in 1850 gives the following particulars : " Collegiate Seminary, Monastery, Mount St. Joseph, Clondalkin. (Patrons : Archbishop Murray, Dean Meyler, V.G., P.P.; V. Rev. R. J. O'Hardon, Provincial, Clarendon-street chapel). Terms : under 12 years, 21 guineas ; over 12, 26 guineas ; parlour boarders, 30 guineas. Elderly gentlemen from 36 guineas, with advantages of resident clergyman and physician. Students of this establishment studying for the church have the privilege of passing direct to the Home and Continental Colleges."[1] This was the mixed community, including the Brothers, whose spiritual life Father Young took charge of.

He was then very feeble, but, according to those who knew him at the period, his animation was remarkable when he began to preach to the boys. His voice and gestures were as strong and vehement as ever, and his emaciated frame seemed to thrill with joyful exultation. His principal subjects were the goodness of God and the joys of Heaven—subjects that appealed to an old man, but which were just as suitable for the discourse of a young man. Faith, Hope, and Charity ran through all his discourses, and he exemplified them for his young hearers by homely examples and illustrations.

During his residence in the monastery, it was his delight to follow the religious rule of the Brothers, and with holy simplicity and humility would hand his letters to the prior to be opened before he would read them, and ask his permission to go to the city once a week for Confession. He went to the city in the market-car with the Brother Procurator and recited the Rosary with him going and returning.

After a time, however, he realised that this religious life,

[1] *New City Pictorial Directory*, 1850.

agreeable as it was, did not fit in with his vocation as a missionary priest. He felt that he still had some years to live, and that they should be employed in active work among the people. The work at St. Joseph's, Portland Row, appealed to him, and he asked the Archbishop to send him back to it. His request was immediately granted, and he returned to St. Joseph's in November, 1863, having spent about eight or nine months in Clondalkin. He returned to his little cell, the coffin-like bed, the single meal, the pious inmates, and the little chapel in the heart of the city. He was at home once more.

Yet he did not forget the happy days he spent at Clondalkin or the kind Brothers who were brothers indeed to him. He wrote them many letters in which he gave expression to his gratitude to them for making his days among them so happy.

In one letter to the Prior he says : " I received too much care and attention, which I can never sufficiently repay." In another letters he says : " I was most happy in your holy and excellent monastery ; too much attention was shown me by your religious."

Again, he said : " I love your monastery and your religious who were too kind to me ; nor would I have left you if I could have fulfilled there *all*, *all* the clerical duties I practise in the asylum church, but which clashed with your choir school duties. I was happy and too much cared for whilst I was with you."

The interesting point is that he felt that his private devotions were being interrupted in chapel by the religious exercises of the Brothers and the pupils, and that he had no scope for his confessional work among the people.

Contrary to the usual practice of the period, he was an ardent advocate of daily Communion. In this he was nearly fifty years ahead of the saintly Pope Pius X's advice to the world. In his letters to Prior Dominick, he recommended daily Communion especially to religious communities. The following extract from one of his letters is worth recording : " ' I am the living Bread,' these and like words from Jesus Himself prove His ardent desire that we should frequently

partake of this Divine Food ; one communion is a preparation
for another. We take daily common bread ; why not take
daily spiritual bread of the soul ? The primitive Christians,
all priests, and very many nuns communicate daily. As
corporal food causes an infant to grow into a man, so daily
spiritual nourishment will raise religious persons to the height
of perfection." He quoted St. Gregory and St. Bernard in
support of his opinions.

If Father Henry did nothing else than write that extract
(in the year 1863), showing that Holy Communion was the
great support of spiritual life, he would have added an
important chapter in the spiritual life not only of religious
communities but of the faithful at large. At all events, he
advocated, for religious and for the people of Dublin, that
Daily Communion was not only the food of spirituality but
the great defence against the spiritual enemy. His ideas, and
his plans of reform, were well thought out, and were the
results of his long experience among the people.

About this time he was amazed at receiving two invitations,
one from the Jesuit Retreat House, Milltown Park, and the
other from Clongowes College, to give retreats to the students.
He wrote : " My backwardness and unsuitable manners
make me unworthy to accept of either."

3. Father Young returns to Portland Row.

A saintly old man, Mr. James Murphy, was one of the
trustees of the Asylum and devoted his life to its welfare.
He was a bachelor, and lived in Eustace-street. Though
Dr. Blake was the great promoter and preacher of the Asylum,
James Murphy was the man who collected the money for
its upkeep and looked after the buildings and the comfort
of the inmates. That continued up to 1888 when the Asylum
was taken over by the nuns ; he then became a mere collector,
and felt he had a grievance.

Another saintly person who was connected with St. Joseph's
was Mr. Keary Cahill, the papal optician of Wellington Quay.
He was a boy of eleven years in 1863, and a pupil of the Christian
Brothers, North Richmond Street, when, as he expressed

it,[1] he had the great honour and privilege of being selected, with two other pupils, to serve Father Young's daily Mass in St. Joseph's for six years, up to 1869, the year of the saintly priest's death. James Murphy, he says, was the President of St. Joseph's, the Matron, Miss Pollard; and Father Young's personal attendant a lady inmate named Miss Fortune. Anne Hughes was the sacristan.

Mr. Cahill relates that, though Father Young occupied a very small room on the right-hand side of the church, he was often found sleeping behind the high altar in an old box. He continued to sleep there until Archbishop Cullen paid him a visit and ordered him to sleep in his little room. When he returned to his room he shortened the length of his box so that he was nearly doubled up in it when he retired to rest, and he had his own back, as he expressed it, on the Archbishop, and chuckled over his triumph. It was one of his little ways of circumventing interference with his austerities.

"Many a time," says Mr. Cahill, "I visited that room with my two companions to help Father Henry to get ready for celebrating Holy Mass. In fact, there was a sort of pious rivalry between us boys to see how one could surpass the other in helping to get him ready to travel to the sacristy to robe for Mass. Then we used to assist and help him on to the altar. As a rule he took an hour to celebrate the Holy Mass. He had a small table on the Gospel side of the altar where he made his thanksgiving after Mass, and many a time he had to be brought away to his scant breakfast, which was simple and meagre."

Mr. Cahill tells of an incident that is said to have occurred during one of Father Young's thanksgivings after Mass. "Mrs. Josephine Curran, who lived opposite St. Joseph's, was a member of the Society of Friends (commonly called Quakers). She was of a most holy and saintly character. Her husband was a professor in Trinity College, Dublin, and a Protestant. She told me, after she became a Catholic, that she often went into St. Joseph's 'to rest.' 'One day,' she said to me, 'I went in and sat down to rest and meditate, and Father Young was kneeling at his little table, and, after looking at the old man for some time, I saw him raised up about three or four feet in the air. I got frightened and cried out, ' Father Young, you will fall,' but he took no heed of me.' "

Mr. Cahill says that Mrs. Curran and her husband were received into the Church, and lived afterwards in Blessington-street where Count Plunkett, when a student, lodged with them.

When Father Young grew very feeble, one of his friends got up a collection to buy him a pony and trap, and gave him the money which he received with great joy. It was soon spent, not on himself, but on his beloved poor. Shortly afterwards, the benefactor met him and inquired about the pony. " Ah," said he, rubbing his hands with glee, " I have got two little ponies, and I think they'll do me very well."

One of his many pious solicitudes was to impress upon all those he could influence the importance of catechetical instruction in order, he used to say, " to encourage close application to the most necessary of all sciences, that of salvation."

His brother, Father James, had translated from Italian Cardinal (now Saint) Bellarmine's Catechism for publication. He died before it appeared in print. Father Henry was anxious to finish the work. He wrote to a clerical friend[1] : ." I hold the manuscript of Cardinal Bellarmine's Cathechism, translated by my late brother James(and also the Italian book), which I wish to show you, that you may give a second revision and correction to it before sending it to press. After which I will show it to the Rev. Canon Pope, of the church of the Immaculate Conception (Marlborough-street), who I hope will obtain Dr. Cullen's sanction for its publication."

His friend replied that as the revised version of Father Henry was no longer his brother's literal translation, and as the completion of the work would entail too much labour on Father Henry, then in his 76th year, it would be advisable for him to think no more about it.

The true facts of the case are, at present, not apparent. The completion of the revision would have entailed no labour on Father Henry for he had already completed it, with the

[1] One of the Vicars-General.

exception of two pages. Yet he submitted willingly to the views of his superiors, and never questioned their judgement, though he had laboured long, snatching odd hours, to pay a last tribute to the memory of his saintly brother.

It would seem that the grounds of objection, on the part of the ecclesiastical authorities, to the publication of the translation of Bellarmine's Catechism, had nothing to do with Father James's literal translation or Father Henry's amplified revision, but with the Catechism itself.[1]

At this time, Dr. Butler's (Archbishop of Cashel) Catechism,[2] in 1st, 2nd and 3rd size, were used throughout the diocese of Dublin, and, indeed, all over the English-speaking world. These Catechisms, with slight emendations, are the catechisms used to-day in most dioceses of Ireland. Many editions, revised and enlarged, were issued by the Dublin printers.

As to Father Henry's resignation concerning his brother's MS. and his own amplification, his letter to the friend is worth recording :

" Dear ——, On the return of my parcel, I stopped my pen, a couple of pages of my manuscript remaining. I determined to forward it to ——, and wrote a letter to him resigning the work. . . . I sent him also the entire of James's MS., so that I have now nothing whatever of Bellarmine's printed or written. I told him to burn my own MS. according to his will, for I do not wish to oppose any advice given me. . . . As it is not God's will that I should prosecute what James undertook, I willingly resign it.—I remain, dear ——,

Your affectionate,

HENRY YOUNG."

[1] Bellarmine (Saint Robert, S.J.) was ordered by Pope Clement VIII, in 1598, to write a catechism for general adoption throughout the world in order to remedy the evils arising from various catechisms written according to different methods. Soon there were two editions of it in English and one in Irish. In 1742 Benedict XIV addressed a special constitution to all the Bishops of the Catholic Church advising its adoption as the official manual of every diocese.

[2] " Butler's Second Size Catechism, Approved and Recommended as a General Catechism for the Kingdom, By the Four Roman Catholic Archbishops of Ireland." (Revised and Corrected by Very Rev. Dr. Blake). James Butler (2) was Archbishop of Cashel, 1774–1791. The Catechism was introduced into Dublin by Dr. Carpenter in 1777. It was commonly used all over the English-speaking world.

Yet, notwithstanding his submission, it would seem that he felt pained that due tribute was not being paid to the memory of his saintly brother who had laboured at the translation of an important and little known work on catechetical instruction at a time when such a work, he considered, would be a powerful help to the priests in the work of instructing the people in the fundamentals of Christianity. Practical Catholicism was a strong point with the Young family.

Father Young always sought the approbation of his Archbishop for all his public devotions, from the greatest to the least. He wrote on one occasion : " If I do not get the approbation of my Archbishop, I am only weaving cobwebs ; whilst acting in according with the will of my prelate I am doing God's adorable will."

On another occasion he wrote : " My reason for this final application to his Grace is that I perform many church devotions on uncertainty as to Dr. Cullen's approbation, and therefore in uncertainty as to God's will and the Divine Blessing."

Enumerating all the devotions he carried out in St. Joseph's, he asked separate permission for each of them. As to Benediction of the Blessed Sacrament, he said : " If you would know my private wish, I should like to give it every day in the year ; but I do not expect this ample indulgence, being content with your will and leave." As to a second Mass in St. Joseph's he wrote : " To tell you my feeling, I would rather lose a hundred pounds or more than forfeit my second Mass on Sundays." In one of these letters he says : " I cannot live much longer, for I am ailing a little. May God's holy will be done." " Our St. Joseph " was the name given to him by a Community of Carmelite Nuns for whom he said Mass at one time every Wednesday. He had a tender devotion to St. Joseph. His favourite saint, however, was St. Mary Magdalen, as " She loved our Lord so much."

He could not endure the perfunctory manner in which so many people made the Sign of the Cross. The Sign of the Cross was to him not only a symbol of the Blessed Trinity but, as he used to express it, " a bearing about us the marks of our Lord Jesus Christ." His Roman training was here apparent. The Sign of the Cross to the early Christians was an act of faith in the Redemption on Calvary. It was ingeniously portrayed in the Catacombs of Rome in the ceilings of the little chapels where Mass was offered. The Mass on the tomb of the Martyrs, during the centuries of persecution, had its symbol in the ceiling paintings in the form of the cross worked in geometrical fashion for the ostensible purpose of ornamentation, but in reality, to the believers, a sign of Redemption. The system of the ancient High Crosses of Ireland was a continuation of the Catacomb idea ; they were catechisms in stone. Father Young wished to revive the value of the symbol in the lives of the people and he had no patience with those who made it in a careless manner, with a short down stroke. He taught the people to make the bold strokes as a profession of faith. He thought it a vital point, for old and young, priests and people.

On the subject of the Sign of the Cross, Father Young's biographer[1] gives a letter written by a young lady who visited St. Joseph's, in December, 1867, when she was thirteen years of age, to get his blessing before leaving Ireland for school abroad. " No light " she writes, " shone at the window of the confessional, and we were leaving the church when a harsh grating cough sounded in the distance. A door leading from the old women's asylum into the church opened, and a feeble old man shuffled out. His head was bowed down, and in one hand he held a long candle and a couple of books. With all the speed he was capable of, he was hastening into his confessional, when a woman from the asylum laid an imploring hand on him, and entreated him not to spend the entire night there in the cold. All his efforts to get free were in vain, and he promised he would not spend the whole night in the cold church ; and 'Father Young, dear,' added she, ' won't you come and take a bit of dinner ? ' ' No, No,' was the answer, ' I have my dinner with me ' ; and in proof of his assertion he took out of his pocket a couple of biscuits. My sister and I then approached, and said, ' Your Reverence, won't you give us your blessing ? ' holding up at the same time our rosary beads. " No, No,' he answered, ' I don't bless

[1] *Life*, pp. 153–55.

anything : I'm only an old man, and my superiors have taken away the power from me to bless anything.' But my sister was not to be denied, and boldly laying her hand on the door of his confessional to prevent him from closing it, she again begged for his blessing. 'Well ! God bless you, God bless you, children,' he said, and was disappearing when he perceived me making the sign of the Cross. Immediately he turned to me, saying, 'Is that the way you bless yourself ? Bless yourself like this,' and with great reverence he made the Sign of the Cross in a manner I could never forget. 'Now do it again till I see how you do it,' and he did not leave us until I had made it reverently enough to satisfy him. Dear saintly old man, it was the last time we were to see him on this earth. He had passed away to his reward ere we returned : but he remains impressed on my memory as I often saw him on Sundays at Catechism—his long white hair falling down on each side of his worn face, sitting surrounded by children, who nestled beside him with the greatest confidence. He used to give out the hymn before and after Catechism in his old cracked voice, so well known to his little flock. Once when prizes were being distributed to the Catechism class, a certain Ned Murphy was called for as entitled to a reward for regular attendance. But no Ned Murphy appeared, he had not been seen or heard of for three weeks. 'He must be sick, poor child,' Father Young ejaculated : 'I must go to him myself, and take him his prize.' "

Miss Fanny Taylor, in her book *Irish Homes and Irish Hearts*, published in 1867, describes St. Joseph's Asylum (p. 108) :

"Not far from the convent of North William Street is a building with somewhat of a conventual appearance, although it is unfortunately not under the care of religious. It is an asylum popularly called the 'Old Maids' Home,' and intended to receive respectable single women when age and failing health have made them unable to earn their own bread. The building is well adapted to its purpose ; and there is a little chapel attached to the house, where Mass is daily said ; a chapel that would be pretty if it were only clean. This institution proved by no means a pleasant sight ; from one end to the other it was extremely dirty, untidy and forlorn looking.

The infirmary, in which were several sick women, was fearfully close, and was in terrible need of ventilation. The matron seemed a most unfit person for the charge. She was too old, bent, feeble, had lost all her teeth—in fact was almost decrepid. It is impossible she can rightly manage such an institution ; none of the inmates looked comfortable or cared for. I wished for a fairy wand to be able to put the institution under the charge of the Sisters of Charity, or the 'Little Sisters of the Poor,' and then to behold the change that their arrival would create. Soap and water, fresh air, and a wholesome atmosphere would attend their footsteps, and the poor inmates' faces would brighten, and peace and content reign in the house."[1]

4. Father Young's Last Years

It is said by his biographer that from the inception of the annual diocesan retreat in Maynooth, in 1820, that Father Young never failed to be present, except in the last few years of his life. Even then, apparently in 1867, at the age of 81 years, he could not deny himself the pleasure of seeing the brethren gathered together though he could not be one of them. As soon as the priests heard he was in the College they flocked to him to Confession. He became so exhausted that his clerical friend had to accompany him back to Dublin. This clerical friend was Father Shelley, curate of Baldoyle, who had taken his place in St. Joseph's during his severe illness. The incident was narrated by Father Shelley.

Shortly before Father Young died, he visited, for the last time, a certain religious community one of the members of which was well acquainted with his family and spoke of his brothers and sisters, mentioning them by name. Contrary to his usual custom he seemed to dwell in loving memory on each cherished name : " O, yes : Joanna, William,

[1] It is a curious coincidence that it was Fanny Taylor's own Order that took over the asylum twenty years afterwards. At the request of Archbishop Walsh, Mother Magdalen Taylor, foundress of the Poor Servants of the Mother of God, took over the care of St. Joseph's Asylum in 1888. In the following year he provided her with a handsome sum, and a new wing was begun. This wing soon became insufficient, and a very fine building, accommodating about 130 " old ladies " now replaces the former dilapidated houses.—(Devon, *Mother Mary Magdalen* (1927), pp. 277–80.)

James," etc., and smiled brightly as he alluded to one of his religious brothers (Father Charles, S.J.) who was still alive.[1]

The last time he visited Howth was in 1868, the feast of the Visitation. His long life was then drawing to a close. No doubt, he felt it as he knelt and prayed a long time in the old graveyard of St. Mary's. Apparently he had some strong attachment to this venerable spot.

He had worked hard in the days of his strong manhood for the fisherfolk, but now he was old and infirm. The friend who accompanied him on this memorable journey noted his palor and exhaustion and advised him "to take refreshment every hour." The saintly old man looked up to heaven, and answered, smiling : " Oh, yes, I do take it every hour of the day and night." His refreshment was of the Spirit ; he cared little for that of the body.

The voice of the people proclaimed him a saint long before the close of his earthly career. In the letters written at the time by those who knew him well are found many illuminating passages. One runs thus : " Often the cabmen of Dublin would leap from their boxes and entreat him to allow them to drive him to his destination that thus a blessing might rest upon them and their vehicles. Coalporters and draymen would stop their carts and kneel down in the street as he went on his way blessing and blessed." The voice of the poor whose instincts seem truest in this matter of adjudging personal sanctity is not one to be lightly put aside. It is true that some held cheap this holy old man ; to them he seemed a strange being, eccentric, rude in his manner, and creating awkward situations. Many saints wished to confound the ideas of the worldly by their eccentric behaviour. St. Philip Neri and St. Teresa resorted to tricks in order to disappoint the great ones of the world in their curiosity as to what a saint was like. Father Young treated even devout people of high rank in a similar way. He was not on show, but wished to do his little missionary work unobtrusively from his little cell in St. Joseph's.

During the thirteen years he spent in St. Joseph's, he ministered day and night to those about him, and carried out

[1] *Life*, pp. 174–75.

the same rigorous penitential exercises that he had practised since his youth. Advancing years seemed only to increase his love for mortification. Indeed, he sometimes found it necessary to resist the efforts of others to procure him little comforts. Nothing but the positive command of his superiors could induce him to relax.

On this subject he wrote a characteristic letter to Canon Murphy, administrator of the Pro-Cathedral, to plead his cause before the Archbishop.[1]

" As the day approaches of Dr. Cullen's decision concerning me, I do ardently wish that he would allow me to make bread and water my diet, which is far more wholesome than any other kind, and would save me very useless expenses, loss of time, and useless talk to my attendant, so that I may be like the Trappists : for of every word that we pronounce, we must render account at the Divine Tribunal. His Grace, you, and I have never heard that my said simple diet injured the constitution of any man. On the contrary the opposite luxurious diet has done much injury, and shortened the lives of many. Any deviation in the least from wholesome bread and water, suppose only tea or plain meat, would involve me in useless extra expenses and breaches of my renewal of religious vows, for I must procure tea, sugar, milk, etc., also kettle, plates, and other breakfast articles, and fires from early in the morning till evening, even in summer. My own mind and inclination are against such lumber, trouble, expense, and what not : all which is cut short by my using wholesome bread and water, and my health far better, like the ancient anchorites and other recluses."

He denied himself the society of his own brothers and other relatives. In his 80th year he wrote to one of his cousins : " I received your kind note a few days ago, but must decline any correspondence, for I do not write even to my only brothers, the Jesuit and Sylvester, much less visit them. As I never read a newspaper, I cannot give you any public news. I never leave this enclosure except to go on Fridays to the Conception church, Marlborough-street."

He settled his affairs about four years before his death and

[1] *Life*, 180.

obtained permission to be interred in the vaults of the Pro-
cathedral : " My ardent wish," he says, " is for my poor
remains to be near daily Masses and the Tabernacle." He was
most grateful to the Archbishop for granting this favour.
When told by his confessor, Father Purcell, that burial in the
vaults necessitated three coffins which would cost about £16,
he was distressed that so large a sum of money should be, as he
termed it, wasted on him. However, his desire to be buried
in the vaults prevailed over all other considerations, and he
asked Father Purcell to order the coffins. Shortly afterwards
he sent him this remarkable letter :

" In my last note I inconsiderately requested that the three
coffins should immediately be made. They are not to be
ordered until I give you the full expense of the three coffins.
I enclosed you £1, and now send another. I would give the
whole price if I had it, but on counting last night the money
I hold, I find that I have no more than about 1l. 10s. The
Rev. Mr. Butler regulated last Christmas two years that I
should receive 50l. yearly, but I since reduced it to 3l. a month,
according to which reduction I should have received 5l. on
the 1st instant. Besides my own personal wants, I have extra
expenses, which I need not detail. I promise that when I
receive the 5l. due, I will enclose you 2l., and thus gradually
lodge in your hands the full price of the said coffins."

Eventually, he was able to gather together the money for
his three coffins, and directed that, if there was any balance
to his credit, it should be disposed of in charity.[1]

During his last days, he used to creep rather than walk out
of his " box " to celebrate Mass in the church. The effort
was too much for him and he got a severe attack, but he made
known his determination to say Mass the following morning.
His brother, Father Charles, S.J., who was on a visit to him
at the time, used every effort to dissuade him, but in vain.

An appeal was made to his friend, Father Shelley of Baldoyle,
to come and entreat him to keep to his " box." Next morning
at 7 o'clock, he found him dressed to say Mass in the church
but so weak that he had to carry him back to the little altar
in his room and place him in a chair. The sacred vestments

[1] *Life,* 184–86.

were put on him as one would dress a child, and he said Mass holding on to the altar and sometimes sitting. When he came to the Consecration he seemed to acquire new strength and was able, without further difficulty, to finish the Mass." [1]

His strength returned somewhat, and he surprised the people of St. Joseph's by attending at his confessional where he remained for hours, giving no indication of the pains he must have endured. He was able to attend the Mission in the Pro-Cathedral, give some fervent exhortations to the crowd assembled in the early morning to await the opening of the church doors, and spend the entire day between the confessional and the altar. He overtaxed his strength, and was found in a faint on the altar steps. Again he recovered, refused wine brought to him, and asked for a cup of water into which a few spoonfuls of tea were put ; that and a little bread were the only refreshment he would accept.

Though he was so weak, next morning, he made his way to his confessional, where he remained for several hours, and then said Mass at 11 o'clock, and preached, without showing any sign of exhaustion.

Again, however, his life was despaired of by his medical attendant as he lay in his " box " in the little room off the church. It was the first Sunday of the month, when the procession of the Blessed Sacrament usually took place. When the procession had passed his room, and his attendant had gone into the church for the Benediction, he got out of his " box," put on the vestments, and said Mass at his little altar.

5. Father Young's Last Illness and Death

The last exercise of his priestly functions was to bless a beautiful statue of St. Joseph and the Divine Child which had been presented to St. Joseph's by a pious lady. He spent the entire day before St. Joseph's altar honouring the patron of a happy death, and his own great patron saint. .

The following morning, 11th November, 1869, he rose as usual to say Mass, but was so weak that he was persuaded to return to his " box " from which he was never more to rise.

[1] *Life*, 180–82.

Gently and gradually mortal life slipped away, and he passed into Eternal Life in whose shadow his mortal life of 83 years had been spent. Perhaps the only thing he ever boasted of was : " I am now the oldest priest in Ireland, and probably in the world, or amongst the oldest."

The last days of his life have been penned by a friend of his who was in close contact with him. He was mindful of the great Vatican Council that was to be opened shortly, to which Cardinal Cullen was about to proceed, and he prayed with extraordinary fervour that the special blessing of God might descend upon the Holy Father and all the prelates engaged in it.

When Cardinal Cullen visited him during those last days, he had to enforce silence on him when he began to proclaim himself an unprofitable servant and unfaithful labourer in the vineyard, and to lament the sins of his life and the opportunities he had neglected. It was left to Father Purcell, of the Pro-Cathedral, to put to rest the scruples of the saintly old man.

He lingered on for a week after his first seizure, and, Wednesday, 17th November, he desired to receive the final Indulgence of the Rosary from one of the Dominican Fathers. Fidelity to the Rosary, in season and out of season, was, as we have seen, uppermost in his mind. He wished to gain, in his dying hours, all the Indulgences of a Dominican Tertiary. A message was sent to Dominick-street, but it was not delivered. It happened that Rev. Dr. Russell, the Superior of the Dominicans, conceived at this time a desire to visit him, and proceeded to St. Joseph's. He found the old man passing away, and immediately gave the final Absolution and Dominican Indulgence. In a few moments, he exclaimed to the inmates gathered around : " A saint has passed to heaven, it is now our turn to ask his intercession for us." [1]

Another account states that, about an hour before his death, he gave his solemn blessing to St. Joseph's, its inmates, benefactors, and all those who used to frequent it.

The Evening Office Societies, that he had promoted in every parish in which he was a curate, gathered in full strength

[1] *Life*, 188–89.

to do honour to their benefactor and to unite in the Church's prayer, the Office for the Dead, for him whose voice had so often led theirs in that great liturgical prayer.

His remains lay for two days before the high altar in St. Joseph's which he had so faithfully served for thirteen years. The devotion of the faithful surpassed all previous experience. The people felt that a saint lay in their midst, and from dawn till midnight they filed past the wooden barriers to honour their guide and friend. It required the constant exertion of the police to preserve order and guard against accidents.

The scene is graphically described by his biographer : " Burly coal porters and dockyard labourers, pale, worn-out women, extreme old age and childhood's dawn, mingled together, all alike swayed by the same sentiment, subdued by the same deep feeling, that the apostle of the poor had passed from his earthly ministry to plead in their behalf before the great white throne. All struggled to touch with their beads, medals, or handkerchiefs, his vestments, or even the coffin ; and grateful indeed was the poor woman who, in the truest spirit of an Irish mother, after hours of patient waiting, succeeded in placing the baby hand of her child on the placid form, invoking with prayers and tears the protection of the holy priest for the little soul so infinitely precious to her maternal heart. Others, who where not able to approach near enough, held out their infants beseechingly towards some man whose strength would enable him to make his way to the bier. And most touching it was to notice the gentle appreciation with which the hard-handed son of toil would fulfil the mother's behest." [1]

The report in the *Freeman's Journal* states : " On Wednesday evening [17th November] he passed serenely out of life, dying the death of a saint. The remains were borne on Wednesday evening to the Asylum chapel. . . . Thousands from all parts of the city flocked to have a last glance of one so eminent for holiness. At 10 o'clock on yesterday [Thursday] morning, the remains which were contained in a cedar shell with a leaden case, and an outer coffin of highly polished

[1] *Life*, 190–91.

Irish oak, with gilt mountings, were removed to a hearse-and-four, with white plumes. The inscription on the coffin, which was engraved on a gilt shield surmounted by a crucifix, was—

THE REVEREND HENRY YOUNG,

DIED NOV. 17TH, 1869,

AGED 84 YEARS.

R.I.P."

The hearse was followed by thousands of the poor. The Rev. Father Young, S.J., Clongowes-wood College, brother of the deceased, was the chief mourner. "The dignitaries and clergy took their places at either side of the remains, and at eleven o'clock every portion of the sacred edifice set apart for the laity was thronged. . . . Very Rev. Mgr. O'Connell, Dean of Dublin, presided at the ceremonies. The sacred music was performed with solemn effect by the choir of priests, aided by the students of Holy Cross College, Clonliffe, led by the Rev. N. Donnelly,[1] the Rev. T. O'Reilly, the Rev. J. McSwiggan, and the Rev. Mark Fricker, who officiated as chanters." High Mass was celebrated by Very Rev. Canon Murphy, Administrator.

" Owing to the dense crowds assembled round the church it was as much as the police, acting under the command of Mr. Superintendent Corr and Inspector McElveeney, could accomplish to make way for the procession to pass on to the vaults, beneath the church." He was placed in the crypt beneath the high altar.

The notice in the *Freeman's Journal* continues : " From the time he arrived at the years of reason up to the close of his patriarchal and honoured life his whole heart and soul were devoted to the service of God and to the welfare of his fellow-creatures. A benign and all-abiding charity was his, and perhaps there never existed a man so utterly unselfish and so thoroughly impressed with a sense of duty. He lived in the world as if he knew it not, but still his was a life of

---

[1] Afterwards the Most Rev. Dr. Donnelly, Bishop of Canea, who had a profound admiration for the deceased, and afterwards in his *Hist. of Dub. Par.*, referred to his apostolic works, and to his dying in the odour of sanctity.

unremitting toil even when the infirmities of age were upon him. He seldom partook of more than a few hours sleep, the greater portion of the night he spent in earnest prayer, when, it is said of him, he became so wrapt in devotion that he used to seem as if he was holding the closest communion with God. He threw all the vigour of his youth and manhood into his sacred calling, and he knew no fatigue when the sinner was to be converted, the sorrowing and the afflicted to be comforted, and the miserable and the destitute to be relieved. For the purpose of relieving the wants of the needy and the destitute he frequently denied himself the mere necessaries of life, and he was often known to have given the coat off his back to cover a naked and shivering fellow-creature."

In the Minutes of the annual meeting of the Committee of St. Joseph's, Sunday, 30th December, 1869, it is recorded[1] : " At his special request a room was prepared off the church porch for his accommodation, to afford every facility for the practice of his well-known piety and vigorous austerity. It was his custom to rise at four o'clock, and immediately repair to the foot of the altar, where he continued engaged in prayer until the opening of the church at six. He then conducted the morning exercises, and after a lengthened stay in the confessional, celebrated the Community Mass. About two o'clock, p.m. he partook of his only daily meal, and having spent the entire remainder of the day, in what he termed his ' Chapel Duties ' partaking of the nature of a perpetual mission, he retired after nine o'clock to repose upon a few boards with a wooden box for a pillow. This he continued until near the close of his holy life when he was compelled by the physicians to mitigate these austerities in consequence of his infirmities. . . . His prominent characteristic was his humility and charity, which never forsook him."

His biographer relates : " The pious inmates of St. Joseph's Asylum say that they were quite unable to satisfy the innumerable demands for relics of the holy servant of God. The Archbishop of Armagh [Dr. McGettigan] requested one to be sent to him, and applications poured in, not only from the

[1] Archives, St. Joseph's.

devout of Ireland, but from England, America, and Australia, on the part of those who either had known Father Henry Young, or were familiar with his great virtues. His soutanes and other articles were cut up into small particles for distribution, and eagerly sought for until the supply was exhausted."[1]

Many accounts were furnished of cures wrought during his lifetime by his prayers, and, after his death, by the application of his relics.[2] There seems, however, to have been no application to the diocesan authorities to deal with these matters. It is thus we must leave this interesting subject, confident that his work and example were of exceptional merit, and hopeful for a recognition of his sanctity.

[1] *Life*, 192.   [2] Ibid., 193

NOTES ADDED IN THE PRESS.

Page 77.   *Charles Young.*

An entry in the " Register of the Confraternity of the Cord of St. Francis, Adam and Eve Chapel, Dublin " (1760–1777), states that Charles Young became a member of the Confraternity on 22nd May, 1768. If this Charles Young be the father of Father Henry Young, as seems quite probable, then he must have come to Dublin when quite a young man.

Page 229.   *Franciscan Orphan Society* (founded 1817).

A printed appeal issued by the Society in 1837 states that, in the space of 20 years, it had rescued " 156 helpless Innocents, 70 of whom now remain on the charity. A great part of these children are the offspring of Parents who have fallen victims to that mysterious and awful visitation [Plague of 1832] which lately spread its destructive ravages throughout the civilized world, and has left in this City the most indelible traces of its terrific progress." Many of the orphans were " apprenticed to useful trades."

(Registers in the Franciscan Library, Merchants' Quay. By courtesy of Rev. Canice Mooney, O.F.M.).

Page 126. *Devotion to the Sacred Heart.*

Tadhg Gaedhlach Ó Súilleabháin (1715–95), a native of Killeedy, Co. Limerick, wrote, after 1767, twenty-five religious songs in Irish at Dungarvan, where some kind of confraternity existed. We have no evidence that this confraternity was one of the Sacred Heart ; all we know is that the recitation of the Rosary was its prominent feature. One of Tadhg's most beautiful religious songs was that to the Sacred Heart— *Gile mo Chroidhe.* Here is the first stanza :

> Gile mo chroidhe do chroidhe-se, a Shlánathóir,
> Is ciste mo chroidhe do chroidhe-se dfhagháil im chomhair,
> O's follus gur líon do chroidhe dom ghádh-sa, a Stóir,
> I gcochall mo chroidhe do chroidhe-se fág i gcomhad.

Thus an Irish poet sang of the Devotion to the Sacred Heart about the middle eighteenth century, very probably before it was preached in St. Michan's by Father Mulcaile, S.J.

(By courtesy of Risteard Ua Foghludha, D.Litt.Celt.)

Page 61. *Recovery of George III.*

Prayers were directed by various Church authorities in Britain to be said at their services for the recovery of the health of George III, who became afflicted with insanity in 1788. The following regulation was issued by the Catholic authorities : " Prayers to be said for the recovery of the King's health in the chapels of the Roman Catholics. In all the masses that are said, let the following prayer for our most beloved King George be added to the post-communion of the day [the prayer is then set out]. After each of the masses, before the priest departs, kneeling at the foot of the altar, let him say : [Antiphon and Psalms XIX and XX, which are set out in full]."

(*The Annual Register, or a View of the History, Politics and Literature, for the year* 1788. London : Printed for J. Dodsley, in Pall-Mall, 1790. Appendix, pp. 251–54.)

EPILOGUE

EIGHT months before Father Young died, one of the most momentous events in the history of the previous three hundred years in Ireland—since the Acts of Supremacy and Uniformity were passed by the Dublin Parliament in Elizabeth's reign (1560)—took place, namely, the Disestablishment of the Protestant Church (March, 1869). For seventeen years Archbishop Cullen had been striving, by voice and pen, to bring it about. The method he adopted was one of waging war on the proselytising institutions whose chief support was the Established Church. If he could show that the Established Church had failed in its primary object (of 1560) to force Catholics to join it, then the existence of the Establishment with its privileged position was an anomaly.

For his personal campaign against proselytism he relied on the platform provided by Margaret Aylward's St. Brigid's Orphanage. Margaret, born 23rd November, 1810, the daughter of a Waterford merchant, came to Dublin in 1846, and formed the Ladies' Association of Charity, 1851, with the consent of Archbishop Murray, at 20 Lower Dorset-street. Protestant institutions to attract Catholic boys and girls had been erected all over the city during those forty years. Margaret Aylward did her best, with the scant funds at her disposal, to provide homes for orphans and manual work for girls, whilst, with her ladies, she tried to induce Catholic girls, as they came out of the Protestant schools in the Coombe and Townsend-street, to avoid them.

From the first meeting of St. Brigid's Orphanage, in 1856, at which Margaret Aylward exposed the wiles of the proselytisers, Archbishop Cullen continued to use its annual meetings as a platform for waging war on the Protestant Establishment. At the 1858 meetings the names of eleven proselytising institutions and their huge incomes were published, and the legislature was publicly denounced as the first and last cause of deliberate proselytism.[1]

[1] *Life of Margaret Aylward,* 270–80.

This view was supported by Mr. Cunningham, a Protestant London Barrister, in an article he wrote in the London press of the time, " Is the Good News from Ireland True ? " He argued that, without the endowments of the Established Church and its institutions, proselytism would be without two of its main supports. It was calculated that every soul purchased by the proselytisers cost them £100,000.

The Rev. Dr. Murray, of Maynooth, put the case in another form : " the whole system is one of pure fraud and bribery. This is clearly evinced by the simple fact that it was first established in the period of Ireland's unparalleled distress, and established, too, in those very districts where that distress was heaviest, and where, therefore, bribery and corruption had a wider field of action and surer prey."[1] Again, he says : " The fourth and last characteristic of souperism is its marvellous spirit of bold, unscrupulous, persistent lying." Dr. Murray quoted from Protestant sources the proofs of his statements.[2]

An important point made by Margaret Aylward was that, considering the relatively small number of Catholics, fewer institutions would have been sufficient for Protestant orphans ; that the hundreds of thousands of pounds provided for the proselytising institutions were not required for Protestant children or orphans ; and that, if the proselytisers were deprived of this endowment, supplied or fostered by the Established Church, she did not fear to face them on their own ground.

The truth of all this had been gradually filtering into the minds of English Protestants. Mr. Cunningham's article had made a deep impression. The Annual Meetings and Reports of St. Brigid's Orphanage, supported by Archbishop Cullen, between 1864 and 1868, brought the English Government to its senses. The lying reports of the proselytising institutions, as to their eager converts, were discredited. " What is the Protestant Church Establishment," said Gladstone, " but an appropriation of the fruits of labour and of skill to certain purposes. And unless these purposes be fulfilled that appropriation cannot be fulfilled." In other words, the so-called Reformation Church had failed to entice Irish Catholics to

[1] *Life of Margaret Aylward*, 287–88. Ibid., 291–95.

attend its services in the sixteenth and seventeenth centuries, and though, in the late seventeenth and early eighteenth centuries, it had tried to impoverish them by depriving them of their industries, commerce and education, and later still, in times of distress, had tried to convert their soul at the expense of their body, yet the Catholic Faith triumphed.

In 1867, Earl Russell moved for a Commission to inquire into the property of the Irish Church and its condition generally. Nothing was said of Disestablishment, but the intention of the motion was obvious. The Commission declared the net income of the Established Church to be £580,000 per annum, and the value of its property 15 million pounds (the fruits of the penal laws). Its reports left no doubt that a determined attack on the Establishment was intended. In March, 1869, Gladstone introduced in the Commons his Bill for Disestablishment, which passed the Commons by an overwhelming majority ; the Upper House did not dare to oppose the will of the people. An interval for the making of needful arrangements was conceded and, 1st January, 1871, the Protestant Church of Ireland ceased as a State Establishment.

In thanksgiving for the Disestablishment, Cardinal Cullen ordered a Solemn Triduum that began, 14th September, 1869, in the Pro-Cathedral, with Father Tom Burke, the great Dominican, as preacher.

When the State Church was disestablished Margaret Aylward received a letter from Mgr. Kirby, Rector of the Irish College, Rome : " A few lines to congratulate you on the fall of the gigantic monster of the Irish Protestant Establishment. How soon it tumbled ! Its head all of gold did not save it as the feet were only of clay. . . . The downfall of the old fortress of heresy is a grand work for God. In the beginning the old enemy of souls will doubtless cause some of them to redouble their efforts. But you know their great support came from the Establishment which with its powerful influences and wealth gave life and strength to all branches of proselytism. But after a time you will find the proselytisers' zeal to cool down, and the daughters of St. Brigid, the Sisters of the Holy Faith, daily adding to their heavenly conquests." [1]

---

[1] *Life of Margaret Aylward*, 300–306.

It was providential that the Christian Brothers and the Sisters of the Holy Faith had refused the Government grant for primary education and were able to carry on their work by popular support, which showed the Catholic strength when properly organised, and which opened the eyes of the Government to the futility of the Established Church. They were the standard-bearers of religious freedom in schools.

To Archbishop Cullen's propaganda was mainly due the attention that was focussed on the Established Church in Ireland and its proselytising institutions which resulted in the Disestablishment. When he visited Father Young some months afterwards (November), he had received the call to Rome to take part in the Vatican Council for the discussion on the promulgation of the Infallibility of the Pope. He bade a last farewell to his old friend, the apostle of Catholic Dublin, who had but a few days to live. He departed with the apostle's blessing for himself and the Church. Father Young had lived to see the real end of the Penal Laws.

INDEX

ACADEMIES, Classical, etc. : Anne-street, North, 128 ; Clarendon-street, 197 ; Clondalkin, 98 ; Harold's Cross, 98 ; Inch, 84 ; Jervis-street, 202 ; Usher's Island, 203. (*Alias* Seminaries) : Castle-street, 196–97 ; St. Patrick's, Arran-quay, 196–97 ; Saul's-court. See under that title.

Aikenhead, Mother Mary, 221, 225, 228, 264, 265.

All Hallows, 204.

Allen, Lord, 58.

Allen's-court, 58.

Ambrogetti, Signor, 135-6-7.

Archbold, Rev. Mr., 178.

Archbold's-court, 38, 231.

Arklow, 16, 271.

Arran-quay, 20, 29, 196, 197, 199.

Ash-street chapel, 17, 20, 24, 25, 196.

Assembly Rooms, 6, 267.

Asylums, 230, 231, 234, 235, 279, 284.

Audeon's Arch, 30, 33.

Augustinians, John's-lane, 20, 114, 225, 276.

Austin, Archdeacon, 24.

Austin, Fr., 38, 35.

Austin's Grounds, 38.

Aylmer, Miss, 44.

Aylmer, Fr., S.J., 242.

Aylward, Margaret, 303, 305.

BALDOYLE, 218.

Baldoyle and Howth, Parish, 243.

Ball, Mother, 101, 102.

Band, Fr. Mathew, 193.

Bar Convent, York, 226.

Barnewall, Friar, 24.

Barnewall, Fr. Barnaby, Shankill, 30.

Barrett, Mr. (Musical Professor), 135.

Bayley, Edward, Rector of Arklow, 271.

Begg, Canon, 218.

Begrez, Signor, 136.

Bellews, 46, 130.

Benedictines, 41, 42, 43, 44.

Betagh, Joseph, Fr., 38, 39, 40, 115, 131, 132, 157, 158, 163, 186.

Bewley, Ephraim, 35.

Birmingham, Archdeacon, P.P., 25, 34.

Bishops, Irish, 133.

Blake, Dr. M., 19, 39, 45, 115, 123, 128, 131, 132, 133, 134, 136, 138, 143, 146, 147, 152, 164, 173, 199, 217, 226, 227, 266, 279, 285.

Bolger, Bryan, 169, 170.

Bond, Oliver, 68.

Bonnet Rouge, 70.

Books, Catechetical, 49.

Booksellers, Catholic, 49.

Bourke, Lady, 44.

Brereton, Sir William 18.

Breweries, 5, 20, 129.

Bridge-street, 17, 20, 22, 29, 33, 51, 58, 60, 68, 77, 172, 213, 236, 237.

Browne, Fr. William, 27.

Brunswick-street, North, 8, 42, 43.

Bryan, Captain George, 130, 131.

Bryans, 46.

Bull-lane, 20, 27, 46, 125.

Burke, Fr. Tom, O.P., 305.

—— Fr. John (Provincial of Franciscans), 42.

—— Fr. Michael, C.M., 98.

—— Edmund, 58.

—— Richard, 58.

Butler, Dame (Abbess of Benedictines) 42.

—— Miss, 44.

—— Dr. James, 49.

—— Dr. (Archbishop of Cashel), 58.

Byrne, Abp., 42, 58.

—— Edward, 62.

—— Fr. Milo, 17.

—— Col., 17.

CAHILL, Keary, 285.

—— Rev., 97.

Cahir, Lady, 44.

Callahan, William (Coolock), 226.

Canavan, Canon George, 275.

Capuchin Fathers, 20, 30, 31.

Carroll, Fr., 222.

Carleton, Alderman, 133.

Carlow College, 198.

Carmelites, Calced, 17, 20, 25, 33, 98.

—— Discalced, 17, 20, 21.

Carpenter, Dr., 55, 57, 59, 60.

Catherine, Mother (Sisters of Charity), 87.

Catechism, Classes, 173, 174, 175, 181, 189.

Catholic Action, 49, 54, 100, 149.

—— Association, 101, 167, 169, 170, 177, 267.

—— Book Society, 127, 203.

—— Burials, 114, 116.

—— Chapels, see under " Chapels."

—— Churches, see under " Churches."

—— Committee, 59, 60, 79.

Catholic Directory, 19, 86, 99, 108, 122,
138, 140, 147, 149, 150, 233.
—— Education, 128, 163.
—— Emancipation, 60, 79, 99, 100,
164, 167, 169, 170, 267.
—— Industry, 10, 13.
—— Merchants, 33, 38, 49, 55–59, 64–5.
—— Printers and Publishers, 49, 50, 51,
79, 147, 180.
—— Relief, 54–65, 80, 114.
—— Religious Instruction, 39, 50, 264.
—— Religious Life, 49, 50.
—— Traders and Craftsmen, 10, 12, 13,
14, 49, 64, 65.
Cemeteries: Glasnevin, 116, 198–9.
—— Golden-bridge, 116.
—— St. James's, 114.
Chapels : Catholic, 34, 51 ; Penal time,
130, 208, 253 ; St. Mary's, 11 ;
Augustinian, 29, 81, 91 ; Mary's-lane,
17, 91, 93 ; St. Francis, 24 ; Harold's
Cross, 95 ; St. Joseph's Infirmary,
280 ; Rosemary-lane, 130, 132 ;
Octagon, 34 ; Phibsborough, 202,
203, 205, 231 ; Meath-street, 179 ;
Jervis-street (1823), 202 ; Adam and
Eve, 24, 34, 229 ; Bull-lane, 126,
130 ; Liffey-street, 131, 148, 225 ;
Denmark-street, 137 ; Finglas, 265 ;
James's-street, 159 ; Bridge-street,
243 ; Clarendon-street, 190, 230 ;
St. Audoen's, 65, 229 ; St. Nicholas'
Metropolitan, 229 ; Francis-street,
25 ; Chapel of Ease to St. Paul, 200 ;
Dirty-lane, 25. See also under
"Churches."
Caulfield, James (Suffragan Bishop of
Ferns), 61.
Cavan, Lady, 44.
Channel Row, 29, 42, 43, 45.
Charity, Ladies Association of, 303.
—— Sermons, 8.
Christchurch-place, 39, 48, 164, 240.
Christian Brothers, 117, 168, 169, 264–65,
306.
Christian Doctrine Confraternity, SS.
Michael and John's, 50, 109, 164–
189, 199, 228, 230.
Cholera, 219, 222, 227, 231, 232, 265.
Churches : St. Andrew's (Westland-
row), 40, 224 ; John's-lane, 94, 181 ;
Immaculate Conception, Marl-
borough-street, 134, 206, 267, 270 ;
St. Michan's, 124, 129, 130, 134 ;
Church-street, 27, 30, 31, 51, 20, 134,
195 ; Of St. Bridget, Bride-street,
166 ; St. Francis Xavier, 242 ;
Dominican, Denmark-street, 134 ;
SS. Michael and John's, 109, 132, 133,
134, 135, 137, 138, 140, 146, 158 ;
John-street, 195 ; Baldoyle, 218 ;
Kinsaley, 232 ; St. Saviour's, 27. See
also under "Chapels."
Church Concerts, 133, 135, 136, 137.
Cistercians, 40, 84.
Clarke, Rev. Eugene, 190.
Clement, Pope, XII, 44.
Clinch, Fr., C.C., 23.
Clongowes, 242.
Cloncurry, Lord, 97.
Cloyne, Bishop of, 119.
Cloney, Thomas, 75.
Clondalkin, St. Joseph's, 97.
Cooke, Robert, O.M.I., 276.
Collier, Mrs, 109.
—— the Widow, 175.
Cotton Manufacture, 3.
Coyne, John (Cook-street), 140, 149.
Coffey, Rev. N., 229.
Colman, Rev. Dr. (St. Michan's), 177.
Commission of the Peace, 268.
Connor, Darby, 100.
Concannon, O. P., Bishop, 89.
Confraternities : Christian Doctrine, 84,
123–4, 140, 149, 158, 162–164, 175–6,
188, 227, 235. See also under "Chris-
tian Doctrine Confraternity, SS.
Michael's and John's." Evening
Office, 139, 148, 150–158, 160, 161,
166, 169, 226, 227, 253, 270 ; Most
Holy Rosary, 44 ; Sacred Heart, 126.
Condran, Charles, 33.
Convents : Poor Clares, 96, 121 ; Adam
and Eve, 99, 100 ; George's-hill, 125,
132 ; Dominican, 8 ; Stanhope-
street, 221 ; Annals of Lanherne, 249.
Coombe, The, 9, 11, 33, 36, 38, 96.
Cook-street, 15, 17, 20, 22, 23, 24, 33,
38, 49, 51, 54, 132.
Copper-alley, 85, 186.
Corn-Exchange, 170, 176.
Cornwall, F.r William Young's
Mission in, 235, 240, 243, 244, 247,
248, 250.
Corri, Hayden, 268.
Craft Guilds, Protestant, 12.
Cullen, Archbishop Paul, 266, 273–276,
306.
Cummins, Mrs., 48.
Cunningham, Mr., 304.
—— Mrs., 48.
Curry, John, 57.
Cure d'Ars, 94, 96.

DANCERS, Tight-Rope, 214.
Dean of Dublin (St. Nicholas's), 95.
Deanery, St. Patrick's, 230.
Death-rate, 183.

Deighan, Paul, 129.
Delaney, Mrs. (Delville, Glasnevin), 6.
—— Daniel (Suffragan Bishop of Kildare and Leighlin), 61.
De Londres, Henry, Archbishop of Dublin, 27.
Dempsey, Rev. Mr., 188, 189.
Derby-square, 39, 152, 157, 158, 163, 164, 172.
Devil's Potstick, The, 256.
Devotion, First Friday, 92.
—— First Saturday, 92, 93.
—— to Sacred Heart, 93.
—— to St. Joseph, 44.
—— to Immaculate Heart of Mary, 237 238.
—— Office of the Sacred Heart, 127.
Devotional Works, 47.
Dillon, Lady, 44.
—— Mr., 98.
Dillons, 46, 130.
Dinan, Fr., S.J., 128.
Directorium, The, 148.
Dirty-lane, 18, 20, 81.
—— —— Chapel, 25.
Disestablishment of Protestant Church, 305.
Dispensaries, 183, 184.
Distilleries, 4, 5, 9, 10.
Dixon, James, 75.
Doctors, Work of (during Fever, 1817), 183.
Dogmatic Works, 47.
Dolphin's Barn, 11, 20.
Dominicans, 17, 20, 22, 27, 43, 45.
Donnelly, Bishop, 21, 273.
Donnybrook, 227.
"Dormitory of the Friars," 95.
Dowdall, Fr. Alexis, 30.
—— Luke, 30.
Dowdalls, 46, 130.
Doyle, Michael (C.C., SS. Michael and John's), 39.
—— Rev. Dr., 186, 190, 241.
—— Rev. Dr. Michael, 196, 197.
—— Bishop of Leighlin, 206.
—— Fr. Michael, 226.
—— Anna Maria, 226, 227.
—— Burses, 198.
Drumcondra-lane, 43.
—— Upper, 204.
—— Road, 230.
Drunkenness, Treatise against, 149.
Duane, John (Suffragan Bishop of Ossory), 61.
Dublin, 1-14, 17, 38-44, 82, 90, 91, 131.
—— Castle Bureaucracy, 34.
—— See of, 57.
Dungan, Rev. M., 190, 193.

Dunleary, 140.
Dunne, Rev. Mr., 99.
Dunsany, Lord, 44.
Dwyer, Michael, 278.

EARL OF MEATH, 1, 2, 11, 25, 34, 35.
Earl Russell's Commission of Inquiry into Irish Church, 305.
Edict, Constantine, 87.
—— Imperial, 89.
Education, 38, 41, 46, 128, 196.
—— Commissioners, 117, 118.
—— Continental, 50, 61, 86.
—— Technical, 46, 98, 185.
—— University, 57.
Elephant, The 58.
—— Lane (Cathedral-street), 229.
Ely, Lord, 25, 26.
Emmet, Robert, 71, 73, 116, 178.
England, Bishop John (of Charlestown), 118, 203.
Ennis, John, 267.
Erasmus Smyth Board, 37.
Esmonde, Fr. (Rector of Jesuit College, Tullabeg), 107, 108, 109.
—— Sir Thomas, 229.
Essex-bridge, 5, 127, 176.
—— -quay, 229.
—— -street, 59, 193.
Established Church, 303, 305.
Eudes, St. John, 237.
"Evening Office,": See under "Confraternities."
Everard, Dr., President of Maynooth, 271.
Evers, Father, 30.
Exchange-street, 192, 229.
—— —— Lower, 132, 135.

FAIRS, 214, 227.
Famine, 182, 231, 263, 269, 275.
Farrell, James, 132.
Ferguson, Fr. (S.J.), 242.
Fever Epidemic (1818), 182, 183, 188.
Field, Fr. John, 39.
Fingall, Countess of 43, 44, 234.
—— Lord, 57, 234.
Finglas, 116, 255, 268.
Fitzgerald, Miss, 44.
—— Lord Henry, 61.
Fitzsimon, Catholic family, 218.
Fitzsimons, Rev. Dr., 29.
Fitzwilliam, Earl, 64, 65, 66.
Flanagan, Fr., P.P. St. Nicholas's, 177.
—— Rev. M., 189, 193, 265.
Flax Manufacture, 11, 185.
Flinn, Rev. Christopher, 81.
—— Dr. (P.P.), 227, 228.
Fordom's-alley, 33.

Forster, Rev. Joseph, 105, 106.
Forty Hours' Adoration, 211.
Foundling Hospital, 52, 54, 55.
Francis-street, 15, 20, 24, 61, 65, 71, 79, 95, 152, 189, 193, 232, 265.
Francis Xaverius, 27, 28.
Franciscans, 17, 20, 24, 33, 54, 73, 99, 100.
Franzoni, Cardinal, 198.
" Freeman's Journal," 134, 135, 267, 272, 299–300.
Freizemongers, 24.
French-street (Upper Mercer-street), 17, 98, 192, 193.
Friars, 17, 20, 24.
Friary, Pre-Reformation Franciscan, 24.
Fullam, Fr. (S.J.), 38.

GAFFNEY, Dean, 238.
Gahan, Fr. (S.J.), 128.
Gallagher, Dr., Bishop of Raphoe, 44.
Garristown, Mission in, 2, 17, 218.
Gentili, Dr., 94.
George I, 17, 18, 19,20, 21, 22, 43, 47, 48.
George III, 45, 58.
—— an Act of, 3.
George's-hill, 121, 126, 128, 230.
—— Glass House, 55.
—— Convent, 47, 132, 133, 227.
Geydon, Widow, 27.
Giovanni, Don, 135.
Glencree, 278.
Glencullen, Mission at, 218.
Glendalough, Archdeacon of, 198.
Globe Coffee-House, Derham's, 58.
Glove-making, 47.
Glynn, V. Rev., St. Mary's, 177.
Golden-Bridge, 116, 127.
Goodwin (Printer), 100.
Gormanstown, Lord, 57.
Grace, R., 237.
Grangegorman, 196, 221.
Gratia Dei, Monastery, 42.
Grattan, Henry, 5, 61, 64, 65, 66.
Graveyard, St. James's, 114.
—— Mulhuddart, 113, 114.
—— St. Kevin's, 115.
Green-street, 178.
Grey, Charles, 31.
Grimshaw, Mr., 9.
Guilds, 11–13.
Guinness' Brewery, 5, 20.

HALSTON-STREET, 130.
Hamill, Dr., 91.
Haly, Fr. (S.J.), 242.
Hammond-lane, 29, 41.
Hand, Fr. J., 204.

Hangman-lane, 27.
Hanley, Catherine, 33.
—— Cornelius, 33.
Hanover-street, 117.
Hardwicke, Lord Lieutenant, 74.
—— -street, 128.
—— Hospital, 8.
Harley, Miss, 227.
Harold's Cross, 11, 70, 80, 99, 100, 105, 106, 109, 111, 120, 121, 131, 146, 148, 149, 150, 175, 207, 230, 264, 283.
Hawkins-street, 25, 182, 184, 186.
Hayden Corrie, 134, 253.
Haydn on children's singing in church, 253.
Hearnon's English school (Church-street), 41.
Henrietta-street, 130.
Herbert-street, 226.
Hevey, Margaret, 77.
—— Catherine, 77.
High-street, 24.
Hoare, Bro. James, 168.
Hohenlohe, Prince Alexander, 102–109.
Holden, William (Music Printer), 255.
Holmes, Rev. T. V., 230.
Howth, 31, 121, 218, 232, 234, 235, 243.
House of Industry, 7, 8.
—— of Mercy (Baggot-street), 222.
—— Refuge, Franciscan, 224.
—— Refuge (Stanhope-street), 226.
Hughes, Axne (Sacristan in St. Joseph's), 286.

INCH, 81, 82.
—— Academy, 86, 143.
Inchicore, 277.
Infirmary of the Foundling Hospital, 52.
Irish Calendar, 153.
—— College, Paris, 85.
—— College, Rome, 131.
—— Sisters of Charity, 196.
Irishtown, 227, 228.

JAMES, Rev. John, 49.
—— II, 22, 30, 40, 41, 42, 267.
—— Bishop of Ossory, 27.
James's-street, 1, 33, 52, 231, 275.
Jervis-street, 28, 268, 269, 270.
Jesuits, 17, 32, 38, 40, 80, 82, 83, 88, 121, 128, 140, 143.
—— General of, 83.
—— College, 82.
John's-lane, 20, 21, 114.
Jubilee, Booklet for the, 148, 206, 209.
—— Devotions for, 207, 209.
Juvenile Delinquents, Institutions for, 277, 278.

KEANE, Rev. J. B., 100.
Kearney, Fr., S.J., 40.
Keary, 218.
Keating, Miss, 44.
Keef, Patrick 33.
Keine's-lane, 22.
Kellett Bequest, 172.
Kelly, Miss, 44.
Kelly, Ignatius, 48.
Kenney, Fr. Peter, S.J., 82, 128, 157, 158, 207, 242.
Kenmare, Lord, 44, 57, 61, 68.
Keogh, Rev. Mr., 31.
—— M. B. Capuchin (P.P. of Howth), 39.
Kilkelly, Dr. Peter, Bishop of Kilmac-duagh, 44.
Killossery, 15.
Kilmacduagh, 89.
Kingsland, Lord, 23.
King-street, 4, 28, 30, 34, 71, 140, 148.
Kinsaley, Chapel at, 219.

LACE-MAKING, 46.
Lace-school, 185.
Lahy's Weekly Conference, 20.
Laithy's Directory, 146.
Laphen, Rev. J. T., 230.
Lazers-hill, 26.
Lecky, 5, 6, 53.
Lennon, S.J., 40.
Leunis, S.J., Fr. John, 82.
Liberty, 1, 2, 3, 7, 9, 11, 19, 25, 32, 34, 36, 37, 71, 80, 186, 187, 189, 208, 265.
—— City, 36, 37.
—— Donore, 34.
—— Earl of Meath, 36.
—— Thomas-court, 34.
Liffey-street, 20, 28, 29, 60, 125.
Linegar, Archbishop of Dublin, 28, 44.
Lloyd, Fr. Silvester, 17.
Loreto Sisters (Rathfarnham), 44, 237.
Louvain, 73, 85, 86.
Lubé, V. Rev. Dean, P.P., 177, 224.
Lucy-lane, 40.
Lurgan-street, 4.
Lusk, 15.
Lynch, Charles, 120.
Lynch, O.M.I., Fr., 278.
—— Family Burial Place of, 78.
Lyster, Miss, 44.

MACDONAGH, Dr., Bishop of Kilmore, 44.
MacDonald, N. H., 192.
MacMahon, Fr. Bernard, 147.
Magee, Dr., Protestant Archbishop of Dublin, 115.

Magee, William, Protestant Dean of Cork, 118.
Malahide, 219.
Mangan, James Clarence, 40.
Manning, Rev. Dr., 275.
Marlborough-street, 198, 204.
Marshalsea, 80.
Mary's-abbey, 193.
Mary's-lane, 27, 41, 46, 48, 51, 55, 58, 91, 92, 98, 190.
Mass-houses, 19, 20, 21, 22, 24, 27, 43, 98.
Mass-lane, 40.
Master-clothiers, 2.
Mathew, Fr., 149, 189, 190, 192, 251.
Maxwell, Brother Anthony, 169.
Maynooth College, 69, 84–5–6, 196, 198, 201, 202, 203, 238, 271.
McAuley, Mother, 222, 226, 227.
McDermot, Lady, 44.
McEgan, Dr. Stephen, Bishop of Meath, 44.
McGloughlin, 41.
McGuirk, 41.
McMahon, Rev. Dr., 128.
McWeeney, Mr., 179.
Meade, Mrs. Mary Catherine, 102.
Meagher, Fr., P.P. of Rathmines, 168.
—— Fr. William, 201.
Meath, 39, 82.
—— Hospital, 187.
Meath-street, 25, 34, 35, 36.
—— Parochial chapel, 89, 258, 259.
—— Fr. Henry as curate in, 175.
Meehan, Fr., 168.
" Memoriale Vitae Sacerdotalis " (M. l'Abbé Claude Arvisenat), 149.
Mendicity Institute, 181–188.
Merchant's-quay, 41, 99.
Meyler, V. Rev. Dr., V.G., 225.
Miley, Dr., P.P. of Bray, 265, 267.
Mill-street, 265, 269.
Mill workers, 98, 99, 101.
Milltown, 98, 99, 105, 131, 198.
Miollis, General, 88.
Miraculous Medal, Devotion to the, 237, 238.
" Missale Romanum," 148.
Missions, College for Foreign, 204.
Mitchell, 178.
Mocharoc of Delgany, 26.
Moira House, 182–189.
Moore-Levins, 152.
Monte Cellino, 89, 205, 211.
Morgan, Lady, 6.
Mori, Signor, 136.
Mount Alverno, 99.
—— Argus, 1.
Mountcashel, Lady, 44.

Mount Melleray, 234.
Mountjoy-place, 231.
Mount-Jerome, 95.
Mulally, Mary Teresa, 46, 47, 55, 119, 121, 185.
Mulcaile, Father, S.J., 17, 38, 46; 47, 48, 126, 128.
Mulhuddart, 78, 113, 114.
Mullinahack, 55, 62.
Murphy, Fr. Michael, 17, 38, 39.
—— Mary, 33.
—— Fr. Barnaby, 81, 129.
—— Bishop of Cork, 133.
—— Rev. Dr., 229.
—— Mr. James, Trustee of St. Joseph's Asylum, 285.
Murray, Dr. Daniel, 90, 97, 102, 106, 109, 121, 163, 168, 179, 192–230, 237, 240–247, 255, 270–273.
—— —— Pastorals and Letters, 102, 195, 220.
Music, Catholic, 45.
—— Church, 134.
—— Sacred, 252, 253, 254.
—— of the Masters, 253.
Musicians, Italian, 45.

Nary, Fr. Cornelius, P.P., 16.
— Dr., 27.
Neal's English School, Hamon-lane, 41.
Netterville, Fr. Nicholas, S.J., 27.
—— Viscount, 44.
Newgate, 1, 17, 178, 179, 269.
New-row, 11, 21, 33, 58, 86, 122.
New-street, 12, 38, 100.
Norton, Taddeus, 33.
Notre-Dame-des-Victoires, 238.
Novices' Directory, Ursuline, 117.
Nuns, Dominican, 43, 45, 46.
—— —— Channel-row, 113, 114.
—— Benedictine, 41, 42, 43, 44.
Nuns' Island, 42.
"New Month of Mary," 237.

O h-Aingli, Bishop Samuel, 26.
O Briain, Murtagh, 26.
O'Brien, Terence, 33.
——Mary, 33.
—— Mrs. John, 196.
O'Connell, Daniel, 100, 115, 116, 133, 167, 169, 176, 190, 191, 192, 193, 194, 198, 199, 204, 227, 266, 267, 269, 270, 275, 282.
—— Rev. Andrew, 159, 189, 207, 225, 229.
O'Grady, Dr., 197.
O'Hagan, Lord, 277.
O'Hurley, Dermot (Archbishop of Cashel), 38, 115.

O'Keeffe, John (Dramatist), 38.
O'Mealy, Mr., 112.
O'Murroghowe, Teige, 30.
Orphan Society, Patrician, 54.
—— —— Malichean, 229.
—— —— Metropolitan Male and Female, 229.
—— —— Patrician, "Adam's and Eve's," 229.
—— —— St. Michan's, Vincent de Paul, 230.
—— —— St. John of the Cross, 230.
—— —— Parochial, 230.
Orphanage, 55, 120.
—— Baggot-street, 22.
—— Trinitarian, 226.
—— Margaret Aylward's, St. Brigid's, 303.
—— Mount Carmel, 230.
Orthodox Journal, 148.
Oscott, 121.
O'Shaughnessy, Colman (Bishop of Ossory), 44.
O'Toole, Fr., 203.
Oxmantown, 29, 196.

Parish, St. Audoen's, 189, 195, 236, 237, 243.
—— St. Andrew's, 19, 25, 65.
—— Blanchardstown, 60.
—— St. Bride's, 14.
—— St. Catherine's, 18, 20, 21, 25, 32, 35 37, 77, 84, 258.
—— Francis-street, 264.
—— St. James's, 19, 20, 33, 199.
—— St. John's, 10, 14.
—— St. John's (Limerick), 77.
—— St. Luke's, 37, 38.
—— St. Mary's, 14, 19, 28, 53, 168, 231.
—— St. Margaret's, 255.
—— St. Michael's, 14, 19, 23, 33, 38, 39, 40, 48, 54, 55.
—— St. Michan's, 14, 15, 16, 17, 18, 19, 20, 26, 29, 40, 41, 42, 46, 47, 53, 92, 94, 123, 125, 127, 128, 132, 167, 180, 185, 237, 256, 266.
—— Meath-street, 264, 266, 267.
—— St. Michael and John's, 131, 132, 148, 152, 153, 189, 163, 166, 167, 173, 191, 198, 199, 203, 204, 207, 209, 213, 217, 266, 267.
—— St. Nicholas's, 71, 94, 95.
—— St. Nicholas Without the Walls, 19, 24, 214.
—— St. Nicholas Within the Walls, 14.
—— St. Paul's, 14, 20, 28, 29, 43, 53, 131, 180, 193, 195, 199, 205, 224, 255.
—— St. Werburgh's, 14.
Panorma, Signor, 136, 137.

Patterns, 216.
Pembroke, Lord, 227.
Penal Laws, 13, 14, 18, 19, 21, 48, 57, 87, 133, 303.
Penitentiary, Grangegorman, 221.
Phrapper-lane, 41, 46.
Pigeon House, 147.
Pill-lane, 41, 46, 48.
Pimlico, 2, 33, 36, 37.
Pius VII, Pope, 119, 126, 139, 238, 240.
Pius X, Pope, 284.
Plague (of 1826), 166 ; Cholera (1832), 56, 219, 222, 224, 228.
Plunkett, Blessed Oliver, Archbishop, 16.
—— Bishop of Meath, 82.
—— family of Loughcrew, 219.
Pollard, Miss (Matron of St. Joseph's), 286.
Poolbeg-street, 26, 184.
Poor Clares, 42, 43, 80, 120, 148.
Portland-row, 234, 279.
Portmarnock Grange, 219.
Porterstown, 60.
Power, Fr. Francis, 84.
Priests, 14, 15, 18, 21, 31, 41, 85.
Prison, Newgate, 178, 179, 269.
Primaria (Parent Sodality) of the Roman College, 82, 83.
Propaganda College, 86–89.
Propagation of the Faith, 87.
Proselytism, 265, 303.
Pro-Cathedral, Marlborough-street, 29.
Protestant Church, disestablishment, 303.
—— —— St. Mark's, 25.
—— —— St. Paul's, 43.
—— —— Workers, 7, 8, 10, 12, 13.
—— —— Dublin, 29, 40, 48.
—— —— Hostility to, 118.
—— —— Population, 35, 46.
—— —— Preachers, 99.
—— —— Schools, Coombe and Townsend-street, 303.
—— —— Vestry Books, North City, 53.
Purgatorian Societies. See under "Society."

Ram-lane, 39.
Ranelagh, 98, 105, 106.
Rathmines, 98.
—— "Our Lady of Victories," at, 241.
Refuge for Girls, 196.
Regan, Miss, 188.
Registration of Papish Parish Priests (1703), 41.
Reile, Bernard, 75.
Reilly, Phil, 41.
—— Miss, 44.
Relief Acts, Catholic, 57, 59, 61–65.

Report (1731), 23–25, 32, 41, 48.
—— (1749), 23, 27–30.
Rhymers, Professional, 213.
Rice, Lady, 44.
—— Brother, 168, 170.
Richardson, Fr., 23.
—— Dr. Lawrence, Bishop of Kilmo e, 44.
Ripoli, Thomas (General of Dominicans), 44.
Rivers, Canon, 18.
Roberti, Padre, 89.
Rogerson's-quay, 70.
Rome, 69, 84, 85, 86, 119, 133, 163, 232.
Romero, Signor, 136.
Rosemary-lane, 19, 23, 38, 55.
Rush, 233.
Russell, Archbishop, 15, 42.
—— Dean (P.P.), 23.
—— Rev. Mr., 113.
Russell's-court, 43.
Russell-street, 169.
Russia, 86.
Ryan, Fr., P.P., Arklow, 271.

St. Vincent's Hospital, 264.
Sanctan of Bohernabreena, 26.
Sandyford, 98.
Saul's-court, 37, 38, 39, 89, 128, 131, 132, 158, 195, 198, 270.
Schwarzenberg, Princess Matilda Von, 105.
Schools : Central Model, 169, 170 ; Christian Brothers, 25, 117, 118, 168, 170, 264 ; Clondalkin Brothers, 97 ; Dr. Betagh's (see " Saul's Court ") ; Dominican, 43 ; English, 40, 41 ; Erasmus Smith, 37, 38 ; Generally, 7, 14, 17, 31–41, 732 ; Kellett's, 172, 200 ; Lambay island, 223 ; Liffey-street, 168 ; Mendicity Institute, 184 ; Protestant, 32, 99, 101, 102 ; Saul's-court (see " Saul's Court ") ; Spinning, 185 ; SS. James's and Joseph's Sunday Male, 224 ; St. John's Society, 173 ; SS. Michael and John's, 164 ; St. Xavier's, 200 ; Sunday, 34, 35, 36, 99, 101, 108, 171, 172, 185.
Schoolhouse-lane, 39, 40.
Sirr, Major, 70, 71, 80, 256.
Sisters of Charity, 220, 221, 222, 225, 234, 263.
—— of Mercy, 220, 222.
—— Presentation, 18.
Sheerin (Printer), 159.
Skinner's-row, 39, 164.
Skerries, 233.
Skipper's-lane, 23.

Smith, V. Rev. J., P.P., 190, 193, 194.
—— Fr. Patrick, 218.
—— Egan, 33, 131.
Smithfield, 30, 60.
Smock-alley, 138, 139, 164, 193.
Smyth, Rev. John, 230, 275.
—— Owen, 99.
Societies : (Royal) Dublin, 2, 3, 26, 182, 231 ; Protestant, 200 ; Purgatorian, 100, 138, 139, 162, 202, 215, 227, 286 ; St. John the Evangelist, 138, 140 ; St. John's Purgatorian, 143, 176, 189 ; of St. Patrick, 140 ; Kildare-place, 169, 177 ; Catholic Book and Tract, 176, 177, 234 ; Roomkeepers, 186 ; Temperance : St. Paul's, 189 ; Metropolitan Total Abstinence, 189, 191, 193, 194 ; Sandyford Temperance, 190, 193, 194 ; Palmerstown Temperance, 190, 193, 194 ; Temperance of St. Nicholas, 189, 193 ; Blanchardstown, 190, 193 ; St. Augustine's, 195 ; Junior Total Abstinence, 192 ; Co. and City of Dublin Orphan, 224 ; Orphan's Friend, 224 ; SS. James's & Joseph's Orphan, 224 ; SS. Michael and John's Orphan, 228, 229 ; St. Catherine's, 263, 268 ; For the Propagation of the Faith, 203 ; Benefit and Burial, 195 ; St. Andrew, Christian Burial, 225 ; Catholic Orphan, 14 ; Magdalen, 100 ; Patrician, 101 ; St. Bonaventura, 100, 107 ; St. Vincent de Paul, 263-65. See also under " Confraternities " and appropriate headings.
Sodality of the Blessed Virgin, 82, 83.
—— —— Living Rosary, 255.
—— —— Sacred Heart of Mary, 238, 240.
Southwell, Henry, 152.
Spratt, V. Rev. Dr., O.C.C., 28, 189, 190, 191, 192, 193, 194.
Stokes, Dr. Whitley, 183, 184.
Stuart, V. Rev., 195.
Sudor, Miracle of the, 232.
Sullivan, Ambrose, 159.
Sweep-boys, 170-174.
Sweetman, John, 65.
—— Michael, Longtown, 264.
Swords, 233.
Synge, Edward, Protestant Archbishop of Tuam, 48.

Tallaght, 1, 107.
Tany (Dundrum), 15.
Teachers, Catholic, 32, 34, 50.
—— Training for Catholic, 169.
—— Female, 33.

Teachers, Illicit, 34.
Teelan, Margaret, 33.
Temperance Movement, 142, 189, 190-194, 213, 240, 256. See also under " Society."
Theatre Royal, 134, 135.
—— Smock-alley, 132.
Thomas-street, 1, 11, 15, 17, 30, 51, 77.
Tholsel, 15.
" Think well On't," 128.
" Three Kingdoms," 109.
" Tides of High Water," 148.
Tombstones, Lynch and Young, 113.
Traders, Catholic, 33, 38, 49, 54, 55, 57, 58, 59.
Trimbleston, Lord, 44.
Troy, Archbishop of Dublin, 8, 57, 60, 64, 66-75, 84, 86, 90, 97, 125, 131, 139, 164, 206, 272.
—— ——Pastorals and Letters, 66-75, 84.
Tullabeg College, 107, 109, 149, 150, 242.
Tynan, V. Rev. Dr., P.P. (SS. Michael and John's), 158.
Tyrconnell, Duchess of, 42, 43, 44.
Tyrrell, Rev. J., 232.

Ullathorne, Dr., 203.
United Irishmen, 66, 68, 70, 84.
Ursuline Convent (Cork), 110, 112, 116, 120 ; (Thurles), 119.
Usher's-quay, 202, 204.
Umbrian College, 163.

Verschoyle, John, 228.
Vincentians, 89, 90, 93, 126, 202, 225, 238.

Wade, Rev. N., 123.
Wall, Father Christopher, 91, 130.
—— Dean of Dublin, 266.
Walsh, B. (Professor of Music), 254.
—— Ralph, 229.
—— William J. (Archbishop of Dublin), 229.
Wakes, Abuses at, 139, 213.
Ward's English school, Mary's-lane (1731), 41.
Ward, P. (Printer, Christchurch-place), 153.
—— Venerable Mary, 226.
Warren (Printer, High-street), 124.
Water-press, Hollybrook, 127.
Watling-street, 19, 20, 224, 275.
Watson, Ann, 115.
Weavers, 2, 3.
Weldon, John, 30.
West New-row, 1, 77, 79, 80.

Wicklow, Missions in West, 163, 173, 214.

Woollen Industry, 2, 4, 77, 122, 185, 234.

Wormwood Gate, 17, 20, 21.

Wyse, Thomas, 57, 79.

YORE, Fr. William, 39, 167, 180, 189, 191, 195, 202, 203, 205, 224, 229.

Young, Anne, 78.

—— Arthur, 2, 6, 13, 77.

—— Catherine, 78, 80, 92, 111, 121.

—— Charles, 77–80, 110.

—— Fr. Charles, 79, 121, 123, 232, 254.

—— Francis, 78.

—— Fr. Henry : Parentage and boyhood, 77–80 ; character, 81–86 ; at Inch Academy, 81 ; Balbriggan, 84 ; at St. Michan's, 91 ; letters to his sisters, 92, 95 ; at Harold's Cross, 94 ; death of parents, 110, 112 ; brothers and sisters, 77–80, 116 ; documents on parochial organisations of, 123 ; booklets, 140–142 ; Purgatorian Society, 146 ; sermons, 91, 262 ; temperance work, 149 ; edition of Evening Office, 158–9 ; Alma Mater, 163 ; missionary work, 205 ; missions at W. Co. Wicklow, 210–4 ; at Ballymore-Eustace and Baltinglass, 214–6 ; at Eadestown, 216 ; Dublin, 217 ; Bray, 218 ; Baldoyle, 219 ; on trial, 215 ; devotions, 237, 289 ; at Finglas, 257, 282 ; Bellarmini's Catechism, 278 ; at St. Joseph's, 273, 280 ; devotion to Forty Hours' Adoration, 280 ; illness, 281 ; at Clondalkin, 283, 284 ; advocate of Holy Communion, 284 ; at Jesuit Retreat House, Milltown Park, 285 ; at Clongowes, 285 ; conversion of two Quakers, 287 ; on Fr. James Young's edition of Bellarmine's catechism, 288 ; on the Sign of the Cross, 290 ; retreat at Maynooth, 292 ; arranges for his burial, 295 ; last days, 295–6 ; death, 297–8 ; relics, 300, 301.

—— Fr. James, 78, 80, 117, 121, 189, 219, 232–4, 255, 282.

—— Johanna, 78, 80, 120.

—— John (Bishop of Limerick), 86.

—— Mary (St. Mary Ursula), 77, 80, 116, 117, 250, 254.

—— Sylvester, 78, 80, 112, 120, 121, 231–5.

—— Fr. William, 77–80, 112, 117 ; at Baldoyle, 121,188, 191, 218, 219, 230 ; pilgrimage to Bari, 232, 240, 243, 247 ; books, 250 ; mission to Cornwall, 254ff.

Made and Printed in Ireland by Browne and Nolan Ltd.
The Richview Press Dublin.